Danny Goodman's
AppleScript™ Handbook

Second Edition

Danny Goodman

toExcel
San Jose New York Lincoln Shanghai

AppleScript™ Handbook

Published by toExcel,
an imprint of iUniverse.com, Inc.

For information address:
iUniverse.com, Inc.
620 North 48th Street
Suite 201
Lincoln, NE 68504-3467
www.iuniverse.com

ISBN: 0-9665514-1-9

LCCN: 98-88412

Contents

In fond memory of David Smith,
a brilliant artist, supreme wit, and best friend
anyone could hope to know.

Introduction

The Promise of AppleScript

As both observer of, and participant in, the personal computing revolution since the late 1970s, I have been fascinated by the evolution of not only the technology, but also computer users' attitudes toward the technology. So many things have changed, yet so many things have remained the same.

I purchased my first serious computer, the original IBM PC, when it appeared on store shelves in 1981. I'm sure I wasn't alone in buying the PC not because of my love affair with technology (although it *was* neat), but because I was tired of retyping draft after draft of articles and correspondence. I figured the computer could save me lots of time and aggravation by letting me edit existing text, and then zip off a final print for submission.

I'm glad to report that my expectations were met. Retyping entire manuscripts became a thing of ancient history. But while the effort that went into producing a given article may have gone down, the hours saved didn't exactly free me for long walks on the beach. Instead, like a gas rushes to fill a vacuum, I churned out more work per week. The productivity gain was a two-edged sword: making any given task easier, but inviting me to take on more tasks.

I think this is a typical response to the introduction of personal computing into most peoples' lives. It also makes it difficult, I believe, to measure productivity gains by the addition of a computer. Add to that the highly magnified occasional lost work when the machine bombs or a hard disk crashes, and the sense is that the computer is a mixed blessing. Still, I believe that anyone who has adopted a personal computer into daily work habits couldn't work tomorrow if suddenly the machine were taken away.

Macintosh users are probably even more dependent on their machines. Having made the transition from DOS to the Mac at the very beginning of Macintosh-time, I find each excursion back to DOS (and now Windows) to be painful.

Even though I am comfortable with the magic incantations a DOS and Windows user needs to type here and there, those environments keep sticking their faces in mine far too much as I try to get something done. Macintosh users have the pleasure of being themselves while running a computer.

Interestingly, the ease of use made famous by the Macintosh has significantly raised the expectations of its users. We Macintosh users are a demanding lot. We're unrelenting in our criticism of something we think can and should be done better. We are also quick to praise a software product or hardware add-on done right—we call it cool, and we mean it.

If there is one thread that seems to run through everything Macintosh, it is that each user likes to have the flexibility to do things his or her own way. It started at the very beginning, when the first Macintosh System software let us design our own Desktop patterns and add fonts. Then we got hold of sounds and sound programs to make each Mac utter its peculiar symphony of film and television soundtrack noises. MultiFinder allowed each of us to keep our favorite suite of applications open at the same time so we could effortlessly switch from one to the next.

HyperCard came along at the same time in 1987. Suddenly, armies of non-programmers were developing special-purpose programs for themselves and colleagues—programs so specialized that they would have never been produced by software publishers. The diversity of the Mac community meant that there were solution needs that could be met only by the individuals conversant with the problems. These problem solvers could roll their own software without two years of programming courses.

System 7 carried this "have it your way" undercurrent even further. On the surface System 7 made it easier for everyday folks to customize their systems. We had additional customizing powers for things like colorizing icons and windows; drop-in system sounds; and an Apple menu to which we add any file, folder, application, or server for instant access.

Less visible in this move to System 7, however, was the foundation for the long-term future of the Macintosh operating system: Apple events. An Apple event is a message that flows entirely behind the scenes from one entity to another. From System 7 onward, the preferred way for the Finder to communicate with an application, for example, is for it to send an "open" message to a program when you double-click the program's icon. Of course, we users don't see any difference—and that's as it should be.

A major advantage of this methodology was that if the infrastructure for handling Apple events were in place, then applications could communicate with each other on the behalf of users—a feature previously not possible. A graphic design program, for instance, could tell a database program that the designer has just selected a particular element for the new layout, and the cost of that item should be added to a bill of materials covering the entire project. To make something like this possible, Apple had to provide the rails and switches in System software; the applications would provide the trains.

Adoption of Apple events by the development community got off to a slow start, partly because there wasn't much incentive to retrofit existing applications to work with Apple events. Initially, the only other program that could communicate with programs was the Finder, and its Apple event vocabulary was limited to four basic events (open, print, quit, and run). Unless a developer had other programs to take advantage of Apple events, why bother?

An independent company, UserLand, demonstrated why it was worth bothering. The company produced a scripting language that hid the complexity of the internal Apple event terminology under a C-like mantle, called Frontier. More importantly, Frontier provided a way for users—albeit advanced users—to perform Finder tasks and link Frontier-aware applications together with Apple events.

At about the same time, Apple formulated a standard that would accommodate future scripting systems into the System software Apple event framework. This standard is called Open Scripting Architecture (OSA). The "open" part of OSA simply means that Apple provides internal mechanisms that any outside scripting environment, such as UserLand Frontier, may use.

A key factor in the OSA concept is something called the Object Model. To successfully bring scripting power to applications, Apple believed it was crucial for applications to be able to have ways to refer to any kind of element in a document that a script may access—paragraphs in a word processing program, cells in a table, blocks in a desktop publishing program. After all, if you want a script to grab a range of cells from a spreadsheet and drop them into a word processing document, the script needs some words to describe those cells and the point in the word processing document where they go. This is not trivial in a graphical interface like the Macintosh, where each action is worth a thousand words. Developers saw the object model as yet more work, to which they again said, "why bother?"

AppleScript is why they should bother.

AppleScript is Apple's system-level scripting language. It relies on the OSA infrastructure to provide a consistent scripting foundation for applications. Newcomers to AppleScript understandably find it difficult to distinguish a language such as AppleScript from the OSA foundation, which is hidden from view. Moreover, the attention paid to AppleScript sometimes overshadows other OSA scripting components, such as the latest releases of Frontier and QuicKeys. But anything built into applications that supports AppleScript also supports all other OSA-compliant scripting environments, since they all revolve around the same technology.

In my view, AppleScript's language constructions are nearly as easy to learn as HyperTalk. The number of language pieces that are built into AppleScript is very small, because scripts use scripting vocabulary that is designed into applications that support scripting. The result is a plain language gateway to the power of Apple events, giving us the power to write scripts for two main reasons: automation and customization.

It's easy to envision automating repetitive processes. I can recall plenty of times when I had to open dozens of files in a program and save them in a different format so they could be read by someone else on a different computer. Unlike system-level macro programs, however, a script can behave with a modicum of intelligence, making decisions based on conditions at any moment, repeating a task until it detects that everything is completed, or even prompting the user to enter information along the way.

More importantly, however, AppleScript lets users, consultants, and in-house developers build custom systems out of existing building blocks. You can literally develop custom applications by scripting the functions of existing software just the way you need them. For example, perhaps you like FileMaker Pro for its data handling, but prefer Excel's chart-making abilities. A brief script can gather data from FileMaker, plug it into a temporary Excel worksheet, generate the chart of your choice, and then plug the chart into a WordPerfect weekly report.

Ah, we're back at the old customization topic on the Macintosh. While today's software products still tend to group themselves around the Big Five categories —word processing, spreadsheets, databases, graphics, and communications— our working (and playing) lives aren't so compartmentalized. Our jobs combine these functions according to our unique requirements. All we want is software that does the same.

The true promise of OSA and AppleScript is to free us from the chains that bind us to the closed worlds of each application—to let us blend the powers that we desire into a desktop or laptop world that works best for each of us. To that end, I look upon AppleScript as the Great Integrator.

For this to happen, of course, Macintosh software developers need to implement the Object Model in their applications. It is happening now, and the ready availability of AppleScript as part of System 7.5 is the incentive for developers to continue the migration. In our search for customized solutions, we who script will flock to those applications that let us script the best.

When I said earlier that some things about personal computing have remained the same, I was thinking about the desire to let the computer let us do more. We turn to the computer for solutions. What has radically changed, however, is that we're less patient in jamming a round software package into a square need. Users' expectations for personalized solutions are extraordinarily high today—and will only go higher. With tools such as AppleScript (and an AppleScript-capable version of HyperCard also in our bag of tricks) the Macintosh stands the best chance of meeting the demands of an increasingly fragmented user world.

What is even more encouraging to me about the potential of AppleScript is the fact that much of the future of Macintosh System software relies heavily on AppleScript as the glue to hold new technologies together. Voice recognition and text-to-speech technologies in the latest Macintosh models depend on AppleScript for their internal communication mechanism. In other words, the System itself will grow around AppleScript.

This is especially true for a technology coming soon from Apple. Called OpenDoc, it represents a breakthrough in ease of use for the Macintosh. Imagine, if you will, a Macintosh document that can accept any kind of data—text graphics, animation, video, sound. When you click on a particular kind of data in this compound document, the appropriate tools appear in the menubar (ClarisWorks 2.0 offers a preview of what this feels like). These tools, however aren't from any giant program, but rather from a multitude of special-purpose components. Instead of buying a monster word processor that has a spelling checker, grammar checker, and thesaurus built in, you would assemble a collection of tools—very likely from different sources. What allows all these software pieces to work together are the AppleScript messages they pass to each other You could then write scripts that summon the powers of any or all components to build a solution that does exactly what we want.

AppleScript today also provides us with a glimpse of another futuristic part of our personal computing world: the agent. An agent carries out a task for us in the background—perhaps keeping an eye on a special folder in a server to let you know when a co-worker's document has been delivered; monitoring your electronic mail in-basket, responding to meeting requests and filling in our schedules for us; even understanding and responding to telephone calls from humans. Most of the technology for these kinds of agents exists today, and AppleScript is again the vehicle that lets us instruct such agents about how to carry out their jobs.

As farfetched as some of these concepts sound, they're either here or imminent —and AppleScript (and other OSA-compliant dialects) will play a major role in the way we control these powers. It's clear, of course, that not every Macintosh user will be writing AppleScript scripts. But AppleScript is the same kind of empowerment tool that gives interested users the requisite access to automation and customization. In my experience, if you have the drive to define a specific need that can be handled by AppleScript, you have more than enough enthusiasm to learn AppleScript. This book is your entry point to implementing your AppleScript solutions.

It's clear to me that AppleScript will become more important to finessing the Macintosh in the years ahead. By getting a head start today, you will be well-positioned to take advantage of the amazing Macintosh applications and System software technologies yet to come.

Getting Started with AppleScript

CHAPTER 1

The Many Flavors of AppleScript

AppleScript currently comes in several varieties (the lineup described here is always subject to change). Your choice depends on what you intend to do with the technology. As this book goes to press, you can acquire AppleScript system software in the following Apple-branded products:

AppleScript Run Time Kit

AppleScript Run Time with System 7.5

AppleScript Finder Scripting Software Upgrade

AppleScript Scripter's Kit

AppleScript Developer's Toolkit

Some AppleScript packages are also available in more than one human language, but we'll be working with the English version in this book.

It is important to understand the differences among the offerings. While a version of the Run Time package is included with System 7.5, you may find that you need the additional software and materials in another package to realize your AppleScript dreams.

AppleScript Run Time Kit

While a "run time" version of other development tools often means a play-only environment, such is not the case with AppleScript. The Run Time Kit comes with not only the requisite system software to make your Mac capable of handling AppleScript, but also a script editor and a sample application (a text editor) to let you experiment with AppleScript.

3

The Run Time Kit is available from APDA [Apple Program Developer's Association, Apple Computer, Inc., P.O. Box 319, Buffalo, New York, 14207-0319, (800) 282-2732 or (716) 871-6555] and on disks accompanying some third-party AppleScript-related products (e.g., HyperCard 2.2) and books. The previous edition of this book included the complete Run Time Kit software on the companion disk. Because the system software is now widely available as part of System 7.5, the companion disk now includes Run Time Kit elements that are not bundled with System 7.5 (allowing more room for other goodies).

Apple's Scripting System Software

The Run Time Kit installer copies the AppleScript extension into your System Folder. The AppleScript extension is Apple's version of a scripting component (UserLand Frontier and CE Software's QuicKeys offer other scripting components).

AppleScript™

Figure 1.1 Extension file necessary
for using AppleScript.

The installation process also places a system-level folder inside the System Folder (more precisely, in the Extensions folder). Called Scripting Additions, this folder contains extensions to AppleScript's internal language. We'll have much more to say about scripting additions in Chapter 7, but for now, just be aware that this folder is tucked away safely in the Extensions folder. The purpose of this folder is to provide AppleScript with a fixed location to look for possible additions to the language (i.e., if AppleScript doesn't understand a command in a script, it looks for a match in the Scripting Additions folder).

Figure 1.2 Scripting Additions folder
delivered with System 7.5.

Script Editor

In the AppleScript Utilities folder is the Script Editor, where you'll spend most of your time using AppleScript. You compose and execute scripts in Script Editor. This program also lets you view lists of valid terms (dictionaries) for other applications that you may wish to script. You'll get to meet Script Editor in Chapter 3.

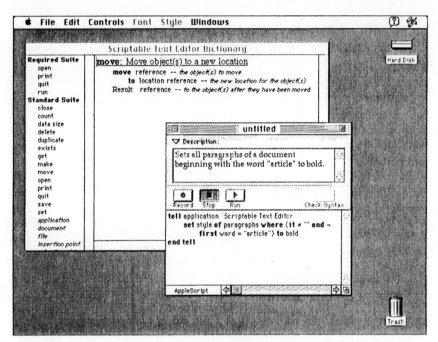

Figure 1.3   AppleScript Script Editor with sample script and dictionary.

Scriptable Text Editor

The AppleScript engineering team created a program as an example for both developers (how to add scripting support to their own programs) and scripters (how to work with a scriptable application). The Scriptable Text Editor is a simple text processing program whose outward appearance is no more complicated than TeachText with styled text. But its scriptable innards offer scripters a convenient way to begin experimenting with manipulating information in applications. For the convenience of learning AppleScript, it's best to keep Scriptable Text Editor in the same AppleScript Utilities folder as Script Editor. When you get more accustomed to dealing with file path names in AppleScript, you can elect to move it wherever you like.

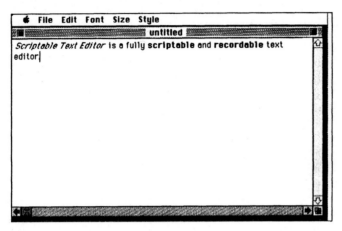

Figure 1.4   Scriptable Text Editor.

Scripting the Finder

A handful of read-only Finder functions (e.g., obtaining a file size or the path name to special folders) are contained in a scripting addition (File Commands) that automatically installs into the Scripting Additions folder. The Run Time Kit includes an extra file, called FinderLib, which filled the gap until the scriptable Finder became available. I cover how to access this library in Chapter 14, but if you have System 7.5, see below.

Other Items

Included with the Run Time Kit is a HyperCard stack file, called Language at a Glance, that contains rudimentary explanations of AppleScript's built-in commands and syntax. This HyperCard stack requires HyperCard 2 (or later) or the HyperCard Player. The remainder of the items include release notes and an extensive set of sample scripts developed by the AppleScript team engineers.

AppleScript Run Time with System 7.5

The run time software that ships with System 7.5 and on new Macs is not the complete Run Time Kit, described above. Included with the system software package are all necessary extensions to get AppleScript working, scripting additions, Finder Scripting Extension, Script Editor, and a number of Finder-related sample scripts. The most important element you don't get with this installation is the sample application, Scriptable Text Editor. Because that program is such a good learning tool, a licensed copy is included on the companion disk to this book.

AppleScript Finder Scripting Software Upgrade

For those scripters who purchased AppleScript prior to System 7.5 and who don't want to upgrade yet to System 7.5, APDA sells the necessary software to make the Finder scriptable. This entails installing a new Finder and a Finder Scripting Extension. The $25.00 (US) scriptable Finder kit includes a detailed manual about the scriptable Finder syntax. This manual (without the software) is also available in technical bookstores (published by Addison-Wesley).

AppleScript Scripter Kit

If you've seen an AppleScript box in your favorite Macintosh software store or in mail order catalogs, that's the Scripter Kit. It includes the run time software, plus an array of manuals (the manuals are also published by Addison-Wesley for distribution in bookstores). But the most important part of this package in my opinion is the inclusion of the FaceSpan interface builder. Covered in Chapter 31, this product by Software Designs Unlimited makes it easy to build friendly front ends to your scripts. All software in this kit is delivered on floppy disks.

AppleScript Developer's Kit

Available exclusively from APDA, the AppleScript Developer's Kit is the most complete AppleScript set you can buy. In addition to everything that comes with the Scripter Kit and Finder Scripting Software Upgrade, this package also comes with a CD-ROM chock full of extra goodies of interest to those who are designing AppleScript into their applications.

While most of the CD-ROM isn't essential for scripters, more advanced AppleScript users may be interested in understanding the details about how the Apple scripting world works. Relevant chapters of *Inside Macintosh* come on the CD-ROM in the DocViewer format, so you can read the pages on screen or print them out (the DocViewer allows you to print odd or even pages separately if you like, so it is possible to print these many hundreds of pages two-sided).

Additional tools are also provided for heavy-duty programming, including utilities for editing "aete" resources, monitoring Apple event messages that circulate throughout your system, plus a couple of other simple application examples and source code. Of course, Pascal and C libraries for linking AppleScript support into your programs are also on the platter. Application programmers and those who want to write scripting additions (Chapter 7) will find the Developer's Kit a worthwhile addition.

What to Buy?

My recommendation is to use the software that comes with System 7.5 to begin your learning process. But then prepare yourself to add either the Scripter or Developer kit, primarily to get FaceSpan.

CHAPTER 2

How to Learn AppleScript

To use AppleScript effectively, there is a fair amount you have to know. Fortunately, that knowledge can be accumulated gradually while putting AppleScript to work.

The reason there is so much to know is that AppleScript does not exist in a self-contained environment, like other programming environments you may have used before. For example, while working with HyperCard, an author has a sufficiently large vocabulary built into the HyperTalk scripting language and a well-defined set of "things" to work with—buttons, fields, cards, and so on. HyperCard even comes with its own painting tools to create an application's graphics without having to leave HyperCard. In other words, your universe is solely within the confines of HyperCard.

AppleScript is an entirely different matter. As you'll learn in subsequent chapters, AppleScript itself has only a handful of words in its vocabulary. The powers that let you control applications are actually contained *in the applications*, not in AppleScript. For example, AppleScript doesn't know anything about spreadsheet cells or graphics blocks in a page layout. It's only when you use AppleScript to, say, automate the process of copying a cell range from a weekly budget spreadsheet to a word processing activity report that you can access the vocabulary built into those programs.

Moreover, the AppleScript vocabulary of one program is not necessarily applicable in another program (although there may be similarities). Spreadsheets have vocabulary entries for cells and ranges; word processors let us talk about words and paragraphs; database programs use the terminology of the record and field.

What this all means is that there are several things to know—even if not in full depth—before it is possible to start making AppleScript work with applications:

- **AppleScript syntax**   The basic construction of statements that Apple-Script can execute.

- **The applications**   Irrespective of AppleScript, it's important to know how to use the application(s) you wish to script. Just as a playwright must know the moral, psychological, and physical makeup of a character before writing lines for him or her, so, too, must a scripter know a program's capabilities before writing scripts that automate its processes.

- **The application's AppleScript syntax**   While the script editor provided with AppleScript (and any third-party editor) lets you display and print each scriptable application's AppleScript dictionary, the dictionary only goes so far to explain intricacies of scripting the application. An important goal of *Danny Goodman's AppleScript Handbook* is to help you interpret the dictionaries that come built into scriptable applications.

The ideal way for beginners to tackle this mountain of information is to do it in horizontal slices of difficulty. Rather than worrying about mastering every tiny bit of AppleScript syntax or an application's dictionary before writing your first line of AppleScript, you can work with the most common items first. Once you have a feel for the pieces you're working with, you can then begin poking deeper as needed.

Gradus ad Scriptum

Whatever your programming experience—even if it is zero—I recommend that you follow a sequence that I've found to be most helpful in getting a handle on AppleScript quickly. The rest of this book is organized according to this sequence.

A number of the chapters in Part II, The AppleScript Language, have topics rated by difficulty. The symbol I chose to represent each level is the pocket protector (hey, if we're scripting, we're programming!). A topic's difficulty will range from one to three according to the following scale:

beginner

intermediate

advanced

In your first time through a chapter, you can spend the most time on the beginner-rated items, and just glance through the others to gain an appreciation for what else is in the vicinity. Come back later to fill in your knowledge in more advanced subjects as you feel ready.

Since over time you will be using this book more as a reference than as a tutorial, I feel it is more important to organize the content as you'll want it later The pocket protector codes, however, will speed your learning because you won't be bogged down with mind-numbing details at first.

Here, then, is a proven sequence for learning AppleScript.

1. **Record scripts.** Some AppleScript-ready programs, including the Scriptable Text Editor on the companion disk, let users walk through operations manually while the programs send a journal of actions to the AppleScript script editor. In other words, you do what you normally do while a perfect working script is assembled for you in the AppleScript editor.

2. **Master AppleScript's basic syntax.** It's vital to know how to construct statements that AppleScript can follow.

3. **Learn AppleScript's built-in commands.** This is a short list, which you'll see early during the mastery of the language syntax (after all, you need some words to work with while learning the syntax).

4. **Understand how scripting additions fill out AppleScript's powers.** You'll see how to use AppleScript and the scripting additions that ship with it to perform some Finder- and system-level actions.

5. **Write self-contained scripts.** These are scripts that perform meaningful actions and purposes on their own, without calling up any other applications.

6. **Start writing scripts for one application at a time.** You'll start to get a feel for accessing a program's scripting dictionary and manipulating information of the same kind. The Finder is a convenient place to start.

7. **Write scripts that integrate multiple applications.** For many scripters, this is the big payoff, since it allows you to essentially create customized solutions from existing programs.

8. **If you have the FaceSpan interface builder, create user-friendly interfaces for your scripts.** FaceSpan is an outstanding tool that all serious scripters should know.

This sequence looks long and arduous, but it can go relatively quickly, because you'll be trying out things along the way. I'll also try to anticipate head-scratching problems you may encounter, and cover them in relevant locations.

If You've Never Programmed Before

To a programming newcomer, the size of this book and the learning sequence above may appear daunting. AppleScript may not be the easiest language in the world to program, but it's darn close. Unlike getting down and dirty into developing full-fledged monolithic applications (like the productivity programs you buy in the stores), AppleScript lets you experiment by writing small snippets of programming code to accomplish big things. The scripting environment in the system software extensions does a lot of technical work for you.

Programming at its most basic level is nothing more than writing a series of instructions for the computer to follow. We humans follow instructions all the time, even if we don't realize it. Traveling to a friend's house is a sequence of small instructions: go three blocks that way; turn left here; turn right there. Amid the instructions we follow are some decisions: if the stoplight is red, then stop; if the light is green then go; if the light is yellow, then gun it. Occasionally, we must even repeat some operations multiple times: keep going around the block until a parking space opens up. Computer programs not only contain the main sequence of steps, but they *anticipate* what decisions or repetitions may be necessary to accomplish that goal (e.g., the stoplight, the parking shortage).

The initial hurdle of learning to program is becoming comfortable with the way a programming environment wants its words and numbers organized inside these instructions. Such rules, just as in a living language such as English, are called *syntax*.

Computers, being the generally dumb electronic hulks that they are, aren't very forgiving if we, humans, don't communicate with them in exactly the language they understand. When speaking to another human, we can flub a sentence's syntax, and there's a good chance the other person will understand fully. Not so with computer programming languages. If the syntax isn't perfect (or at least something within the language's range of knowledge that it can correct), the computer has the brazenness to tell us that *we* have made a syntax error.

It's best to just chalk up the syntax errors you receive as learning experiences. Even experienced programmers get them. Each syntax error you get—and the resolution of that error by rewriting the statement—adds to your knowledge of the language.

If You've Done a Little Programming Before

Programming experience in a procedural language, such as BASIC or Pascal—especially if it was for computers other than the Macintosh—may almost be a hindrance rather than a help to learning AppleScript. While you may have an appreciation for precision in syntax, the overall concept of how a program fits into the world is probably radically different from AppleScript. Part of this has to do with the typical tasks a script performs (automating processes or exchanging information between programs), but a large part also has to do with the nature of object-oriented programming.

In a typical procedural program, the programmer is responsible for everything that appears on the screen and everything that happens under the hood. When the program first runs, a lot of code is dedicated to setting up the visual environment. Perhaps there are text entry fields or clickable buttons on the screen. To know if a user clicks on a particular button, the program examines the coordinates of the click, and compares those coordinates against a list of all button coordinates on the screen. Program execution then branches to carry out instructions (probably in a subroutine) that are reserved for clicking in that space.

Object-oriented programming is almost the inverse. A button is considered an object—something tangible. An object has properties, such as its location, color, size, label, border style, and so on. An object may also contain a script. At the same time, the system software can send a message to the object—depending on what the user does—that triggers the script. For example, if the user clicks on a button, the system software tells the button that somebody has clicked there, leaving it up to the button to decide what to do about it. That's where the script comes in. The script is part of the button, and it contains the instructions the button carries out when the user clicks on it. A separate set of instructions may be listed if the user double-clicks on the button, or holds down the Option key while clicking.

Some of the scripts you'll write may seem to be procedural in construction: they contain a simple list of instructions that are carried out in order. But when dealing with information from programs or the Finder, these instructions will be working with the object-oriented nature of programs. A range of spreadsheet cells becomes an object, as does a word processing paragraph.

In advanced uses of AppleScript, you can even create your own objects—scripts that create entities consisting of specific properties and behaviors. We'll build an object in Chapter 15. The script creates a daily alarm clock object. This object continually operates in the background, comparing the Macintosh's internal system clock against the top item in a list of alarms set to go off. When the times match, the object comes to life, displaying a dialog with the alarm details.

Making the transition from procedural to object-oriented concepts may be the most difficult challenge for you. When I was first introduced to object-oriented programming a number of years ago, I didn't "get it" at first. But when the concept clicked—a long, pensive walk helped—so many lightbulbs went on in my head, I thought I might be glowing in the dark. From then on, object orientation seemed to be the only sensible way to program.

If You've Programmed in HyperTalk Before

I suspect that a lot of HyperCard developers will be trying their hands at AppleScript. After all, the concept of scripting little bits of code was popularized through HyperCard—a self-contained programming environment for non-propellerheads. Although it avoids the terminology of object orientation (classes, methods, etc.), HyperCard is very object-oriented. You won't have any trouble with AppleScript's object orientation.

What may drive you crazy, however, is that HyperTalk and AppleScript have enough similarities and differences to make the learning process confusing at first. For example, you can get and set properties of objects in both environments. But in HyperCard when you get a property, the information goes into a special variable called It; in AppleScript the information goes into a special variable called Result. AppleScript also has an It word in its vocabulary, but the meaning is different from HyperTalk's It. You also don't "put x into y"; you "copy x to y" or "set y to x". I'll have more to say about syntax differences in specific discussions later.

Probably the biggest difference you'll notice right off the bat is that AppleScript scripts are not dependent on system messages, as HyperTalk scripts are. While a HyperTalk script (say, a stack script) may contain handlers for any of the possible system messages that reach it through the message hierarchy (e.g., openStack, mouseUp), most AppleScript scripts you write have a main sequence of statements that simply run from top to bottom when they're told to run. The initiating force is a click of a Run button in the script editor, or, if the script has been saved as a standalone application, opening it from the Finder (plus other ways we'll see later).

You'll also welcome AppleScript's syntax forgiveness—sometimes doing even better than HyperCard. For example, the greater than (>) operator has five synonyms:

```
comes after
greater than
is greater than
is not less than or equal [to]
isn't less than or equal [to]
```

Some other constructions, such as if-then and repeats, however, are slightly more restrictive. Still, the differences are easily surmountable.

Enough Talk: Let's Script!

If I haven't frightened you away by now, we're ready to get underway. Be sure you have installed AppleScript from your System 7.5 master disk(s) and the additional files from the companion disk. In the next chapter we'll be using Script Editor and Scriptable Text Editor to record some scripts.

CHAPTER 3

Your First AppleScript Script

In this chapter we'll start using the Script Editor, the primary user gateway to AppleScript. The Script Editor is where you will write scripts, even if your scripting travels take you to other applications. We'll make one of those journeys—to the Scriptable Text Editor—in this chapter. In the end, you'll see how to let AppleScript record your actions in a program, and convert them to AppleScript in the Script Editor.

Scriptable Applications

By far the most common method of AppleScript support in applications is *scriptability*. This means that by way of an external editor, such as Apple's Script Editor, you can write scripts that automate processes or capture data from documents.

Each application's level of scriptability is entirely up to the program's designers. For some programs, the designers give scripters access to almost every conceivable element and characteristic of a document. Others may have their own scripting language built in (which they likely share with Windows versions of the products). Rather than reinventing the scripting wheel for the program, the designers let scripters run the program's internal scripts. That means, of course, that a scripter must also be sufficiently knowledgeable of the program's own scripting language to do those scripts first—and then trigger them from an AppleScript script.

The majority of scriptable applications are in the middle, offering some level of scriptability support for elements of a document. Over time, as scripters demand more from application developers, the average level of scriptability will improve across all applications.

Recordable Applications

While the Scriptable Text Editor sample application that comes with the Run Time lets you record a script of your actions, not all AppleScript-capable programs support this feature. A program that supports script recording is said to be *recordable*.

It is no trivial task for commercial software developers to retrofit existing applications to be recordable. Just because an application is scriptable doesn't mean that it is recordable. As a result, the number of recordable applications will for a long time lag behind those that offer other levels of AppleScript support. It won't be immediately apparent from working with a program whether it is recordable. Only when you try to record a script from the Script Editor—and nothing appears in the Script Editor window as a result of actions in a program—will you know that the program is not recordable.

Recording's Learning Value

Experimenting in a recordable application is a valuable learning experience. For one thing, you see immediately how the program "thinks" in AppleScript terms as you make menu selections, move data around, and so on. Even more important is that recordable applications record in the precise syntax they prefer from scripts. You'll see syntax details in recorded scripts that don't necessarily show up while viewing a program's AppleScript dictionary (Chapter 6). It's these pesky details—which can vary from program to program, even when they appear to do the same thing—that can make learning an application's scriptability time-consuming.

Recording's Limitations

Before you get all excited and think that recordability will write all your scripts for you, I have some sobering news. Aside from the fact that precious few programs are recordable, it's not possible to record powerful AppleScript operations, such as if-then decision trees or repeat loops.

Recording goes in a kind of brute force straight line. For example, you may record a sequence of steps that involves opening a document file. But what if that document file isn't available when the script runs some time in the future? Even if you walk a recording through the same series of steps 20 times, the recorder duly lists those steps 20 times, rather than putting them efficiently inside a repeat loop—as you would do if writing the script from scratch.

Still, you can combine a program's recordability with manual scripting to help out. In the missing file situation, above, let the recording track the steps when the file is there. Later, manually add error checking to handle the case when the file isn't available to script. For the repetitive action scenario, use the recorder to snag one instance of the sequence, and then manually build a repeat loop around that sequence.

Attachable Applications

While on the subject of AppleScript support, I'll mention here the third type: *attachability*. This feature will work its way into applications slowly. It means that an element in a document—a spreadsheet cell, a button on a database form—can contain a script. More than likely, the program will have a script editor of some kind built into the program so you can write scripts that are to be attached to an information element in a document. Such a script might send a query to a remote computer based on information in a field or cell, copy the query results, and paste them someplace else in the document.

One of the best examples of an attachable application is HyperCard. For every object you create in a HyperCard stack (button, field, card, background, or stack), you can give that object an AppleScript script to execute when the user acts on that object (e.g., clicks a button, enters text into a field, or navigates to another card). Eventually, OpenDoc parts (e.g., text blocks, pictures, buttons in a document) will be able to contain scripts that might fetch data from a server, speak the text, or send a message to a colleague.

Script Editor

It's time to get acquainted with the Script Editor, where you'll spend a lot of your AppleScripting life. The Script Editor is an application that works very closely with the AppleScript system extension.

Opening the editor, you see its primary editing window. It contains two fields. One lets you enter a description of what the script does. If you ultimately save the script as a double-clickable application, then the contents of this description field appear in the splash screen when the script opens (more about this later in the chapter). The other field is where you enter the script.

One of the first tasks you want to perform is establishing the size of the window each time a new script window appears. The default size in a fresh copy of Script Editor is too small for productive work. Drag the lower right corner of the window so that the window resizes to approximately the proportions shown in Figure 3.1. Then choose Set Default Window Size from the File menu. You can adjust this default setting anytime.

Figure 3.1 AppleScript Script Editor
window.

The Record Button

Two of the editor's four buttons are dedicated to script recording tasks: Record
and Stop. When you click the Record button, Script Editor tells the system that
recording is on. In turn, the system alerts all running applications that support
script recording to send copies of its actions to the system, which then passes
them on to Script Editor. At all times while recording is on, the Apple menu
icon flashes between the Apple and cassette tape symbols.

Figure 3.2 Record
button and flashing
Apple menu icons.

Because of the quasi-multitasking environment of System 7, you can watch
the script filling in Script Editor while you perform the real actions in the programs (provided you have enough screen real estate to view it all). Don't be
shocked, however, if absolutely every action isn't immediately set to script.
Some applications queue up recorded events until they sense by another action
that what you have just performed is finished, and ready for recording. One or
more lines of script may then flow to Script Editor.

Only applications designed to be recordable will know how to send copies of their events to the system and Script Editor. If, while recording a script, you switch to a non-recordable application, not one line of new script appears in Script Editor.

What to Record

Just like recording a videotape with a camcorder, AppleScript recording captures virtually everything you do in a recordable application—including mistakes. Even if an Undo were recorded, it would mean that the script still contained the gaff. The good news is that because the recording is translated into human readable form, you can edit out the mistakes.

More important, however, is figuring out exactly the state of your applications and documents at the beginning and end of a script. These states may be different when you're recording a script than when you want to run it later.

The script you'll be recording later in this chapter is a good example. The purpose of the script will be to assemble portions of a document into one master copy (each portion having been prepared and revised by different people). Ultimately, we just want to run the script on each day's submissions to assemble the latest version of the whole document.

In the course of recording the script, the Scriptable Text Editor is already open, and a blank document window greets us, ready to accept the pieces. But that may not be the state of the text editor program when we run the script next week. There may already be one or more other open windows, which we don't want to disturb. The proper thing to do would be to create a new window before doing anything else. In the recording process, this seems redundant, since a blank window is already waiting for us. Still, it's a case of anticipating the environment in which the script may be used in the future.

Stopping Recording

When you're finished with the process you want to record, switch back to Script Editor (either clicking in its window, if exposed, or using the Application menu), and click the Stop button. One or more lines may complete the script, and it's ready to run.

You'll see that the script begins with a tell statement, which indicates where the rest of the commands in the recorded script are sent. An end statement finishes the script. If you then turn on recording a second time, a second tell statement is added to the bottom of the script—there is no magic that knows to blend the commands into the previous script.

Running the Script

Clicking the Run button (or typing ⌘-R) in Script Editor plays back what you've recorded. While the script runs, you see the programs' windows open, and other actions you had done manually. There is rarely a problem running unmodified recorded scripts, but if something doesn't work correctly, script execution stops, the Script Editor comes to the foreground, and an error message appears. Unless you've had some experience debugging scripts, the error message probably won't be very helpful in telling you what's wrong.

Saving the Script

Since the idea of a script is to automate processes, you will want to save the script so you can use it later. There are a number of save options available as indicated by the File menu and Save dialog box choices illustrated in Figure 3.3.

The complete list is shown in Table 3.1.

Your choice between the two major categories—editable or run-only—depends solely on whether you use the script yourself (in which case it's best to leave it in an editable state for later adjustment) or you hand the script over to others (and you don't want them to view or modify your script).

Figure 3.3 Save menu and dialog options.

Table 3.1   Save Script Choices

Save As	Type	Finder Icon
editable script	text only	Text Only
	compiled script	Compiled Script
	application (run and quit)	Application
	application (run and stay open)	Application
run-only	compiled script	Compiled Script
	application (run and quit)	Application
	application (run and stay open)	Application

We'll have more to say about saving scripts as applications, and what a compiled script really is, but it's valuable to understand the main differences between the types at this juncture.

Saving a script as text or as a compiled script means that you can run the script only by loading it into Script Editor and clicking the Run button. Use the text-only version only when you're having difficulty with a script of your own design (it won't compile—explained later).

If the script does what you like, however, it is more efficient from a user perspective to save the script as an application (most will be "run and quit" types, as you'll learn later). AppleScript applications occupy very little disk space, since they depend on the system software to do most of the work when they run. To run a script saved in this form, double-click it in the Finder—just as you would any application. You can also place aliases to script applications in the Apple Menu Items folder for quick access via the Apple Menu (or use the Automated Tasks folder created during System 7.5 installation).

When you open an AppleScript application, you usually see what is called a *splash screen*—just like you do on many commercial programs (Figure 3.4). The window displays the contents you entered into the Description field of Script Editor for that particular script (you can also save a script application so that it doesn't show the splash screen). You also see a Quit button and a Run button. Clicking this Run button is the same as clicking the Run button in Script Editor. After the script completes executing its statements, the AppleScript app automatically quits (unless it was saved as a Stay Open application).

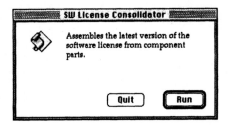

Figure 3.4 **A typical script application splash screen.**

Deciding What to Script

The first class ticket to an unenjoyable scripting experience is sitting down in front of Script Editor and trying to dream up something to script. Scripting is no meandering Sunday drive.

Instead, any attempt to script should be driven by a desire to accomplish a task. The better you can visualize the goal of the script, the easier it will be to record or write a script. Even if the goal changes during the scripting process, you need to know where you're going before you begin.

Recording Your First Script

Since you may not know exactly what you'd like to script at this point, I'll make that part of the scripting process easy for you. In the folder Handbook Scripts:Chapter 03 (installed from the accompanying disk) is a set of Scriptable Text Editor files. These files represent portions of a legal document (in this case, a mythological software license). In this scenario from a big law office, each segment of the license is written by a different junior associate. Since the final license and its constituent parts will be going through many revisions, we need a script that assembles the current versions of parts into a complete license for review by the partners and client.

Script Overview

The manual process for this consolidation consists of the following steps:

1. Open Scriptable Text Editor if it isn't open.
2. Create a new blank window for our consolidation.
3. Open the file containing the first portion of the license.
4. Select all of the text.
5. Choose Copy from the Edit menu.
6. Switch back to our consolidation document window.
7. Choose Paste from the Edit menu.

8. Repeat steps 3 through 7 for each of the remaining components.

9. Save the consolidation with the file name "Software License."

When you multiply the number of steps for each component by the five components in this document, you can see that this is a good solution to script. By saving the script that does this as a script application, all you do is double-click the app each time you want to assemble the latest version.

Setting the Stage

Follow along as we go through the recording process that takes us up to the point of actually working with the components.

1. Open Script Editor if it isn't already open.

    If you have a large monitor, you may want to drag the editor window to the right or bottom of the screen to watch what happens during recording.

2. Enter a description of what this script does.

    Styles vary about the language of these descriptions, but I try to envision what a user would see in this script application's splash screen. For this script, you might use: "Assembles the latest version of the software license from component parts." Don't be afraid to be verbose in these descriptions if they will help users fully understand what clicking the Run button accomplishes.

3. Click the Record button.

    After a few seconds, the flashing recording icon alternates with the Apple menu icon.

4. Switch to the Finder and open Scriptable Text Editor.

    If Scriptable Text Editor is already open, make it the active application.

5. Choose New from the File menu.

    Even though you may be looking at a new, untitled window before doing this, you have to anticipate that the user of this script may already be using the application with another document window already open. There is no penalty for having two untitled windows open in an application. This new window is where we'll assemble the components into a fresh copy of the whole license.

Bringing in the Components

In this segment, we'll go through the repetitive drudgery of copying and pasting each component in sequence.

1. Choose Open from the File menu, and open the component named *0. Introduction.*

2. Choose Select All from the Edit menu.

3   Choose Copy from the Edit menu.

4.   Close the *0. Introduction* window.

This is important so we don't leave a trail of window clutter after the script executes.

5.   Choose Paste from the Edit menu.

Doing one of these manually isn't so bad. Avoid clicking in the document window, which may reposition the text insertion pointer someplace other than at the end of the text. We want the pointer to always be at the end of text so that succeeding components are pasted to the end of the document.

6.   Repeat steps 6 through 10 for each of the remaining components: *1. License*; *2. Restrictions*; *3. Warranty*; and *4. General*.

This is mind-numbing drudgery that you'll only have to perform once. Do these repetitions slowly, because it's easy for your mind to wander while doing repetitive stuff like this.

Saving the Whole

We're nearing the end. All that's left is to save the document and stop recording.

1.   Choose Save As from the File menu.

2.   Enter the name Software License, and click the Save button (or press Return).

3.   Switch back to Script Editor.

4.   Click the Stop button.

Saving the Script

Before running the script for the first time, be prudent and save the script. While it's not as big an issue for recorded scripts, you never know what may happen when you run a script the first time. The vast majority of the time, things will work fine or some safe error will occur. But should there be some instability in your system (what, your Mac has never crashed or some application has never unexpectedly quit?), you could lose the script. Saving the script is an insurance policy that will let you get back to this state should the worst happen.

I'll help you decide here how to save this script. We'll turn it into an application, since we will probably want to give it to another Mac user who may not appreciate the scary look of Script Editor or have Script Editor installed on his or her machine. Also, we'll leave it in its editable form, since we'll come back to it later in the book and enhance it.

1.   Choose Save As from the File menu (not Save As Run-Only).

2.   In the pop-up menu below the file name, choose Application.

3.   Enter the file name *SW License Consolidator*.

Especially in the case of script applications you intend to give to others, the script's name should help the user know what the app does from the Finder, and pick out one script from perhaps dozens.

Checking the Script

We won't go through the contents of the script at this point (we'll come back to it after you've seen more about AppleScript syntax). But it's still a good idea to give the script a run-through before turning it over to someone else to use. Click the Run button. You'll see those dozens of steps reduced to a single click.

If you should receive an error message that indicates something is wrong with the syntax, select and delete the contents of this script and re-record it. The steps in this example should work as described. Make sure during recording that you perform no steps other than the ones described above.

The Next Step

You've just recorded a pretty powerful script for automating a dull process. From here we go into writing AppleScript scripts. Later we'll write AppleScript to increase the power and apparent intelligence of the SW License Consolidator script. But before we can do that, we must get down to some syntax basics.

PART II

The AppleScript Language

CHAPTER 4

Writing AppleScript Scripts—An Overview

To gain an appreciation for writing scripts, we'll spend some more time in Script Editor. The goal is not to learn specific commands just yet. Rather, you'll recognize what runs in a script and how.

Back to Script Editor

If you're still in Script Editor from the last chapter, close all windows, and choose New Script from the File menu. You see a blank, untitled script editor window.

Notice the small triangle icon above the top left corner of the Description field (Figure 4.1). When it is in the down position, the field is visible and ready for editing. Click the icon to close up the field (Figure 4.2). This position leaves more screen space for your script.

Figure 4.1 The triangle icon pointing down reveals the Description field.

Figure 4.2 Hide the
Description field by clicking
on the triangle icon.

If you want all new script windows to open with the Description field hidden, then hide the field, and choose Set Default Window Size from the File menu. The Script Editor remembers the size, location, and other attributes of the current window as the default.

Results

I now want to introduce you to another window available in Script Editor: the Result. Open this window by choosing Show Result from the Controls menu.

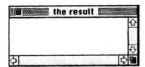

Figure 4.3 The Result window.

The vast majority of script lines produce a result of some kind. For example, if you enter a script line that adds two numbers, and then click the Run button, Script Editor displays the result of that script execution in the Result window (Figure 4.4). Only the result of the last executing line of a multiple-line script

Figure 4.4 The resulting
value of the last script line
appears in the window.

appears in the Result window. Nine times out of ten, you won't even bother viewing these results. But at this crucial learning stage, you can use the Result window as a tool to understand how scripts work.

Checking Syntax

I haven't yet mentioned the Check Syntax button, which sits by itself to the right of the Run button. For strict script recording, the syntax is supposed to be accurate, so it's usually not necessary to check a recorded script's syntax (although there is no penalty for doing so).

Figure 4.5 The Check Syntax button.

The minute you enter any text into the script field of Script Editor, the Check Syntax button activates. You can type utter gibberish into the script, and the Script Editor won't mind—until you click the Check Syntax button. At that point, Script Editor summons its AppleScript powers to doublecheck what you've typed against its own dictionary of AppleScript terms, plus some other places, as we'll see later. It also makes sure you've followed the syntax rules, such as putting commands before the things they're commanding.

What Syntax Checking Does

For those who are experienced in programming environments, the Check Syntax button actually triggers the AppleScript compiler to produce (in memory) a compiled version of the script. This is the same compiled version that gets saved to a compiled script and script application. Compiling the script does not run the script, although clicking the Run button on an uncompiled script compiles it first.

For those without programming experience, the brief explanation is that compilation converts the human readable script you type into a more computer-readable version, which the Mac can perform much faster than having to translate the script each time you click the Run button. As you'll see later, this compilation step also makes sure that any commands you summon from other programs are, in fact, available to the script. So syntax checking performs double duty.

The Outcome

If syntax checking uncovers a problem, a syntax error alert appears. The contents of these error messages can be all over the board, and we'll get into them later. It takes a bit of AppleScript experience to understand the real meaning of some of these messages.

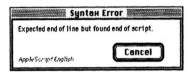

Figure 4.6 A typical syntax error alert.

You'll know if syntax checking was successful by two clues. First, you don't see any error messages. Second, the font of the script changes. As you type any new characters into a script (including one that has already successfully compiled), the characters appear in a distinctive font and size (the default is Courier 10). After successful compilation (see Figure 4.7), the font changes to Geneva 10 (with some words possibly boldfaced and italic). You can change these font settings by choosing AppleScript Formatting from Script Editor's Edit menu, and adjusting individual settings via the Font and Style menus (Figure 4.8).

Let's try a bogus script to see what happens when attempting compilation fails:

1. In a new script window, type the command **do my laundry**.

    This may be a valid command for some future Macintosh, but not the ones we're using today.

2. Click Check Syntax (a handy shortcut for this button is the Enter—not Return—key).

Figure 4.7 A script statement before (above) and after (below) compilation.

AppleScript Formatting

Select keyword categories, then choose
commands from the Font and Style menus to
change their formatting.

New text (uncompiled)	Courier 10pt
Operators, etc. (+ & ,)	Geneva 10pt
Language keywords	Geneva 10pt bold
Application keywords	Geneva 10pt
Comments	Geneva 9pt italic
Values (numbers, strings, lists)	Geneva 10pt
Variables and subroutine names	Geneva 10pt
References	Geneva 10pt

Dialect: [AppleScript English ▼]

[Use Defaults]   [Cancel]   [OK]

Figure 4.8 Script Editor dialog for
adjusting font characteristics of scripts.

The first two words highlight, and a Syntax Error window appears
(Figure 4.9). The error, we're told, is that the word "my" cannot go after
the identifier "do". We know, of course, that there is far more wrong
with this command than what it's telling us, but what AppleScript tells
us is as much as it knows from the information we've given it.

3. Click the Cancel button.

The script is still in Courier font, and the Check Syntax button is still active,
meaning that the script has not compiled.

Now, try a valid command:

1. Select all the text in the script, and press the Delete key to remove it
   all.

2. Type the command **beep**.

Figure 4.9 Words responsible
for the syntax error highlight in
the script.

3. Click Check Syntax.

This time there is no error window, and the font of the beep command turns to Geneva. Notice, too, that the Check Syntax button has become inactive (Figure 4.10). This indicates that the current script in the window is compiled, and no further syntax checking is required. Making even a one-character change to the script reactivates the button, because the compiled version is not what's in the script field.

(a)   (b)

Figure 4.10 The Check Syntax button before (a) and after (b) a successful compile.

Click the Run button to try your beep command. Certainly not the most impressive script in the world, but you've just *written* your first AppleScript script.

Smart Checker

The syntax checker/compiler also tries to clean up messy scripts if it can, replacing a source script with a prettier version if necessary. For example, the beep command, when followed by a space and a number, plays the beep as many times as the number indicates. But if you type multiple spaces between the command and number, the compiler returns the proper version, with a single space. Try it:

1. If it's not already there, place the text insertion pointer at the end of the beep command.

2. Type six spaces and a 3.

The Check Syntax button activates after the first space, because the script has changed since the last compilation. The numeral appears in Courier font, because that part of the script hasn't be compiled yet (the spaces are in Courier, too, but you can't see that).

3. Click Check Syntax.

After successful compilation, the command displays with a single space between it and its number (Figure 4.11).

4. Click Run to hear the beep three times.

During compilation, AppleScript dissects each line, and figures out how each word fits into the grand scheme of things. Thus, as you see in the AppleScript Formatting window (Figure 4.8), you can instruct Script Editor to highlight certain categories of words. In other programming environments, this feature is called "pretty printing," but its goal is not aesthetic: it is to help someone reading the script—including you—more quickly understand how the

(a)   (b)

Figure 4.11 **The sloppy command before (a) and after (b) compilation.**

script works. The default formatting is straightforward, with only one type of word in an active line of script highlighted in boldface. Gradually, you may evolve a different style of your own. There are no rules you must follow in this regard.

The formatting information from the Formatting window (Figure 4.8) is not saved with a script file. Rather, these settings govern how your copy of Script Editor displays scripts from all sources. This includes scripts that may have been written in another AppleScript dialect (see the pop-up menu in Figure 4.8). An AppleScript script originally written in "AppleScript French," for example, appears in whatever dialect is selected in the pop-up window. In the version supplied with System 7.5 in the U.S., only one dialect, AppleScript English, is installed. You can, however, make your formatting "stick" in your copy of Script Editor by choosing Set Default Window Size in the File menu.

Making a Statement

Every line of an AppleScript script is known as a *statement*. A script may consist of any number of statements, including a single line, such as the one-line **beep** statement you wrote earlier.

Another type of statement, called the *compound statement*, begins with only one of a few special AppleScript keywords (you'll learn about these later), and must end with an **end** statement. The compiler performs special indenting of statements nested inside the outer edges of a compound statement. The script you recorded in the last chapter produced a compound statement, starting with the **tell** command. Notice that it had a balancing **end** statement—a requirement for all compound statements.

Commandments

At the minimum, a statement must contain a *command*, a word that acts like a verb to indicate some action that is to take place. Here is an abbreviated version of the script you recorded in the previous chapter (it brings in only a single component of the software license).

```
tell application "Scriptable Text Editor"
    activate
    make new document at beginning
    open file "Hard Disk:Handbook Scripts:Chapter 03:0. Introduction"
    select contents of document 1
    copy
    close document 1 saving no
    paste
    -- the ™ symbol in the next line is typed Option-2
    save document 1 in file "Hard Disk:AppleScript™ Utilities:Software License"
end tell
```

In the indented list of statements, there are three one-word statements (activate, copy, and paste), each one a command that the Scriptable Text Editor knows how to execute.

More common, however, are statements that include additional words after the command. Collectively, items coming after a command are called *parameters*. In the statement, make new document at beginning, make is the command, and new document at beginning are its parameters.

Telling an Object What to Do

A command generally performs an action on an *object*. This is an object in the object-oriented world I spoke about in Chapter 2. What the object is depends entirely on the objects that the application's designers have defined for their product.

For example, in the make statement of the script above, the object it's supposed to make is a document (the new part of the command is optional—you'll learn later how to determine that). Additional parameters (at beginning) provide instructions as to the sequence the new document window should appear if multiple windows are already open.

In the next line, the open command also works on an object: a file with a valid pathname. And so it goes.

Common Actions

While it doesn't show up so much in a recorded script, a significant percentage of actions you'll be writing in scripts have to do with obtaining and inserting information. The AppleScript commands for these actions—get and set—will be the first word of most of the statements you'll write, especially for scripts that exchange information between documents.

For the moment, let's think about getting and setting in the context of one of those large warehouse type stores. In an organized warehouse, each location has some kind of location identifier, like a bin number or row and shelf number. Getting something with AppleScript is like picking out an item from a bin;

setting is like putting the item someplace else—in another bin or your shopping basket.

If this warehouse were a scriptable application, the bin would be an *object*. An item you pick from a bin would be an *element* of that bin. And the bin, itself, has a number of *properties*, such as location, size, minimum reorder point, and so on. The element, too, is an object, with its own properties, such as price, color, size (completely independent of the size property of the bin), and perhaps others.

We can summarize the purchase of an item at one of these stores in Apple-Script terms:

1. Standing in front of the bin, we *get* the price property for one item.
2. If the price fits within a predefined budget, we *get* the color property of the item on the top of the pile.
3. That color isn't what we want, so we *get* the color property of the second item in the pile.
4. It's the one we want, so we *get* the second box object in the pile (in the store, we actually remove the item from the bin, while in AppleScript, we only get a copy of the original, so we don't disturb the original item by getting it).
5. Finally, we *set* the contents of our shopping basket to what was already in there plus the new item object.

In the process of working with real applications, your scripts will get and set elements and properties all over the place. In word processing programs, you'll encounter elements such as characters, words, and paragraphs, with properties for font characteristics, character length, and the like. Spreadsheets elements include cells, columns, rows, and ranges of cells, featuring properties such as widths, formulas, borders, and format. These objects, elements, and properties shouldn't be new to you if you've used these programs, but you probably didn't think about such items quite in those terms before. For these applications to be scriptable, their documents *must* be defined by these bits and pieces.

Where the Wording Comes From

I must emphasize again that the definitions of an application's commands, objects, elements, and properties are entirely up to the program's designers, and are not built into AppleScript. There is no guaranteed uniformity across similar applications (e.g., all databases) that the elements and properties (or the specific syntax for describing them) will be the same.

Application Dictionaries

Script Editor provides a tool for viewing the AppleScript terms that an application knows. Choose Open Dictionary from the File menu (Figure 4.12). The

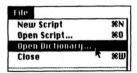

Figure 4.12 The Open Dictionary
command in Script Editor's File menu.

only kinds of applications that appear in the resulting open file dialog box are
those that have the proper add-on ('aete' resource for those who know what
resources are) that signify that the program is scriptable.

Figure 4.13 shows the dictionary window for Scriptable Text Editor. The left
column lists all the AppleScript terms that this application understands. When
you click on a word in the column, the details for that word appear in the right.
I won't go into the specifics of the words here, but it's important to understand
the basic structure of a dictionary.

How Suite It Is

All of Apple's scripting technology (which accommodates other scripting components, such as UserLand Frontier) relies on a behind-the-scenes mechanism
called Apple events. Scripting languages, such as AppleScript and Frontier,
shield scripters from the significant complexity of working with Apple events
directly.

Apple publishes guidelines for various groups of events to help developers
make their programs capable of sending and receiving Apple events. Each
group is called a *suite*. Among the suites commonly in use are:

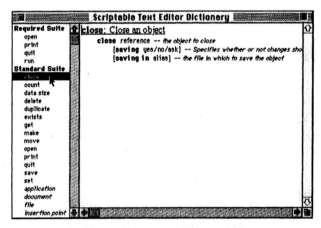

Figure 4.13 Scriptable Text Editor's dictionary

Suite Name	Description
Required	If the application is Apple event–aware, these must be here
Standard	Highly recommended, but not essential
Text	For working with textual data
QuickDraw	For working with graphical data
Table	For representing tabular data
Finder	Definitions for Finder actions
Miscellaneous	Catch-all for common items

Other suites for areas such as communications and personal information management have been developed with the help of applications developers.

Developers who make their programs scriptable have the freedom to pick and choose specific events from whatever suites they like—all in the interest of supporting the functions of their products. The number of suites and number of definitions in each suite varies from program to program. Moreover, most products have a special suite that is specific to that product.

The Scriptable Text Editor divides its dictionary into three suites: Required, Standard, and Scriptable Text Editor. Suite names appear in the left column of a dictionary listing in bold face.

Not So Suite

Beneath each suite name are any commands or objects that belong to that suite. Commands appear in regular font, while objects appear italic (Figure 4.14). One of the things that makes learning an application's AppleScript implementation difficult at times is that there is no specific roadmap in the dictionary that links commands to objects. Some commands work with only a limited number of objects listed for that suite.

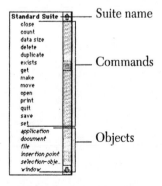

Figure 4.14 Suite names are in bold; commands in plain; objects in italic.

For example, if you're new to scripting Scriptable Text Editor, you may think that you can create a new document by the statement:

make new file

since the **make** command and file object are listed under the Standard suite (and the definition of the **make** command just says it requires an object as an argument). What you can't tell directly from the definition is that the make command works only with window and document objects. Nothing in the application's resources (from which all information shown in the dictionary window comes) can tell us or the dictionary view specifically which command works with which objects. Initially, it becomes a trial-and-error experience or requires a study of whatever external documentation might be supplied by the application's developer.

In future chapters, we'll spend more time in the dictionary, since it is a valuable tool to help you know what a scriptable application can do. But as you've just seen, the dictionary doesn't tell the whole story.

CHAPTER 5

A Crash Course in Programming Fundamentals

As with a lot of programming environments I've seen, learning AppleScript sometimes seems to require knowing many parts before you can learn the first part. Subject A requires a knowledge of subject B; but you can't learn subject B without knowing subject A. If AppleScript is your first programming experience, this can be frustrating. It seems as though everything whirls around like a carousel without a brake. 'Round and 'round it goes—when you try to hop on, forces of nature repel you.

The goal of this chapter isn't necessarily to stop the wheel, but to slow it down enough so an inexperienced programmer can hop on safely. I'll introduce you to important terminology and concepts that will make learning AppleScript comparatively easy. If you are an experienced programmer or HyperTalk scripter, you can skim this chapter to make sure that your understanding of these terms is the same as the way they're used in AppleScript.

Open Script Editor, because we'll type some things there to reinforce the meaning of these concepts. Don't worry of you don't fully comprehend everything, because we'll revisit all these terms in more detail in succeeding chapters.

Statements

In the previous chapter, you saw that a script consists of a series of statements. They may be all simple statements—one-line statements that appear aligned along the left margin of Script Editor's window:

```
tell application "Scriptable Text Editor" to open file "Software License"
```

More commonly, especially when scripts perform a number of steps inside an application, the statements are grouped into a compound statement:

41

```
tell application "Scriptable Text Editor"
    open file "Software License"
    print front window
    close front window
end tell
```

Compound statements begin with only a limited number of AppleScript words (predominantly tell, if, repeat, try, on, and to), and always end with an end statement. After compilation, compound statements are formatted so that the simple statements within a compound statement are indented. In the example above, the tell compound statement contains three simple statements.

Commands and Objects

Statements, as you've also seen, usually consist of at least one command, such as the beep command. Many commands also accept or require additional words—parameters—to help them carry out the action.

The beep command has an *optional* parameter: the number of times the beep sounds. If you don't specify a parameter, then the command has a default parameter of 1. Therefore,

```
beep
```

and

```
beep 1
```

achieve the same action. But if a command *requires* a parameter, then a parameter must follow the command in the statement. For example, the open command in Scriptable Text Editor requires a parameter signifying what should be opened. Thus, in the statement

```
open file "Hard Disk:Chapter 03:Software License"
```

the parameter to the open command is file "Hard Disk:Chapter 03:Software License".

The formal definition of the open command in Scriptable Text Editor's dictionary says the following:

open reference

The word "open" is clearly the command here. The parameter, however, is defined merely as something called a reference. In AppleScript, a *reference* is the manner in which we distinguish one object from all the rest. Recall I said in the last chapter that commands perform actions on objects. For AppleScript to know precisely which object you mean—among perhaps thousands of possible objects "living" in your Macintosh at any instant—you signify the object by its reference. Take the statement

```
open file "Hard Disk:Chapter 03:Software License"
```

as an example. The object of our **open** affections is a file whose Finder path name is "Hard Disk:Chapter 03:Software License." The wording—file "Hard Disk:Chapter 03:Software License"—is a valid reference for a file as far as Scriptable Text Editor is concerned. Remember that virtually every command and object we write about in a script is defined by the application we're scripting Scriptable Text Editor wants its files referred to by the word "file" and the full pathname to the file. In this case, the word "file" specifies what kind (class) of object the text between the following pair of quotes refers to: a file.

Object Elements and Properties

An object's dictionary definition includes what component parts (*elements*) make up that object, and what *properties*—characteristics or attributes—help define the object. For example, in Scriptable Text Editor, the document is one of the main objects. Among the elements of a document are paragraphs and words. If we want to refer to a particular word in the document, we assemble a reference from the point of view of the document:

word 3 of document 1

If that word 3 happens to be the first word of the second paragraph, then we can also refer to it in the context of the paragraph

word 1 of paragraph 2 of document 1

because paragraphs, themselves, have words as elements. Both object references point to the same word, and either one would be valid in an AppleScript script directed to Scriptable Text Editor (Figure 5.1). This element business sounds more complicated than it is. The more familiar you are with a program you'll be scripting, the more logical become the relationships between objects and the elements they consist of.

More important are the properties of an object. Also listed in an application's dictionary, object properties define the characteristics of the object—sometimes visible, sometimes not. Table 5.1 shows the properties of a Scriptable Text Editor window object:

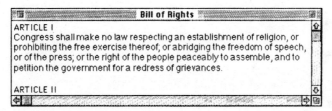

Figure 5.1 In this document, a word has position relative to the entire document and to its own paragraph. "Congress" is both word 3 of the document "Bill of Rights" and word 1 of paragraph 2 of the document "Bill of Rights."

Table 5.1 Properties of a Scriptable Text Editor Window Object

Property	Read-Only	Description
bounds	no	Boundary rectangle for the window
closeable	yes	Does the window have a close box?
titled	yes	Does the window have a title bar?
index	no	Number of the window in sequence
floating	yes	Does the window float?
modal	yes	Is the window modal?
resizable	yes	Is the window resizable?
zoomable	yes	Is the window zoomable?
zoomed	no	Is the window zoomed?
name	no	Title of the window
selection	no	Selection visible to the user
visible	yes	Is the window visible?
modified	yes	Has window been modified since last save?
position	yes	Upper left coordinates of window

You don't have to remember these at all, but once you start working with an application, it will be helpful to acquaint yourself with the range of properties for the objects you'll be dealing with. In this case, most of them govern the visible appearance and behavior of a window. One, the modified property, isn't so obvious, because it tracks whether the contents of the window have changed since it was last saved. Simple properties may be either on or off (true or false), while others consists of coordinates or text. Many properties here are read-only, which means that scripts can only find out what their settings are, and cannot change them.

To retrieve the contents of a property at any instant, you use the AppleScript get command, as in:

```
tell application "Scriptable Text Editor"
   get modified of document 1
end tell
tell application "Scriptable Text Editor"
   get position of document 1
end tell
```

Changing the value of a property involves the set command, as in:

```
tell application "Scriptable Text Editor"
   set bounds of window 1 to {20, 59, 481, 305}
end tell
```

with the items in curly braces representing screen coordinates in pixels. Try running this script yourself with Script Editor.

Working with Information

Virtually every statement you write in a script contains information—data. Even setting a property, like the bounds of a window, above, contains data about the coordinates. Any kind of data that can be shuffled around inside AppleScript is called a *value*. AppleScript values come in a number of different varieties, called *value classes*. One reason for this is that parameters for commands often accept only a specific kind of value.

For example, in the statement

beep 3

the **beep** command accepts an optional value to specify how many times to beep. The parameter must be an integer (a number without any decimal fraction). Trying to feed another kind of value, such as a series of letters between quotes (called a string value), would result in an error (you'll learn more about this in a moment). Table 5.2 lists examples of the most common value classes used in AppleScript.

Table 5.2 Common Value Classes in AppleScript

Class	Example	Description
Boolean	TRUE	A logical true or false
integer	233	A positive or negative whole number (no decimals allowed)
list	{1,2,3}	A series of other values of any class—arranged in a specific order inside curly braces
real	2.5	A positive or negative number with decimal fraction
string	"Howdy"	A series of characters inside quote marks

There are additional value classes, which you'll meet in Chapter 9. By and large, values do their work automatically, as long as you help them when necessary (e.g., putting quotes around strings or curly braces around lists). Occasionally, however, it will be necessary to change one value class to another. For example, a script may fetch some real numbers, perform some math on them, and then have to insert them into another document as a string. This conversion process is called *coercion*, but we can save that discussion for later.

Variables

In the course of any kind of programming, it is often necessary to hold values in temporary baskets while the script gets additional data or performs operations on the original values. Consider this script:

```
tell application "Scriptable Text Editor"
    set oneBlock to paragraph 1 of document 1
    make new document at beginning
    set the contents of document 1 to oneBlock
end tell
```

Let's focus on the three statements inside the compound statement. The first uses the **set** command to place a copy of the first paragraph of an opened document into a basket we've arbitrarily named oneBlock. Since the contents of that paragraph are now safely in the basket inside our script, we can forget about document 1 and move on. The script next creates a new document window and sets the contents of that window to whatever the oneBlock basket holds at that instant. In AppleScript, this kind of holding basket is called a *variable*.

You assign values to variables with either the **set** or **copy** commands. The following two statements accomplish the same task:

```
set myMac to "PowerBook 280c"
copy "PowerBook 280c" to myMac
```

They both put the string "PowerBook 280c" into the variable named **myMac**. For the most part, you can use either syntax, depending on which one reads better to you, but as you'll learn in Chapter 6, the **set** command has additional powers that may be useful in certain situations.

An AppleScript variable can hold any type of value (string, integer, list, etc.). And unlike many programming languages, you don't have to predetermine what kind of value a particular variable will hold. In fact, a variable's contents may change radically during script execution, holding a reference to a file in one statement and a text string in the next—if your script so requires.

The names you assign to variables can play a critical role in your understanding of how a script works. AppleScript allows single-word variable names without any coaching. You may, however, use multiple-word variable names, provided the words are contained between vertical bar characters (the shifted backslash key). For example, the following variable names are valid in AppleScript:

```
oneBlock
one_Block
|one Block|
```

My personal preference for single-word names consisting of two or more plain language words is to have each word after the first capitalized (e.g., one-Block). I find this style easiest to read and also the least likely to conflict with words reserved (now or in the future) by AppleScript or scriptable applications.

I also often use single-letter variables for repeat loop counters, as you'll see in Chapter 10. The important point to remember is to assign names that describe the contents of the variable. I'll have more to say about variables in Chapter 9.

Expressions and Evaluation

We've seen that any piece of data—an integer, a string—is a value in Apple-Script. Another concept that is closely related to the value is the *expression*.

We use expressions in everyday language. Consider the sentence:

"I want to watch television."

The word "television" is universally understood to be the box that replays sound and pictures carried to it from an antenna or cable. We use the word "television" as an expression to stand in for the meaning of a more formal or complete definition of that device. But it's not uncommon for us to use other expressions for that television:

"I want to watch *TV*."
"I want to watch *the tube*."
"I want to watch *the idiot box*."

All three sentences end with different words, but in our minds, we know what they mean. We automatically (often unconsciously) *evaluate* each term to our mental picture of the device.

In an AppleScript statement, all values are automatically evaluated to their true meanings. For example, an expression that is already at its truest form, say the integer 3, can be evaluated no further. But a value of 3 + 4 evaluates to 7.

Variables also get involved here. When we set a variable to hold some value, the variable becomes an expression that evaluates to whatever the contents of the variable are. For example, after executing the statement

```
set x to 5
```

the variable x evaluates to its contents: 5. In the next example,

```
set y to 5 + 5
```

before y is assigned its value, the arithmetic expression, 5 + 5, is evaluated to 10. The variable y holds the value 10.

Why this expression evaluation stuff is important in AppleScript is that it grants scripters great flexibility in working with values as parameters to commands. Consider the open command from Scriptable Text Editor we've used before. We saw that it requires as a parameter a reference to a file. We had hard-wired the parameter before, as

```
open file "Hard Disk:Chapter 03:Software License"
```

But we can substitute any expression after the open file command that evaluates to the string that is expected for the file's path:

```
set pathName to "Hard Disk:Chapter 03:Software License"
open file pathName
```

Here, the pathName variable contained a string. Before the **open** command executed, AppleScript evaluated all expressions in the statement to their true form. Once the pathName variable evaluated to the string, the command read internally just like the hard-wired version. This is particularly useful if you intend to use that value many times in a script—you need only the short variable to stand in for the long, quoted string.

The key point to remember about expressions and evaluation is that you can substitute any expression for a value, as long as the expression evaluates to the kind of value that is expected at that instant.

Operators

It's quite common to use *operators* in expressions. In fact, in one example we used above,

```
set y to 5 + 5
```

we used the addition operator, signified by the plus symbol. An operator generally performs some kind of calculation or comparison with two values to reach a third value. Arithmetic operators are easy enough to grasp, since they let us add, subtract, multiply, or divide two values (integer or real number classes of values) to arrive at the answer.

Another kind of operator lets us join two string values into a longer string that is the combination of the two. That operator, represented by the ampersand (&), is called the *concatenation* operator. The expression

```
"John" & "Doe"
```

evaluates to "JohnDoe", because the concatenation operator is very literal when it comes to joining strings. If you want a space between concatenated strings, then you've got to put it there yourself. One way to put the space between the strings is to put the space inside one of the component strings, as in

```
"John " & "Doe"
```

Or, you can concatenate three strings, one of which is merely a space, as in

```
"John" & " " & "Doe"
```

Depending on the source of your strings, you may end up using both forms in your scripting.

You will often use multiple layers of expression evaluation with operators. In the script fragment

```
set x to 5
set y to 20
set z to x + y
```

the last statement first evaluates each of the variables, x and y, before adding them. Only then does AppleScript set the value of z to 25.

AppleScript is also loaded with operator vocabulary to help you compare values. Not just to find out if things are the same, less than, or greater than, but whether one item comes before another in a list and whether one string contains another string. You'll see what all these operators are in Chapter 11. These kinds of comparison operators return only one kind of value, a Boolean—TRUE or FALSE. Boolean values are used frequently as on/off indicators for object properties. But where these comparison operators and their Boolean results come into play is constructing scripts that make decisions based on the results of comparisons. We do this in real life all the time: if the room is dark when we enter it, then we turn on the lamp first; otherwise we go straight ahead with what we planned to do there. We'll cover this in detail in Chapter 10, when we start working with if-then decisions.

Continuation Symbols

I'll introduce here a symbol (¬) that you will see in many scripts throughout this book. The symbol is called a *continuation symbol*. A statement may be too long to fit comfortably in the margins of this book or within the viewable area of your Script Editor window. You can break up the line into smaller chunks, provided you put a continuation symbol at the end of the broken line.

While the symbol is normally typed as Option-L, Script Editor lets us insert one by holding down the Option key while pressing the Return key. It's like a "soft" return. There are some tricks involved if you want to break up a line in the middle of a string, but we'll cover that in Chapter 9.

Comments

The last item I'll cover here is something else you'll see often in scripts throughout this book. They're called *comments*, and are pieces of a script that do not compile or execute. Comments are useful as extra plain language guides to let someone reading the script understand a statement that may not be obvious.

To instruct the compiler to ignore comments, they must be formatted in one of two ways. One is a double hyphen preceding the comment. In this fragment

```
-- we set the x variable
set x to 5 + 5 -- x is now 10
```

the only part that compiles and executes is set x to 5 + 5. Because all other items began with the double hyphen, the compiler ignores them. The double-hyphen is useful for one-line or in-line (i.e., at the end of a valid statement) commands.

Comments may also be bracketed by special symbol combinations. The comment begins with (* and ends with *), as in

```
(* This is a long comment,
which can go
on for many lines. *)
```

Comment sections of any script appear in italic after compilation (this is the default behavior of Script Editor, although you can choose a different font or style for comments). Good scripts use comments liberally, because they help you remember why you did certain things in your scripts.

A Lot of Stuff

This chapter has crammed a lot of terminology and concepts into a small space. If you didn't get it all, don't worry too much, because we'll cover everything in more depth in succeeding chapters. It was important, however, to acquaint you with these concepts, because they'll help you work with the details. We begin with the details in the next chapter with commands.

CHAPTER 6

Issuing Commands and Getting Results

In previous chapters, you've seen three of AppleScript's built-in commands—get, set, and copy—in action. In this chapter, we'll learn more about them, as well as see what else AppleScript comes with. Before we get to the actual commands, however, there is some other ground to cover, namely where the commands come from, how commands return information back to a script, and how we direct commands to the proper target.

Commands Provoke Action from Something

AppleScript commands are the verbs of the language. As the first word of any simple statement, a command signals the action that is to take place as a result of the statement. You may wonder, though, that if a human language command has an intended audience, what about an AppleScript command?

AppleScript does, too. In formal terminology, the recipient of a command is considered an *object*. But which object? Consider the command

    beep

in a script all by itself. When you run this script, AppleScript looks for an object to send it to. Since none is specified in this statement or elsewhere in the script, AppleScript sends the command to itself. If there is a command within AppleScript's own dictionary to match, then it carries out the command without complaint.

When it comes time to direct a command to an application, the script must specifically do so with a tell statement. Here's how a tell statement looks in simple form:

    tell application "Scriptable Text Editor" to make new document

In other words, you're sending the command, make new document, to Scriptable Text Editor. That program has the make command in its dictionary, and knows what to do with it. If your script had been the single line

```
make new document
```

you would receive an error when you try to run the script, because AppleScript doesn't have the make command in its vocabulary.

Ganging Statements

It would be exceedingly cumbersome to designate the object of every command in a script. AppleScript provides a shortcut for grouping commands directed at a single object. By creating a compound tell statement, all commands inside it are directed to the *default object*—the last application signified by a tell statement in the script. For example, look at the following script:

```
tell application "Scriptable Text Editor"
    activate
    make new document
end tell
```

Both the activate and make new document statements have Scriptable Text Editor as their objects.

Nested Tell Statements

As scripts get more complex and work with multiple applications, it may be necessary to temporarily redirect the default object of some steps within a compound tell statement. Schematically, such a script might look like this:

```
tell application "ScriptWord"
    ScriptWord-compatible statement 1
    ScriptWord-compatible statement 2
    tell application "ScriptSheet"
        ScriptSheet-compatible statement 1
        ScriptSheet-compatible statement 2
    end tell
    ScriptWord-compatible statement 3
    ScriptWord-compatible statement 4
end tell
```

The important item to notice here is that ScriptSheet understands only commands in its dictionary—not those from ScriptWord's dictionary. The tell statement defines the focus, no matter how nested it may be.

If the script you're writing works with two applications in a serial, rather than nested, fashion, you could also structure your script like this:

```
tell application "ScriptWord"
    ScriptWord-compatible statement 1
```

```
      ScriptWord-compatible statement 2
    end tell
    tell application "ScriptSheet"
      ScriptSheet-compatible statement 1
      ScriptSheet-compatible statement 2
    end tell
```

Scripts continue to execute down the statements until there's no more to execute.

HyperTalk Watch

In HyperTalk you get used to execution stepping through only single handlers—an **end** statement that balances a handler's **on** statement finishes up all execution. AppleScript compound **tell** statements are not in any way like HyperTalk handlers. A script executes in full, with the exception of subroutines (in the familiar on-end handler format you're used to in HyperTalk). Therefore, in the script above, execution runs from one **tell** statement to the next without any interruption.

Mixed Bag

You can also combine a single statement directed at a different object within a compound **tell** statement. Here's an example of how this might look:

```
    tell application "Scriptable Text Editor"
      -- puts a paragraph from default object,
      -- STE, into the variable oneBlock
      set oneBlock to paragraph 1 of document 1
      -- the next statement goes to a desktop publishing
      -- application that has defined a text block object
      -- where text can be dropped in
      tell application "Scriptable DTPer" to ¬
          set text block 3 of document 1 to oneBlock
      -- back to STE as default object
      set paragraph 1 of document 1 to "√" & oneBlock
    end tell
```

More Specific

So far we've just been directing commands toward applications. But a script can be even more specific about a default object if it helps the cause of the script. For example, if a script performs a lot of actions in a single document window, and you know there will be only one document window, then the script can set up the document window of a specific application as the default object. Instead of:

```
tell application "Scriptable Text Editor"
   set oneBlock to paragraph 1 of document 1 -- directed to document 1
   close document 1 saving no -- and here, too
   make new document
   set contents of document 1 to oneBlock -- and here
end tell
```

we can make the script a bit more compact by saying:

```
tell document 1 of application "Scriptable Text Editor"
   -- document 1 is understood as default object
   set oneBlock to paragraph 1
   close saving no
   -- new document becomes document 1, in front of others!
   make new document
   set contents to oneBlock
end tell
```

So, you see, you can be as granular as you like in establishing a default object.

The purpose of these exercises in default object-ry is to demonstrate that every command needs an object as a recipient. You can specify the object in a simple statement, in a compound tell statement, or ignore the object entirely if the default object you want is AppleScript or a scripting addition.

Networked Applications

With the ease of setting up a Macintosh network, you may have to write scripts that summon the scripting powers of applications that reside on another Mac on the network. AppleScript lets you do this by being specific about the location of the application on the network. You specify as part of the application parameter (of a tell statement) the name of the Macintosh, as defined in that machine's Sharing Setup control panel. If the network is divided into multiple zones, you can specify the zone as well. A volume from the other Mac does not have to be mounted on your Desktop for this feature to work.

The format for the reference to an application on another machine is:

```
application applicationName of machine computerName ¬
   [ of zone AppleTalkZoneName ]
```

The brackets in these vocabulary definitions mean that the contents are optional.

Here is a networked version of our software license example. In this scenario, each user has the license section on his or her machine. The job of the script is to use the Scriptable Text Editor application on each user's machine to open and copy the segment, and then bring it back into the combined document:

```
tell application "Scriptable Text Editor" -- our copy
   activate
   make new document at beginning
   -- here we go to Steve's machine for the Introduction
   tell application "Scriptable Text Editor" of machine "Steve's Mac" ¬
      of zone "Associates"
      -- Steve had set up a folder that he leaves available for sharing
      open file "SteveHD:Shared Documents:0. Introduction"
      copy contents of document 1 to oneDoc
      close document 1 saving no
   end tell
   -- now we're back in our own STE
   copy oneDoc to end of document 1
   -- do the same for other parts on other Macs
end tell
```

You'll notice that we don't use the copy and paste scheme from the recorded script. The reason is that by working through Steve's copy of Scriptable Text Editor, the copy command would have used his Clipboard—and Clipboards don't transfer from machine to machine. Therefore, we place the data in a variable, which lives in our machine in our script, and makes the journey to our document.

As an author of scripts that perform actions across Macintoshes on a network, you must be aware of this and other scripting limitations. One, in particular, will affect your design. While a tell statement to an application on your own Mac opens the application before sending the commands, *scripts do not have the power to launch applications on a remote Mac*. When the application object of a command is on another Mac, the application must already be open. For additional information about these kinds of accesses, see the notes about the choose application command, in Chapter 7.

Where the Words Are

You probably got the point already that AppleScript, by itself, comes with only a small handful of commands. The rest of the language comes from outside of AppleScript. Here are the four places commands (and objects) are made available:

1. **AppleScript** All these commands are built into the AppleScript extension, and can be called anywhere in a script.

2. **Scripting additions** These are system extensions of a very special type, and must reside in the Scripting Additions folder, nested inside the Extensions folder. Scripting additions transparently extend the vocabulary of AppleScript as far as the scripter is concerned, because these commands can be called anywhere in a script. In fact, Apple, in its documentation for AppleScript, includes the scripting additions it

supplies as part of the AppleScript dictionary. I don't like to do that for a number of reasons:

a. A scripter can't count on the AppleScript Run Time to be properly installed in a user's machine.

b. The user may have mistakenly deleted the scripting addition before knowing your script needed it.

c. The scripting additions supplied by Apple may change over subsequent releases of AppleScript.

In any case, scripting additions (sometimes called OSAXes, after their file type) provide enormous flexibility for AppleScript, allowing C and Pascal programmers to extend AppleScript's native abilities. You can find a number of scripting additions on electronic bulletin boards frequented by AppleScript scripters. Many are included on the companion disk, and are explained in Chapter 33.

3. **Scriptable application** These commands can be used only when directed to the application. You can look up these commands in the application by choosing Open Dictionary in Script Editor.

4. **User-defined commands** These are subroutines that scripters can design and make a part of a script. You can think of a user-defined command as a scripting addition written in AppleScript. A user-defined command may exist inside the script that calls it, or may be loaded into the script when the script runs (see Chapter 14 for more about script libraries).

Who Gets What?

Each of the four kinds of commands has a different scope. The question is, then, what does AppleScript do with a command that isn't in the scope of the default object? For example, in the following script, I'll comment as to the location of the command vocabulary for each statement inside the tell statement:

```
tell application "Scriptable Text Editor"          -- STE, for short
    activate                                        -- AppleScript
    open file "Hard Disk:Chapter 03:Software License"   -- STE
    set oneBlock to paragraph 1 of document 1       -- AppleScript
    make new document                               -- STE
    set contents of document 1 to oneBlock          -- AppleScript
    display dialog "The job is done!"               -- scripting addition
end tell
```

Yet in all cases, the commands first go to the default object, Scriptable Text Editor. The mechanism, however, provides a pathway for these commands to follow if nothing intercepts them. This mechanism is analogous to the HyperTalk message passing hierarchy, but the hierarchy depends on where the command is located. Here are the rules:

1. If the command has AppleScript as the default object (i.e., it is not inside a tell statement directed at an application), then the command follows this path:

    user-defined command

    AppleScript command

    scripting addition command

    Here is an example you should try in Script Editor:

    ```
    choose file with prompt "Pick a file, any file:"
    doMyCommand()
    -- a user-defined command that is the same as a scripting addition
    on choose file with prompt promptText
        display dialog "I trapped the choose file command."
    end choose file


    -- a user-defined command just for this script
    on doMyCommand()
        display dialog "The command reached this user-defined command."
    end doMyCommand
    ```

    When you run this script, you get two dialog boxes that show how both commands were trapped by user-defined command handlers in the same script (even though one of them, choose file, is a scripting addition).

2. If the command has an application as the default object (i.e., it is inside a tell statement), then the command follows this path:

    application command

    AppleScript command

    scripting addition command

    If we modify the example, above, so that the two primary statements are directed to Scriptable Text Editor:

    ```
    tell application "Scriptable Text Editor"
        choose file with prompt "Pick a file, any file:"
        doMyCommand()
    end tell


    -- a user-defined command that is the same as a scripting addition
    on choose file with prompt promptText
        display dialog "I trapped the choose file command."
    end choose file
    ```

```
    -- a user-defined command just for this script
    on doMyCommand()
        display dialog "The command reached this user-defined command."
    end doMyCommand
```

then when you run the script, you get the actual choose file dialog from the scripting addition (the command never looked for a user-defined match in the script). When the running script reaches the doMyCommand( ) statement, it generates an error message that says Scriptable Text Editor doesn't know this command. In other words, AppleScript has entirely different hierarchies, depending on the default object of the command (although see Chapter 14 for ways to alter the message hierarchy for user-defined commands).

More About Parameters

We saw in earlier chapters that commands sometimes have extra words appended to them that supply necessary information for the command to do its job. These words are called *parameters*. An important part of a command's definition in this book is the description of what parameters, if any, accompany the command.

In the command definitions, you'll see two different kinds of parameters: direct and labeled parameters. Both kinds were used in the script you recorded in Chapter 3.

A *direct parameter* generally consists of the object that the command is to work with. For example, in the statement

```
select contents of document 1
```

the select command's direct parameter is an object reference to the contents of a document. The ever popular get, set, and copy commands all use direct parameters.

In contrast is the *labeled parameter*, a parameter whose value is preceded by a plain language word describing what the value is supposed to represent. From our recorded script, we had the statement:

```
close document 1 saving no
```

The close command (as defined in Scriptable Text Editor) has both a direct parameter (a document) and a labeled parameter (saving no). When the designers specified the behavior of the close command, they realized that if a document is edited in any way, the program will ask the user about saving changes before closing the document. In real life, we have the choice of not saving those changes. We have the same choice while scripting. The command includes a labeled parameter, called saving, which requires either a yes, no, or ask value—yes to save changes; no to ignore changes; ask to query the user about saving. Labeled parameters make statements much more meaningful to someone reading a script. Instead of a gibberish list of parameter data, the statement almost reads like a sentence.

Labeled parameters also let you write the statement in any order that makes the most sense to you. For example, the formal definition of the choose file command (which displays an open file dialog box) indicates a statement syntax like this:

choose file with prompt "Select something:" of type "TEXT"

From a plain language syntax point of view, however, it's the file of type "TEXT" we want, not a prompt of that type. Because this command uses labeled parameters, you could just as easily reorder the statement to read:

choose file of type "TEXT" with prompt "Select something:"

Parameters of any type may be required or optional, depending on how the command was defined by its designer. If a parameter is required, then there must be a parameter of the required class provided. You can detect whether a command has required or optional parameters (or both) from the command definitions in this book. Optional parameters are surrounded by brackets, as in the following:

beep [*numberOfBeeps*]

If you don't supply a parameter to the beep command, it uses its default value: 1. But you can also supply any other integer, if needed.

Here's an example of a command that has both required and optional parameters (a lot of them):

display dialog *questionString* [default answer *answerString*] ¬

[buttons *buttonList*] [default button *buttonNumberOrName*] ¬

[with icon *iconNumberOrName*]

The first parameter, *questionString*, is a required parameter. It also doesn't have a label, so it must go where it does, immediately after the display dialog command. The rest of the parameters are optional (in brackets), and they are labeled. You can use only the one(s) you need to specify the dialog box. We'll cover what these parameters mean in Chapter 7.

Getting Results

Unlike a lot of other programming languages, AppleScript commands almost always return a result of some kind. There are no functions, per se, in AppleScript. Most of the time, your script will ignore the results that come back after issuing a command, but they're there if you need them (e.g., for debugging purposes—see Chapter 13).

After a command executes, the result is stuffed into a special AppleScript variable called result.

HyperTalk Alert

The result variable in AppleScript operates very much like the It variable in HyperTalk. In HyperTalk, for example, the value of a **get** command is placed into It; in AppleScript, the value of a **get** command is placed into result. Of course, HyperTalk places some returned values in the result variable (e.g., from **ask** or **answer** dialogs), so there is ambiguity across the language. You don't have that ambiguity in AppleScript—everything comes back in result.

Script Editor lets you show a separate window, which displays the value of the result variable at the end of a script's execution. If for debugging purposes you need to view results of lines as they execute, use the Event Log window (Chapter 13).

Show the Result window in Script Editor, and type the following statements—one at a time—into the script window. Run each script to view the value that comes back as result:

```
3        -- this expression evaluates to itself

3+4      -- evaluates to the sum

"Fred"   -- evaluates to its own string

get 3

set genius to "Einstein" -- result is the value assigned to genius

current date -- the date and time from Mac's clock

count of {"larry", "moe", "curly"} -- the number of items in the list: 3
```

You can then use the result variable in a script to convey the value from a command to a more durable variable (result will change with the next command). For example:

```
count of {"larry", "moe", "curly"}
set numOfStooges to result
```

You can now use the numOfStooges variable throughout the script, even though the contents of the result variable will be changing with each command.

In later chapters, you'll also see how you can use commands as parameters to other commands. This is logical, because a command returns a value—which may then be used as a direct parameter to another command in the same statement. Here's a preview of what such a construction might look like:

```
set numOfStooges to count of {"larry", "moe", "curly"}
```

The count command evaluates to a value (3), which is then assigned to the numOfStooges variable.

"Standard" Application Commands

From what you may read in Apple's *AppleScript Language Guide*, Apple has gone out on a limb to document commands commonly found in applications—the so-called *standard application commands*. While this documentation effort is helpful in many ways (especially for scriptable applications that provide little or no documentation for scripters), it is equally risky. One risk is that newcomers to scripting may believe that these "standard" commands are a part of AppleScript and/or are supported by every scriptable application. Moreover, there may be the expectation that the way these commands are documented by Apple is the way they work in all scriptable applications. Such is the myth.

The reality is that this presentation is more guidance for developers to implement the common Apple events in their scriptable applications. As a scripter, you can use these definitions as starting points, but don't be surprised to find applications implementing commands slightly differently or providing additional capabilities for a particular command. Apple's own Scriptable Text Editor (STE) is a good example. While Apple defines the copy command as a standard application command (as well as an AppleScript command), STE defines the copy command not in the Standard Suite of events, but in the Scriptable TE Suite. Also, don't be surprised if not every command is supported by every application.

Application Commands

Table 6.1 lists all standard application commands identified by Apple, and indicates in italic which ones are also in AppleScript's own vocabulary.

Even though several items are the same as AppleScript's own commands, they are implemented with some enhancement in an application. In any case, it is important to check the syntax of the commands presented here against the scripting dictionaries of scriptable applications you intend to work with.

Table 6.1 Application and *AppleScript* Commands

Close	Make
Copy	Move
Count	Open
Data Size	Print
Delete	Quit
Duplicate	*Run*
Exists	Save
Get	*Set*

You will see these commands again in Chapter 18's discussion about their implementation in Scriptable Text Editor. But later you'll see how these commands can be implemented differently in Chapter 19's discussion about Table-Server's dictionary—TableServer's objects are about tables, not paragraphs. For example, compare the parameters to the make command in STE (Chapter 18) against those to the same command in TableServer (Chapter 19).

If there is an advantage to these standard application commands, then, it is not that you learn one command for all programs, but that when you are scripting a newly acquired program, you know what command to look up in the dictionary. For example, rather than wonder if a program requires a make, new, or create command to generate a new document or object, you should look first for a make command, because it is the accepted standard command for such an operation. Then use the details in the dictionary to fill in the blanks of parameters for the unique objects and document environment of that application.

AppleScript Commands

The following commands are the ones that are hard-wired into the AppleScript system extension. If a user's computer has this extension, then the commands listed in this section will be available. The list is small, but the items listed here account for a majority of the commands you will write in scripts.

activate *referenceToApplication*

Result
None.

Purpose
Makes the referenced application the active application among all open programs on your Macintosh. For crowded screens, it allows the person running the script to see the action in that application.

When to Use
Recorded scripts always record the activate command, because you can't help but activate the program to perform recordable actions. But activating every program in a script is not necessary. You may see an application open beneath current programs while a script runs. Unless the comfort of witnessing each action is required (to some, seeing is believing), you can leave out this step on most scripts. On slower machines, the activation may also slow down the elapsed time required to execute the script as the Mac must refresh more of the screen as applications switch.

Some application commands require that the application be the active one to work. For example, if an application lets you cut, copy, or paste with the

Clipboard, the laws of Macintosh operation insist that the application be active to access the Clipboard.

Parameters

This command requires only one direct parameter in the form of a reference to an application. Such a reference begins with the word "application" or "app" plus a quoted string containing the name or pathname to a program. Most commonly, the application reference is handled by a preceding tell statement, as happens during script recording. In this case, the object of the **activate** command is the default object, the application referred to in the tell statement.

If you don't specify a full pathname as part of the application reference, and the application is not already open, you may receive a file dialog box that asks where the program is. AppleScript does not search a volume (or volumes) for the specified application.

The application must be capable of receiving AppleScript commands for it to respond to the **activate** command. If you specify a non-scriptable application that isn't running, any number of things can happen depending on the application. Here are some of the behaviors I've observed with numerous non-scriptable applications:

- The program launches, but in the background.
- The program launches in the background, and locks the screen except for the Application menu, which you can use to access the newly launched app—but switching back to Script Editor, the script waits for an acknowledgment from the app, and times out after two minutes.
- The program launches in the foreground.
- The program launches, but AppleScript issues the error "The application does not respond to Apple Events."

If the non-scriptable application is already open, the response ranges from no response to a temporary delay until the underlying Apple Event times out.

As with any application reference parameter (this goes for such a parameter to a tell statement, as well), if the application is on the same machine as the script, the application will open automatically when it is called by the script. The application must be available on a mounted volume on your Mac for the script to compile (but the application doesn't open for compilation).

For applications on a different machine on an AppleTalk network, the reference must include the machine name (and zone name if the network is divided into multiple zones). See the discussion earlier in this chapter about references to networked applications. The most important point to remember is that an application on another machine must be open for both script compilation and script execution. Also, the other machine must: (a) have Program Linking turned on in its Sharing Setup control panel; and (b) have the target application set for sharing (select the application in the Finder, choose Sharing from the File menu, and turn on program sharing for this app). Users of scripts that call shared applications also must go through the System 7 Program Linking logon process the first time the application is accessed (even if the volume containing that application is already mounted on your Mac's Desktop).

Examples

```
activate application "Scriptable Text Editor"
```

```
activate application "SteveHD:Applications:Microsoft Excel" ¬
    of machine "Steve's Big Mac"
```

You Try It

Enter the following script and run it:

```
tell application "Scriptable Text Editor"
    activate
end tell
```

Common Errors

Forgetting the word "application" in the application reference parameter; not putting the entire pathname to an application in the parameter; trying to activate a non-scriptable application; File and Program Sharing turned off for remote access; remote application isn't running.

Related Items (Chapters)

Choose file (7); choose application (7); recording applications (3); default object (6); networked applications (6); application object references (8).

copy *expression* to *variableOrReference*

Result

Value that was copied (any class).

Purpose

Places a duplicate of a chunk of data into an object or variable.

When to Use

The copy command lets you put any kind of information into an object or variable. It is in many ways synonymous with the **set** command, although the latter has additional powers. Since much of what goes on in scripts that link documents or applications together is moving information around, the copy command can be used to fetch information from one document (placing the information into a variable), and then putting the information (from the variable) into another document.

Parameters

Both parameters are required. The first, *expression*, is the item that is to be copied. Any valid expression can be used here, since it is the evaluated value that is placed into the object or variable. The expression could also be a reference to an object, in which case AppleScript retrieves the value of the object before putting it into the object or variable.

When the second parameter is written as a single word (but not an Apple-Script reserved word), then AppleScript assumes that word to be the name of a variable. As a result of the copy command, the variable contains a copy of whatever the first parameter evaluated to. In the simplest example,

```
copy 90210 to ZIPCode
```

the value, 90210, is copied to the ZIPCode variable. But the first parameter could also be a reference to an object, as in

```
tell application "Scriptable Text Editor"
    copy paragraph 1 of document 1 to niceGraph
end tell
```

Here, the expression parameter is a reference to a particular paragraph of a particular document. AppleScript evaluates this expression to the actual text of the paragraph. The variable, niceGraph, then contains just the text. NiceGraph is ignorant of the source of the text or anything about Scriptable Text Editor documents.

The second parameter may also be a reference to an object. If the reference doesn't indicate a position within the object (e.g., beginning or after), then the object is replaced by the value of the first parameter. With this script, we replace document 2's first paragraph with the first paragraph from document 1:

```
tell application "Scriptable Text Editor"
    copy paragraph 1 of document 1 to niceGraph -- variable niceGraph
    copy niceGraph to paragraph 1 of document 2 -- replaces paragraph
end tell
```

But if insertion point references are supported in the application (as they are in Scriptable Text Editor), then you can also insert data:

```
tell application "Scriptable Text Editor"
    copy paragraph 1 of document 1 to niceGraph -- variable niceGraph
    copy niceGraph to before paragraph 1 of document 2 -- inserts at beginning
end tell
```

Also valid in this scenario would be one longer statement that has references for *both* parameters:

```
tell application "Scriptable Text Editor"
    copy paragraph 1 of document 1 to ¬
    before paragraph 1 of document 2
end tell
```

Examples

copy "Fred" to oneName

copy formula of cell "R1C1" to firstFormula

copy bounds of window 1 to windowCoords -- *copying an object's property*

You Try It

On the companion disk, in the Chapter 06 folder, are two Scriptable Text Editor files, named "Sample 6.1" and "Sample 6.2". Open both files. Position them, a Script Editor window and the result window, as shown in Figure 6.1. Then enter and run each script separately below:

```
tell application "Scriptable Text Editor"
    copy paragraph 1 of document "Sample 6.1" to oneGraph
end tell
```

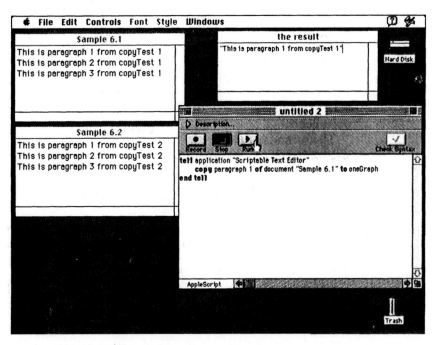

Figure 6.1 Window layout for experiments.

The result contains the value of the data copied to oneGraph—the contents of the first paragraph of the document.

```
tell application "Scriptable Text Editor"
    copy paragraph 1 of document "Sample 6.1" to oneGraph
    copy oneGraph to paragraph 3 of document "Sample 6.2"
end tell
```

The script replaces paragraph 3 of Sample 6.2 with the contents of one-Graph.

```
tell application "Scriptable Text Editor"
    copy paragraph 1 of document "Sample 6.1" to oneGraph
    copy oneGraph to paragraph 3 of document "Sample 6.2"
    copy return to end of document "Sample 6.2" -- append a carriage return
    copy oneGraph to end of document "Sample 6.2"
end tell
```

In this script, we use the **copy** command to copy a constant value—a carriage return, known by the word **return**—and a paragraph to the end of Sample 6.2. Because the second parameter of the last two **copy** statements indicate a position reference (end of), the data is inserted at that point, rather than replacing some other text. When you're finished with this example, close both text files without saving changes.

In our final example, we'll use the **copy** command twice to fetch vice presidential data from a TableServer table, and place the data in a Scriptable Text Editor document. For best results, place the Presidents file in the same folder as TableServer:

```
tell application "Scriptable Text Editor"
    activate
    make new document
    tell application "TableServer"
        if not (table "Presidents" exists) then
            open file "Presidents"
        end if
        copy Value of cell "Vice President" ¬
            of row "James K. Polk" of table "Presidents" to Veep
        close table "Presidents"
    end tell
    copy Veep to end of document 1
end tell
```

Inside TableServer, we open a table (delivered on the companion disk) that contains Presidents, their parties, and Vice Presidents. The script copies the value from one cell to a variable, which we later append to a Scriptable Text Editor document.

Common Errors

Incorrect object reference syntax; an object named in the second parameter cannot accept the type of value contained in or referred to by the first parameter.

Related Items (Chapters)

Get (6); set (6); object references (8); variables (9).

count [of] *directParameter* [each *className*]

Result

An integer representing the number of elements in an object. Applications may enhance this command so that it returns multiple values in the form of a list of integers.

Purpose

Provides a count of elements in lists, records, or application objects.

When to Use

Obvious applications for this command are when a script needs to know how many objects there are, such as the number of characters in a word or the number of words in a document. But a script often needs to know how many elements there are in an object so it can set up a repeat loop that performs some action on only as many items as there are elements.

Because the value returned by the count command often goes into a variable, it is common to employ count statements as parameters of other commands, such as copy and set, as in:

```
set wordCount to (count words in document 1)
```

To help AppleScript figure out your meaning in such a statement, place the parentheses around the nested statement.

Parameters

The *directParameter* must be one of the following:

a. The actual data to be counted

b. Variable that evaluates to the data to be counted

c. A reference to an application object whose data is to be counted

Types (a) and (b) can be used within AppleScript by itself, and are generally lists, records, or strings; type (c) must be used inside a tell statement directed to an application.

Here is an example of the command working with a list of various pieces of data:

```
count {"Red Sox", 3, "Yankees", 2}
    -- result: 4
```

But we can add a parameter to more narrowly define classes of items we want to count. For example, if we want to know how many teams are in the list, we actually want to know how many strings there are. Therefore we can add the each *className* parameter, as in

```
count {"Red Sox", 3, "Yankees", 2} each string
   -- result: 2
```

Here is an interesting alternative to the last example. Rather than specify "each string," we use a reference form, strings in {"Red Sox", 3, "Yankees", 2}, as the *directParameter*. This reference evaluates to another list, containing just the strings: {"Red Sox", "Yankees"}—try it yourself in Script Editor to see the result. This evaluated reference is what gets counted, as follows:

```
count strings in {"Red Sox", 3, "Yankees", 2}
   -- evaluates to:
count {"Red Sox", "Yankees"}
   -- result: 2
```

Incidentally, if the *directParameter* is a simple string (i.e., not in a list), then the default behavior of the count command is to count the characters (including spaces), as in:

```
count "Knowledge Navigator"
   -- result: 19
```

Scriptable Text Editor enhances the count command by letting us count things like characters in a word, words in a paragraph, paragraphs in a document, and so on. Other programs may allow you to count cells in a spreadsheet or graphic objects in a document. Here is how you might use the count command to set the first character of every paragraph of a document to bold:

```
tell document 1 of application "Scriptable Text Editor"
   set graphCount to (count of paragraphs) -- perform this command just once
   repeat with i from 1 to graphCount -- step through each paragraph
      if (count of words of paragraph i) > 0 then -- omit blank paragraphs
         set the style of character 1 of paragraph i to bold
      end if
   end repeat
end tell
```

We used the count command in two in-line statements, because we needed the values that the count command returned. One value became the maximum number for a repeat loop; the other let us know whether the paragraph had a character to set to bold (in Scriptable Text Editor, a blank line is still a paragraph, because it ends with a return character).

There is a lesson here in how to examine components of a statement in case you get errors you don't understand. Take the in-line command, count of words of paragraph i. The reference to words of paragraph i evaluates to a list of words in the paragraph; the count command then counts the number of items. You can dissect a reference like this, and experiment in Script Editor to see exactly how a reference evaluates, so you know what the count command will be counting. See more about this as a debugging technique in Chapter 13.

Examples

```
count of {1, 3, 5} -- result: 3

count {1, 1.5, 2} each real -- result: 1

count words of "Now is the time" -- result: 4
```

You Try It

Enter and run each of the following commands in Script Editor one at a time. Keep the Result window open and visible so you can see the result of the count.

```
count of {"Eeny", "Meeny", "Miney", "Moe"}

set charCount to count "Antidisestablishmentarianism"

count integers in {1, 2, 3, "four", "five", "six"}
```

Open a new window in Scriptable Text Editor, and type several words in a single line. Then enter the following script to see how the reference works:

```
tell application "Scriptable Text Editor"
    get words of paragraph 1 of document 1
end tell
```

The result will show a list of all the words. Now, replace the **get** command with the **count** command:

```
tell application "Scriptable Text Editor"
    count words of paragraph 1 of document 1
end tell
```

The result is the number of words in the list.

One more example, this time counting the rows of a table, reveals information about the size of the table:

```
tell application "TableServer"
    if not (table "Presidents" exists) then
        open file "Presidents"
    end if
    set numOfPresidents to (count of rows of table "Presidents")
    close table "Presidents"
end tell
numOfPresidents
    -- result: 42
```

We assign the count to a variable (numOfPresidents), which we repeat after the script to view its value in the Result window.

Common Errors

Incorrect reference form for the *directParameter*; trying to count an application's objects without specifying the application (e.g., in a tell statement).

Related Items (Chapters)
List value class (9); record value class (9).

[get] *expressionOrReference*

Result
The value of the expression or reference.

Purpose
Assign a value to the result variable.

When to Use
Because this command does little more than copy a value to the result variable—which changes value after the very next statement in a script—the get command is often used for retrieving throwaway information. By this I mean information whose lifespan doesn't need to extend beyond the next statement. This can come in handy immediately preceding an if-then or repeat construction, in which the result variable is examined for some comparison or repeat value.

```
tell application "Scriptable Text Editor"
   get font of paragraph 1 of document 1
   if result is not "Helvetica" then
      display dialog "The first paragraph isn't in Helvetica."
   end if
end tell
```

In practice, it's more efficient to avoid get statements if you can. For example, the above script can be shortened to read:

```
tell application "Scriptable Text Editor"
   if font of paragraph 1 of document 1 is not "Helvetica" then
      display dialog "The first paragraph isn't in Helvetica."
   end if
end tell
```

It is also a waste of script to get a value, and then copy the result to a variable: Just copy the value to the variable directly using the copy or set commands. But sometimes, a reference or expression may not evaluate for use in one side of an if-then statement. If that's the case, then use the two-step method with the get command.

The get command—especially the version that doesn't use the "get" word for the command—does come in handy, however, for debugging purposes. As you begin to write a script, you can test it up to a certain point, and use a get statement as the last line of the script to check the value of an expression or reference. See Chapter 13 for debugging guides.

Parameters

Perhaps the most striking part about this command is that the command, itself, is optional. We've actually seen this action in previous discussions. If you type any value (a number or quoted string) into a script, and run it, the result contains that value. Therefore, these two statements are identical:

```
"Jane"
```

```
get "Jane"
```

Both statements place the string, "Jane", into the **result** variable (and displayed in the Result window). The same goes for expressions that evaluate to other values:

```
3 + 4
    -- result: 7
```

```
"John" & " Doe"
    -- result: "John Doe"
```

```
paragraph 1 of document 1
    -- result: the actual contents of that paragraph as a string
```

For your own use, the **get** word is usually superfluous. But if you intend to use one of these statements in a script that others will read, it's best to use the **get** word to make the script easier to read and follow.

The main parameter of this command is an expression or a reference to an object (including an object's properties). It is always the value of that expression or reference that goes into **result**. Therefore, in the statement:

```
get 3+4
```

the result contains the evaluated value, 7, not the characters of the arithmetic problem. Similarly, the statement:

```
get words 1 thru 5 of paragraph 1 of document 1
```

as defined by Scriptable Text Editor, places the actual words as a list into **result**, not the wording of the reference.

When working with some application objects, the object reference may evaluate to data you cannot see in the Result window, such as a chart or Quick-Time movie (they are, after all, data that can be copied and set just as numbers and strings).

Examples

```
10
    -- result: 10
```

```
10 + 10
    -- result: 100
```

```
get 10 + x
    -- result: nothing, because it's an invalid expression
```

get name of window 1
-- *result: "untitled 2"*

words 1 thru 3 of document "Preamble"
-- *result: {"We", "the", "people"}*

You Try It

Enter several one-line arithmetic problems, and run each one as a script. Look for the answers in the Result window.

Next, create a compound tell statement directed at Scriptable Text Editor. Open any document or enter some a couple lines of text yourself. Try each of the following one-line **get** statements and examine the results. Some of these get contents of the document, while others get properties of objects:

get contents of document 1
get paragraph 1 of document 1
get words of paragraph 1 of document 1 -- *words are returned in a list*
bounds of window 1
font of paragraph 1 of document 1
size of word 1 of document 1   -- *font size*
length of word 1 of document 1   -- *number of characters*

Common Errors

Incomplete application object references; trying to force an evaluation of mixed value classes (e.g., integer + string); confusion over an application's dictionary, mistakenly trying to get a property that doesn't exist for a particular object.

Related Items (Chapters)

Copy (6); set (6); object references (8); if-then constructions (10); repeat loops (10); debugging scripts (13).

run *variableOrReference*

Result

For an application reference, no result.

When to Use

It's not often that you need to use this command to start up an application, because any statement directed at a scriptable application (via a tell statement) automatically launches the application anyway. The run command encounters the same kinds of problems with non-scriptable applications as the activate command.

Issuing the command to an application that is already open, however, may be useful if the program performs some initializations in response to the command. For example, Scriptable Text Editor always opens a new untitled window whenever it runs—either from a Finder launch or as a recipient of the run command. This can give you a known state to start a series of statements. But not all programs react this way. If you want to launch an application but not allow it to go through its initialization, use the launch command (below).

A scripting addition with a similar sounding command, run script, is described in Chapter 7.

Parameters

Parameters for the run command may be a variable or reference that evaluate to the name of the application. If an application is already running, the file name without pathname is understood to mean running (i.e., sending the run Apple event to) the copy already open. Otherwise, a pathname to the application is required (unless the app and script file or Script Editor are located in the same folder). Be sure to include the word "application" as part of an application reference, as in:

```
run application "Scriptable Text Editor" -- for application
```

The surefire way to provide a valid pathname to an application or script file is to let the user choose the file via the choose file command:

```
set fileToOpen to (choose file with prompt ¬
    "Choose a program to run:" of type {"APPL"}) as string
run application fileToOpen
```

Since the choose file command returns the chosen file as a class of alias, your script must coerce the value to a string (see more about value classes in Chapter 9).

Forcing the user to open the desired application every time would be an unwelcome user interface "feature." Fortunately, you can have your script (saved as an application) store the pathname as a property, so the user is faced with the file dialog only the first time the script runs in the same session (i.e., without closing the script):

```
property fileToOpen : ""

if fileToOpen is "" then
    set fileToOpen to (choose file with prompt ¬
        "Choose a program to run:" of type {"APPL"}) as string
end if
run application fileToOpen
```

Examples

```
run application "HD:Applications:Microsoft Excel"

run application myFile -- variable containing pathname
```

You Try It

Close Scriptable Text Editor if it's running. Then enter and run the following script:

```
get (choose file with prompt "Open STE") as string
run application result
```

Leave Scriptable Text Editor running, and position Script Editor windows such that you can see part of the Text Editor's window. Then enter the following command, and run it twice:

```
run application "Scriptable Text Editor"
```

Notice how the run command provoked the program's initialization process to create a new window.

Common Errors

Omitting "application" from parameter; trying to use an alias class value as a parameter, when a string for the pathname is required; trying to open non-scriptable applications.

Related Items (Chapters)

Launch (6); choose file (6); run script (7); value classes (9); script objects (15).

launch *variableOrReference*

Result

None.

When to Use

The launch command is a kinder, gentler version of the run command. While the run command not only launches an application or script object, it also sends a run Apple event to the launched object. It is this run Apple event, for instance, that makes Scriptable Text Editor go through its initialization paces to produce a new untitled window. It is also the event that tells a script object to do its work (if there is a matching run handler in the script object to obey).

This activity proves to be unacceptable for script objects designed to run and stay open (things like background agents). They end up opening and quitting before they get to run their scripts—and AppleScript eventually times out because one of its events fails to get handled.

AppleScript provides this launch command as a workaround, specifically for run-and-stay-opened script objects. It tricks the script object into launching without letting it perform its implicit run duties. You can then safely issue the AppleScript run command at a later time to get the script to do its thing.

Should you try launching an already-open application, nothing happens. You can also use this command to launch non-scriptable applications without the problems and timeouts inherent in using the **activate** and **run** commands.

Parameters

The **launch** command's parameters are the same as the **run** command's parameters. The same guidelines and cautions apply.

Examples

```
launch script "HD:System Folder:Script Objects:Find New Folders"
```

You Try It

Close Scriptable Text Editor if it's running. Then enter and run the following script:

```
get (choose file with prompt "Open STE") as string
launch application result
```

Leave Scriptable Text Editor running, and position Script Editor windows such that you can see part of the Text Editor's window. Then enter the following command, and run it twice:

```
launch application "Scriptable Text Editor"
```

Notice how the **launch** command does not cause the program's initialization process to create a new window, as the **run** command does.

Common Errors

Omitting "application" or "script" from parameter; trying to use an alias class value as a parameter, when a string for the pathname is required.

Related Items (Chapters)

Run (6); choose file (6); run script (7); value classes (9); script objects (15).

set *variableOrReference* **to** *expression*

Result

The value assigned to the variable or reference.

When to Use

The **set** command is perhaps the most used command in AppleScript scripts. Its job is to assign a value to a variable or application object (including properties of objects). You may freely mix **copy** and **set** statements in the same script, since they perform the same basic value assignment tasks. But it will be easier on someone reading your scripts if you are consistent.

While the **set** command does everything that the copy command does (albeit with parameters in a different syntactic order), it does have an extra, unseen power when the item being set is a list, record, or script object: *data sharing*.

A demonstration of data sharing reveals more about it than a long explanation. Consider this series of statements:

```
set stoogeList to {"Larry", "Moe", "Curly"}
set comedyGroup to stoogeList
set item 3 of stoogeList to "Shemp"
```

We first assign a list of strings to a variable. Then we assign that variable to a second variable, comedyGroup. Finally, we change the third value in the original variable, replacing Curly with Shemp. What's the value of comedyGroup?

Without data sharing, the value of comedyGroup would remain what it was when it was assigned. But because the **set** command automatically performs data sharing with variables that evaluate to lists, records, and script objects, the value is updated in comedyGroup as well. Therefore, if you run these four script lines:

```
set stoogeList to {"Larry", "Moe", "Curly"}
set comedyGroup to stoogeList
set item 3 of stoogeList to "Shemp"
comedyGroup -- examine value in result window
```

you'll see that comedyGroup is updated to be {"Larry", "Moe", "Shemp"}—the same as stoogeList. As long as the initial **set** statement for the second variable doesn't try to modify the value of the second value (e.g., concatenating an additional item in the process), data sharing will survive any subsequent modification to the second variable:

```
set stoogeList to {"Larry", "Moe", "Curly"}
set comedyGroup to stoogeList
set item 1 of comedyGroup to "Larry Fine"
set item 2 of comedyGroup to "Moe Howard"
set item 3 of stoogeList to "Shemp Howard"
comedyGroup
    -- result: {"Larry Fine", "Moe Howard", "Shemp Howard"}
```

Moreover, data sharing is bi-directional. Any change you make to one variable appears in the other. After the above script, the stoogeList variable evaluates to the same as comedyGroup.

Data sharing is more memory-efficient, especially for large data collections. Instead of creating multiple copies of the same data for use in various parts of a script, data sharing lets one copy be shared among multiple variables. Data sharing can extend anywhere throughout a single script (and all activity must be on the same Mac). For example:

```
set stoogeList to {"Larry", "Moe", "Curly"}
set comedyGroup to stoogeList
```

```
shempify(comedyGroup)
stoogeList
-- result: {"Larry", "Moe", "Shemp"}
```

```
on shempify(comedyGroup)
   set item 3 of comedyGroup to "Shemp"
end shempify
```

In this version of our earlier script, we break the replacement of Curly with Shemp out to a subroutine. We create a shared copy (comedyGroup), which we pass as a parameter to the subroutine. The subroutine merely modifies one item of the list. But in so doing, the other shared list is updated without having to return the "shempified" value.

Parameters

Both parameters are required. The second, *expression*, is the item that is to be evaluated and assigned to the object defined by the first parameter. Any valid expression can be used here, since it is the evaluated value that is placed into the object or variable. The expression could also be a reference to an object, in which case AppleScript retrieves the value of the object before putting it into the object or variable.

When the first parameter is written as a single word (i.e., not an AppleScript reserved word), then AppleScript assumes that word to be the name of a variable. As a result of the **set** command, the variable contains whatever value the second parameter evaluated to. In the simplest example,

```
set ZIPCode to 90210
```

the ZIPCode variable is assigned the value, 90210. But the second parameter could also be a reference to an object, as in

```
tell application "Scriptable Text Editor"
   set niceGraph to paragraph 1 of document 1
end tell
```

Here, the *expression* parameter is a reference to a particular paragraph. AppleScript evaluates this expression to the actual text of the paragraph. The variable, niceGraph, then contains just the text. It is ignorant of the source of the text or anything about paragraphs or documents.

The first parameter may also be a reference to an object. If the reference doesn't indicate a position within the object (e.g., beginning or after), then the object is replaced by the value of the first parameter. With this script, we replace document 2's first paragraph with the first paragraph from document 1:

```
tell application "Scriptable Text Editor"
   set niceGraph to paragraph 1 of document 1 -- variable niceGraph
   set paragraph 1 of document 2 to niceGraph -- replaces paragraph
end tell
```

But if insertion point references are supported in the application (as they are in Scriptable Text Editor), then you can also insert data:

```
tell application "Scriptable Text Editor"
    -- assign contents to variable niceGraph
    set niceGraph to paragraph 1 of document 1
    -- insert text at beginning
    set beginning of paragraph 1 of document 2 to niceGraph
end tell
```

Also valid in this scenario would be one longer statement that has only references for both parameters:

```
tell application "Scriptable Text Editor"
    set beginning of paragraph 1 of document 2 to ¬
        paragraph 1 of document 1
end tell
```

Examples

```
set oneName to "Fred"

set firstFormula to formula of cell "R1C1"

set windowCoords to bounds of window 1 -- copying an object's property

set locked of file "myFile" to true
```

You Try It

On the companion disk, in the Chapter 06 folder, are two Scriptable Text Editor files, named "Sample 6.1" and "Sample 6.2". Open both files. Position them, a Script Editor window and the result window, as shown in Figure 6.1. Then enter and run each script separately below:

```
tell application "Scriptable Text Editor"
    set oneGraph to paragraph 1 of document "Sample 6.1"
end tell
```

The result contains the value of the data assigned to oneGraph—the contents of the first paragraph of the document.

```
tell application "Scriptable Text Editor"
    set oneGraph to paragraph 1 of document "Sample 6.1"
    set paragraph 3 of document "Sample 6.2" to oneGraph
end tell
```

The script replaces paragraph 3 of Sample 6.2 with the contents of one-Graph.

```
tell application "Scriptable Text Editor"
    set oneGraph to paragraph 1 of document "Sample 6.1"
```

```
      set paragraph 3 of document "Sample 6.2" to oneGraph
      -- append a carriage return
      set end of document "Sample 6.2" to return
      set end of document "Sample 6.2" to oneGraph
   end tell
```

In this script, we use the **set** command to assign a constant value—a carriage return, known by the word **return**—to the end of Sample 6.2. Because the first parameter of the last two set statements indicate a position reference (end of), the data is inserted at that point, rather than replacing some other text.

In our final example, we'll use the **set** command twice to assign vice presidential data in a TableServer table to a variable, and place the data in a Scriptable Text Editor document:

```
tell application "Scriptable Text Editor"
   activate
   make new document
   tell application "TableServer"
      if not (table "Presidents" exists) then
         open file "Presidents"
      end if
      set Veep to Value of cell "Vice President" ¬
         of row "James K. Polk" of table "Presidents"
      close table "Presidents"
   end tell
   set end of document 1 to Veep
end tell
```

Inside TableServer, we open a table (delivered on the companion disk) that contains Presidents, their parties, and Vice Presidents. The script copies the value from one cell to a variable, which we later append to a Scriptable Text Editor document. Compare the syntax of this version with the version using the **copy** command earlier in the chapter.

Common Errors

Incorrect object reference syntax; an object named in the first parameter cannot accept the type of value contained in or referred to by the second parameter.

Related Items (Chapters)

Copy (6); object references (8); variables (9).

Onward to Scripting Additions

In the next chapter, we examine commands that are external to AppleScript, but are supplied by Apple as scripting additions. We'll also look at how application dictionaries describe an application's commands.

Scripting Addition Commands and Dictionaries

AppleScript's internal vocabulary is intentionally small. It is meant to supply only the basic structure and wording for shuffling data from point A to point B, leaving the more powerful work to scripting support inside applications. But often we scripters need more help with file, data, and interface issues on a universal scale—not just when we're inside applications with those powers.

To fill the gap, AppleScript provides a mechanism whereby the commands available to all scripts can be extended to include some of these helpful extensions. These extensions are called *scripting additions*. You use these commands in AppleScript statements just like you do the built-in commands. When you call one in a statement, AppleScript looks for its specifications in a special folder—Scripting Additions—installed inside the System's Extensions Folder.

HyperTalk Alert

Scripting additions have the same feel as XCMDs and XFCNs in HyperTalk. You will often see references to these additions by this file type: OSAX. Details and examples for writing OSAXes in C or Pascal can be found in the AppleScript Developer's Toolkit.

Apple supplies a number of useful scripting additions, which we'll discuss in this chapter. To help you get an overview of what you'll have at your scripting fingertips, I've divided Apple's scripting additions into categories by type of operation:

System Commands	Finder Commands	String Commands
beep	path to	ASCII character
choose application	list folder	ASCII number
choose file	list disks	offset
choose folder	info for	
new file		
scripting components		
AGStart		
monitor depth		
set volume		

Numeric Commands	Script Commands	User Interface Command
round	load script	display dialog
random	run script	
	store script	

File Commands	Debug Commands	Date/Time Commands
open for access	log	current date
close access	start log	timeToGMT
read	stop log	
write		
get eof		
set eof		

We'll cover these commands within the groupings to help you learn them initially, and then to make them and related commands easy to find later as a reference.

System Commands

beep [*numberOfBeeps*]

Result
None.

When to Use
Beep sounds are intended to alert the user when some user interaction is required, often before displaying a dialog box that signals an error or other problem. The actual sound that plays is the beep sound set in the Macintosh's Sound

control panel. I find multiple beeps that serve as alert sounds to be very annoying. Scripters can also use beeps in the debugging process to know whether certain parts of a script (e.g., a branch of an if-then construction) execute as expected. By placing beep commands with varying number of beeps, you can get an aural clue about where inside a script the current execution is taking place. Be sure to remove such beep statements before releasing the script to other users.

Parameters

If you omit the parameter for this command, the beep sound occurs once per command. Any parameter you supply, however, must evaluate to an integer value.

Examples

```
beep

beep 4
```

You Try It

Enter and run the following script:

```
display dialog "How much is 2 + 2" default answer ""
if {"4", "four"} contains text returned of result then
    display dialog "Awright!"
else
    beep -- alert that something is wrong
    display dialog "Since when?"
end if
```

Common Errors

Sound control panel sound is turned off; variable value used as parameter does not evaluate to an integer.

Related Items (Chapters)

Display dialog (7).

choose application [with prompt *promptString*] ¬
[application label a*ppListLabel*]

Result

Clicking the OK button returns a reference to an application (in the form application *applicationName* of machine *computerName* of zone *AppleTalk ZoneName*) chosen by the user in the choose application dialog box. Clicking the Cancel button returns error number –128 and error string "User canceled".

When to Use

The choose application dialog box (Figure 7.1) became a part of the Macintosh toolbox when the first interapplication communication (IAC) concepts were built into the Macintosh system. The intent of this dialog box is to allow users to choose a program on another Macintosh for program linking—the ability of one program to send Apple events to another program on another machine.

Figure 7.1 The choose application dialog box.

Since an AppleScript script in a networked environment may well need to send commands to other Macintoshes, the **choose application** scripting addition lets you build this user interface element into your scripts. From the dialog, your script can obtain a complete pathname to an application on another Macintosh, including machine and zone names. That's all you need for describing an application as an object for things like **tell** statements. While you can use this to access a pathname to applications on your own Mac, user interface guidelines strongly suggest using the **choose file** command for that purpose.

If there are no zones set up in the network, the user doesn't see the zone list, nor does the command return a zone name. Here are some examples of returned values:

```
application "Scriptable Editor" of machine "Steve's Mac"
```

```
application "Microsoft Excel" ¬
    of machine "Giga Server" of zone "MIS Dept"
```

From a practical standpoint, the potential downside of this command (and the whole concept of program linking, for that matter) is that to see a list of programs on another Mac, that other Mac must be set up (via the Sharing Setup control panel) for program linking, and only programs that are running on that other Mac appear in the list of available programs. If you're setting up a networked script and can enforce which applications must stay open, this may not be a problem, but be prepared to do some error checking in scripts that utilize this command.

Also be aware that users whose scripts link to an application on the remote Mac will have to go through the Program Linking log-on process, and hope they either have been granted guest access or have the password assigned to them by the remote Mac's owner (also see Chapter 33's discussion of an OSAX that automates the network log-on). Connecting Macs to a network is easy; making the experience friendly isn't always so easy.

Parameters

Both labeled parameters are optional, and both must be strings. One, *promptString*, specifies the text that goes across the top of the dialog. This should contain as specific instructions as necessary to guide the user to select the right kind of application. The second parameter, *appListLabel*, lets you specify the label that appears atop the list of programs. If you omit a parameter, the command supplies default values. For promptString, the default is "Choose a program to link to:"; for appListLabel, the default value is "Programs" (see Figure 7.1).

Examples

```
choose application

set targetApp to (choose application with prompt "Pick a program:")
```

You Try It

If you don't have access to a network of one or more Macintoshes with program sharing turned on, there isn't much need to try this command. But if you have the network setup to do it, enter and run the following script, watching the Result window for what the command returns:

```
choose application with prompt "Select a scriptable application:"
    application label "Apps"
```

Try selecting other machines and programs to view the results of those choices.

Common Errors

Program sharing isn't turned on at other machine; other Mac is not running System 7 or later; any one of dozens of common networking problems with cables and control panel settings.

Related Items (Chapters)

Choose file (7).

choose file [with prompt *promptString*] [of type *fileTypeList*]

Result

Clicking the Open button (see Figure 7.2) returns a reference to the file chosen by user in the form alias *pathname*. Clicking the Cancel button returns error number –128 and error string "User canceled".

When to Use

The choose file command provides a standard open file dialog box for users to select a file from any mounted volume on their Desktop. This is a common user interface device, so users of your script should know how to locate a file. To select a folder, see the choose folder command, below.

Figure 7.2 The choose file dialog box.

The command does not open any files, but does return the full pathname of the selected file in a quoted string, preceded by the word alias, making the value an alias class, as in:

    alias "HD:Documents:Presentations:Overhead Template"

But if you want to perform any operations just on the name of the file, the returned value must be coerced to a string value. You can combine the choose file command and value class coercion in a single statement, such as:

    set myFile to (choose file with prompt "Select a file:") as string

The result from this command would look like this:

    "HD:Documents:Presentations:Overhead Template"

If you want only the name of the file, and not its pathname, you can perform some magic on the string, by changing a property of AppleScript—text item delimiters. Since colons are the delimiters of pathnames, you can change the text item delimiters to be a colon, and then extract the last text item. Here's a complete script that does this:

    set myFile to (choose file with prompt "Select a file:") as string
    set oldDelims to text item delimiters of AppleScript -- *save existing*

```
set text item delimiters of AppleScript to {":"} -- set new
set justFileName to last text item of myFile
set text item delimiters of AppleScript to oldDelims -- restore
justFileName
```

It's very important to restore the text item delimiters property of AppleScript to its original setting. Unlike HyperCard (in which many properties like this automatically reset to default values after a script runs), AppleScript properties remain in effect until you quit Script Editor (or your script application quits). AppleScript's default text item delimiters property is an empty string within a list {""}.

If the user selects a Finder alias to a file, choose file returns a reference to the original file, not to the alias. This command does not support getting the pathname to an alias file.

Because this command provides an interface element that the user controls, your script should anticipate all actions the user could make in a situation like this: selecting the desired file; selecting the wrong file; clicking the Cancel button. See Chapter 13 for more about error trapping in scripts.

Parameters

Two optional parameters—both of them labeled parameters—let you insert a prompt into the file dialog and limit the kinds of files that appear in the lists of files.

The with prompt *promptString* parameter makes room for one line of prompt text in the file dialog. The length of the string that will show up depends on the width of various characters in the Chicago font, but it's generally fewer than 50 characters—still plenty to give instructions to most users. The *promptString* part of the parameter must evaluate to a string class variable.

A file type is a four-character identifier that helps the Finder differentiate between different kinds of files (and display their icons accordingly or let them open applications along with documents). Because the choose file command without any restrictions displays every file (including invisible files), things can get confusing for users. You can instruct the command to filter the views so that only folders and files of the desired type(s) are displayed. Table 7.1 demonstrates popular file types.

Notice that each file type is four characters (no more, no less). Also notice that uppercase and lowercase characters make a difference. If, while designing a script, you're unsure about the file type of a document, use this one line script to help you:

```
file type of (info for (choose file))
```

The of type parameter for the choose file command requires a list class variable. By placing multiple file types in the list, your script can allow more than one type of file to be listed.

Table 7.1   A Sampling of File Types

File Type	Description
TEXT	Plain text file
APPL	Any application
PICT	Graphic file saved in PICT file format
PNTG	Graphic file saved in the MacPaint file format
QUIL	Scriptable Text Editor document
osas	Compiled script
osax	Scripting addition
W6BN	Microsoft Word 6 document
XLS5	Microsoft Excel 5 spreadsheet
STAK	HyperCard stack

Examples

```
choose file

set myFile to (choose file with prompt "Pick a file, any file:")

choose file with prompt "Select a spreadsheet:" ¬
    of type {"XLS4"}

choose file with prompt "Select a document:" ¬
    of type {"TEXT", "QUIL"}
```

You Try It

Enter and run each of the script lines below, selecting a file in the dialog, and watching the result window to see the values returned by the command:

```
choose file

choose file with prompt "Select a file of your choice:"

choose file of type {"QUIL"}

choose file with prompt "Select an STE file:" ¬
    of type {"QUIL"}

get (choose file of type {"TEXT","QUIL"}) as string
```

Common Errors

Expecting just the file's name or pathname being returned as a string; not observing proper capitalization of file types; forgetting to place file types in a list.

Related Items (Chapters)

Choose application (7); choose folder (7); alias and text value classes (9); info for (7); text item delimiters property (8).

choose folder [with prompt *promptString*]

Result

An alias reference to the selected folder.

When to Use

This scripting addition is a sister command to the **choose file** command. Issuing the command creates a special file dialog (Figure 7.3), which allows the user to select a folder. For many Finder-based operations (e.g., locating files within a given folder whose modification date is after a certain date), it is important that users have the ability to select a folder.

Figure 7.3 The choose folder dialog box.

The dialog has three unique features to it. The first is that only folders appear in the item list. Second is a Choose button, which is the one the user clicks to select a folder for further action. The default button, Open, opens a selected folder to view its contents. If there are no folders within the opened folder, then the item list is empty. Last, an extra button below the item list allows the user to select the current folder without backing out one more level to select it. This is also how the user would be able to select the Desktop folder, by, indeed, backing all the way out to the Desktop and clicking this button.

Like other file dialogs, this one's Cancel button generates a –128 error, halting script execution. Therefore you should place statements using this command inside a Try-Error construction if you want to gracefully bow out of a script when the user cancels the dialog.

The returned value of the **choose folder** command is an alias reference form, but the last item in the quoted part of the reference is the folder name, followed by a colon, as in:

    alias "Macintosh HD:Documents:Correspondence:"

This form is the one preferred by various other scripting addition commands that require a folder reference as a parameter (although see Chapter 17 for folders and the scriptable Finder). Moreover, you can coerce the reference to text, append a file name, and create a file or alias reference for some other file-based command, as in

```
set myPath to (choose folder with prompt "Choose your AppleScript folder:") as
text
set myPath to myPath & "Test Script Data"
set myFile to (open for access file myPath with write permission)
(* do file writing here *)
close access myFile
```

Parameters

One optional parameter lets you insert a prompt to help the user locate the kind of folder your script requires. If no *promptString* parameter is included with the command, the choose folder command inserts a default prompt: "Choose a folder:". A custom prompt may be up to 255 characters long.

Examples

```
choose folder

set folderPath to (choose folder ¬
    with prompt "Where should we store the backup file?")

size of (info for (choose folder))
```

You Try It

Enter and run each of the script statements in the Examples section, above, watching the intermediate values in the Event Log window.

Common Errors

Using "alias" or "file" in commands with results from this command, when "alias" is already part of the resulting data.

Related Items (Chapters)

Choose file (7).

new file [with prompt *string*] [default name *string*]

Result

File reference for an as-yet uncreated file.

When to Use

The new file command is perhaps poorly named, because it might imply that the command creates a file. In truth, the command is a simple, but useful, user interface element for scripts that need to write data out to a new file. The command displays a standard Save As dialog box, allowing the script user to locate a folder location for a new file and assign a name to the file (Figure 7.4).

Figure 7.4 The new file dialog box.

A helpful feature of the Save As dialog is that if the user enters the name of a file that already exists in the current folder, then the user is prompted about replacing the existing file. To meet the expectation of the user in this case, your file writing should overwrite the old file. Remember, even though the Replace dialog appears here, nothing happens to the existing file until other parts of your script write to the disk.

The returned value of the new file command is a file reference, containing the pathname to the file as named by the user (see Chapter 8 for details about the differences between file and alias references). It is then up to the script to pass that information to the command (in AppleScript or other scriptable application) that creates the new file. In AppleScript, the open for access command does the job. In many scriptable applications, the make command is the one to use. In either case, the commands expect a file reference, and the resulting data from the new file command fits the bill.

Because the user may cancel out of the Save As dialog box, it is vital for your script to use this command in a Try-Error construction. Here is a typical sequence using AppleScript to create the file:

```
try
    set myFile to (new file with prompt "Save today's data as:")
on error errMsg number errNum
    if errNum = -128 then
        display dialog ¬
            "Data was not saved." buttons {"Cancel"} default button 1
    else
        display dialog errMsg & ¬
            " Call the Help Desk." buttons {"Cancel"} default button 1
```

```
      end if
   end try
   set myFileRef to (open for access myFile)
   (* more statements assembling and writing data to file*)
   close access myFileRef
```

Notice that the open for access command near the bottom does not have the word "file" in its parameters. That's because the word is part of the file reference returned by the new file command (e.g., file "Macintosh HD:Documents: Today's Data")

Parameters

The first optional parameter lets you enter a prompt for the user. The prompt is similar to the one in the choose file command. The second optional parameter is the name of the file you may wish to suggest as a default value. In the following example, illustrated in Figure 7.4, the script suggests a file name containing part of today's date:

```
new file with prompt ¬
   "Save today's data as:" default name "Data » " & ¬
   (text from word 2 to word 3 of date string of (current date))
```

When possible, recommend a file name. This lets the user perform the save action with as little keyboard work as possible.

Examples

```
set myFile to new file with prompt "Save as:"
```

```
set myFile to new file with prompt "Store information in:" ¬
   default name "Backup"
```

You Try It

Enter and run the Try handler above with the Event Log window open so you can see the events being sent and values returned.

Common Errors

Expecting the command to generate a file; using "alias" or "file" in commands with results from this command, when "file" is already part of the resulting data.

Related Items (Chapters)

Open for access (7); close access (7); file and alias references (8).

scripting components

Result
A list of all OSA-compatible scripting components installed in the Macintosh's system.

When to Use
With this command, your script can make sure that a scripting component other than AppleScript is installed in the system before branching to a script that requires that component. For example, an AV-model Mac comes with both AppleScript and QuicKeys scripting components pre-installed in the system software. A call to the command reveals all components:

```
scripting components
   -- result: {"QuicKeys", "AppleScript"}
```

Most typically, you would use this command in an if-then construction, as in

```
if scripting components contains "QuicKeys" then
   (* run QuicKeys-based script *)
end if
```

If you call this command from AppleScript, you can be assured that the AppleScript component will always be listed.

Parameters
None.

Examples

```
scripting components
```

You Try It
There isn't much to play with here except entering the command and checking the result.

Common Errors
Forgetting that even a single component result comes back as a list value.

Related Items (Chapters)
None.

AGStart

Result

None.

When to Use

This scripting command works only with System 7.5 or later, because it starts Apple Guide as a background process. Apple Guide is a scriptable process, allowing any program capable of running OSA scripts to control navigation through an Apple Guide database. To make sure Apple Guide is running before issuing any commands to it, use the AGStart scripting addition command. If Apple Guide is already running, the command is ignored, and no errors occur.

Parameters

None.

Examples

AGStart

You Try It

There isn't much to play with here because no visible action takes place after issuing this command.

Common Errors

Forgetting to issue the command prior to running a script that controls an Apple Guide database.

Related Items (Chapters)

None.

monitor depth
max monitor depth
min monitor depth
set monitor depth *<numberOfColorBits>*

Result

For the first three commands, AppleScript returns integers representing the bit depth of the primary monitor (1, 2, 4, 8, 16, or 24). No result for the set version of the command.

When to Use

Some programs operate best in very specific monitor bit depths. Also, a 24-bit large color screen may take longer to refresh the screen, making it appear as though the Mac is running slowly. These commands, which were released with System 7.5, let your scripts determine whether the monitor is set to the desired setting for running scriptable applications.

The first three commands reveal the current setting and the outside ranges possible with the given Macintosh and monitor setup. If your applications rely on 24-bit color, your script should make sure the Macintosh it's running on is capable of that bit depth (whether it has sufficient video RAM for the size of the screen). Use the set monitor depth command to make any adjustments.

All four of these commands are located in a single scripting addition named "MonitorDepth."

Parameters

The set monitor depth command requires an integer of possible bit depths (1, 2, 4, 8, 16, or 24 depending on monitor and video RAM installed). You are not allowed to set the value to one beyond the machine's range. Therefore, check max monitor depth prior to setting the bit depth.

Examples

if max monitor depth ≥16 then set monitor depth 16

You Try It

Enter the following statements one at a time to view the resulting values, changes to your video screen, and error messages:

monitor depth

set monitor depth min monitor depth

set monitor depth 32

max monitor depth

set monitor depth 8

Common Errors

Inserting a "to" preposition after the set monitor depth command.

Related Items (Chapters)

None.

set volume *<integer0thru7>*

Result
None.

When to Use
Whenever your script needs to adjust the volume level while working with various applications, use this command (new with System 7.5). Unfortunately, Apple supplies no corresponding command to obtain the current setting, so your script cannot save and restore an arbitrary original setting.

Parameters
The parameter must be an integer between zero and 7, inclusive. These values correspond to the possible positions of the volume slider control in the Sound control panel. At zero, the sound is turned off.

Examples
```
set volume 3
```

You Try It
Experiment at will with this command and the beep command.

Common Errors
Inserting a "to" preposition after the set volume command.

Related Items (Chapters)
None.

Finder Commands

path to *applicationOrFolder* [as *class*]

Result
The pathname to the designated application or folder as an alias.

When to Use
This command is intended to help your script locate the pathname to specific system-related folders and applications on the startup disk of your Mac. With this command, you can locate the paths to nested system folders (e.g., Preferences). Typically, a script would use the value returned by this command to

assemble a complete pathname for a file in the system-related folder, and then open or save the file there.

Values returned from this command are in the alias class, such as:

alias "HD 160:System Folder:Extensions:"

unless you include the optional coercion parameter:

```
get path to control panels as string
set panelPath to result & "General Controls"
set genControlsFileSize to ¬
    size of (info for alias panelPath)
```

The last line of this script re-coerces the value back to an alias, as required by the info for command. Notice, too, that the value returned by the path to command ends in a colon when the item it's working on is a folder. This eases any concatenation that may be necessary, as above.

Parameters

This command requires one of a specifically worded list of items as a parameter. Only the following parameters may be used:

Folders	Applications
apple menu	frontmost application
apple menu items	printmonitor
control panels	
desktop	
extensions	
preferences	
printmonitor documents	
startup disk	
startup items	
system folder	
temporary items	
trash	

The only non-system-oriented item in the list is for the frontmost running application.

Using the optional command parameter for class coercion is faster than letting AppleScript perform the coercion. Therefore, while these two statements yield the same result,

path to preferences as text

(path to preferences) as text

the first version runs faster.

Examples

```
path to apple menu items

path to startup disk

set extensionsPath to (path to extensions as string)

set libraryPath to (path to extensions as string )& ¬
   "Scripting Additions:FinderLib"
```

You Try It

Enter and run each of the following scripts, watching the returned values in the result window:

```
path to control panels

path to control panels as string

path to frontmost application

tell application "Scriptable Text Editor"
   activate
   path to frontmost application
end tell
```

Common Errors

Not using one of the predefined parameters; forgetting that unless coerced by the second parameter, the result is an alias value class.

Related Items (Chapters)

Info for (7); list folder (7); alias and string value classes (9).

list folder *folderReference* [invisibles *Boolean*]

Result

A list of file and folder names (but not pathnames) in the designated folder.

When to Use

With this scripting addition you can retrieve a list of all items in a folder. From here, you can see if the list contains a particular item your script may be interested in. This can be especially valuable for folders that hold transient information, such as Trash, PrintMonitor Documents, or Temporary Items. The Desktop level and Trash are treated as folders, so you can use this command to see if any files or folders are in these locations. Your script can determine if these folders are empty or full, as in:

```
list folder (path to trash)
```

If the Trash folder is empty, the result would be:

{ }

Results come back as a list. Therefore, the results of a Desktop with two items on it would look like this:

{"Documents", "SuperDweeb"}

Items in a list do not distinguish between file and folder items. They're all listed as equal citizens.

Parameters

The required parameter, *folderReference*, is an alias class value, but the notation must indicate a folder—ending with a colon, as in:

list folder alias "HD:Trash:"

If you omit the trailing colon after a valid folder name, the colon is inserted for you at compile time.

For listing special system folders, nothing beats nesting the path to command as a parameter to the list folder command. The path to command returns the required alias class value, as in:

list folder (path to extensions)

Using the path to command for files (e.g., path to frontmost application) generates a run-time error.

If your application requires a list of pathnames to items in a folder, consult the listFiles command in finderLib (Chapter 16).

The optional second parameter allows you to filter out invisible items. If you don't specify the Invisibles parameter, the default value is true, so that all items come back in the result. In the startup disk folder, for example, that would include the Move&Rename folder and the various Desktop files and folders.

When you enter the command and set the invisibles property to false, the compiler turns the phrase around a bit, but the meaning is the same. If you enter

list folder alias "Macintosh HD:" invisibles false

the compiler displays

list folder alias "Macintosh HD:" without invisibles

The revised version reads better, and you can enter it that way if you prefer.

Examples

list folder "Hard Disk:System Folder:" without invisibles

list folder (path to preferences)

count of (list folder (path to extensions))

You Try It

Enter and run each of the script statements below, watching the returned values in the result window:

list folder (path to system folder)

list folder (path to startup disk)

list folder (path to startup disk) without invisibles

count of (list folder (path to preferences)) -- *frightening!*

Common Errors

Forgetting to supply an alias class value as a parameter; trying to list a file.

Related Items (Chapters)

Path to (7); alias class values (9); list class values (9); listFiles (16).

list disks

Result

A list of all volumes mounted on your Desktop.

When to Use

This command offers a convenient way to check whether a particular volume—especially a networked volume—is mounted on the script runner's Macintosh. If your script expects files or applications to be available on the local Mac, the script can use this command to check before it makes any calls to the desired volume, and elegantly handle any user messages or other actions (e.g., use a Finder command, described in Chapter 17, to open an alias to a server).

This command treats all volumes—hard disks, floppies, CD-ROMs, servers—the same, and does not distinguish one type from another in the list of volumes it returns:

list disks

    -- *result: {"Hard Disk", "Backup Floppy", "Alice to Ocean"}*

There will always be at least one item in the list: the name of the startup disk.

Parameters

None.

Examples

list disks

count of (list disks)

if (list disks) does not contain "Big Daddy" then

    mountServer -- *subroutine that opens a server alias*

end if

You Try It

Enter and run the following scripts:

list disks -- *returned list in results window*

display dialog "You have " & (count of (list disks)) ¬
    & " volume(s) mounted."

Common Errors

Forgetting that returned values are in a list.

Related Items (Chapters)

If-then (10); list class values (9).

info for *fileOrFolderReference*

Result

A record containing fields for the following information for the designated item. The precise collection of fields in the record depends on whether the item in question is a folder, application, or data file. Table 7.2 shows what properties apply to each type of item.

Table 7.2 Info for Results by Item Type

Property	Folder	Application	Data File
name	•	•	•
creation date	•	•	•
modification date	•	•	•
icon position	•	•	•
visible	•	•	•
size	•	•	•
folder	•	•	•
folder window	•		
locked		•	•
file creator		•	•
file type		•	•
short version		•	•
long version		•	•
default application			•
alias	•	•	•

When to Use

There is a strong likelihood that a number of Finder related tasks you need to perform involves one or more properties of a file or folder. These properties are generally the kinds of things you get from an item's Get Info dialog box. This command lets a script read that information about any file or folder. Moreover, the command returns the four-character file creator and file type strings that don't appear in the Finder (but do in Finder supplements, such as CE Software's DiskTop).

The info for command only allows reading of these properties. Some of these properties may be changed via the scriptable Finder (Chapter 17).

Because the data comes back in a record value format, each of the items is labeled, making it comparatively easy to extract the data in readable scripts. For example:

```
set fileToExamine to choose file
get size of (info for fileToExamine )
```

A script can directly extract the labeled item from the result of the info for command. The key is knowing the exact names of the labels—and then knowing the class for a particular field's data for further manipulation. Here are the property names, classes, and examples of the data returned for these properties:

Property Name	Value Class	Example
name	string	"Letter to Amy"
creation date	date	date "Sunday, June 5, 1994 10:20:33 PM"
mod date	date	date "Monday, June 6, 1994 3:45:00 PM"
modification date	date	date "Monday, June 6, 1994 3:45:00 PM"
locked	Boolean	true
visible	Boolean	true
folder	Boolean	false
folder window	rectangle	"0,0,150,150"
file creator	string	"ToyS"
file type	string	"APPL"
default application	alias	alias "Mac HD:Apps:ClarisWorks"
alias	Boolean	false
size	integer	155673
short version	string	"1.0.1"
long version	string	"1.0.1, Apple Computer, Inc. 1992-93"
icon position	point	"75,320"

An item's name property is the name for that item as it appears in the Finder. The mod date and modification date property labels represent the same property, one offering a scripting shortcut for us. The version properties values come from the file's 'vers' resource. Additional properties include:

visible A Boolean value indicating whether the file or folder is visible in a Finder window. Many times you don't want to perform operations on hidden files or folders, so checking for this property can tell your script whether the item is worth messing with.

folder window The global screen coordinates of the window of a folder. This property is available only for folders, and applies even to a closed folder, which knows the size to which it would open if double-clicked by the user.

default application An alias reference to the application that would open with the document if the document were opened from the Finder. Document files that are not linked to applications (or whose applications may not be on the script runner's hard disk) may present problems for your script, because the property does not come back in the result of the Info For command. Instead you receive an error that the script can't get that property (we'd expect the property to come back empty, but such is not the case). Therefore, if your script must extract this information about a document file, it is best to do so in a Try-Error construction to avoid breaking scripts on plain document files.

alias A Boolean value that reveals whether the item is an alias to another item. No property, however, reveals the name of the original of the alias.

icon position The coordinate point of the upper left corner of the icon, within the Finder window that contains the icon for the file or folder. The icon referred to here is the one that shows when the Finder's View menu is set to "by Icon." When an icon is snapped to the upper left corner of the window (i.e., by holding down the Command key while dragging to the corner), the icon position property value is 0,0.

Syntax for extracting a property from a record is flexible. For example, below we assign the record of a file's info to a variable. Succeeding statements show two methods of extracting the mod date property from that variable:

```
set fileData to info for alias "HD:Documents:Letters Template"
get mod date of fileData
     -- or --
get fileData's mod date
```

Your choice depends on which version seems more readable to you. While this is an AppleScript command, it works on any Macintosh folder or file available in the Finder—it is not limited to scriptable applications and their documents. The command simply makes toolbox calls, which apply to all Finder items.

Parameters

This command requires an alias class reference to a folder or file, as in

```
info for alias "HD:Applications:MacProject Pro" -- for file
info for alias "HD:Applications:" -- for folder
```

Other AppleScript commands, particularly **choose file**, provide results that feed the info for command parameters directly. In fact, the combination of the two commands is helpful to scripters who, in the course of developing a script, are in need of a file type for a document. This one-line script can get the info you need for just such a task:

get file type of (info for (choose file))

The returned value appears in the Result window.

Examples

info for "Hard Disk:System Folder:System"

creation date of (info for "Hard Disk:Documents:")

get modification date of (info for (path to preferences))

You Try It

Enter and run each of the following scripts, watching for returned values in the Result window:

info for (choose file)

info for (choose file of type "QUIL")

info for (path to system folder)

size of (info for (choose file))

display dialog (creation date of (info for (choose file))) as string

icon position of (info for (path to system folder))

Common Errors

Not taking into account the class of a returned value before performing further manipulation with the result; forgetting the alias reference in the parameters; trying to get a file-only property of a folder.

Related Items (Chapters)

Choose file (7); path to (7); record value class (9); date value class (9); Boolean value class (9).

String Commands

A CII character *integer0to255*

Result

A single-character string of the character corresponding to the integer value in the ASCII table.

When to Use

This command is a common programming capability that allows you to convert an ASCII number to the actual character it represents. The value returned will be the same in all fonts for characters 32 to 127. For integer values above 127, the actual character returned may differ from font to font, since those characters are not part of an established standard, even among Macintosh fonts (and certainly not among fonts from other types of computers).

While AppleScript often ignores the case of a character for things like file names, uppercase and lowercase characters have different values in an ASCII table. Changing characters of a string from one case to another is a common application of this command (and its counterpart, ASCII number). Table 7.3 is an ASCII table for values zero through 127.

It's important to note for the high characters (greater than 127) that some values will convert to what looks to be a square in the Result window. Be aware that the Result window displays in Geneva only. Copying the value to a word processor and changing the font may create a real character or symbol from that font.

Table 7.3   ASCII Table

ASCII	Character	Name	ASCII	Character	Name
0	NUL	Null	24	CAN	Cancel
1	SOH	Start of Heading	25	EM	End of Medium
2	STX	Start of Text	26	SUB	Substitute
3	ETX	End of Text	27	ESC	Escape
4	EOT	End of Transmission	28	FS	File Separator
5	ENQ	Enquiry	29	GS	Group Separator
6	ACK	Acknowledge	30	RS	Record Separator
7	BEL	Bell	31	US	Unit Separator
8	BS	Backspace	32	SP	Space
9	HT	Horizontal Tab	33	!	Exclamation Point
10	LF	Line Feed	34	"	Double Quote
11	VT	Vertical Tab	35	#	Number Sign
12	FF	Form Feed	36	$	Dollar Sign
13	CR	Carriage Return	37	%	Percent Sign
14	SO	Shift Out	38	&	Ampersand
15	SI	Shift In	39	'	Apostrophe
16	DLE	Data Link Escape	40	(	Open Parenthesis
17	DC1	Device Control 1	41	)	Close Parenthesis
18	DC2	Device Control 2	42	*	Asterisk
19	DC3	Device Control 3	43	+	Plus
20	DC4	Device Control 4	44	,	Comma
21	NAK	Negative Acknowledge	45	-	Hyphen
22	SYN	Synchronous Idle	46	.	Period
23	ETB	End of Transmission Block	47	/	Slant

Table 7.3 (*continued*)

ASCII	Character	Name	ASCII	Character	Name
48	0	Zero	88	X	
49	1		89	Y	
50	2		90	Z	
51	3		91	[	Open Bracket
52	4		92	\	Reverse Slant
53	5		93	]	Close Bracket
54	6		94	^	Circumflex
55	7		95	_	Underline
56	8		96	'	Grave Accent
57	9		97	a	
58	:	Colon	98	b	
59	;	Semicolon	99	c	
60	<	Less Than	100	d	
61	=	Equals	101	e	
62	>	Greater Than	102	f	
63	?	Question Mark	103	g	
64	@	Commercial At	104	h	
65	A		105	i	
66	B		106	j	
67	C		107	k	
68	D		108	l	
69	E		109	m	
70	F		110	n	
71	G		111	o	
72	H		112	p	
73	I		113	q	
74	J		114	r	
75	K		115	s	
76	L		116	t	
77	M		117	u	
78	N		118	v	
79	O		119	w	
80	P		120	x	
81	Q		121	y	
82	R		122	z	
83	S		123	{	Open Brace
84	T		124	|	Vertical Line
85	U		125	}	Close Brace
86	V		126	~	Tilde
87	W		127	DEL	Delete

Parameters

The only valid ASCII table values range from 0 through 255 (for a total of 256 values), and the ASCII character command accepts integers within this range only. A parameter is required. You can supply only one parameter at a time.

Examples

```
ASCII character 65
    -- result: "A"

ASCII character 97
    -- result :"a"

ASCII character 13
    -- result: "
        " -- a return character
```

You Try It

Enter and run the following script, which changes any string you enter to all uppercase:

```
tell application "Scriptable Text Editor"
    display dialog "Enter text to be made into uppercase:" ¬
        default answer "sample"
    set mainString to text returned of result
    activate
    make new document
    set contents of document 1 to mainString
    -- check each character of the string
    repeat with i from 1 to count of mainString
        set testChar to (ASCII number item i of mainString)
        -- see if character is in lowercase ASCII value range
        if testChar ≥ 97 and testChar ≤ 122 then
            -- adjust corresponding character in document
            set character i of document 1 ¬
                to ASCII character (testChar - 32)
        end if
    end repeat
    -- replace variable with adjusted copy from document
    set mainString to contents of document 1
    close document 1 saving no
end tell
mainString -- in the result window
```

Among the lessons in this script, perhaps the most important is that we're using an application's commands and objects to help out with a chore. We chose an available application that provided text object services that make substituting one character for another much easier. When we're finished with the task, we close whatever windows we opened, and still have the data in a local variable.

Common Errors

Confusing this command with ASCII number; value of the parameter is not an integer.

Related Items (Chapters)

ASCII number (7).

ASCII number *characterAsString*

Result

An integer value between 0 and 255.

When to Use

This command performs the inverse action of the ASCII character command. This version converts a character to its equivalent value in the ASCII table (Table 7.3). As demonstrated in the You Try It section of the ASCII character command description, it is common to use the two ASCII commands together in a script: one converts characters to numbers for calculations, while the other puts the numbers back into characters for reinsertion into a string.

Parameters

The required parameter must be a single character in quotes. If you need to obtain ASCII values for multiple characters (e.g., all characters in a word), your script will need to perform this command on each character.

Examples

```
ASCII number "G"
   -- result: 71

ASCII number (item 1 of {"a","b","c"})
   -- result: 97
```

You Try It

First enter and run the examples, above. Then consult the "You Try It" section for the ASCII character command, which includes a hands-on example of both commands.

Common Errors

Confusing this command with ASCII character; value of the parameter is not a string.

Related Items (Chapters)
ASCII character (7).

offset of *containedString* in *containerString*

Result
An integer that signifies the character number of *containerString* at which *containedString* begins.

When to Use
Many operations involving strings require knowing precisely where a substring starts within a larger string. For example, you can build a subroutine that performs a search-and-replace within a chunk of text. On the companion disk (Handbook Scripts:Chapter 06 folder) is a script called Offset Script (Search&Replace), which works with a pre-formatted document (Offset Document) to demonstrate the offset function. The script grabs the contents of the document, and then sends it off to the generic search-and-replace subroutine:

```
-- We use Scriptable Text Editor and pre-written document
-- as the source of text for the search and replace
-- subroutine.
tell application "Scriptable Text Editor"
    activate
    choose file "Locate the file "Offset Document":" of type "QUIL"
    open result
    -- grab text, but preserve font style adjustments
    set theDocument to text of document 1 as styled text
    -- Call the searchReplace subroutine, passing three parameters:
    -- 1) the document text
    -- 2) the text to search for
    -- 3) the text with which to replace the found text
    searchReplace of me into theDocument at "• • •" ¬
        given replaceString:"SuperSubScript Plus"
    -- since the subroutine returns value in result,
    -- we place result back into document
    set contents of document 1 to result
end tell

-- universal search and replace subroutine
-- operates strictly in AppleScript, not an application
on searchReplace into mainString at searchString¬
    given replaceString:replaceString
    -- keep going until all instances of the searchString are converted
    repeat while mainString contains searchString
        -- we use offset command here to derive the position within
```

```
        -- the document where the search string first appears
        set foundOffset to offset of searchString in mainString -- <<<<<<<<
        -- begin assembling remade string by getting all text
        -- up to the search location, minus the first character of
        -- the search string
        set stringStart to text 1 thru (foundOffset - 1) of mainString
        -- get the end part of the remade string
        set stringEnd to text (foundOffset + (count of searchString)) ¬
            thru -1 of mainString
        -- remake mainString to start, replace string, and end string
        set mainString to stringStart & replaceString & stringEnd
    end repeat
    return mainString -- ship it back to the statement that called me
end searchReplace
```

At the very core of this script is the **offset** command, which, every time through the repeat loop, returns the number of the character in the string at which the search string begins. That value then becomes a fixed point to be used to extract text before and after the search string, and assemble a new string around the replacement string.

It's best to use the **offset** command in AppleScript-only environments, rather than while executing commands directed to an application. The reason is that the word "offset" is a common name of a property within text-based applications (like Scriptable Text Editor). You cannot use the **offset** command as you would expect inside a compound statement directed at Scriptable Text Editor. You can, however, pass the data to a subroutine, which works strictly within the confines of AppleScript. The Mail Merger application in Chapter 20 demonstrates how to do this.

Parameters

Both parameters for this command are required, and both must evaluate to strings. Since application objects are generally not usable (their offset property conflicts with the **offset** command), **offset** command parameters tend to be literal strings (in quotes) or variables containing strings.

There is no penalty for the *containedString* not being in the *container String*. All that happens is that the command returns 0 (zero) as the result. Consequently, the repeat loop in the subroutine above could have been controlled this way:

```
repeat while offset of searchString in mainString > 0
```

The loop would end when the search string no longer exists in the main string.

Important

Unlike most of AppleScript, the **offset** command *is* case-sensitive. These two examples should demonstrate that fact:

offset of "World" in "We are the world"
-- *result: 0*

offset of "world" in "We are the world"
-- *result: 12*

This behavior can be a real gotcha while scripting.

Examples

offset of "We" in "We the people"
-- *result: 1*

offset of "people" in "We the people"
-- *result: 8 (spaces count)*

offset of "America" in "We the people"
-- *result: 0*

offset of "row" in "row, row, row your boat"
-- *result: 1 (first instance in a string)*

You Try It

Enter and run each of the following scripts with the Result window open and visible so you can see the values returned by the offset command:

offset of "a" in "abc"

offset of "b" in "abc"

offset of "desire" in "A Streetcar Named Desire"

offset of "Desire" in "A Streetcar Named Desire"

set temp to "We compile no script before it's time."
offset of "script" in temp

Common Errors

Forgetting one of the prepositions in the parameters; specifying a parameter that does not evaluate to a string; conflict with offset parameter in an application.

Related Items (Chapters)

String values (9); repeat loops (12).

Numeric Commands

round *realNumber* [rounding up | down | toward zero | to nearest]

Result

An integer representing the rounded value.

When to Use

The round command performs double duty. Its obvious function is to round a real number to a whole number in whatever direction you specify in the optional rounding parameter. But since so many properties and parameters of other commands require integer values, you can use the round command to prepare a real number to be sent along as a parameter.

Parameters

One required parameter is any real number that evaluates to an integer in the range from –536,870,912 to +536,870,911. If you script a large number as the parameter, it is converted to scientific notation at compile time:

```
round 123456.7
   -- becomes
round 1.234567E+5 -- after compilation
```

If you specify no additional parameters, the real number is rounded to the nearest integer, with .5 being rounded up. But you can alter the way rounding is performed on any value by adding the rounding parameter. This optional parameter requires one of four hard-wired parameters: up, down, toward zero, to nearest. For example, you can force a value that would normally round up to round down:

```
round 35.74 rounding down
   -- result: 35
```

Remember, too, that you can nest this command in a statement as an argument to another command that requires an integer value.

Examples

```
round 3     -- result: 3

round 6.5   -- result: 7

round 0.23 rounding up -- result: 1
```

You Try It

Enter and run each of the following script lines, watching for values (when appropriate) in the Result window:

```
round 25.4

round 25.5

round 0.9 rounding down

beep (round 2.3)
```

Common Errors
Forgetting to specify the correct rounding method.

Related Items (Chapters)
Integer value class (9); real value class (9).

random number [*number*] [from *number* to *number*] [with seed *string*]

Result
For integer parameters, a random integer; for real number parameters, a random real number.

When to Use
Random numbers come into play quite often in entertainment applications (e.g., the roll of the dice) and in education applications, in which the random presentation of quiz items prevents a lesson from turning into rote exercises time after time.

Parameters
How your script specifies parameters to this command has a great deal of impact on the results returned by the command. If you specify no parameters, then the command returns a real number value between zero and one, displayed with precision to 13 digits to the right of the decimal, as in:

```
random number
  -- result: 0.8225142273435
```

Supplying a single value as a parameter instructs the command to return a value between zero and that number—in the same value class as the parameter. If the parameter is an integer, then the command returns an integer; if the parameter is a real number, then the result is a real:

```
random number 3
  -- result: 2

random number 3.0
  -- result: 2.8721084350796
```

Another parameter allows you to set different low and high limits to the range of random numbers. Both the from *number* to *number* parameters must be provided together to work properly, even though their dictionary definitions make them look like independent parameters.

Finally, random numbers are a misnomer in most personal computers, because they tend to repeat the same series of random numbers from session to session. You can, however, send the series off on an entirely new way by adjusting the seed value. The with **seed** parameter works as advertised when the seed value is a string of any length.

Examples

```
random number 10

tell application "Scriptable Text Editor"
    repeat 10 times
        set style of word (random number ¬
            (count words of document 1)) ¬
            of document 1 to underline
    end repeat
end tell
```

You Try It

Enter and run the script below, which appears to roll two dice, and supplies their values in a dialog box:

```
repeat
    set die1 to random number 6
    set die2 to random number 6
    display dialog "The dice values are: ""¬
        & die1 & "" and "" & die2 & ""." ¬
        buttons {"End", "Roll Again"} default button 2
    if button returned of result is "End" then exit repeat
end repeat
```

We set up this script in a repeat loop, so we can continue to roll the dice by pressing the Return or Enter keys. Only if we click the End button does the script exit the repeat and end. To enter the curly quote symbols, type Option-[(left quote) and Option-Shift-[(right quote).

Common Errors

Forgetting the word "number" in the command.

Related Items (Chapters)

Integer value class (9); real value class (9).

Script Commands

One group of commands deals exclusively with script objects. These three commands help scripts use other script objects in their execution without having to duplicate script lines everywhere.

load script *fileOrAliasReference*

Result

A script object, which displays in the Result window as <<script>>. The resulting object should be copied to a variable or property and treated like an application object.

When to Use

It is often helpful to incorporate a pre-written library of AppleScript routines into one of your scripts. First of all, it fosters the idea of reusable code, because multiple short scripts you write can share the same library of sophisticated code with essentially no RAM overhead penalty. Second, it lets your scripts take advantage of successful work others have done to write these libraries, which you may have obtained from a commercial publisher or through an on-line bulletin board or user group diskette.

In the AppleScript Runtime Samples:Libraries folder on the companion disk are some libraries that provide useful utility handlers for areas such as string and list manipulation. Many of the routines in each library call other routines as components—a very compact way of handling a library of things.

One library, stringLib, contains a replaceString handler, which lets you specify a string, a word to be replaced, and the text that is to replace it. Here's a script that loads the script and calls the routine:

```
set mainString to "Now is the time for all good men " & ¬
    "to come to the aid of their country."

set targetLib to (choose file "Locate StringLib:") as string
load script file targetLib
set StringLib to result

tell StringLib -- like working with an application
    set mainString to (replaceString into ¬
        mainString at "men" given replaceString:"people")
end tell
mainString -- view result in the Result window
```

The replaceString command is defined in the library, and we call it just like a command in an application—with the library as the application object. None of this can happen, however, unless we load the script as an object.

While script libraries typically do not have scripts that execute automatically (i.e., as they would with run script), there's nothing that prevents from having these kinds of executable lines. They won't execute, however, unless you send a run command to the script object. If your only goal is to run executable lines of a script, use the run script command (below) instead of load script.

Parameters

The required parameter is a file or alias reference to the script library you want to load, as in:

```
load script file "HD:System Folder:Script Libraries:StringLib"
```

The only kind of scripts you can load this way, however, are those that have been saved as applications or compiled scripts. In other words, they must be pre-compiled before being loaded into another script. Scripts saved as text won't work.

For more about creating and using script libraries, and making calls to them, see Chapter 14. See Chapter 9 for more about file and alias references.

Example

```
load script file ((choose file "Locate a library") as string)
```

You Try It

Enter and run the script above that loads the string library (stringLib). Run the script a second time, but opening a library other than stringLib to see the same error message you'd get by asking an application to perform a command not in its dictionary.

Common Errors

Forgetting the word "file" in the *fileReference* parameter; forgetting to assign the result of the command to a variable for a later tell statement; incorrectly including the word "application" in a tell statement directed at a script object.

Related Items (Chapters)

Run script (7); file and alias references (9); script libraries (14).

---

run script *variableOrReference* [with parameters *parameterList*] ¬
    [in *scriptingComponent*]

Result

Whatever value (if any) the script or script object returns.

When to Use

The run script command is more flexible than you may think at first glance. Used one way, the command gets into the realm of script objects (Chapter 15). In other guises, it lets you mix scripts written in different OSA scripting languages (e.g., adding a Frontier or QuickKeys script to an AppleScript script).

A script object is a software object that you can define, much like a subroutine saved as a separate script file. Script objects have properties and behaviors as you see fit. You can pass them parameters, and they can return values. As separate files, their value is in their reusability by any number of other scripts, provided they are designed to be called as generic operations.

When you need the services of such an object, you use the run command to make that script go. If the script returns any data, it goes into the result variable, just like any other command.

For run-and-stay-opened scripts, use the launch command (Chapter 6) before the run command.

Script files, of course, may be written in any OSA scripting language. When they are run with the run script command, they are run as compiled scripts, so their language of origin is of no concern to your AppleScript script.

But you may want to use the facilities of another scripting language in a simple one-line statement within your AppleScript script. Instead of having to write a separate script file for that one line, you can tell AppleScript to compile that line using the other language. For example, if you want to use QuicKeys' alert box that can close itself after a number of seconds, the statement would be:

```
run script "Message \"Howdy\" No_OK Continue 5" in "QuicKeys"
```

Here, you're telling AppleScript to use QuicKeys' own command (Message) as if the scripting language popup menu in Script Editor were set to QuicKeys.

The run script command should not be confused with the do script command found in scriptable applications that have their own scripting languages. Run script is strictly for OSA-compatible scripts and script objects.

Parameters

The required parameters for the run command must be an alias or file reference to the script file. Be sure to include the word "script" in a script object reference, as in:

```
run script alias "HD:Scripts:DateRecord"
```

The surefire way to provide a valid pathname to a script file is to let the user choose the file via the choose file command:

```
set fileToOpen to choose file with prompt ¬
  "Choose a script to run:" of type {"osas"}
run script fileToOpen
```

The choose file command returns the chosen file as a class of alias.

Forcing the user to open the desired script object every time would be an unwelcome user interface "feature." Fortunately, you can have your script store the pathname as a property, so the user is faced with the file dialog only the first time:

```
property fileToOpen : ""
if fileToOpen is "" then
  set fileToOpen to choose file with prompt ¬
    "Choose a program to run:" of type {"osas"}
```

```
      end if
      run script fileToOpen
```

You may pass parameters to the script being run with the run script command. To see this form in action, create a script object containing a Run handler and positional parameters. Here is an example of a handler that adds any number of days and hours to the current date and time, based on the values passed as parameters:

```
      on run {deltaDays, deltaHours}
         set theDate to current date
         if deltaDays ≠ "" then
            set theDate to theDate + (deltaDays * days)
         end if
         if deltaHours ≠ "" then
            set theDate to theDate + (deltaHours * hours)
         end if
         return theDate
      end run
```

If you enter this script into the Script Editor and try to run it, you will get errors, because the run command sent by the Run button in the Script editor does not send any parameters. In any case, save this script as a compiled script with the name "DeltaTime."

In another Script Editor window, you can now run the script and pass parameters to it:

```
      run script file "Delta Time" with parameters {2, 6.5}
         -- result: date "Thursday, December 9, 1993 5:13:53 PM"
         -- (which is 2 days and 6-1/2 hours after running the script)
```

Parameters for the run script command are positional parameters (not named parameters in list format), so each parameter must have a value, even if it is zero.

You can also pass parameters when the script has been loaded with the load script command:

```
      copy (load script file "Delta Time") to deltaTime
      run script deltaTime with parameters {2, 6}
         -- result: date "Thursday, December 9, 1993 5:13:53 PM"
```

Examples

```
      set newFolders to (run script ¬
         alias "HD:System Folder:Script Objects:Find New Folders")

      run script "Choosy \"ImageWriter\" in "QuicKeys"
```

You Try It

On the companion disk's Handbook Scripts:Chapter 07 folder are two scripts that demonstrate script objects. Use Script Editor to open the one named Run

Script Script. The first time you run this script, it asks you to find a script named DateRecord. Open it when asked. Texts of both scripts are listed here:

Run Script Script

```
property scriptObjectPath : ""

if scriptObjectPath is "" then
    set scriptObjectPath to ¬
        choose file with prompt "Find DateRecord script" of type "osas"
end if

copy (run script scriptObjectPath) to todaysDate -- <<<run script here>>>
display dialog "Today is " & dayOfWeek of todaysDate & "." buttons {"OK"}
```

DateRecord

```
on run
    set todaysDate to (current date) as text
    set theDay to word 1 of todaysDate
    set theMonth to word 2 of todaysDate
    set theDate to word 3 of todaysDate
    set theYear to word 4 of todaysDate
    return {year:theYear, month:theMonth, date:theDate, dayOfWeek:theDay}
end run
```

Run the first script. It runs the second script, which places elements of today's date (as supplied by the current date scripting addition) into a record, and returns those values as a result of running that object. The last line of the first script extracts on field of that returned record (the day of the week), and displays some knowledge in a dialog box.

Common Errors

Omitting "script" from parameter; forgetting to use an alias class value as a parameter.

Related Items (Chapters)

Launch (6); choose file (6); run (6); scripting components (7); value classes (8); script objects (15).

store script *scriptObject* in *aliasOrFileReference*
[replacing ask | yes | no]

Result

None.

When to Use

The store script command is specialized in that it works only with values that represent compiled script objects—precisely the kind of objects that you get into your scripts via the load script command. In other words, you can't store a script unless you've previously loaded an existing script. Why would you want to do that? Actually, for a number of reasons.

The most obvious is that your script may have to save a copy of a library to another location on your hard disk or to another Mac on the network. In practice there is little need for this action.

The need for saving a copy of a script comes from a script object's ability to store data in the form of properties (discussed fully in Chapter 15). It's very possible that a script application will contain updated information (such as: how many times the script has been run; the date and time of the last database transaction; the latest delinquent customer list) that needs to be propagated to other Macintoshes on the network. A script can automate that process by running the store script command after a loaded script has been run and its properties modified.

Parameters

As the first parameter, the *scriptObject* must be a variable that evaluates to a script object. Script object values are hard to come by, but the load script command returns everything that the store script parameter needs. Also required is an alias or file reference to the path and name for the saved script object.

You can also use this command in a script to save itself—valuable for updating property values of a script object not saved as an application (Chapter 15). The parameter for *scriptObject* is the self-referencing me variable, as in

    store script me in file "HD:Scripts:MyObject"

To compile and save the script the first time, use the file reference so the compiler doesn't choke on an alias to a non-existent file.

An optional parameter lets you control the user interface for asking about overwriting an existing copy of the file. Hard-wired choices for the replacing parameter are ask, yes, or no. Without the parameter, the default is replacing ask. In some senses the default is the best choice for knowledgeable users, since the resulting dialog box (Figure 7.5) gives you a chance to locate and name the file differently. But if you're trying to do this updating behind the scenes, the replacing yes parameter is a better choice: the name and location of the saved copy will be under script control, and your script will know where to find the object the next time it's needed.

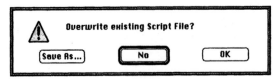

Figure 7.5 The replacing ask alert.

Even though the dictionary indicates that a result is returned for errors, the errors come back as error messages. Therefore, it is a good idea to incorporate the store script inside a try statement with trapping for errors, as in:

```
try
    store script theLib in alias targetLib replacing ask
on error errMsg number errNum
    if errNum is -128 then -- user canceled
        display dialog "Network update was not made!"
    end if
end try
```

If the user cancels, you can then handle what needs doing to maintain the integrity of the system you've scripted.

Examples

```
store script transactionLog ¬
    in alias "Server:Shared Objects:Transaction Log"¬
    replacing yes
```

You Try It

It will be pretty boring, since you can't see much of what's going on behind the scenes, but enter and run the following script. It loads a library of your choice, and saves it back to itself (unless you save a copy elsewhere). Since we don't do anything to the libraries (and they may or may not have any properties to change anyway), the contents of the library you choose won't be harmed (unless there is a disk error, so make sure you have a backup).

```
set targetLib to (choose file "Select a library:") as string
load script file targetLib
set theLib to result
try
    store script theLib in alias targetLib replacing ask
on error errMsg
    display dialog errMsg buttons {"OK"}
end try
```

Common Errors

Specifying an object of the wrong class for the *scriptObject* parameter; forgetting the alias word in the *aliasReference* parameter.

Related Items (Chapters)

Load script (7); file and alias references (9).

User-Interface Command

display dialog *string* [default answer *string*] ¬
    [buttons *buttonList*] [default button *integer* | *string*] ¬
    [with icon *integer* | *string*]

Result

A record consisting of one or two labeled fields: Button Returned:
buttonNameString and Text Returned: *string.*

When to Use

The display dialog scripting addition is an important user interface device when
your scripts run without the aid of any interface builders. In lieu of a full debugging
environment, it also helps scripters read intermediate values of variables while a
script is under construction.

    With one command, you control whether the dialog is a read-only dialog or
is the kind that provides a field for the user to enter some information via the
keyboard. Even a read-only dialog can be a user-input interface device, because
the command lets a script display up to three buttons, each of which can contain a different meaning (and send the script on a different branch or subroutine for each).

    When the dialog appears as a read-only type of alert, the returned value is a
record with a single property, as in

```
{button returned:"OK"}
```

Only one button can be returned for each invocation of the dialog.

For a user-input dialog, the returned record has two properties, as in

```
{text returned:"David", button returned:"OK"}
```

You can then use the powers of record class values to extract the information
that comes back. Here's a series to demonstrate an example for a read-only
dialog:

```
display dialog "Make an ice cream flavor choice:" ¬
    buttons {"None", "Vanilla", "Chocolate"} ¬
    default button "Chocolate"
set favFlav to button returned of result -- <<returned value here
if favFlav is "Vanilla" then
    display dialog "Potentially boring." ¬
        buttons {"OK"} default button 1
else if favFlav is "Chocolate" then
    display dialog "Now you're clicking!" ¬
        buttons {"OK"} default button 1
else
```

```
    display dialog "Sorry you don't like these." ¬
        buttons {"OK"} default button 1
end if
```

With the result containing a record, we can extract the data from a property by name (button returned of result), and perform some if-then decisions on the text of that button.

Here's another version, this time for a dialog that asks the user for some input:

```
display dialog "Enter a number between 1 and 10:" ¬
    default answer ""
set userValue to (text returned of result) as real
if (userValue < 1) or (userValue > 10) then
    display dialog "That value is out of range." ¬
        buttons {"OK"} default button 1
else
    display dialog "Thanks for playing." ¬
        buttons {"OK"} default button 1
end if
```

The answer supplied by the user (the text returned value of result) comes back as a string, which we coerce to a real number. We do this because the if-then construction tests whether the number is within the specified range.

The Cancel button in a dialog has a special power. When a user clicks it, script execution stops, but not before an error message ("User canceled.") and number (-128) are sent back to the script. If your script needs to perform some other action as a result of a user cancellation, build the display dialog command within a try statement, and trap for the error (Chapter 12).

Exercise care when building dialogs into your applications. Too much of a good thing gets in the way of the user. Good practice also dictates that dialogs allowing the user to make a choice about proceeding with an action provide a Cancel button to let the user back out at the last minute. If you need more complex dialogs for your scripts, consider applying an interface builder, such as FaceSpan, to this application.

Parameters

A key to success with this command is understanding its many parameters. Only one, the hard-wired string that appears in either style of dialog, is required. It can be any string up to 255 characters long. If the message extends beyond one line, the dialog automatically deepens to fit the text.

Little known is that the string can contain return characters to allow the script to control to some degree the formatting of text within the dialog (beyond the automatic word wrapping). There are a few different techniques, but one of the most readable styles builds strings with the return constant placed where necessary, as in:

```
display dialog "From one line..." & return & "to two."
```

Figure 7.6 Multiple line text in a dialog.

As an alternative, you can use the \r constant, which accomplishes the same thing, but at compile time often divides the string in the script into two lines, making the script look funny and more difficult to read:

```
display dialog "From one line...\rto two."
   -- compiles to...
display dialog "From one line
to two."
```

If you want the dialog to contain a field for the user to enter some text, then the command must contain a **default answer** parameter. Many dialogs supply default answers for users, making it a simple task of clicking the OK button or pressing the Return key to accept what's there. That **default answer** string is an argument to the default answer parameter. But if you want the field to be empty when the dialog opens, then an empty string must be the argument, as in:

```
display dialog "Enter your age:" default answer ""
```

Figure 7.7 Dialog box with a field for user entry.

You have many choices about how to handle the buttons that appear in these dialogs. If you do nothing about it in the parameters, the dialog displays a Cancel and an OK button, with the OK button being outlined as the default button (the one that takes effect when the user presses Return or Enter). By providing one, two, or three string values in a list class parameter for **buttons**, however, you can change the contents and order of all the buttons.

Buttons start filling in from the right (i.e., one button appears at the right edge of the dialog), and their order in the dialog from left to right is the same as the order of items in the list. Here are some examples of the buttons parameter and the corresponding button appearances (see Figures 7.8, 7.9, 7.10):

```
buttons {"OK"}
```

Figure 7.8 One dialog button.

    buttons {"Cancel","OK"}

Figure 7.9 Two dialog buttons.

    buttons {"General Motors", "Chrysler", "Ford"}

Figure 7.10 Three dialog buttons.

Size of the buttons depends on the amount of text in the longest button. But there is a limit (defined more by space of the proportional Chicago font than by character count), so you should try your long button's names and make sure they don't look too goofy or aren't longer than the longest button can possibly be.

Note that the buttons parameter says nothing about which button, if any, should be highlighted as the default button: that's what the default button parameter is for. The argument for this parameter can be either a number representing the number of the button (with the leftmost button being number 1) or a string representing the text of a particular button in any location, as in:

```
display dialog "Pick a car company:" ¬
    buttons {"General Motors", "Chrysler", "Ford"}¬
    default button 3
        -- or
display dialog "Pick a car company:" ¬
    buttons {"General Motors", "Chrysler", "Ford"}¬
    default button "Ford"
```

Figure 7.11 Three dialog buttons with default.

The final parameter, with icon, allows your script to display one of several possible icons in the dialog. These are useful primarily for read-only, alert kinds of dialogs, since the icon can often convey subtle meanings about the message or choice to be made.

Icons come from ICON or cicn (color icon) resources from a variety of places. All such resources have ID numbers associated with them, and occasionally names. Either the number or name can be used to specify the desired icon for the with icon parameter.

The display dialog looks for an icon described with this parameter in a specific order (hierarchy) of places:

1. Script file.
2. Current application object.
3. System.

The first ICON or cicn resource to match the number or name supplied as a parameter is the one that shows up in the dialog. Use a resource editing tool, such as ResEdit, to edit and insert icons into a compiled or self-running script file. If you create a cicn resource, and provide a color version of the icon, the color version appears in the dialog on Macintoshes with color displays. To be on the safe side and avoid possible conflicts with icons in other parts of the hierarchy, assign an ID number above 128 (choose Get Resource Info from the Resource menu in ResEdit to change the resource's ID number).

Virtually every scriptable application you'll encounter will have its own icon—the one that appears in the Finder. Almost universally, the application's icon has an ID number of 128.

Finally, the System offers three of its special icons, which are the same ones that appear in various system alert dialogs. These three icons have meanings according to the Macintosh User Interface Guidelines:

Icon	Icon Name	Icon Number	Meaning
(stop hand)	Stop	0	It's not recommended to go any further down the original path. Offer ways out for the user (e.g., Restart).
(note)	Note	1	Information for your benefit, but nothing serious.
(caution)	Caution	2	Something may be overwritten or lost if you proceed. Confirm that you want to continue.

You can mix an icon with an answer field in a dialog box, but the icon takes up width that may be better devoted to the user field. Also, this combination is highly unusual in Macintosh usage.

Examples

display dialog "Howdy, pardner!"

display dialog "What is your name?" default answer ""

display dialog "What color would you like?" ¬
    buttons {"Red","Green","Blue"} ¬
    default button 1 with icon 1

set theAnswer to text returned of ¬
    (display dialog "What is the meaning of life?" ¬
    default answer "Dunno")

You Try It

Enter and run the following scripts. When prompted, enter text into a field, and/or click a button, watching for the records displayed in the Result window:

display dialog "How ya doin'?"

display dialog "What city do you live in?" default answer ""

display dialog "Pick a card..." buttons {"Jack","Queen","King"}

display dialog "Place your bets..." buttons {"Win","Place","Show"}¬
    default button 1

Run the Display Dialog Icons script from the Handbook Script:Chapter 07 folder on the accompanying disk. This file contains a cicn resource number 400. The script shows all system icons, plus icons for the script file and Scriptable Text Editor.

Common Errors

Leaving out a word in one of the optional parameter labels; forgetting to put button names in a list; forgetting to specify a default button.

Related Items (Chapters)

List value classes (9); error trapping (13).

File Commands

open for access *fileOrAliasReference* [write permission *Boolean*]

Result

File reference number (integer) generated by the Macintosh Toolbox File Manager. You can use this number—which will likely be different each time you issue the command—for further commands that act on the file, including reading, writing, and closing.

When to Use

To access or modify the data from any file directly from a script, you must first open the file with this command. This is also the command you use to create a new file. This scripting addition creates files of creator 'ttxt' (TeachText) and file type 'TEXT'—the same kind of files generated by TeachText.

That doesn't mean, however, that only text files can be opened with this command. Existing binary files may also be opened, but you had better know what you're doing with the data in such files before mucking around with them.

It is very important to balance each **open for access** command with a **close access** command (below). Keep the file open only as long as needed for reading from or writing to the file.

Parameters

The required parameter is the pathname of the file to be opened. While you may use either a file or alias reference, you will be able to compile a script for an as-yet uncreated file only with a file reference. Use alias references only for pre-existing files. If the file is to be created with the command, the name you use for this parameter is the one assigned to the new file (see New File, above, for user interface help in this regard).

Unless specified with the optional Write Permission parameter, a file opened with the **open for access** command is set to be read-only. Before you can write to the file, it must be opened with the Write Permission parameter set to true. You cannot change the status of a file once it is open: close it and reopen it with the desired write permission. When you enter the Write Permission parameter with the true or false Boolean value, the compiler converts the statement to the with or without version, as in:

```
open for access file "Test File" write permission true
```

becomes

```
open for access file "Test File" with write permission
```

Examples

```
open for access file "Macintosh HD:Memo"

set fileRef to (open for access alias "HD-120:Documents:My Data")

open for access alias "HD-120:Names" with write permission
```

You Try It

Enter and run the script below, watching the process in the Event Log window:

```
set theFile to open for access file "Test File" with write permission
write "Howdy" to theFile -- using file reference number
close access theFile
```

This script created a file named "Test File" in the same folder as the Script Editor. Open it with Teach Text, SimpleText, or Scriptable Text Editor to see the results. Delete the file when you are finished.

Common Errors

Using an alias reference for a new file; not including the entire pathname for the file; forgetting to set the Write Permission parameter to true; opening a file that was not closed the last time the script ran; opening a file already open in another application.

Related Items (Chapters)

Close access (7); read (7); write (7); new file (7).

close access *fileReference*

Result

None.

When to Use

Any time a script opens a file for access, the script should also close the access once all file reading and writing has been completed.

Parameters

An acceptable *fileReference* parameter may be a pathname (in either file or alias reference style) or, more easily, the file reference number that comes back as the result of the **open for access** command. Because file pathnames get clumsy when used multiple times within a script (and they are prone to typographical errors when entering them), the file reference number mechanism makes the job of working with files (including using the other file scripting additions) much easier. As demonstrated in the **open for access** command, capture the reference number in a variable upon opening a file, and then use that variable for the file reference in all commands directed to that file. Because the number will likely be different each time, don't rely on any hard number for the file reference: let the variable do the work.

Examples

    close access myFile -- *myFile is a variable with a reference number*

    close access alias "HD-120:Memo to Linda"

You Try It

See the You Try It section in the **open for access** command, above, for an exercise of the **close access** command.

Common Errors

Forgetting the word "access" in the command; typographical error in a file or alias pathname.

Related Items (Chapters)

Open for access (7); read (7); write (7).

read *fileReference* [from *startInteger*] ¬
  [for *numberOfBytes* | to *endInteger* ¬
  | until *includedDelimiter* | before *excludedDelimiter*] ¬
  [as *dataType* | *class* [using delimiter[s] *delimiterList*]]]

Result

Data from the file referred to in the *fileReference* parameter. The amount of data, position of data from within the file, and form of the data are determined by additional, optional parameters.

When to Use

This is the command that retrieves data from a file previously opened via the **open for access** command. Files that may be read are not limited to text files. Binary data files may also be read, but unless you fully understand the nature of the data in such files, the retrieved data won't mean much to you or your scripts.

While Apple's *Scripting Additions Guide* goes to great lengths to demonstrate using the **read** and **write** commands to replicate a flat-file database, you are far better off using an application, such as TableServer (included with this book), to work with simple data collections.

Just the same, the **read** and **write** commands can be quite useful for creating data collections for your scripts that may not fit into structures handled nicely by programs such as TableServer or for data that you might wish to save independently of persistent properties. For example, you may wish a script to save snippets of data each time the script is run—data from script object properties about the number of times a shared script is accessed (the "Bean Counter" example in Chpater 15)—so that others on a network may access the information. The file commands give you the power to create and massage such files while a script runs. Then let others access the resulting files in TeachText or other text editing program.

The bottom line, therefore, is to use these file commands for quick access to small collections of data that apply to the script (whether the data be rigidly structured or not). Leave the job of database management to scriptable applications better suited to the task.

AppleScript from Apple offers no facilities to read or write resources. But see the discussion of the GTQ OSAX collection (Chapter 33) for ways to accomplish resource access.

Parameters

The array of parameters to the **read** command may seem daunting, but they're not that complex when you examine the job of the command. For the most part, you'll use only a couple of parameters at a time.

A helpful concept to understand about reading a file is that of the *file mark*. When a file opens for access, the Macintosh automatically places this mark immediately before the first character of the file. The mark indicates where the next **read** command will begin grabbing a copy of data from the file (reading does not disturb the contents of a file in any way). As you'll see in the next few paragraphs, the **read** command can be instructed to read a specific sequence of characters. After one **read** command, the file mark moves ahead in the file, past the characters grabbed by the first **read** command. The next **read** command then starts where the marker is—somewhere further within the file. This file mark advancement continues until the mark reaches the end of the file, at which point the **read** command returns no further data.

The file mark moves only in one direction: from the beginning toward the end of a file. Therefore, if you read a segment near the end of a file and then need another segment from the beginning, you cannot move the file mark back to the beginning of the file during this access. You may, however, close access to the file and reopen it to re-set the marker to the beginning of the file.

The only required parameter to the **read** command is a reference to the file to be read. A file reference number obtained from the **open for access** command is the best bet. If you specify no more parameters, the command reads the entire file, and returns its contents as the result, ready for assignment to a variable, as in

```
set myData to (read myFile)
myData
    -- result: [entire contents of the file]
```

In file mark terms, the marker reaches the end of the file after a single **read** command (with no other parameters). Any subsequent reads return End of File errors.

To begin the file reading from a character other than the first character, use the From parameter. Specify the number of bytes from the beginning of the file (the first byte is byte number 1) where the file mark should be placed prior to reading. For text files, one byte equals one character. For example, to read a file beginning with the 20th character,

```
set myData to (read myFile from 20)
myData
    -- result: [file contents from character 20 to end]
```

If the need is to read just the last x characters of a file, you may use a negative number, relative to the very end of the file. For instance, to obtain the last 50 characters of a file,

```
set myData to (read myFile from -50)
myData
    -- result: [last 50 bytes of the file]
```

Be aware, however, that if the file ends with a carriage return (as most data-base-style files do), the final carriage return counts as the very last character, and must be taken into account when figuring the number of bytes to read.

Without further parameters specifying an end to the read segment, the file mark is at the end of the file after this command. No subsequent reads are possible without closing and re-opening the file.

Whether the file is read from the very beginning or from some other starting point (with the From parameter), you may specify one of four types of limits on any Read command. They are:

for *numberOfBytes*

to *endInteger*

until *includedDelimiter*

before *excludedDelimiter*

The argument to the For parameter is a positive integer representing the number of bytes to be read from the file mark. Like all four of these choices, the For parameter may be used with or without the From parameter. Two examples are:

```
set myData to (read myFile for 100)
```

```
set myData to (read myFile from 201 for 100)
```

Here, after the first read command, the file mark is located immediately before byte 101 of the file. If the next read command were identical, it would retrieve bytes 101 through 200. But in this example, we start the next read at byte 201 for another 100 bytes. After this second command, the file mark is located before byte 301.

Another way to express the end point of a read command is with the To parameter and an integer representing the byte of the last character to be read. If the integer is positive, then the count is from the beginning of the file; for a negative argument, the count is from the end of the file. See the Examples section, below, for samples of this parameter.

While we said earlier that the file marker moves only from front to back, a combination of the From and To parameters, coupled with a negative number, produces some interesting results. If the last seven characters of a file were "Kennedy," notice the results from the following command:

```
set theData to (read myFile from -1 to -7)
theData
    -- result: "ydenneK"
```

Still, the file mark remains at the further point along the file (in this case at the end of the file) after the command, even though the reading started from that location.

The Before and Until parameters both require arguments consisting of a single character. The read command starts from the file mark and grabs a copy of all bytes from that point to the first instance of that character (or end of the file, whichever comes first). The distinction between the two parameters is how the read command treats this delimiting character. In the case of the Before parameter, the delimiter is not returned as part of the data; for the Until parameter, the delimiter is part of the returned data. Importantly, specifying the Before parameter causes the file mark to jump *past* the delimiting character, so that the next read command starts *after* the delimiter.

All of this makes sense particularly if you are reading a file with delimiters between chunks of data, and you want to retrieve just the data. In fact, you may use constants (such as return, space, and tab) as delimiter arguments for these parameters, as in:

```
set theData to (read myFile before tab)
```

The final optional parameters for the read command (As and Using Delimiters) let you determine the form of the data from a file for further manipulation by your script. Acceptable value classes are: list, record, integer, text, real, short, Boolean, and data. There are limitations to many of these, primarily revolving around the suitability of the data for coercion into a particular value class. For example, a text file containing words can't be coerced into an integer class; similarly, only an AppleScript record format data file can be read as a record.

Perhaps the most common coercion will be converting a comma- or tab-delimited file into an AppleScript list. For illustration purposes, we'll use the tab-delimited States file generated for Chapter 19 (we'll also assume that the examples here are surrounded by the requisite open for access and close access commands, and that the file reference number is in a variable called myFile). The default method of extracting data is as text, as follows:

```
set theData to (read myFile until return)
    -- result: "State    Entered Union    Abbreviation    Capital
    "
```

To retrieve data from this file such that each row (record) is an item of an AppleScript list, we can direct the read command to recognize the return character as a delimiter between list items:

```
set theData to (read myFile as {text} using delimiters {return})
    -- result: {"State    Entered Union    Abbreviation    Capital", ¬
        "Alabama    1819            AL              Montgomery", ... ¬
        "Wyoming    1890            WY              Cheyenne"}
```

The tab characters between items in each record are preserved in this arrangement, and this may be the way we want it. But it is also possible to pass two delimiters as arguments to the Using Delimiters parameter, such that the read command recognizes each of the named delimiter characters as item delimiters for the AppleScript list that comes back:

```
set theData to (read myFile as {text} using delimiters {return, tab})
-- result:{"State", "Entered Union", "Abbreviation", "Capital", "Alabama", ¬
    "1819", "AL", "Montgomery", "Alaska", ..."Cheyenne"}
```

As an alternate to specifying a value class, you may use a four-character data type, again provided that the file data is of that type. For example, if you open a file consisting of a PICT, you can copy the data from that file into a variable as a PICT, and then use that data in another program that can accept PICT data:

```
set theData to (read file "HD:Pretty Picture" as "PICT")
-- result: [PICT data]
```

Examples

```
read myFile
read myFile from 25
read myFile for 20
read myFile to 20
read myFile from 25 for 50
read myFile from 25 to 74
read myFile before tab
read myFile until return
read myFile from -20
```

You Try It

Because we don't know the location of various files on your hard disk, we'll have to leave it to you to locate the States database file (from the Chapter 19 folder) on your disk. Open the event log, enter the following script, and then run the script, watching the returned values in the Event Log window:

```
set myFile to (open for access (choose file))
read myFile for 11
read myFile from 20 to 32
read myFile from 33 for 9
read myFile until return
read myFile before return
read myFile until return as {text} using delimiters {tab, return}
read myFile from -10
close access myFile
```

Common Errors

Inserting the word "file" between the **read** command and file reference number (from HyperTalk experience); reaching end of file; trying to read more bytes than there are in the file.

Related Items (Chapters)

Open for access (7); close access (7); write (7).

write *expression* to *fileReference* ¬
    [for *numberOfBytes*] [starting at *integer*]

Result

None.

When to Use

Use the write command to modify a file opened by the open for access command. Before you may write to the file, the open for access command must include the parameter that allows write permission.

Also see the discussion in the read command about the kinds of files you should work with from AppleScript directly, and when scriptable applications are better vehicles for reading and writing data.

AppleScript from Apple offers no facilities to read or write resources. But see the discussion of the GTQ OSAX collection (Chapter 33) for ways to accomplish resource access.

Parameters

The write command requires at the minimum parameters containing the data to be written to the file and a reference to the file. The data can be any data that is appropriate for the file. That may include a tab-delimited text record that you've assembled in your script or from other documents, plain text, binary data extracted from other sources, or any AppleScript value class, such as lists and records.

Writing AppleScript value classes brings up an important point about the read command when reading such data. Consider the following script, which writes an AppleScript list to a file:

```
set myFile to (open for access file "Test File" with write permission)
set eof myFile to 0 -- empty anything previously in the file
write {30, 40, 50, "forty"} to myFile
close access myFile
```

If you were to open the file in TeachText or other editor, this is what you would see:

```
list    long    -long    (long    2TEXT    forty
```

This is how AppleScript writes a list to a file. If you then perform a plain read on the file, your script would grab exactly that text—something your script would have no use for. But that's why the read command contains a parameter that lets you retrieve AppleScript data in a particular value class. Therefore, to retrieve this list from a file in its original list format, the script would be:

```
set myFile to (open for access file "Test File")
set myData to (read myFile as list)
```

```
close access myFile
myData
  -- result: {30, 40, 50, "forty"}
```

Back to parameters, the file reference may be any file or alias reference, or most efficiently, a file reference number, as demonstrated above.

When you write to a file, you must pay attention to the file mark, just as you do for reading. Upon opening the file, the marker is at the very beginning of the file. If the file contains data, and you write data to the file, the Write command overwrites existing data for only the length of the data you're writing. Notice that it overwrites, rather than inserts, data. But that also means that if the file contains 20 bytes, and you write 10 bytes, bytes 11 through 20 of the original data remain in the file.

If your goal is to completely overwrite a file, however, you can do so with the help of the **set EOF** command (detailed below). This command essentially lets you determine where the end of the file is. By setting the EOF to zero, you tell AppleScript to delete everything in the file, cleaning the slate for your next **write** command.

An optional parameter lets you determine where in a file you wish the **write** command to place your data. The Starting At parameter requires an integer as an argument. The integer represents the character (counting from the beginning) where the data should be written (or negative numbers from the last character). To append data to an existing file, there is a shortcut for this parameter: substitute the eof constant for the integer, as in

```
write return & "Bill Clinton" to presFile starting at eof
```

a statement that adds a new line of data to a file of U.S. presidents.

You have a number of ways to delete data from a file, depending on where in the file the data to be deleted is located. In general, however, the task requires reading the file's data into one or more variables, performing text manipulations upon those variables, and then rewriting the entire file again (after setting EOF to zero). Hence my recommendation to use scriptable applications that provide easier support for inserting and deleting data in their documents—rather than AppleScript's file access capabilities.

One last parameter, the For parameter, lets you write only a portion of a chunk of data to the file. For example, if you have a body of text to write, but you only want to write the first 100 characters of that text to the file, the statement would be something like this:

```
write bodyText to myFile for 100
```

You may also combine the For and Starting At parameters to perform tasks such as overwriting a fixed number of bytes within a file.

Examples

```
write date string of (current date) to myFile
```

```
write myText to myFile starting at 25
```

> write myText to myFile starting at -25 for 10
>
> write myText to myFile starting at eof

You Try It

Enter and run the following script:

> set myFile to (open for access file "Test File" with write permission)
>
> set eof myFile to 0
>
> write "My first file writing!" to myFile
>
> close access myFile

Replace the middle two lines with each of the following statements, which build on the data entered with the previous script. Execute each script, and then open Test File with TeachText or other text editor to see the results. You must close the file between script executions.

> write "my" to myFile
>
> write ", NOT!" to myFile starting at -1
>
> write " Cool." to myFile starting at eof
>
> write " was a blast. A real trip." to myFile starting at 22 for 14

Common Errors

Inserting the word "file" after the **write** command from HyperTalk experience; the file is already open from a previous **open for access** command when an error interrupted the script (solution: create a separate script that closes the file by name); accidentally overwriting existing data; failing to clear a file with **set EOF** before writing entirely new data.

Related Items (Chapters)

Open for access (7); close access (7); read (7); new file (7); set eof (7).

get eof *fileReference*

Result

Integer representing the number of bytes of data in the file (i.e., the offset of the end of the file). Zero for application files.

When to Use

You may obtain the length of a file with this command. As with other commands that access a file, the file must already be open for the **get EOF** command to work. As described in the **read** command discussion, it isn't necessary to specify the end of file if you plan to read the file from the current position of the file mark to the end of the file: the plain **read** command automatically reads to the end of the file.

Parameters

The only parameter is a reference to the file, either by name, alias, or reference number.

Examples

```
copy get eof myFile to fileLength

write myData to myFile for (get eof myFile)
```

You Try It

Enter and run the script below several times, choosing different data files each time. Watch the returned values in the result window:

```
set myFile to (open for access (choose file))
set fileLength to get eof myFile
close access myFile
fileLength
```

Common Errors

Failing to open the file for access prior to the command; failing to include the fileReference parameter; forgetting that "get" is part of the command name, and omitting it.

Related Items (Chapters)

Open for access (7); close access (7); read (7); write (7); set eof (7).

set eof *fileReference* to *integer*

Result

None.

When to Use

This command lets you control where you wish the end of a file to be. That means you may truncate a file to any length, or, by setting the value to zero, empty the file of all data (but this does not delete the file). As demonstrated in the write command discussion, above, this command is most often used to empty a file prior to rewriting its entire contents from a script. And, as with any file command that alters the content of a file, the file must be open with write permission enabled for the set EOF command to work.

Parameters

Two parameters—a reference to a file (file, alias, or file reference number) and an integer—are required. The integer represents the offset value where you want the file to end. All bytes beyond that offset value will be erased from the file.

You cannot specify a negative number to set the eof as a negative offset of the original eof. Instead, use the get EOF command, as in

    set eof myFile to (get eof myFile - 10)

Examples

    set eof myFile to 512

    set eof myFile to 0

You Try It

Enter and run the script below to establish a starting point for further experimentation:

    set myFile to (open for access file "Test File" with write permission)
    set eof myFile to 0
    write "Now is the time for all good men." to myFile
    close access myFile

Replace the middle two lines with each of the following statements, which build on the data entered with the previous script. Execute each script, and then open Test File with TeachText or other text editor to see the results. You must close the file between script executions.

    set eof myFile to (get eof myFile - 1)

    set eof myFile to 15

    write "." to myFile starting at eof

    set eof myFile to 0

Common Errors

Failing to open the file for access and write permission prior to the command; failing to include the fileReference parameter.

Related Items (Chapters)

Open for access (7); close access (7); read (7); write (7); get eof (7).

Debug Commands

log *string*
start log
stop log

Result

None.

When to Use

See Chapter 13, Debugging Scripts, about using these commands in conjunction with the Script Editor's Event Log window.

Date/Time Commands

current date

Result

A value of class date.

When to Use

This scripting addition gives your scripts the ability to retrieve the current date and time from your Mac's internal clock. A date class value is more powerful than it may look at first glance. See the discussion about date class values and date arithmetic in Chapter 9.

The returned value looks like this:

```
date "Friday, June 11, 1993 4:23:26 PM"
```

The command returns the date format specified by the Date & Time control panel setting (which is also influenced by different localized versions of the System). Different date formats scramble the order of the words, so it makes parsing the string unreliable to extract, say, the word for the month.

It is possible to use the data from this command for things like comparisons, as we do in the alarm agent script described in Chapter 15.

For scripting of times and dates, an understanding of date class objects and their properties (Chapter 9) is essential.

Parameters

None.

Examples

```
set timeStamp to current date

if (current date) is greater than or equal to ¬
    date "Saturday, September 11, 1993 5:00:00 PM" then
    soundAlarm -- calling a subroutine
end if
```

You Try It

Enter and run the following script line, watching the returned value in the Result window:

```
current date
```

Common Errors

Forgetting that the value is a date class, rather than a string; parsing the returned value for one date and time format setting when the user's control panel is set differently.

Related Items (Chapters)

Date class values (9).

time to GMT

Result

A positive or negative integer representing the number of seconds difference between the local time zone set in your Map control panel and Greenwich Mean Time (also known as Coordinated Universal Time, or UTC).

When to Use

For this command to be of any value to a script, the Macintosh on which the script runs must have its local time zone set correctly. In practice, few Macintosh users know to do this when they set up their machines. The local time zone is set by locating the nearest city in the Map control panel. Only then should you synchronize the Mac's internal clock with a local time signal.

Unfortunately, neither the Map control panel nor the time to GMT command take into account changes in time zone differences due to what North Americans call Daylight Saving Time. The difference between New York and GMT is five hours all year 'round, according to the Time to GMT command, yet in real life the difference shortens to four hours during the summer months of Daylight Saving Time. System 7.5's Date & Time control panel has a checkbox for Daylight Savings Time, but it's questionable whether all users will know to use it for changing their Mac clocks twice a year.

As a result of this unreliability, it is best to use this command guardedly, and perhaps only for personal use (or built around your own correction for Daylight Saving Time).

You may use the date and time objects in AppleScript to help with the math in calculating the number of hours or minutes between your Mac's local time and GMT. For example,

```
(time to GMT)/hours
    -- result: -8.0
```

meaning that the difference is that a Macintosh in the Pacific time zone is eight hours earlier than GMT. See Chapter 8's details about the date reference for more about working with date and time arithmetic in AppleScript.

Parameters

None.

Examples:

time to GMT
(time to GMT)/hours

You Try It

There isn't much to play with here, but by entering the command and checking the result, you will see if your Mac's Map control panel has been set correctly.

Common Errors

Incorrectly set Map control panel.

Related Items (Chapters)

Date and Time arithmetic (9).

Understanding Application Dictionaries

This section could be better be titled *"Trying* to Understand Application Dictionaries." A dictionary supplies a great deal of information about an application's scriptability, but it also isn't selective enough to provide as specific a roadmap to scripting as a scripter would like, especially when you're just getting to know a program.

When you use Script Editor to open a dictionary, the window has two panes (Figure 7.12). In the left is a list of Apple Event suites, commands, and objects. Click on any item(s) in the left, and a fuller explanation appears on the right. These explanations come from resources in the application—put there by the programmers who made the application scriptable.

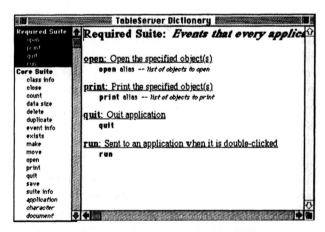

Figure 7.12 Dictionary window in Script Editor.

If you look at the outline of information supplied in a typical application, here's what it comes down to:

Apple Event Suite
    command
        purpose
        syntax
        result
    object
        [plural form name]
        [elements]
        [properties]

Let's look at each of these items, and see what's great about the definitions, and what's usually missing.

Apple Event Suites

Event suites are groups of Apple event messages (commands, in AppleScript). These labels in the dictionary (Required, Standard, etc.) are important to programmers, but not all that useful to scripters. Where they do help, however, is letting a scripter know what parts of the dictionary are specific to the application. These are usually listed last as a suite named after the application. Figure 7.13 illustrates this point in the TableServer dictionary.

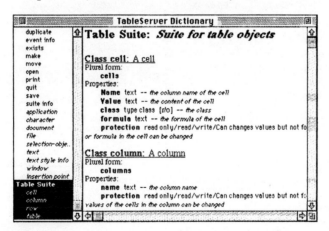

Figure 7.13 TableServer-specific commands in the dictionary.

Almost all applications support the Required Suite in a standard way. The so-called Standard Suite, however, is another matter. Any given application may support some or all of the standard commands, and often enhance some of the standard ones to work better with specific data or interface elements of the application. It's always a good idea to check through each of these commands for a new application, and see if there is something you haven't seen before for a given command. Its deviation from the standard won't necessarily be noted in any of the comments.

Commands

These are vital to your scripting the application. A command definition usually consists of the syntax form and a note about the result that the command returns after execution. How well the syntax is described can make the difference between success and failure your first few times out with a command. The more detailed the better. Ideally, the syntax description should provide an explicit listing of the classes of values required for each parameter.

Here is an unfortunate example that tells a scripter absolutely nothing:

open: Open the specified object(s)
  open reference -- *list of objects to open*

I'm not making this up. It comes from Scriptable Text Editor. A better representation would be:

open: Open the specified file
  open fileReference -- *reference to a file to open*

At least this tells you that the parameter must be a file reference (which more than likely means it accepts a file or alias reference). Unfortunately, to get from the first version to a more understandable version takes either supplementary documentation or enough experience to try different kinds of things to find out what works and what doesn't.

Command definitions also rarely describe which objects they work with. When you look at the list of commands and objects for a given suite, you may be led to believe that the commands work with all objects in the suite. Most of the time this is impractical, but nothing in the command definition helps you narrow down the objects that the command can affect.

Also, be aware that the comments supplied are not tied to the way a command has been written or modified (at the last minute) to behave. I have seen numerous examples of incorrect information about the result produced by a command or the default behavior of a command when a parameter is omitted.

Objects

Object definitions can simply boggle the mind with superfluous information, particularly about the supposed element classes that are related to the object. Figure 7.14 shows the object definition for a paragraph in Scriptable Text Editor. This object is specific to the program, and is not shared by AppleScript.

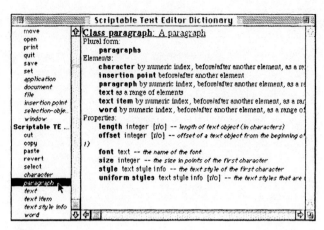

Figure 7.14 Paragraph object definition in Scriptable
Text Editor's dictionary.

Notice the list of elements. The element listed as "insertion point" turns out to be an object you don't access from a script. Details provided in the more fully detailed documentation for Scriptable Text Editor omits that item as an element of a paragraph.

Early scripters of Microsoft Excel 4.0 ran into difficulty with its AppleScript dictionary. For example, nowhere in the dictionary does it explain exactly how to compose a reference to a specific cell in a spreadsheet. If you were used to the A1 type of cell addresses in Excel macros, you'd be frustrated as all get-out in AppleScript. Only by some trial and error did early scripters figure out that cell references were in the "R1C1" format. To compound matters, if your script retrieved a formula for a cell, it would retrieve the formula in whichever format it was written in, including the A1 format. But then Excel would not accept that formula in another cell, because the data was in the A1 format, rather than the R1C1 format.

Scripting by Dictionary Alone

The bottom line is that until you get a lot of scripting under your belt, learning an application's scriptability only by its built-in dictionary is fraught with peril. If an application you intend to use frequently offers documentation for scripters, it will be well worth obtaining it if it's not part of the program's regular documentation. For example, the printed version supplied for TableServer (on the companion disk in two parts) includes a list of what commands can work with each object.

Just the same, be prepared for lots of trial and error as you gain comfort with the way each program expects its commands and object references. Eventually, as applications developers learn more about how we scripters use their products, the information available in the on-line dictionary should improve in quality.

Next Stop

Learning the AppleScript commands and scripting additions is a big part of AppleScript. But an equally important piece of the puzzle is how to work with objects. Learning how to refer to objects in scripts can be one of the most challenging parts of AppleScript, but once you've got a good feel for that in the next chapter, you're well on your way to successful scripting.

CHAPTER 8

Describing Objects—
References
and Properties

I've said it before, and I'll say it again: commands perform actions on objects. In the previous two chapters we looked at lots of actions. This chapter focuses on the "objects."

Objects in Real Life...

Most of the commands we issue in real life have well-defined objects as part of the command statements. For example, if you ask Joe to open the window, there are actually a couple of objects involved. First, Joe is an object, and the fact that he was the only person named Joe to be within earshot at the moment means that he is the sole target of your request. Your request then triggers Joe to do something with another object: the window.

While this may be a simple request in real life, you don't realize the hidden parts of the command you issued. For instance, by asking Joe to perform a certain task, you first assume that there is only one Joe who could possibly hear your request. Your second assumption is that Joe is capable of doing that task: that he knows what a window is and how to open one. And as for which window you mean, you may not have noticed the glance, nod, or other gesture that indicated to Joe which window you had in mind.

...Translated to Computer

Computers tend to ignore subtlety. As a consequence, they require extreme precision in how we label things. If our window opening request of Joe were part of a computer script, the computer wouldn't be able to see our gestures or nods to help it know what objects we're talking about. In fact, it may not even know precisely which Joe we mean from the dozens it may know.

We've already seen how this affects tell statements. Consider this statement fragment:

```
tell application "Microsoft Excel"...
```

We help the script narrow down who it is we're going to tell something to. First we supply an application's file name. Technically, this isn't enough for AppleScript, because your disk may contain more than one copy of an application. Without any prompting, AppleScript looks for the named application in the same folder as Script Editor. If it's not there, then we are presented with a file dialog and the instructions to locate the application. By our selection, we retrieve the pathname to the application, which Script Editor retains during the course of the session (and also stores with the script when it is saved). In other words, the parameter includes a strict pathname to a particular copy of the application—a kind of roadmap for the command.

The same goes for other objects. In our window opening example, a computer script needs a roadmap to the precise window. The window we want Joe to close is one window of a certain wall, of a certain room, of a certain building, and so on, until there is an ample description to make it clear exactly which window we mean.

For objects we'll be working with in AppleScript, we need these same kinds of object roadmaps. The length of the directions on the roadmap depends on how small the object is within the scope of the application and its realm of objects. Watch the progression of depth the following statements encounter as the objects become smaller components of the outermost object, the application:

```
-- application level
tell application "Scriptable Text Editor"
    quit
end tell

-- document level
tell application "Scriptable Text Editor"
    get name of document 1
end tell

-- paragraph level
tell application "Scriptable Text Editor"
    get paragraph 3 of document 1
end tell

-- word level
tell application "Scriptable Text Editor"
    get word 2 of paragraph 3 of document 1
end tell

-- character level
tell application "Scriptable Text Editor"
```

```
    get character 1 of word 2 of paragraph 3 of document 1
end tell
```

As each object becomes more deeply nested within others, the description of the object grows. Yet this is necessary, since each part of the description is an integral part of the object description.

References

These verbal roadmaps to objects are called object *references*. Knowing how to write proper object references is one of the most important aspects of mastering AppleScript. The difficulty lies not so much in knowing the various kinds of references there are, but in the fact that each application can—and does—treat references differently, even among similar applications.

If you dissect any object reference, you will discover that it has three pieces:

1. Type of object—called the class
2. Form—distinguishing characteristic about a particular object
3. Container—the object that holds the specific object you're referring to

The first word of a reference identifies the class of the object of your command's affections. Class names—terms such as word, paragraph, cell, row, record—clearly state what kind of object is to receive the action of the command.

The form that distinguishes one object in a class from another object of the same class is some identifier, such as a number or name.

A container is any object that can consist of other, smaller objects. For example, a document contains paragraphs. When you view the dictionary of an application, you see the inverse of the container metaphor: elements. For instance, a document object may list as its elements paragraphs, words, and characters. The container of a particular object is simply part of the roadmap to the object, and must be part of the reference to the object.

When an object is deeply nested, the reference must include the series of containers that point to the object. An extreme example with the Scriptable Text Editor character object is:

```
character 1 of word 2 of paragraph 3 of document 1 ¬
    of application "Scriptable Text Editor"
```

Notice that the series of containers are listed in this reference from the smallest to the largest. In other words, we're referring to the first character of the second word of the third paragraph of document 1 of a specific application. The sequence demonstrates the logical steps AppleScript or the application follows to reach the object.

As you'll see later in this chapter, the extreme case above can be shortened if your script can accommodate a different frame of reference. Consider the three-paragraph text entry in a Scriptable Text Editor document shown in Figure 8.1.

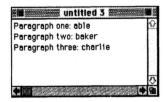

Figure 8.1 A three-
paragraph document.

Here are the various ways we can refer to the first letter of the word "baker":

character 1 of word 3 of paragraph 2 of document 1

character 1 of word 6 of document 1

character 36 of document 1

The index (i.e., numeric) values that signify character, word, and paragraph count are all intertwined in the sequence of objects. When the frame of reference is the document and its character elements, the script can get straight to the character by its count among all the character elements of the document.

Container Syntax

So far, all of our examples use the of preposition between elements. AppleScript accepts the in preposition as an alternate. The following references get you to the same Scriptable Text Editor object:

word 3 of paragraph 2 of document 1

word 3 in paragraph 2 in document 1

word 3 of paragraph 2 in document 1

AppleScript also recognizes the possessive form of containers. For example, the reference

paragraph 3 of document 1

can also be written as

document 1's paragraph 3

The possessive form is more often used in concert with object properties and the ordinal form of numbers, as in

first window's bounds

For references that feature a series of containers, the possessive form can become quite cumbersome. Use this form only when it helps the readability of the script.

Default Object References

When sending a command to an application's object, the application must also be part of the reference. Therefore, to send a command to the third word of document 1 inside Scriptable Text Editor, the formal reference is:

```
word 3 of document 1 of application "Scriptable Text Editor"
```

A reference that includes the application name, like this one, is called a *complete reference.*

When a reference doesn't have enough information to fully specify the object, the script looks to the default object to fill out the reference. If no default object is explicitly named, then the *default object* is AppleScript, itself. Chances are, however, that AppleScript won't understand the command or object described in the statement.

But we can shift part of a complete reference to a tell statement. In fact, we've been doing a lot of that in the book thus far. When a script says

```
tell application "Scriptable Text Editor"
    get word 3 of document 1
end tell
```

Scriptable Text Editor is the default object for all commands inside the tell statement. AppleScript completes the *partial reference* in the get statement with the application name, as required. We can also go further along this line by defining a narrower default object, if it suits the needs of the script. Therefore, we can also say

```
tell document 1 of application "Scriptable Text Editor"
    get word 3
end tell
```

to accomplish the same thing. In this case the partial reference is filled out with default object information about document and application identifiers. We can use this behavior to our advantage when a number of statements apply to a specific object belonging to the application. It makes for shorter, more readable script lines. Thus,

```
tell of application "Scriptable Text Editor"
    set style of word 1 of paragraph 1 of document 1 to bold
    set style of word 1 of paragraph 2 of document 1 to bold
end tell
```

becomes:

```
tell of document 1 of application "Scriptable Text Editor"
    set style of word 1 of paragraph 1 to bold
    set style of word 1 of paragraph 2 to bold
end tell
```

You have the power to make any container the default object, as long as the objects in the remaining partial references are elements of the default object.

Creative uses of tell statements can provide interesting flexibility in how you structure a script. Here is how nesting tell statements can be used for efficiency:

```
tell application "Scriptable Text Editor"
    tell document 1
        tell paragraph 1
            (* commands for objects in paragraph 1 *)
        end tell
        tell paragraph 2
            (* commands for objects in paragraph 2 *)
        end tell
    tell document 2
        tell paragraph 1
            (* commands for objects in paragraph 1 *)
        end tell
        tell paragraph 2
            (* commands for objects in paragraph 2 *)
        end tell
    end tell
end tell
```

Object Properties

Now that we've been introduced to the concept of referring to an object, how does a script get or set information about that object? In most applications, it all relies on an object's *properties*. Properties of an object consist of a well-defined series of specifications that help shape the appearance and characteristics of an object.

Real-life objects have properties as well. If we were to define a pencil object, the kinds of properties we might give it are: length; diameter; outer color; lead number; point sharpness; lead color; has eraser; eraser height; has toothmarks. Every pencil has those properties, although the values (or settings) of those properties likely differ from one pencil to another.

Scriptable object properties are often more complex than that, but it is quite common to find the contents, value, or text of a property bearing the data your script is interested in. Here are some examples from various scriptable programs:

```
text of paragraph 1 thru 5

value of cell "Cost Each" of row "Product 4"

formula of cell "R35C12"

cellValue of cell "Name" of record 200
```

Each of these property references point to data stored in a document—very likely the kinds of things your scripts will be shuffling about.

Because the dictionary for an object may not be clear on the subject, you may also have to use trial and error to discover what the mere reference to an object returns. In some cases, it may be the data you're looking for; in other cases the returned value is a detailed record of the object's properties, from which you must still extract meaningful data as a property.

Object Reference Syntax

AppleScript has defined a number of object reference forms, or rules for the structure of object references. For the rest of this chapter, we'll examine each of these forms in detail. The form types are:

Property	Index
Relative	Name
ID	Middle Element
Range	Arbitrary Element
andFilter	Every Element

Before you get too involved with all these forms, I must give you one important caution that should make learning these easier:

Not every application and not every object supports every form.

In the next pages, you'll see some very interesting, if not exciting, ways to refer to objects or groups of objects. Be aware that while AppleScript provides a framework that allows these references to work, their implementation is solely the responsibility of the AppleScript implementation in a program. Scriptable Text Editor, designed to be a shining example for other application developers, supports all of these forms, but most programs support only a subset of these forms. Sometimes information about what forms an object supports is provided in printed documentation about a program's AppleScript support. You won't, however, get much help from most dictionaries. Trial and error will be the course of action in many cases.

In the syntax descriptions to follow, recall that a reference includes a class, an identifier, and a container. To help make the property syntax more readily understandable, I will include the container part inside angle brackets (e.g., *<object>*). This should help you place these references in better context as you learn them or look them up for reference.

Property References

Syntax
[the] *propertyLabel* <of *objectOrRecord*>

How to Use

The property reference form is perhaps the simplest and most reliable, because it's relatively easy to determine an application object's properties (from the dictionary) and know what kinds of values to set or get. All properties are values, but some properties are read-only.

As an illustration, examine Figure 8.2, which shows the properties for a word object in Scriptable Text Editor. Let's look more closely at one property's definitions and how it translates to the property reference form.

Figure 8.2 Scriptable Text Editor's properties for a word object.

The value of the length property is an integer, representing the number of characters in the word object. Assuming the default object of a statement is the Scriptable Text Editor application, the reference to the length property of the first word of an open document would be:

```
length of word 1 of document 1
```

The name of the property, length (as listed in the dictionary), is the *property-Label* part of a property reference form.

Notice that the length property is specified as being read-only (the [r/o] designator). This would be a natural assumption, since you can't adjust the length of a word just by giving it a different value. Other properties can be adjusted, particularly those that affect font characteristics.

You also use the property reference form to get or set values inside a record. For example, a record from an employee object might look like this:

```
{ name: "Morris Sloan", hourly rate: 9.35, department: "Manufacturing" }
```

You can think of each field within this record as a property, with the field value corresponding to a property value. Syntax for referring to the data within a record is the same as referring to a property of an object, as in:

```
set oneRecord to ¬
    { name: "Morris Sloan", hourly rate: 9.35, department: "Manufacturing" }
hourly rate of oneRecord
    -- result: 9.35
```

If you like, you can precede any or all property reference forms with the word "the". This can add to the readability and friendliness of a script for new-comers. These two scripts produce exactly the same results:

```
set font of document 1 to "Times"
```

```
set the font of document 1 to "Times"
```

Here are some examples from various scriptable applications plus an Apple-Script list object:

```
bounds of window 1 -- Scriptable Text Editor
```

```
name of column 3 of table 1 -- TableServer
```

```
the formula of cell "R3C15" -- Microsoft Excel
```

```
enabled of menu item "Copy" of menu "Edit" -- MacProject Pro
```

```
cellValue of cell "City" -- FileMakerPro
```

```
the ZIP of { city: "Chicago", state: "IL", ZIP: 60611 }
```

The more you work with scriptable applications other than Scriptable Text Editor, the more importance you will give to properties. While Scriptable Text Editor allows your script to access the contents of a text object directly (e.g., word 3 of paragraph 1), many other application objects don't offer such shortcuts. For example, in most table-oriented programs (such as TableServer), you only get to the contents of a cell by referencing the value property of the cell, as in

```
value of cell 4 of row 5
```

If your script references the cell object in its entirety, the program likely returns a long record of properties, values, and other gibberish that won't do your script much good.

You Try It

Enter and run each of the following scripts, watching the returned values in the Result window:

```
tell application "Scriptable Text Editor"
    name of window 1
end tell
```

```
tell application "Scriptable Text Editor"
    bounds of window 1
end tell
```

```
tell application "Scriptable Text Editor"
    activate -- so we can watch
    -- grab bounds property value for a window
    set windowRect to the bounds of window 1
    -- add 50 to each value
    repeat with i from 1 to 4
        get item i of windowRect
```

```
        set item i of windowRect to (result + 50)
    end repeat
    -- set the property for the window
    set the bounds of window 1 to windowRect
end tell

set teamRecord to { team: "Mudhens", wins: 40, losses: 32 }
set theWins to wins of teamRecord
set theLosses to losses of teamRecord
set gameTotal to theWins + theLosses
display dialog "This team has won" & ¬
    theWins & " out of " & gameTotal & " games."
```

Enter and run the following script to see what happens in an application that requires a property reference form to access its data:

```
tell application "TableServer"
    if not (table "Presidents" exists) then
        open file "Presidents"
    end if
    set testValue to cell 1 of row 20 of table "Presidents"
    close table "Presidents"
end tell
testValue
    -- result: {class:cell, name:"President", «property data»:"James Garfield"}
```

The result here is some of that gibberish I was talking about earlier. This data is actually a record of all the characteristics of the cell. To get the data, however, we must access its value property. Modify the script's set statement as shown below, and run the script:

```
tell application "TableServer"
    if not (table "Presidents" exists) then
        open file "Presidents"
    end if
    set testValue to Value of cell 1 of row 20 of table "Presidents"
    close table "Presidents"
end tell
testValue
    -- result: "James Garfield"
```

Common Mistakes
Forgetting the second word of a two-word property or field name; forgetting to complete the reference when addressing a property of a deeply nested object (e.g., paragraph of document).

Related Items (Chapters)
Record value class (9); get (6); set (6); copy (6).

Indexed References

Syntax

[the] *className* [index] *index* <of *objectOrItem*>

[the] (first | second | third | fourth | fifth | sixth | seventh | eighth |
   ninth | tenth) *className* <of *object OrItem*>

[the] *index*(st | nd | rd | th) *className* <of *objectOrItem*>

[the] (last | front | back) *className* <of *objectOrItem*>

How to Use

An index is nothing more than an integer that represents the count of elements from the beginning or end of a containing object. For example, in a table, your script may have to refer to the first cell of the third row. The index reference form would be:

    cell 1 of row 3 of table 1

In truth, there are three indexed references in that phrase. The first one is the 1 indicating which cell of row 3; the second one is the 3 indicating which row among all rows in the table; the final one is the 1 indicating which table object we're talking to. The syntax, then, says to name the class of object, followed by the index count (the word "index" is optional and rarely used, since it adds nothing to readability).

In an effort to offer alternatives that read more like a natural sentence, AppleScript's designers provide other versions of the index reference form. Therefore, instead of saying

    cell 1

your script can refer to that object as

    first cell

AppleScript knows about the special ordinal numbers as words—"first" through "tenth"—and accepts them without a blink as long as the ordinal word is followed by a space and the class name of the object being counted. It's even smart enough to know that any integer immediately followed by the ordinal endings ("st", "nd", "rd", or "th") is a valid index (again followed by a space and class name of object to be counted). The following index references are valid:

    first word

    1st word

    word 1

    the 234th word

    92th word

That last one ("ninety-twoth word") may seem odd, but AppleScript accepts it as one of the ordinal endings, regardless of the numeral preceding it.

Nothing limits you from mixing the regular and ordinal indexed references in the same statement. Therefore,

third paragraph of document 1

paragraph 12 of first document

are both acceptable.

So far, the descriptions and examples have been for index counts from the beginning of objects in a series. What if the operation you need to perform is at or near the end of the series of objects? While you can usually find out how many objects are in its container (e.g., **count of words in paragraph 1**), and use that value as an index, some types of data (like lists and some objects in Scriptable Text Editor) let you use a shorthand notation. They consider the value −1 to represent the last object in a series. Here are some examples:

```
item -1 of {10,20,30}
   -- result: 30
```

```
item -2 of {10,20,30}
   -- result: 20
```

```
tell application "Scriptable Text Editor"
   get word -1 of document 1
      -- result: (last word of the document)
end tell
```

The formal definition of this reference form also indicates the words "last", "front", and "back" are accepted as ordinals (i.e., followed by a class name). In truth, not all kinds of data support this syntax. Aside from definitely working with items of lists, these variants work with layered objects, such as windows:

```
front window -- topmost window (i.e., window 1)
```

```
back window -- most hidden window
```

You won't, however, find these front/last/back references working for some other kinds of data, such as cells in a table.

To find out if a certain object can be referenced by index, check the application's dictionary for the containing object. For example, if you were unsure about using an index reference for a character in Scriptable Text Editor, look at definitions of its possible containers (word, paragraph, document). Where you see the character element listed (Figure 8.3), the comment indicates whether you can refer to character within that container by an indexed value. For Scriptable Text Editor, all three containers say they accept the character element referred by an indexed value.

```
Class word: A word
Plural form:
    words
Elements:
    character by numeric index
```

Figure 8.3 The dictionary indicates a character element can accept indexed references.

You Try It

Open the Bill of Rights document (Scriptable Text Editor document) in the Handbook Scripts:Chapter 08 folder on the accompanying disk. Position this document and the Script Editor windows so you can see as much of the document as your screen allows. Then enter and run the following script in Script Editor, watching for returned values in the result window:

```
tell document 1 of application "Scriptable Text Editor"
    get paragraph 1
end tell
```

Substitute the "get paragraph 1" line, above, with each of the following lines and run the script:

```
get paragraph 2

get word 1 of paragraph 2

get front word of paragraph 2 -- same as word 1

get last character of first word of paragraph 2

get 11th character -- of document 1

get 11th character of paragraph 5

get character 20 of paragraph 1
    -- error, because there aren't 20 characters there
    -- the index is therefore invalid

get paragraph 3
    -- result: empty because it's the blank line between paragraphs
```

Enter and run each of the next lines by themselves, since AppleScript knows how to handle items:

```
item 3 of { "Chico", "Harpo", "Groucho", "Zeppo", "Gummo" }

first item of { "Chico", "Harpo", "Groucho", "Zeppo", "Gummo" }

back item of { "Chico", "Harpo", "Groucho", "Zeppo", "Gummo" }

last item of { "Chico", "Harpo", "Groucho", "Zeppo", "Gummo" }
```

Common Mistakes

Incomplete references when referring to a deeply nested object; invalid index number (for more objects than are available).

Related Items (Chapters)

Partial and complete references (8); list class values (9).

Relative References

Syntax

[*className*] (before | [in] front of) *baseReference*

[*className*] (after | [in] back of | behind) *baseReference*

How to Use

A relative reference is an object whose location is defined by its position in relation to another object. For example, in the (vintage TV show title) phrase:

Who Do You Trust

the word "Who" is before (or in front of) the word "Do"; the word "Do" is after (or in back of or behind) the word "Who". This can be useful for a script that is moving objects around. Be careful with this reference, however: it is not universally supported in applications (in fact, it doesn't work on AppleScript items). Scriptable Text Editor (and probably most other text processing and layered object kinds of applications, such as draw-type graphics programs) supports this reference form fully, so all examples in this section will be from that application.

The key to working with a relative reference is knowing how to specify the *baseReference* parameter. Typically, the *baseReference* is a more absolute reference, such as an indexed or named reference. Think of the *baseReference* as the anchor, with the relative reference being an object on either side of that base object.

Going back to our "Who Do You Trust" phrase, we could use a relative reference to refer to the first word, as in:

`word before second word`

This is kind of clumsy, since when dealing with like objects (words and words), other reference forms are usually simpler to write and easier to read. One strength of the relative reference form is that if the application is willing (as Scriptable Text Editor is), your script can mix and match objects, as in:

`word before paragraph 3`

`paragraph before word 30`

Some rules apply here, however. The objects are usually related by their class-element definition. For example, in

`word before paragraph 3`

a word is an element of a paragraph object, so there's no problem for AppleScript to pick out what you mean. But for

`paragraph before word 30`

things get trickier, especially if word 30 is in the middle of a paragraph. AppleScript interprets this request to mean "paragraph before the paragraph containing word 30". In other words, if the base object isn't an element of the relative object, AppleScript tries to make the base object into the same class as the relative object.

Common sense also applies here. While it's fine to say

window behind window 1

you cannot mix unlike objects as in

paragraph behind window 1 -- <<No can do!

The prepositions for the two syntax descriptions need just one point of explanation. When the reference is to something in front of a base object, it means *immediately* in front of. If the items were indexed, and the base object were indexed as value 3, the object in front of it would have an index of 2. For an object after the base object, we're talking immediately following (the imaginary index value would increase by one).

Notice that the syntax description lists the leading *className* parameter as optional. It is in some circumstances. For Scriptable Text Editor, omitting the *className* parameter is telling the program that you mean the insertion point object (a strange object, but helpful to know about if you work with programs that use it). An insertion point object is a location relative to another object (it may hard to think of a location as an object, but strictly speaking, it is). When you click the cursor at the beginning of a paragraph and the flashing text insertion pointer flashes there, the insertion point object is defined by its location:

beginning of document 1

Press the right arrow key to move the pointer, and the object is defined by its new location:

after character 1 of document 1

Therefore, when a script says,

copy "Fred" to after word 1 of document 1

the relative reference (**after word 1 of document 1**) means the insertion point immediately following word 1 of document 1. Insertion points don't know about spaces (in fact, an insertion point can go between a space and a character), so you have to supply spaces with your text, as in

copy ", I must emphasize, " to before word 12

Working with this somewhat invisible insertion point object takes some getting used to, but it becomes essential for inserting text into existing text.

Earlier I said that the relative reference form also works well with layered objects. You can experiment with that concept with document windows, which are treated as layers that can go before, in front of, after, in back of, or behind other windows. For instance, Scriptable Text Editor supports the move command as it applies to windows:

move window "Main" to back of window "Demo"

As a final note (and I don't know why you'd want to do this), the *className* parameter must be just a valid class name for the default application of the script. You cannot use another kind of reference (as in tenth word before paragraph 2 of document 1) for this parameter. You should probably be using an indexed reference for this kind of object location.

You Try It

Open the Bill of Rights document with Scriptable Text Editor. Enter and run the following script:

```
tell document 1 of application "Scriptable Text Editor"
    word after first paragraph
end tell
```

Substitute the word after first paragraph line, above, with each of the following lines and run the script:

```
move paragraph 1 to before paragraph 3
```

```
move paragraph 3 to before paragraph 1
```

```
move paragraph 1 to after paragraph 2
    -- becomes part of paragraph 2, no space
```

Close the Bill of Rights document, and click "No" to the save changes alert. Now open the three Scriptable Text Editor documents named "Layer 1", "Layer 2", and "Layer 3" in that order. Enter the following script, and envision how the windows will behave when you run it. Then run the script, watching how well the action of the windows matches your expectations:

```
tell application "Scriptable Text Editor"
    activate
    move window "Layer 1" to front
    move window "Layer 1" to behind window "Layer 3"
    move window "Layer 2" to in front of window "Layer 3"
    move window "Layer 3" to before window "Layer 2"
end tell
```

Common Mistakes

Incomplete reference for the *baseReference* object parameter; relative reference form not supported by the application or object.

Related Items (Chapters)

Indexed reference form (8); partial and complete references (8).

Name References

Syntax
className [named] *nameString* <of *ObjectOrItem*>

How to Use

If an object has a name property in its definition, then your scripts can use the name reference form to identify that object. Two required parameters for the name reference form are the class of object, followed by the name (in quotes or a variable that evaluates to a string) assigned to that object. Sometimes the name is assigned by an application (e.g., the "untitled" name of a new window), while in other cases, your scripts can assign names (via the **set** command). Optionally, you can insert the word "named" between the two parameters if you believe it helps the readability of your scripts.

Name references are most often used in concert with other references to get or set specific information about that object. If the reference is simply to the named object (and the program accepts it as a valid reference), you may get more information than you bargained for. For example, in Microsoft Excel, we can assign a name to a cell, because a cell object in that program has a name property (also settable in the program via the Define Name command in Excel's Formula menu). Let's say you've assigned the name "Product" to the first cell, which contains the value 456. If your script says:

    get cell "Product"

Excel returns a record of properties and other gobbledygook that is useless for most scripts. What you really want is the data from the cell, covered by the value property of that cell. Therefore, the reference to the value consists of a property reference form combined with a name reference form:

    get value of cell "Product"

Name reference forms are commonly required for parameters to commands (AppleScript's and an application's commands). Look at these commands:

    open file "HD:Documents:Bill of Rights"

    close window "Jane Doe"

    activate application "HD:Apps:Microsoft Excel"

    list folder alias "HD:Trash:"

Each one contains a command followed by a required name reference form. The *className* sets up the type of data the command needs (file, window, application, and alias, in the examples above). The command chokes without the *className* parameter part of the reference.

Whenever an application you'll be scripting can have many objects available for a command, it is vital that you use name reference forms if at all possible. The value of a name reference over an indexed reference will become readily apparent the instant a user disturbs the order of objects (e.g., window, documents), and your script expects a particular object to be in a particular order. Assigning unique names to objects and then using those names in references go a long way to avoiding unexpected execution errors.

Of course, there may be times when more than one object in the default object (e.g., multiple cells in a spreadsheet document) have the same name. If that happens, the name reference will apply to only one of those objects. Which one depends on how the application handles it. Chances are, the program will pick the one whose indexed reference would be the lowest number.

Where necessary, you may have to include a series of name references. A good example is accessing an application on another Macintosh connected to a network:

```
tell application "Scriptable Text Editor"¬
    of machine "Gonzo" of zone "Marketing"
```

Here, a series of three name reference forms identify the precise object we want (amongst all the Scriptable Text Editors available on the network).

You Try It

Open the three Layer documents (Handbook Scripts:Chapter 08 folder) in Scriptable Text Editor. Enter and run the following script:

```
tell application "Scriptable Text Editor"
    contents of window "Layer 1"
end tell
```

Substitute the contents of window "Layer 1" line, above, with each of the following lines and run the script:

```
contents of document "Layer 3"
```

```
bounds of window "Layer 2"
```

TableServer provides excellent examples of how to use name references. In the Presidents table, we've named the three columns: President, Party, and Vice President. One of the behaviors of a TableServer table is that unless directed otherwise, a row automatically assumes the name of the value in the leftmost cell. For the Presidents table, that means the President's name is the name of the row. We can then use the name of a row and a column to access the value of any cell in the table. Enter and run this script:

```
tell application "TableServer"
    if not (table "Presidents" exists) then
        open file "Presidents"
    end if
```

```
        set testValue to ¬
            Value of cell "Vice President" ¬
            of row "William McKinley" of table "Presidents"
        close table "Presidents"
    end tell
    testValue
        -- result: "Garret Hobart/Theodore Roosevelt"
```

Substitute various Presidents' names for the row name parameter and run the script. Also check out the "President" and "Party" cells of any given row.

Common Mistakes

Incomplete reference to a named object; forgetting the property name when accessing values of a named reference object.

Related Items (Chapters)

Indexed reference form (8); partial and complete references (8); properties (8); string class values (9).

ID References

Syntax

className id *IDvalue* <of *Object*>

How to Use

A few applications assign unique ID (identifier) values to each object they create. This value is like a serial number stamped in steel on the object. Hyper-Card, for example, creates an ID for each button, field, card, and background object in a stack. An object's ID number (usually an integer) stays with that object for its entire life. Applications that do IDs correctly (like HyperCard) won't let the same ID be assigned to any other object in the file—even if an object is deleted, no new object of the same class will ever receive the same ID.

An ID guarantees a uniqueness to a property that cannot be altered by the user changing the object's order (index) or name. Therefore, an ID reference is guaranteed to work while the object is still "alive" in the file.

Two required parameters are the class of the object containing the ID property and the property value (usually an integer). Between them is the hard-wired word "id" (in any combination of uppercase and lowercase), which is pronounced as if the letters were two initials (not like the Freudian term). Here are some examples of what the syntax looks like in real life:

```
window id 9029

background field id 23
```

Be prepared, however, to not be able to access the ID of some objects whose property list includes an ID. Often such properties are present for internal use only, but end up in the dictionary, causing scripters no end of trial and error—mostly error.

You Try It

Unfortunately no applications included on the accompanying disk define accessible ID properties for its objects. You'll have to try it on other scriptable applications that may come your way.

Common Mistakes

Forgetting the "id" word; incomplete reference.

Related Items (Chapters)

Partial and complete references (8); properties (8); integer class values (9).

Middle Element Reference

Syntax

middle *className* <of *objectOrItem*>

How to Use

Some objects allow this reference form, which points to the center element of a series. For example, in a three-item list, the middle reference form points to the second item:

```
get middle item of {"Executive","Legislative", "Judicial"}
    -- result: "Legislative"
```

When the number of items in the series is even, the reference points to the item that is the last item of the first half of the group [the actual formula is ((n + 1) div 2), where n is the total number of objects in the series]. Therefore,

```
get middle item of {"parsley", "sage", "rosemary", "thyme" }
    -- result: "sage"
```

Scriptable Text Editor supports this reference for some objects, as in:

```
middle word of paragraph 1
middle character of word 3 of paragraph 7
```

You may see similarities between the middle and indexed reference forms. In a way, the middle reference form is a special case of the indexed form, where AppleScript does the math of figuring out which is the middle (between the first and last).

You Try It
Open the Bill of Rights document in Scriptable Text Editor. Then enter and run the following script:

```
tell document 1 of application "Scriptable Text Editor"
    get middle paragraph
end tell
```

Substitute the get middle paragraph line, above, with each of the following lines and run the script:

```
get middle word of paragraph 1
```

```
set middle word of paragraph 1 to "Right Number"
```

```
set size of middle word of paragraph 2 to 48
```

```
middle word of paragraph 1
```

Close the Bill of Rights document, without saving changes. Next, open the three Layer files in order. Run the following script:

```
tell application "Scriptable Text Editor"
    name of middle window
end tell
```

While previous examples were calculating horizontally, the middle reference can work "vertically" through layers of objects of the same class, such as these three windows.

TableServer does not support this reference form, but you may want to try a script that gets the value of the middle cell of a row—and experience the error message that comes back.

Common Mistake
Incomplete reference.

Related Items (Chapters)
Partial and complete references (8); indexed reference form (8).

Arbitrary Element References

Syntax
some *className* <of *objectOrItem*>

How to Use
Related to the indexed reference, the arbitrary element reference points to a random item in a series of objects. AppleScript handles the random number generation for things like lists, but not for an application's objects—that's entirely up to the application if its designers elect to support this reference form.

This form is not appropriate for some classes of data, so don't expect it to be present in all instances (although it is available for several object classes in Scriptable Text Editor).

HyperTalk Alert

HyperTalk's equivalent to "some" is the word "any."

As with any kind of indexed reference form, the arbitrary reference requires a complete reference, as in:

```
some word of paragraph 1 of document 1
```

```
some paragraph of document 1
```

You can also use this form with lists, as in,

```
some item of {20, 40, "sixty", 80, 100}
    -- result: (could be any item)
```

Even though random numbers are involved here, there is no relation between this reference form and the random scripting addition discussed in Chapter 7.

You Try It

Open the Bill of Rights document in Scriptable Text Editor. Then enter and run the following script:

```
tell document 1 of application "Scriptable Text Editor"
    get some paragraph
end tell
```

Substitute the get some paragraph line, above, with each of the following lines and run the script a few times to see random results:

```
get some word of paragraph 2
```

```
set size of some word of paragraph 2 to 48
```

```
some word of paragraph 1
```

Enter and run this script, which sets ten random words of the document to bold:

```
tell document 1 of application "Scriptable Text Editor"
    activate
    repeat 10 times
        set style of some word of paragraph 2 to bold
    end repeat
end tell
```

Close the Bill of Rights document, without saving changes.

Common Mistake
Incomplete reference.

Related Items (Chapters)
Partial and complete references (8); indexed reference form (8).

Every Element References

Syntax
every *className* <of *objectOrItem*>
pluralClassName <of *objectOrItem*>

How to Use
This variation of the indexed reference form points to all items of the class named in the *className* parameter. It's a little tricky to work with sometimes, because programs may react differently to this reference. The best way to use it, however, is to retrieve all the values of a particular property of an entire collection of objects, as in

```
text of every word of paragraph 1
```

```
value of every cell of row 12 of table 1
```

As it turns out, some programs, like Scriptable Text Editor, assume that when we ask for an object, we mean its text. Therefore, for that program, the following reference also works:

```
every word of paragraph 1
```

Most other programs, such as TableServer, don't make that assumption, and require the property name as part of the reference, as demonstrated above.

What you may not expect from this reference form, however, is that data shuffled about in commands that use the every element reference is in the list format. For example, if the first paragraph of a Scriptable Text Editor document is

```
"Four score and seven years ago..."
```

and we

```
get text of every word of paragraph 1
```

the result is:

```
{"Four", "score", "and", "seven", "years", "ago..."}
```

In other words, the command asks for all the words, and AppleScript returns an itemized list of them. By asking for the text of every word—instead of the text of the paragraph—we get just that: every word in a form that allows us to perform convenient AppleScript item-by-item parsing or looping.

If you look at the last word AppleScript extracted from the paragraph, you also get a clue about how important spaces are to Scriptable Text Editor's definition of a word. Any punctuation immediately preceding or following a word from the language is part of the word object. This definition, I emphasize, is determined by Scriptable Text Editor, and may be different in other text-based scriptable applications.

As another example of this item-ness, we can ask Scriptable Text Editor to give us the length property of all the words in that "Four score" paragraph:

```
tell document 1 of application "Scriptable Text Editor"
    length of every word of paragraph 1
end tell
    -- result: {4, 5, 3, 5, 5, 6}
```

Things can get pretty granular, if you like:

```
get every character of "Big Bird"
    -- result: {"B", "i", "g", " ", "B", "i", "r", "d"}
```

Or if you go the other way:

```
get every paragraph of document 1
```

the returned value is a list, with each paragraph as a quoted string item in that list.

AppleScript returns an empty list (instead of an error) if your reference to a list specifies every object of a class that is not contained in the list. For example,

```
get every string in {1,2,3}
    -- result: { }
```

while referring to classes of objects contained in the string will return desired values:

```
get every string in {1, "two", 3}
    -- result: { "two" }
```

For application objects, you will most likely get an error when mismatching objects (e.g., every window in paragraph 1).

Some applications also define a plural class definition for objects your scripts tend to use all the time. Figure 8.4 shows how this looks in a dictionary entry for an object with a plural class form. Plural class forms are usually just the plural of the object. You can substitute this plural class form for every element references. For example, the following two statements are identical:

```
get text of every word of paragraph 1
```

```
get text of words of paragraph 1
```

Both return an itemized list of all the words in paragraph 1.

Class word: A word
Plural form:
    words

Figure 8.4 A plural class form in a dictionary.

You Try It

Open the Bill of Rights document in Scriptable Text Editor. Then enter and run the following script:

```
tell document 1 of application "Scriptable Text Editor"
    get every word of paragraph 1
end tell
```

Substitute the get every word of paragraph 1 line, above, with each of the following lines and run the script:

```
get every word of paragraph 2
```

```
get words of paragraph 2
```

```
get every paragraph
```

```
set size of every word of paragraph 1 to 18
```

```
set style of every word of paragraph 2 to bold
```

```
get length of every word of paragraph 2
```

```
get length of every paragraph
```

Close the Bill of Rights document, without saving changes.

To see how this reference works in TableServer, enter and run the following script:

```
tell application "TableServer"
    if not (table "Presidents" exists) then
        open file "Presidents"
    end if
    set testValue to Value of ¬
        cells of row 42 of table "Presidents"
    close table "Presidents"
end tell
testValue
    -- result: {"Bill Clinton", "D", "Albert Gore, Jr."}
```

Here we get the values of every cell in row 42. Notice that the property name is singular, while the references are plural—this is an important syntax point for this reference form. If you substitute "every row" for "row 42," the result is a list of lists. Try it. Also try getting "cell 3 of every row".

Common Mistakes

Incomplete reference; forgetting to specify a property for the objects; using a plural class form when none is defined for that object.

Related Items (Chapters)

Partial and complete references (8); list value classes (9).

Range References

Syntax

className startIndex (thru | through) *stopIndex*

pluralClassName startIndex (thru | through) *stopIndex*

every *className* from *boundaryReference1* to *boundaryReference2*

pluralClassName from *boundaryReference1* to *boundaryReference2*

How to Use

A range reference is a powerful extension to the every element reference. While the every element reference applies to all items of a class, you can use the range reference to target a smaller, consecutive group (or subset, for math-prone folks) of items. You specify the range by indicating the starting and ending points as indexed references.

Let's walk through an example, using a Scriptable Text Editor paragraph that reads:

When in the course of human events...

Starting with the every element reference form,

```
get every word of paragraph 1
  -- result: {"When", "in", "the", "course", "of", "human", "events..."}
```

But we can limit the range to be just the first three words by saying:

```
get every word from word 1 to word 3 of paragraph 1
  -- result: {"When", "in", "the"}
```

The indexed references (word 1 to word 3) are inclusive. And, like the every element reference, the data is generally conveyed in a list form.

Notice an important point about this construction: When you compile the statement, AppleScript automatically converts it to the following:

```
get words 1 thru 3 of paragraph 1
```

which is valid syntax for the range reference form. Why did it do this? Because it recognized that all the objects referred to in the original statement were of the same class and were contained by the same paragraph object. In the process of reducing the statement to the *startIndex* variation of this reference form's syntax, AppleScript has made the statement more readable. When an object supports a plural class name (as many objects do in Scriptable Text Editor), the conversion automatically turns the *className* parameter to the *pluralClassName* during compilation—all it means is that AppleScript can accept either from us humans, and knows what to do with them during compilation.

For both the *startIndex* and *boundaryReference* parameters of this form, you can use the AppleScript words beginning and end to signify the respective locations among a series of objects. Therefore for the previous statement, the script could have also read:

> get words beginning thru 3 of paragraph 1

or

> get every word from beginning to 3 of paragraph 1

You can also obtain a list of objects in from the end of a group of objects. For example,

> get words end thru -3 of paragraph 1
> *-- result: {"of", "human", "events..."}*

But while the way the statement reads you might expect the objects to come back in reverse order (i.e., the last object listed first), such is not the case.

Lists also can take part in this reference form. For example,

> get items 2 thru 4 of { "Classic", "LC", "Mac II", "Centris", "Quadra" }
> *-- result: { "LC", "Mac II", "Centris" }*

You use the *boundaryReference* version of this reference form when the objects involved are of different classes. For example, Scriptable Text Editor (and most scriptable text processing programs) defines a text object, which is the actual text within a document. If you supply the statement:

> get text of document 1

AppleScript (and Scriptable Text Editor) returns the text of the entire document as one long quoted string value (not as an itemized list). But if we want just a range, we can limit what comes back, as in:

> get text from paragraph 1 to paragraph 3

Here we're mixing objects: text and paragraphs. Therefore, the *boundary Reference* syntax is required. Notice that the reference for each boundary is a complete reference (coupled with the default document and application object, of course). AppleScript won't accept:

> get text from paragraph 1 to 3 *-- <<No way!*

If the application is up to the task, you can even mix *boundaryReferences*, as long as they make sense. Scriptable Text Editor easily accepts the statement:

> get text from word 3 to paragraph 5

meaning all the text from the third word of the document to the end of the fifth paragraph of the document, inclusive.

Working not with the text object, but other elements of programs like Scriptable Text Editor, the results you get with mixed objects may confuse you at first. Let's start with this paragraph:

> To be or not to be.

If we want to extract the individual characters (as a list) of the first two words, the proper reference would be:

> get characters from word 1 to word 2
> *-- result: {"T", "o", " ", "b", "e"}*

But you might be tempted to use another construction, which produces quite different results:

```
get characters of words 1 thru 2
  -- result: {{"T", "o"}, {"b", "e"}}
```

What gives? If you examine this statement more closely, you'll recognize that it actually contains two references. The first is an every-element reference (in plural class form) to all the characters; the second is a range reference to the first two words of the paragraph. AppleScript begins its evaluation process of the statement by getting the value of the range reference:

```
words 1 thru 2
  -- result: {"To", "be"}
```

Then it gets the characters of that list, which ends up being a list of characters for each word nested within a list of words.

What this last issue demonstrates is that you need to be careful with range references that involve mixing object types. Think the reference through, and make sure you haven't combined multiple references that get evaluated differently than you expected.

You Try It

Open the Bill of Rights document in Scriptable Text Editor. Then enter and run the following script:

```
tell document 1 of application "Scriptable Text Editor"
  get words 1 thru 2
end tell
```

Substitute the get words 1 thru 2 line, above, with each of the following lines and run the script:

```
get words 1 thru 10 of paragraph 2
```

```
get text from word 1 to word 10 of paragraph 2
```

```
get text from end to word -5 of paragraph 2
```

Close the Bill of Rights document, without saving changes. Next, open the three Layer documents. Enter and run the following scripts to see range references work with other kinds of application objects:

```
tell application "Scriptable Text Editor"
  get name of windows 2 thru 3
end tell
```

```
tell application "Scriptable Text Editor"
  get text of paragraph 2 of documents 1 thru 3
end tell
```

Close the three Layer documents. TableServer doesn't support range references.

Common Mistakes

Incomplete reference; nesting multiple references when mixing objects; the application doesn't support range references for some object(s); forgetting to specify a property for an object range.

Related Items (Chapters)

Partial and complete references (8); every element reference forms (8); indexed reference forms (8); list value classes (9).

Filtered References

Syntax

reference whose | where *BooleanExpression*

How to Use

The filter reference form is the most powerful of all in AppleScript. Unfortunately, it is limited to application objects in scriptable applications that support them (like Scriptable Text Editor and scriptable Finder). They may not be used on AppleScript objects, such as lists or other types of values.

In the real world, when you run a liquid through a filter, you are trying to filter out impurities, ending up with only the stuff you want. That's precisely what a filter reference does with a series of objects: it lets a script extract just the information you want from the whole. Let's start with a Scriptable Text Editor document with a single paragraph:

My sister Susie sells sea shells by the sea shore.

If we ask AppleScript for all the words with the every element reference form, we get them all in a list:

```
tell document 1 of application "Scriptable Text Editor"
    every word
end tell
    -- result: {"My", "sister", "Susie", "sells", "sea", ¬
        "shells", "by", "the", "sea", "shore."}
```

But with the filter reference, we can ask for only those words whose first letter is an "s":

```
tell document 1 of application "Scriptable Text Editor"
    every word whose first character is "s"
end tell
    -- result: {"sister", "Susie", "sells", "sea", "shells", "sea", "shore."}
```

What makes this work is that Scriptable Text Editor tests each of word object in the container (the whole document, here) to see whether it is true that its first character is the letter "s". If the test returns a true (internally), then the word is added to the list of values to be returned to the script. This true value is what we mean by the *BooleanExpression* parameter of this reference form.

Let's go further, and see how this might be useful in our example. We can extract all the words of the document that match a particular word. A first effort at such a reference might be something like:

```
every word whose word is "sea"
```

but this doesn't work, because the *BooleanExpression* parameter cannot evaluate correctly at the same object level as the original. To accommodate this dilemma, AppleScript has a special predefined variable: it. In a filter reference form, "it" points to each successive occurrence of the object within the series as AppleScript performs its tests through the group. The correct syntax, then, is:

```
tell document 1 of application "Scriptable Text Editor"
    every word where it is "sea"
end tell
    -- result: {"sea", "sea"}
```

It may not seem that you can do much with this information, but on the contrary. You now have a list of items that match your filter criteria (like the every element reference form, the filter form returns a list of data matching the criteria). You can count items:

```
tell document 1 of application "Scriptable Text Editor"
    get every word where it is "sea"
    count of result
end tell
    -- result: 2
```

Your choice between the whose and where words in a filter reference is entirely up to your taste in how a phrase reads. The words are interchangeable, although the common terminology for this kind of reference is that an application "supports whose clauses."

To take full advantage of this reference form, you should have a good grasp of the AppleScript's Boolean operators (Chapter 11). They provide a very full range of possibilities for constructing filter references. Here are some examples to give you ideas:

```
words of document 1 whose length > 10

every paragraph where it contains "normal"

words whose style contains bold

every word where it contains "ing"

every paragraph where it starts with "Once"
```

You could say that these examples use the filter reference to find "things that are." You can use other Boolean expressions, however, to filter results to show "things that are not":

> words of document 1 whose length is not 10

In theory, we should be able to use the Not operator to invert the returned value of another Boolean expression. For example, to find all words whose style is not bold, we should be able to say:

> words whose style not (contains bold)

Using the synonyms available for AppleScript's comparison operators (whose results are Booleans), we should then be able to make that statement more readable:

> words whose style doesn't contain bold

Incidentally, a Boolean expression can be the aggregate of multiple Boolean expressions. For example, if you want to refer to every paragraph whose first word is "The" and whose last word is "end", you can combine the two expressions with the Boolean AND operator. This is what the reference would look like (parentheses added for help in showing the two components:

> paragraphs where (it starts with "The") and (it ends with "end.")

This filter catches only paragraphs that meet both criteria. If one or the other would do, use the OR operator:

> paragraphs where (it starts with "The") or (it ends with "end.")

Feel free to string as many of these smaller Boolean expressions into one larger one as needed to make your selection criteria clear.

A script can also narrow its scope for objects within a container, such as words within a specific paragraph of a document. Here's an example of what that reference would look like:

> every word of paragraph 2 whose first character is "a"

Filter references can be tricky to work with, especially the first time you work with them in a new application. If the acceptable syntax for such references isn't documented with the application, it could take some trial and error to make one work the way you expect. One way to help figure these things out is to test the *BooleanExpression* parameters on some known sample data first. Let's try this out with the following reference:

> paragraphs where it contains "telephone"

Since the Boolean test is whether a paragraph contains a specific word, try each of these scripts:

```
tell application "Scriptable Text Editor"
    paragraph 1 contains "telephone" -- assuming paragraph 1 really does
end tell
```

```
tell application "Scriptable Text Editor"
    paragraph 2 contains "telephone" -- assuming paragraph 2 does not
end tell
```

You should get "true" and "false" returned values, respectively, in the Result window for these two scripts, meaning that the Boolean expression does work, and its place in the filter reference is secure.

One final note about testing filter references. If there are lots of objects that the filter reference needs to check (characters or words of a document), be prepared for a wait. You'll see the beachball cursor appear, but not spinning as AppleScript performs its object-by-object tests. This is not script execution, per se, so Command-Period won't halt it. You'll just have to wait until it's finished or AppleScript times out.

You Try It

Open the Bill of Rights document in Scriptable Text Editor. Then enter and run the following script:

```
tell document 1 of application "Scriptable Text Editor"
    paragraphs where it starts with "article"
end tell
```

Substitute the paragraphs where it starts with "article" line, above, with each of the following lines and run the script:

```
words where it contains "mm"
```

```
set style of paragraphs where it starts with "article" to bold
```

```
copy "(blank paragraph)" to paragraphs where it is ""
```

```
copy "" to paragraphs whose contents = "(blank paragraph)"
```

Close the Bill of Rights document, without saving changes. Next, open the three Layer documents. For good measure, open a couple new, untitled windows, and make them small enough so you can see the Layer windows. Enter and run the following scripts to see range references work with other kinds of application objects:

```
tell application "Scriptable Text Editor"
    name of windows whose name contains "Layer"
end tell
    -- result: names of Layer windows only
```

```
tell application "Scriptable Text Editor"
    bounds of windows whose name contains "Layer"
end tell
    -- result: bounds properties for Layer windows only
```

Close all documents.

With the scriptable Finder, you can witness the power of whose clauses in the following script:

```
tell application "Finder"
    activate
```

```
    open startup disk
    select (every item of startup disk whose kind is "folder")
end tell
```

In a production script, additional commands could now act on the selected items.

Common Mistakes

Invalid Boolean expression; improper or unsupported Boolean operator synonym; incomplete reference.

Related Items (Chapters)

Boolean operators (13); partial and complete references (8); every element reference forms (8); list value classes (9).

File and Alias References

Syntax

file *<pathname>*

alias *<pathname>*

How to Use

There is considerable confusion about the differences between file and alias references. Part of the confusion comes, I believe, from the fact that "alias" has a specific meaning to most Mac users: a small file that stands in for a Finder item located elsewhere on a hard disk or network. AppleScript alias references are not related to these kinds of alias files.

The distinctions between the two reference types revolve around the way file pathnames are treated during and after script compilation. To help explain the differences, let's use the following example references:

file "HD-120:Correspondence:Memo to Mike"

alias "HD-120:Correspondence:Memo to Mike"

Both references point to the same file.

When a script contains a file reference, AppleScript does not search the disk volume(s) for the file indicated by the pathname when the script compiles. In other words, the file does not even have to exist for the script to compile (it may need to exist, of course, for the script to execute, depending on the command that uses the reference as a parameter). AppleScript leaves any error detection about the file's existence for runtime. If the file exists where stated, then the script runs fine, looking for the file in the precise location in the reference each time. Incidentally, this behavior is what allows the open for access command to compile with the name of an as-yet uncreated file when the parameter is a file reference instead of an alias reference.

When a script contains an alias reference, however, AppleScript looks for the file according to that path during compilation. If the file does not exist at that path, then you receive a compilation error indicating that the file does not exist. This is where some extra magic comes into play. As part of the compilation process, AppleScript creates its own internal alias for the file. AppleScript treats this internal alias just as a user treats an iconized alias in the Finder. No matter where the original file is moved, the alias will know how to find it. Therefore, if you compile a script with an alias reference, you may move the file into another location on the hard disk—the next time the script runs, it will know how to find the original.

You must be careful, however, about moving a file bearing an alias reference in a script. Each time you compile the script (even if it is to correct a problem in a different place of the script), AppleScript must go through its internal alias creation—the original file must be in the spot indicated in the path of the alias reference. Before you start moving your aliased files around, the script should be completed and compiled (or saved as an application).

One further distinction between file and alias references is that only alias references may be stored in variables directly (for use as parameters to other commands in a script). For example,

```
set myFile to alias "HD-120:Tables:States"
tell application "TableServer"
   open myFile
...
```

For file references, however, the variable must contain a reference class value to the file, as in

```
set myFile to a reference to file "HD-120:Tables:States"
tell application "TableServer"
   open myFile
...
```

In both cases, of course, you can save just the string part of a pathname in a variable, and turn it into the desired reference with the file command:

```
set myFile to "HD-120:Tables:States"
tell application "TableServer"
   open alias myFile
...
```

The upside of this clarification is that virtually every command that works with existing files compiles and runs with either a file or alias reference. Therefore, there is rarely a need to convert one reference to another. But should the need arise, here's how to coerce an alias reference to a file reference:

```
set myFile to (choose file with prompt "Pick one") -- returns alias
set myFile to a reference to file (myFile as string)
```

Converting any pathname string to one of these references is as simple as prepending the reference name to the string. For example, here we assemble a pathname string to a file in the System Folder, and then pass the alias form to a command:

```
set pathname to ((path to system folder) as string) & "Finder"
set finderVersion to short version of info for alias pathname
```

In the first line, we extract the text-only pathname from the alias reference returned by the path to command, and stick the file name on the end. Then we convert the value to an alias reference in the second line as we pass it as a parameter to the info for command.

Common Mistakes

Assigning a reference to a variable already containing the reference; trying to compile an alias reference to a non-existing file.

Related Items (Chapters)

File-related scripting additions (7); scriptable Finder (18).

Next Stop

So far we've seen the commands we send to objects and how we make sure the commands get to the desired objects. In the next chapter, we cover the third and last big topic: working with the information that our scripts shuffle about.

CHAPTER 9

Working with Data— Values, Variables, and Expressions

A strong argument exists for saying that computing is all about information— data. Most of us use our Macintoshes for retrieving, creating, storing, and massaging information in the form of words, pictures, sounds, animations, and combinations thereof. Scripting's role in this information-filled world is still evolving. By and large, scripting is moving away from simple macro processing—the electronic equivalent of clicking buttons—and moving toward manipulating information. I'm not just talking about grabbing one piece of information from here and applying it over there—something that Publish and Subscribe does (if anyone bothers). A scripting language, such as AppleScript, can extract or insert information and even make decisions based on the content.

AppleScript calls any kind of information a *value*. Think about a paper application form from the real world. One of the blank spaces would be a kind of object, and what you write in the blank becomes the value of that object.

Kinds of Values

Some blanks on a form expect certain kinds of information to consider the information valid. For example, a field for someone's name wouldn't look strange if letters and numbers appeared in there (John Smith, 3rd). But the field asking for an age is usually small, denoting its expectation of the entry of numbers only ("32," not "thirty-two"). Therefore, the value of the name field could be any combination of numbers and letters, while the value for the age field must be a number.

AppleScript calls each different type of value a *value class*. This class terminology comes from the object-oriented programming world. You can think of a class as a master copy of something: anything belonging to the same class behaves the same way. Therefore AppleScript treats all values of the same class identically (e.g., you can use arithmetic operators with all values of the integer class).

By dividing values into classes, it helps scripters know how to work with data that flows through a script. We know, for instance, that to join two values of the string class, we use the concatenate ("&") operator. Classes also help us know what kinds of information can work together. For example, the expression

```
3 + "Fred"
```

won't work, because it applies an operator (+) to a value ("Fred") that doesn't understand that operator. Conversely,

```
3 & "Fred"
```

is invalid, because the concatenate operator ("&") doesn't work with integer class values.

But if we turn that integer into a string value, then the operator works, creating a valid expression:

```
"3" & "Fred"
  -- result: "3Fred"
```

One more advantage to classifying values is that when we look at a formal definition for a command or reference, the definition generally states what class of value is required for the various parameters. Therefore, when we see that a property of an application's object requires a value of the Boolean class, we know that any value that satisfies the definition of a Boolean class value can go into that slot.

Variables and Value Classes

I introduced you to the concept of variables in Chapter 5. There you saw how a variable is a named holder of a value or series of values. A variable name is formally known in AppleScript as an *identifier*—a term you will see in error messages that refers to a variable. Most of the data we work with in scripts spends at least part of its time in variables. Even if we use the **get** command to extract a piece of information, the value goes into the predefined AppleScript variable named **result**:

```
get 5 + 5
display dialog result
```

We can plug variables into slots for command and reference parameters (like we just did for **display dialog**), because AppleScript always evaluates the variable to its contents before the contents are passed as parameters.

While a variable you define in a script can contain a value of any class (unlike some other programming languages, you don't have to tell the variable ahead of time what class of value it will be holding), a variable evaluates to the class of the data it holds. For example, if we assign an integer to a variable, we can use that variable in any operation that works with integers:

```
copy 25 to yourAge
yourAge + 1
    -- result: 26
```

But as with a hard-wired value, a variable evaluates to the same class as the value that goes into it, so the following doesn't work:

```
copy 25 to yourAge
yourAge & " Fred"
    -- result: {25, " Fred"} -- a list value of the components
```

While we could turn an earlier example (3 & "Fred") into a valid expression by placing quotes around the integer—turning the integer into a string—you cannot do that directly with a variable:

```
copy 25 to yourAge
"yourAge" & " Fred"
    -- result: "yourAge Fred"
```

To accomplish the task, you must use a facility of AppleScript that allows a script to change a value from one class to another: *coercion.*

Coercing Value Classes

AppleScript uses the dictionary definition of coercion (the application of force) in the way it lets us alter a value's class. The most readable method is to use an AppleScript operator—**as**—to force the class issue. This operator is covered in Chapter 11, but it's important to understand it in the context of the values we're discussing here.

A script can change the class of a value by adhering to this syntax:

expression as *className*

where *expression* is the value you want changed, and *className* is the class you want it to become. Here are some examples of coercion with hard-wired values and their results:

```
100 as string
    -- result: "100"

"Joe Blow" as list
    -- result: {"Joe Blow"}

45 as real
    -- result: 45.0

"1024" as integer
    -- result: 1024 (they're both integers)
```

Coercion is an important concept to master, because quite often a command will receive results of one class, which your script must then feed as a parameter to another command in another class. We've seen this with some of the file commands and scripting additions. If we use choose file to get an alias class value of a file, we need to convert the value to a string that we can feed the open file command in an application. Here's one way to do it:

```
tell application "Scriptable Text Editor"
    get (choose file with prompt "Pick a file") as string
    open file result -- open command from application
end tell
```

In this case, the choose file command returns an alias class value, which is immediately coerced to a string class value before going into the result variable. We then use the variable as the parameter of the correct class in the open command. Incidentally, we could have also done the coercion later:

```
tell application "Scriptable Text Editor"
    choose file with prompt "Pick a file"
    open file (result as string)
end tell
```

In both scripts, parentheses help AppleScript more accurately perform necessary evaluations. In the first, we want AppleScript to get the alias reference from the choose file command intact—and then we coerce it. In the second script, we need AppleScript to perform the coercion on the result variable before sending it as a parameter to the open command.

With all this in mind, we can go back to the yourAge example above, and coerce the variable containing the age value from its original integer value to a string for the desired concatenation:

```
copy 25 to yourAge
(yourAge as string) & " Fred"
    -- result: "25 Fred"
```

Coercion Caveats

As neat as coercion sounds, you must be realistic about it. Just as you cannot turn yarn into gold (except in fairy tales), some values simply can't be coerced to specific classes. For example, a string of alphabet characters can't be made into a numeric class of any kind. Also, a real number with a decimal fraction cannot be made into an integer (although you can round the number, and then coerce it).

One other gotcha afflicts primarily the application, script, file, and alias class values, all of which use a file path name as a further parameter. Coercion among these classes doesn't work the same way as for other class coercions. That's why we have to use a construction like this:

```
tell application "Scriptable Text Editor"
    choose file with prompt "Pick a file"
    open file (result as string)
end tell
```

instead of:

```
tell application "Scriptable Text Editor"
    choose file with prompt "Pick a file"
    open (result as file)
end tell
```

If we try the latter, AppleScript advises us that it's not possible to coerce an alias class to a file class. For these kinds of classes, it's best for now to coerce one type to a string, and then pass the string as an argument after the command and the class name, as demonstrated in the prior example.

Value Class Details

In the next several subsections, we'll examine each of AppleScript's value classes. To help you learn about them in the first place, and refer to them later for reference, I've divided the classes into three categories:

Common	Less Common	Rare
Boolean	Date	Class
Integer	Record	Constant
List	Reference	Data
Real		
String		

As you learn AppleScript for the first time, you can get pretty far just with the common value classes. You can become familiar with the rest as you run into them in the course of expanding your AppleScript experience.

Boolean Class

Computerdom owes a big debt to the nineteenth-century mathematician, George Boole. He developed an arithmetic system based on the logic of true and false properties. These two states play a large role in computer languages, because they can be used to specify common real world states: on/off; yes/no; true/false; one/zero.

AppleScript uses Boolean class values of TRUE and FALSE (no quotes around the words, and may be upper or lowercase) for these situations. For example, one property of an application's document may be whether its contents have changed since the last time it was saved. The property is defined as being TRUE if the contents have been modified; FALSE if they're the same as when the document opened. The minute a user or script changes the contents, the program internally and automatically changes the property from FALSE to TRUE. Our scripts can obtain that property, which comes back as the unquoted text:

```
true
```

Variables can hold Boolean values just as they can any other value. For example:

```
set modifiedState to modified of document 1
```

stores TRUE or FALSE into the modifiedState variable.

I devote the majority of Chapter 11 to making comparisons in scripts—actions that rely on Boolean results from operators, such as:

```
4 > 3
   -- result: true

10 = 20
   -- result: false

"mouse" contains "us"
   -- result: true

"Microsoft" comes before "Apple"
   -- result: false
```

All these expressions evaluate to Boolean values. As a result, they are considered Boolean expressions.

Multiple Boolean expressions can be combined into a single expression that evaluates to a single TRUE or FALSE. The glue that holds these Boolean expressions together are the And and Or operators. Consider the expression:

```
(10 < 20) and ("a" comes before "b")
   -- result: true
```

This expression evaluates to TRUE because *both* smaller expressions evaluate to TRUE. Then the And operator, working on the two TRUE values (TRUE And TRUE), returns the final evaluation: TRUE. If one of the smaller expressions had evaluated to false, then the entire expression would be false:

```
(10 < 20) and ("z" comes before "a")
   -- result: false
```

That's because the And operator worked on dissimilar values (TRUE And FALSE).

The Or operator returns a true if either of the two sides of the expression returns a TRUE:

```
(10 < 20) or ("z" comes before "a")
   -- result: true
```

In other words if the left side is TRUE or the right side is TRUE, then the expression is TRUE.

All this And/Or operator stuff explains how we can combine multiple Boolean expressions into things like filtered references:

syntax: *reference* whose | where *BooleanExpression*

example: **every paragraph where (it starts with "The") and ¬**
                    (it contains "general")

The two smaller Boolean expressions are applied independently to each paragraph of the document. If both expressions prove to be true, then the paragraph qualifies for this filter.

See Chapter 11 for more about operators that affect Boolean values. Chapter 10 shows Boolean values in use for if-then decisions.

Integer Class

An integer is any positive or negative number (including zero) that does not also contain any decimal fraction. The following values are integers:

0

–1

1

495

23948570

The following values are *not* integers, because they are represented as having a fractional part:

0.1

1.0

–45.0

3.14159

The distinction between integers and other kinds of numbers (real number values, below) is primarily necessary because of the way computers and programs work. Internally, computers work with integers and real numbers (also called floating point numbers) very differently. As a result, we who write programs or scripts are saddled with having to make the distinction in our values (unless we use an environment that handles that for us, such as HyperTalk). While we may think 12 and 12.0 represent the same amount of anything, the computer has to treat them differently for calculation purposes.

AppleScript integers may be in the range between –536870911 to +536870911. Any number outside that range is automatically coerced to a real number value class during compilation (and displayed in exponential notation). Note that all large numbers in AppleScript (integer or real) do not allow commas or other delimiters between numerals. The value for 100,000 must be entered as:

100000

In some dictionary entries, you may see class references to "small integer." AppleScript makes no distinction between categories of integers, as some compilers for other programming languages do. Typically, a short integer means any value in the range of 0 to 255. This works for something like the ASCII character scripting addition, whose parameter must be within that range. To AppleScript, an integer is an integer is an integer. I'd rather see dictionary definitions simply state the integer class for the parameter, and supply the required range in the comment following that item.

List Class

AppleScript relies heavily on the list value class. It's worth the effort to spend time learning about lists early in your AppleScript learning process, because you'll use them a lot for carrying and manipulating data.

A list is defined as an ordered collection of values. What this means is that a single list value can carry around multiple values. We've seen that some commands expect or are ready to receive multiple pieces of information for a single parameter. For example, the display dialog scripting addition command lets a scripter pass to the buttons parameter the names of up to three buttons. The convenient method of passing the names as a group is the list value.

Each component of a list is called an *item*, and a single list may contain any number of items whose individual values may be from any class (i.e., they don't have to be the same within a list).

You can recognize a list by its curly braces. An empty list looks like this:

{ }

That is a valid list class value, whose contents are empty.

More likely, you'll see lists of similar data:

{ "Howdy", "Doody" }

This list contains two string values. Here's a list with values of three classes (string, real, and Boolean):

{ "piano", 88.0 , true }

The majority of the lists you will deal with in scripts come as the returned values of commands to objects. A number of reference forms (particularly the every element reference form and those derived from it) return the contents of an application object as a list. In fact, if a result has an ability to contain multiple pieces of information, the returned value will be in the list class, even if the actual data returned is one or zero items. For example, if a Scriptable Text Editor document consists of this sentence,

Let them eat cake!

then here's a script that gets all the words of that document:

```
tell application "Scriptable Text Editor"
   get every word of document 1
end tell
   -- result: {"Let", "them", "eat", "cake!"}
```

Once the data is in this form, a script has a great deal of flexibility due to the special status a list has in AppleScript.

A List Object

While every value is considered an object within AppleScript, a list has more of the traditional pieces you would expect: defined elements and a complement of properties to help you work with contents of the list.

The elements of a list are called *items*. An item is one of the values inside a list, separated from other items by commas:

```
{ 1, 3, 5, 7, 11 } -- five elements

{ "Joe", true, 45 } -- three elements
```

To set or get the value of one item, a script refers to the item by its index value, with the leftmost item being item 1:

```
item 4 of { 1, 3, 5, 7, 11 }
  -- result: 7 (an integer)

item 2 of { "Joe", true, 45 }
  -- result: true (a Boolean)
```

You can place a list in a variable, and then manipulate the items of the list via the variable:

```
set bigCities to { "London", "Tokyo", "New York" }
set item 3 of bigCities to "Los Angeles"
  -- result: { "London", "Tokyo", "Los Angeles" }
```

A script may also add items to the beginning or end of the list with the help of the concatenation (&) operator:

```
set bigCities to { "London", "Tokyo", "New York" }
set bigCities to bigCities & "Los Angeles"
  -- result: { "London", "Tokyo", "New York", "Los Angeles" }
```

This also works if the two groups you're joining are both lists. The result is one list consisting of elements from both original lists.

Three properties of lists are useful in scripts. They are:

Property	Value Class	Description
rest of	list	items in the list except for the first one
reverse	list	items in the list in reverse order
length	integer	number of items in the list

The rest of property can be useful when a script needs to examine or operate on the content of each element in turn:

```
tell application "Scriptable Text Editor"
  set wordList to words of document 1
```

```
        repeat until wordList is { }
            (* do something with each word *)
            set wordList to rest of wordList
        end repeat
    end tell
```

The example shows an alternate to performing a repeat loop using the number of items in the list as a repeat counter. But you can also use the **rest of** property to construct a list when you know the original data coming back from another command has a leading item in the list that you don't want.

The reverse property allows a script to extract a copy of a list, but with items in reverse order:

```
reverse of { 1,2,3}
    -- result: {3,2,1}
```

Getting this property does not alter the order of the original list.

A list's **length** property is a read-only value of the number of items—of all value classes—in the list:

```
length of { "sunny", 65, "35%" }
    -- result: 3
```

Notice that this property ignores the contents of the items, themselves. If you want to get the length of an item, construct the reference accordingly:

```
length of item 1 of {"sunny", 65, "35%"}
    -- result: 5
```

The **length** property duplicates the work of AppleScript's **count** command, which works on lists. Thus,

```
count of { "sunny", 65, "35%" }
    -- result: 3
```

provides the same results as requesting the **length** property. It's a good habit, however, to use the **count** command, because it can be more selective in what it counts:

```
count of integers of { "sunny", 65, "35%" }
    -- result: 1
```

Like many other objects, you can use a number of reference forms to access items within a list. Here are the ones that work:

Reference Form	Example
Property	length of { 1, 2, 3 }
Index	item 3 of { 1, 2, 3 }
Middle	middle item of { 1, 2, 3 }
Arbitrary	some item of { 1, 2, 3 }
Every Element	every item of { 1, 2, 3 }
Range	items 1 thru 2 of { 1, 2, 3 }

The last two references, since they have the capability of returning multiple items, return their results also as lists. All the rest return results in the class of the item extracted from the list (integer, string, etc.). Some of the more powerful reference forms—relative, filter, name, and ID—don't work with lists.

Nested Lists

You may encounter lists within lists. Applying the rules above, you should be able to work with them (or figure out how you got them in the first place when you didn't expect them).

If we take our "Let them eat cake!" document from above, we saw what happened when we get the words of the document:

```
tell application "Scriptable Text Editor"
    get words of document 1
end tell
    -- result: {"Let", "them", "eat", "cake!"}
```

But look what happens when we alter the get command to get all the characters of all the words in the document:

```
tell application "Scriptable Text Editor"
    get characters of words of document 1
end tell
    -- result: {{"L", "e", "t"}, {"t", "h", "e", "m"}, ¬
        {"e", "a", "t"}, {"c", "a", "k", "e", "!"}}
```

We end up with lists within an outer list. That's because the command first acted on getting the words as a list, followed by dissecting the words into smaller elements. To work with the data, however, we have to be cognizant of the item status of this giant list. There are four items of the outer list:

```
tell application "Scriptable Text Editor"
    get characters of words of document 1
    length of result
end tell
    -- result: 4
```

Each of those items is a list:

```
tell application "Scriptable Text Editor"
    get characters of words of document 1
    count of lists of result
end tell
    -- result: 4
```

To work with the characters of a given word, we need to extract the word's list of characters, as in:

```
tell application "Scriptable Text Editor"
    get characters of words of document 1
    get item 1 of result
```

```
end tell
    -- result: {"L", "e", "t"}
```

Now we can treat those items as we would any list. Of course, we could also directly reach one of the characters by combining item references:

```
tell application "Scriptable Text Editor"
    get characters of words of document 1
    get item 1 of item 1 of result
end tell
    -- result: "L"
```

Let's apply some of this list knowledge to a real script example that neatly overlaps all open windows in Scriptable Text Editor. The script, below, is available on the accompanying disk in the Handbook Script:Chapter 09 folder:

```
-- Item Value Practice
tell application "Scriptable Text Editor"
    -- start with number of windows
    set windowCount to count of windows
    -- prepare first window's bounds property value
    if windowCount = 0 then
        display dialog "There are no open windows to arrange." ¬
            buttons {"Phooey"} default button 1
    else
        -- do this only if there are open window(s)
        activate -- so we can watch
        -- for each window...
        set nextWindowBounds to {1, 39, 481, 305}
        -- loop through all the windows
        repeat with i from 1 to windowCount
            -- set the bounds property
            set bounds of window i to nextWindowBounds
            -- bring window to front of pile
            move window i to front
            -- add 20 to each value of bounds property
            repeat with j from 1 to 4
                set item j of nextWindowBounds to ¬
                    (item j of nextWindowBounds) + 20
            end repeat
        end repeat
    end if
end tell
```

The first steps include getting a count of the open windows at the moment. We assign that number to a variable which serves double-duty: first as a value to check to make sure at least one window is open (if not, display a dialog alerting of the fact); second as a counting value later on to make sure we cycle through all open windows.

If there is at least one window open, then we bring Scriptable Text Editor to the front and assign the first window's bounds property (a list of four coordinates) to a variable, nextWindowBounds. Now we use the windowCount variable as a limit to the number of times through an activity loop. In that loop we set the actual property of the designated window to the contents of the nextWindowBounds variable. In the next line, we bring the newly sized window to the front so it overlaps any other windows previously set. Finally, we include yet another repeat loop, this one working with each of the items in the nextWindowBounds property. To effect the overlap in a uniform fashion, we add 20 pixels to each of the four coordinates. Since AppleScript doesn't let us perform math operations directly on a list item (not like the HyperCard's add command), we set each value of the list to its original value plus 20. This action sets up the coordinates for the next window if execution goes through another loop for another open window. As soon as Scriptable Text Editor runs out of windows, so does the repeat loop, and execution continues uninterruptedly out to the end.

Real Class

In AppleScript, a real number is any positive or negative number that includes a decimal point. The number doesn't have to include any fractional part: a whole number is represented with a decimal point and zero. Here are some real numbers:

0.92

1.0

−45.5

0.0

AppleScript accepts scientific notation for real numbers (in fact, all scientific notations compile to real values). The format for scientific notation starts with a real number, followed by the letter "E", followed by an exponent integer (positive or negative). Any hard-wired number you write into a script that has more than four digits on either side of the decimal is automatically compiled to scientific notation. Here are some examples and their decimal equivalents:

```
1.0E+4      -- 10000.0
−1.0E+4     -- −10000.0
1.0E−5      -- 0.00001
```

When performing math with all real numbers, the results also come back as real values:

```
3.0 + 0.14159
   -- result: 3.14159
```

But if you perform math with a mixture of real and integer values, the class of the result varies, depending on which side of the arithmetic operator the real value is, and what that value is. If the real value is on the left side of the operator, you are guaranteed that the result will be a real (AppleScript essentially coerces the integer on the right side to a real for the math):

```
10.0 + 5
    -- result: 15.0
```

When the left operand is an integer, two things can happen, depending on the real operand's value:

```
5 + 10.0
    -- result: 15
5 + 10.1
    -- result: 15.1
```

In most cases, as you'll learn in Chapter 11's discussion about operators, AppleScript takes the clue from the left operand to try to coerce the right operand to the same value class to make the operator work. In the first example, that's true: the real operator (10.0) was coerced to an integer, and the result is that of integer arithmetic. But in the second example, the real-ness of the right operand took precedence, causing the arithmetic and result to be in real number terms. Without this reverse coercion, potentially valuable information (the decimal fraction of the operand) would have been lost. If you intended to lose that fraction, your script should first round the real, and then let the left integer operand govern the action.

It's unlikely you'll run into this limit, but the range of values for real numbers is from the smallest (positive or negative) values with an exponent of –324 to the largest with an exponent of +308. If you ever outrun these limits in the course of applying AppleScript to an everyday solution, telephone Dr. Carl Sagan.

String Class

The term, string, goes way back in computer programming, but it doesn't seem to be a ready metaphor for something in the real world, except as a string, or series, of characters. String values in AppleScript are always placed inside standard quotation marks. I make the distinction between standard ASCII character quotes instead of the so-called smart quotes (or curly quotes) used in desktop publishing. Curly quotes don't work in AppleScript scripts (much to the chagrin of the person assembling pages for this book) unless they are surrounded by standard quotes. Here are some string value examples:

```
"Pride and Prejudice"
"a"
"Beverly Hills 90210"
".285"
```

The instant you place quotes around any characters—including numbers—the characters become strings. Numbers lose whatever arithmetic abilities they may have had prior to becoming a string (although they can be coerced to numbers if needed).

Because the double-quote symbol, which must surround a string, may also need to be inside a string, AppleScript provides a mechanism that lets us designate a quote inside a string. By preceding the in-string quote with a backslash symbol (\), we instruct AppleScript to look at the next quote not as the end of a string but an in-string quote:

```
"Have you read \"Walden\" lately?"
```

If you then want a real backslash character in your string, you extend the rule to mean that you enter two backslash characters:

```
"The backslash character (\\) has special meaning in AppleScript."
```

Since the value of a string displayed in the Result window is also a string, these backslash-coded characters don't convert to what you'd expect until you copy them to a document. Still, the length property of a string, which returns the number of characters in the string, takes these special characters into account:

```
length of "\"Walden\""
   -- result: 8
```

Here, the length property ignored the leading backslashes, and counted the double-quotes we want. Without the double-quotes:

```
length of "Walden"
   -- result: 6
```

AppleScript has two more of these backslash special characters. One represents a return character (\r); the other a tab character (\t). For example, if you tell a Scriptable Text Editor document to

```
copy "Line 1\rLine2" to beginning
```

the following text appears at the start of the document:

```
Line 1
Line 2
```

Quite often in the compilation process, a string containing \r and \t characters get put back into the editor window in their true form. For example, if we type:

```
tell document 1 of application "Scriptable Text Editor"
   copy "Line 1\rLine2" to beginning
end tell
```

after compilation, the script reads:

```
tell document 1 of application "Scriptable Text Editor"
   copy "Line 1
Line2" to beginning
end tell
```

This true-to-life formatting of strings can really throw off the look and readability of scripts, but you can't control the compiler's behavior using this backslash notation. As a slightly more wordy but definitely more readable alternative, you can concatenate helpful constants for three useful string values:

Constant	Value
return	"\r"
tab	"\t"
space	" "

Here's how the previous example would look:

```
tell document 1 of application "Scriptable Text Editor"
    copy "Line 1" & return & "Line 2" to beginning
end tell
```

We join two strings together with an intervening constant. This format is identical to HyperTalk string construction.

Continuation Strings

Mixing the continuation character (¬) and strings requires some care. If you need to break a statement into two lines, and the break falls within a string, you cannot simply insert the continuation character, as in

```
"Now is ¬
   the time."
```

Instead, you must break the string into two pieces, and insert both a concatenation and continuation symbol, as in

```
"Now is " & ¬
   "the time."
```

You are also responsible for maintaining spaces between words, if you break up the string between words.

String Objects

AppleScript strings, as objects, have four elements: character, paragraph, text, and word. In concert with a number of reference forms, script statements can get and set any one or all of an element of a string. How AppleScript defines these elements is important to understand your expectations for their behavior.

Character. Any single character that can appear in a string.

Paragraph. A series of characters that meets any of the following criteria:

Starts At	Ends With
beginning of string	return character
beginning of string	end of string
character after return	return character
character after return	end of string

Text Item. A series of characters between text item delimiters (see below). Used primarily to extract the running characters of a subset of a string (getting just the characters results in a list value being returned).

Word. A series of characters that starts at either the beginning of a string or after any character not counted as part of a word (e.g., space, en-dash symbol, em-dash symbol, leading or trailing apostrophe). Characters that count as part of a word include letters, numerals, non-breaking spaces (Option-Spacebar), currency symbols, percent signs, commas between numerals, periods preceding numerals, apostrophes between characters, and plain hyphens. Here are examples of Apple-Script words:

```
alpha
semi-transparent
45,000
it's
$19.95
```

Given these element classes and the length property of the string value class, the following reference forms are valid for strings:

Reference Form	Example
Property	length of "Now is the time"
Index	word 3 of "Now is the time"
Middle	middle character of word 3 of "Now is the time"
Arbitrary	some word of "Now is the time"
Every Element	every word of "Now is the time"
Range	words 2 thru 3 of "Now is the time"

As with any use of the Every Element and Range reference forms, the returned values for strings are lists:

```
words 2 thru 3 of "Now is the time"
    -- result: {"is", "the"}
```

If, however, your script needs the running text, you'll need to summon the text item element and text item delimiters property. Note that AppleScript strings do not respond to whose clauses (filtered references).

Text Item Delimiters

AppleScript maintains a global property, called text item delimiters. Values of this property are stored in a list value, although for now only the first value in the list is recognized as the current property.

Normally set to empty, the text item delimiters property defines how Apple-Script picks out text items from a string (this has nothing to do with items in a list). For example, with the default property value, each text item consists of a single character (i.e., to the next "non-character"):

```
text item 1 of "Now is the time."
  -- result: "N"
```

But if you set the property to a space character (space is another AppleScript string constant), the text item element behaves as if each word is a text item:

```
set AppleScript's text item delimiters to space
text item 1 of "Now is the time."
  -- result: "Now"
text items 2 thru 3 of "Now is the time."
  -- result: {"is","the"}
```

Notice how the last example returned all items in a list. Yet if you coerce the result to text while text item delimiters are still set to space, you get the original text with the proper word spacing:

```
set AppleScript's text item delimiters to space
(text items 2 thru 3 of "Now is the time.") as string
  -- result: "is the"
```

This property also comes in handy for other kinds of parsing. For example, folder and file path names are colon-delimited strings. To extract the file name from a full pathname, you can do the following:

```
set pathName to "HD:Documents:Letters:Linda 6/3/93"
set AppleScript's text item delimiters to ":"
last text item of pathName
  -- result: "Linda 6/3/93"
```

Do not confuse text items with AppleScript's character, word, and paragraph objects. These are very independent concepts, and changing the text item delimiters property makes no change to how AppleScript views characters, words, and paragraphs of strings.

You must exercise care, however, when changing this property. It is the most global you can get—AppleScript global (not script global)—so any setting you make in one script remains in effect during execution of any other script. A safe way to work with this property is to save the existing setting in a script variable, and restore the property at the end of the script:

```
set oldDelim to AppleScript's text item delimiters
set AppleScript's text item delimiters to space
```

```
(* do your text item stuff here *)
set AppleScript's text item delimiters to oldDelim
```

Safer still, is to surround a script that changes the text item delimiters property in a try statement (Chapter 12), as in:

```
try
    set oldDelim to AppleScript's text item delimiters
    set AppleScript's text item delimiters to space
    (* do your text item stuff here *)
    set AppleScript's text item delimiters to oldDelim
on error
    set AppleScript's text item delimiters to oldDelim
end try
```

This way, if your script should fail with an execution error, the global property will still be restored to its original setting before the script bails out.

Styled Text

Normally, when a script grabs a chunk of text from a document, it takes just the characters. There is nothing in there about font, size, or style. But it will become vital at times to preserve this information, particularly when extracting formatted data from one document and inserting it into another. AppleScript provides a mechanism, called *styled text,* whose syntax makes it appear to be another value class, but is actually a variation of the string class.

To obtain a string and its style, a script must explicitly request the data as styled text:

```
tell document 1 of application "Scriptable Text Editor"
    set goodGraph to paragraph 2 as styled text
    (* do something with goodGraph *)
end tell
```

I must emphasize, that the "as" word here is not a coercion operator, coercing a regular string to a styled text class of value. The value is still a string, but one that contains more information about itself than a plain string. Also, the application must support this scriptable styled text mechanism for it to work in either direction (getting or setting). Just because a program offers its users font and style menus doesn't automatically mean strings can be operated on as styled text.

Date Class

Values of the date class are in many ways similar to the classes that signify things like applications, files, aliases, and scripts: the class name appears as part of the value, and you cannot coerce it to a date class with the **as** operator. The **current date** scripting addition, for example, returns a date value:

```
current date
    -- result: date "Tuesday, June 20, 1995 3:53:02 PM"
```

The leading word, "date," is required for any subsequent string to be viewed as a date value.

While the amount of information in a date value appears rather large (day, month, date, year, hour, minute, second, AM/PM designation), it's not necessary to give AppleScript every part of the information for it to consider a string a date. Here are examples of date values AppleScript accepts (e.g., when assigning these values to a variable):

```
date "9/11/95"

date "9/11/95 1:01 PM"

date "Sep 11, 1995 1 PM"

date "1:01 PM"
```

In all cases, when some pieces are missing, AppleScript does its best to fill in the blanks. For example given any date, AppleScript calculates and returns the full day name, month name, four-digit year, and the midnight time (12:00:00 AM) for that date. Given any time, AppleScript applies today's date. In fact, if you simply enter any date value (like the above examples) as a script and run that script, AppleScript returns the full value of what you entered (although it does not change the script upon compilation, as happens with some other kinds of values).

A number of valuable operators work on date values—primarily those that let you test for the equality of dates or whether one date precedes another. Bear in mind that the date value includes whatever time is attached to it. For example, let's say today's date is 9/11/93. A script that performs this test:

```
date "9/11/93" = current date
    -- result: false
```

returns a false, because the left operand evaluates to midnight on the date, while the current date command will most likely return a time on the same day that is after midnight. The current date evaluates to a value greater than "9/11/93."

Working with Dates and Times

AppleScript 1.1 improved the flexibility of working with date and time in scripts, but perhaps not to the satisfaction of experienced HyperTalk scripters. Still, new properties of the date value class and new constants make the job easier.

Date Objects

The date class value by itself is not particularly helpful for performing calculations with dates such as figuring the number of days between dates or finding the date two weeks from today. Fortunately, AppleScript treats dates as objects that contain a number of properties that help in this arena (but perhaps not to the satisfaction of experienced HyperTalk scripters)

Here are the properties for a date object:

Property	*Example*
weekday	Wednesday
month	December
day	8
year	1993
date string	"Wednesday, December 8, 1993"
time string	"5:25:12 PM"
time	36000 (seconds since midnight)

It's important to note that the values for weekday and month properties are not strings, but object class names in themselves. Unfortunately, these class names cannot be coerced to strings, and are therefore usable primarily for comparison operations, as in

```
if weekday of (current date) is Friday then beep
```

You can, however, change a date by setting the month, day, and year properties of a date value. AppleScript does its best to calculate the meaning of the adjustment. For example, if you assign a date value to a variable, and set the year property, AppleScript recalculates the date based on that year:

```
copy date "Wednesday, December 8, 1993" to myDate
set year of myDate to 1994
myDate
    -- result: date "Thursday, December 8, 1994 12:00:00 AM"
```

where the day changes to Thursday, which is the day of the week for the date in the following year. Moreover, if you set the day value to an integer greater than the number of days in the month of the date value, then AppleScript calculates the date of the fictitious day:

```
copy date "Wednesday, December 8, 1993" to myDate
set day of myDate to 35
myDate
    -- result: date "Tuesday, January 4, 1994 12:00:00 AM"
```

Even so, see below for better ways to deal with date arithmetic.

One potential disappointment among scripters is that the date string and time string properties come in only one flavor each, corresponding to the long formats in HyperTalk. Without the help of third party scripting additions on this book's companion disk (see the GTQ OSAX collection, Chapter 33), you cannot have AppleScript deliver short versions of those strings (e.g., "12/8/93" or "5:25 PM") with reliability across Date & Time control panel settings.

Date and Time Arithmetic

You may perform the following kinds of arithmetic on dates and times:

- Subtracting one date from another to achieve the difference in seconds
- Adding time (in seconds) to a date to achieve a new date
- Subtracting time (in seconds) from a date to achieve a new date

The second is the key unit of time and date measurement in working with AppleScript dates and times. When you subtract one date from another, the result of the operation is returned in seconds. For example:

```
set firstDate to date "1/1/94"
set secondDate to date "2/1/94"
secondDate - firstDate
   -- result: 2678400
```

The result in this example is the number of seconds in the 31 days between the two date values.

To help make the math appear more like plain language, a new set of constants define standard chunks of time:

Constant	Number of Seconds
minutes	60
hours	60 * minutes
days	24 * hours
weeks	7 * days

To let AppleScript figure out the number of days between the dates in the previous example, we'd modify the script as follows:

```
set firstDate to date "1/1/94"
set secondDate to date "2/1/94"
(secondDate - firstDate) / days
   -- result: 31.0
```

To add time to, or subtract time from, a date value, you must use either seconds or the constants listed above. For example, if your script wants to record the date for ten days from today, the script would look like this:

```
set nextAppointment to (current date) + (10 * days)
```

You aren't restricted to integer calculations here, either. To get the time 3½ hours from now,

```
set nextAlarm to (current date) + (3.5 * hours)
```

The only restriction in using these constants in addition or subtraction operations is that the date value must come first in the algebraic expression for AppleScript to know how to evaluate the constants. Also, the constants are defined only as plurals, so you must use the plural form even if the amount of time is singular, as in:

```
set nextWeek to (current date) + (1 * weeks)
```

or

```
set nextWeek to (current date) + weeks
```

These date object enhancements arrived with version 1.1 of AppleScript. Let's hope future releases provide even more time and date powers for scripters.

Year Formats

While date references can accept a number of variants (above), you should exercise care when depicting a year with fewer than four digits. The re-use of the last two digits every century wreaks havoc with the Macintosh's internal date tracking. To be somewhat helpful, the Mac toolbox interprets two-digit years to be years near the mid-1990s. For example:

```
date "Sep 11, 94"
    -- result: date "Sunday, September 11, 1994 12:00:00 AM"

date "Sep 11, 05"
    -- result: date "Sunday, September 11, 2005 12:00:00 AM"
```

But beyond a very specific range, the results may be other than what you expect. Use this table as a guide:

Two-digit Entry	Converted to Year
0–10	2000–2010
11–99	1911–1999

These two-digit entry conversions apply only to date class entries, not to the year property of a date value. For example, if you attempt to set the year property of a date value to a two-digit value, the year will be the actual two-digit year:

```
copy date "3/4/1994" to someDate
    -- result: date "Friday, March 4, 1994 12:00:00 AM"
set year of someDate to 95
    -- result: date "Friday, March 4, 0095 12:00:00 AM"
```

To be on the safe side, use four-digit years whenever specifying dates as date value classes.

Record Class

While the formal definition of a record is a collection of properties, I like to think of a record as a labeled list. Look at the items in the following list:

```
{ "Quadra", "950", "68040" }
```

The list contains three strings, each referring to specific information about a Macintosh model. If we turn this list into a record by assigning names to the pieces of information, we are said to be establishing properties of a record:

```
{ Family:"Quadra", Model:"950", CPU:"68040" }
```

A property name is not in quotes and is separated from its value by a colon. Like items in a list, properties are separated from each other by a comma. Values of any property can be of any value class (including lists or other records).

It may be easy to confuse an AppleScript record value class with database records. The similarity exists when you see that a property name is like a field label in a database record. But an AppleScript record is not an entry in a database. It is a convenient way to pass along multiple values together (as a single record value), and make those values more readable and accessible because of their names.

A script gains access to data in a record via a property reference (just like accessing properties of an application object). Let's take the Mac record above. If we want to find out what the Model property is, the script would be:

```
get model of { Family:"Quadra", Model:"950", CPU:"68040" }
    -- result: "950"
```

This example is not particularly realistic, because it's kind of goofy getting the named property you just typed into a hard-wired record in the script. Where records come in handy is when some application object property returns a record value, which typically would go into a variable in your script. The display dialog scripting addition is a good example.

As described in Chapter 7, the display dialog command returns a record value. Properties of that record are text returned (i.e., typed into the editable field of a dialog) and button returned (i.e., text of the button clicked to close the dialog). Here's a script you can try, which demonstrates how to access the data of a record class value:

```
-- request user's age
set dialogResult to ¬
    display dialog "Please enter your age:" default answer "21" ¬
        buttons {"None of your business", "OK"} default button "OK"
-- build in error detection for non-integer entries
try
    -- first get button returned property
    if button returned of dialogResult is "OK" then
```

```
            -- check text returned property value is an integer
            set myAge to (text returned of dialogResult) as integer
            display dialog (myAge as string) & " is a fine age." ¬
                    buttons {"OK"} default button "OK"
        else
            display dialog "Sheesh! I wasn't going to tell anyone." ¬
                    buttons {"OK"} default button "OK"
        end if
    on error errMsg -- if coercion to integer fails
        display dialog text returned of dialogResult & ¬
            " is not a good answer." buttons {"OK"} default button "OK"
    end try
```

The first task of this script is to place whatever results come from the initial display dialog command into a variable named dialogResult. This variable contains the record containing information about what was typed into the dialog and which button was clicked. Because we need to check whether the user entered an integer, we build the rest of the script into a try statement, allowing an error handler at the end to take care of erroneous entries.

The script next checks one of the properties of the dialogResult record value: the button clicked. If it is the "OK," then the script tries to coerce the entry (derived from the text returned property of dialogResult) to an integer and then displays a friendly message. A user's click of the other button displays an air of disappointment. In the error handler, we summon the text returned property of the dialog's resulting value so we can display it as an example of an invalid entry.

Scripts not only extract information from a record by its label, but they can set data as well. It's just like setting an object property:

```
set oneRecord to ¬
    {model:"SuperDorf", price:9.95, taxRate:0.08}
set price of oneRecord to 10.95
oneRecord
    -- result: {model:"SuperDorf", price:10.95, taxRate:0.08}
```

Once a record has been defined by its property labels, you cannot insert a new property. You can, however, prepend or append new properties with the help of the concatenation (&) operator:

```
set employee to {name:"Joe", age: 32}
set department to {dept:"Manufacturing"}
set fullRecord to employee & department
fullRecord
    -- result: {name:"Joe", age:32, dept:"Manufacturing"}
```

Finally, the count command and length property both work with records. Results from these actions produce the number of properties in a record:

```
count of {name:"Joe", age:32, dept:"Manufacturing"}
   -- result: 3
```

I encourage the application of record values in your scripts. Property labels make scripts much more readable for others to follow, and should also make the script writing easier for you as well.

Reference Class

In Chapters 6 and 7, we saw some commands whose parameters require references to objects. The value expected there is of the reference class. These are the same kinds of references we saw in Chapter 8's exposition of reference forms—but here we're talking specifically about those reference forms that point to an entire object, not a subset. The most common reference forms to fit the bill of a reference class value are indexed, named, and property reference forms.

Some examples of reference class values are:

```
word 1 of document 1 of application "Scriptable Text Editor"
```

```
item 3 of {"Yankee", "Red Sox", "Tigers"}
```

```
row "Total Sales" of document "Sales Spreadsheet" of ¬
   application "Microsoft Excel"
```

```
bounds of window 3 of application "Microsoft Project"
```

When used in an AppleScript statement (particularly as a parameter to a command), reference values evaluate to the value of the reference.

```
tell document 1 of application "Scriptable Text Editor"
   get paragraph 1
end tell
```

Here the get command's parameter is a reference to the first paragraph (the full reference also includes the default document and application objects in the tell statement). AppleScript, however, automatically evaluates the reference so that the get command gets the actual paragraph. This can be a valuable shortcut if you want to use the value from the contents of an object as an argument to a command:

```
display dialog "Total errors: " & ¬
   (value of cell "errorCounter" of last row of table 1)
```

where the contents of cell errorCounter in the last row is a value you insert into the message of a display dialog command—even concatenating it to some hard-wired part of the parameter. This is probably the most common way you'll consciously use the reference value (unconsciously, you'll use references as parameters to commands).

Contents Property of Reference Classes

The reference class works very much like a programming pointer. For example, if we work with the Bill of Rights document in Scriptable Text Editor, we can create a variable that contains a pointer to the first paragraph:

```
tell application "Scriptable Text Editor"
    set oneObject to a reference to paragraph 1 of document 1
    oneObject
end tell
    -- result: paragraph 1 of document 1 of application "Scriptable Text Editor"
```

The script can then use that value to represent whatever may be in paragraph 1 at the time it is called. In other words, if we had simply set oneObject to paragraph 1, the value would contain the text of paragraph 1. If the contents may change in the course of running a script, however, we'd have to re-do the assignment of data to oneObject. Instead, we set oneObject to a reference to the paragraph. Each time oneObject is used in a statement, it points to that spot in the document.

To get to the actual contents of the paragraph by way of that reference, we can access the Contents property of a reference class. Therefore,

```
tell application "Scriptable Text Editor"
    set oneObject to a reference to paragraph 1 of document 1
    contents of oneObject
end tell
    -- result: "ARTICLE I"
```

While Scriptable Text Editor also allows getting the text of a reference value class, other programs may not. AppleScript, on the other hand, can get the contents of virtually any reference value.

Class Class

No, this isn't doubletalk, but this value class starts to make all this class stuff sound somewhat recursive. Anything in the AppleScript world that is considered an object belongs to a class. For example, in our Chapter 8 discussions about references, most references require a parameter called *className*. In these object references, the class name is the type of object we're referring to (e.g., word, paragraph, cell, row). The definition of the indexed reference form:

> *className* index

the *className* parameter expects a class value—one of the object class names defined for the application (the words listed in italics in a dictionary listing for a program). Therefore, in the partial reference

> word 6

"word" is the class value, and "6" is the index value.

This probably sounds more complicated than it is. By and large, you won't think much about the class value, because it becomes a virtually automatic part of object references.

But micromanagement of this value can be helpful at other times. For example, every value we've been discussing in this chapter has a class property, which allows a script to determine what type of value—class—it is. A script can use this information to decide how to handle a value. Let's say a script subroutine handler receives some data as a parameter that may be a real or integer class value. The handler can make sure it handles each type accordingly:

```
on mySubroutine(passedValue)
    if class of passedValue is real then
        (* do real number processing *)
    else
        (* do integer processing *)
    end if
end mySubroutine
```

Each of the value classes covered in this chapter has a class property consisting of the name of the value class (boolean, class, constant, data, date, integer, list, real, record, reference, string). Notice, too, that the class name, when referred to in a script, is not a quoted string:

```
class of "Howdy Doody"
    -- result: string
    -- not "string"
```

To bring this discussion full recursive circle, the class property of the class value is, well, class. The first time you encounter this stuff, it can make your head hurt, but once you see enough value class references in property descriptions in application dictionaries, it begins to makes sense.

Constant Class

Several commands and objects provide in their definitions a number of words that appear to be hard-wired as possible parameters. For example, in Scriptable Text Editor, an optional parameter to the **close** command lets you specify how to handle the saving of a changed document. The syntax definition is:

close reference [saving yes/no/ask]

Arguments for the saving parameter can be one of the three choices provided. These three words are constant class values. Their contents are predetermined by the application and cannot be changed. They are also represented in script lines without quotes (which would turn those words into strings). Therefore, if we ask for the class of one of these values, AppleScript tells us it's a constant class:

```
class of yes
    -- result: constant
```

A constant class is different from what other programming languages might call a constant. For example, while TRUE and FALSE are reserved words in AppleScript (and are even listed as constants in the *AppleScript Language Guide*), their value class is Boolean.

By and large, you won't have to worry about the class of these values, since the values are presented as options in definitions where needed. The only thing you have to remember is that when a definition specifies one of these constants, you must use one of the ones provided. Incidentally, you cannot coerce a string to a constant to fill one of these parameters, although AppleScript does allow assigning a constant to a variable, which then assumes the constant class.

Data Class

Because scripts and results deal only in text, there are other kinds of information that can't be represented or viewed in the scripting environment. But very often, our application of AppleScript depends on moving this kind of data—graphics, sounds, movies—from one document to another.

AppleScript accommodates this with the data class value. These kinds of values are stored in variables in their binary form, and can be passed from document to document without the script ever looking at the data (if a variable is like a basket of information, a variable containing a data class value would be like a covered basket).

In Microsoft Excel 4.0, for instance, a script can retrieve the data of a chart:

```
tell application "Microsoft Excel"
    copy Chart 1 to myChart
end tell
```

The result variable contains information of no use to the scripter:

```
-- result:«data PICT021F0000000000C701»
```

About the only thing you can tell about this data is that it is a PICT format—the most common graphics format for the Macintosh.

As with any value class, you can use the = and ≠ operators to test whether two values are the same. For data class values, the comparison is a comparison of all the binary data of the values on each side of the equation.

Class Name Synonyms (Text, Number)

While we previously emphasized using the string class name when working with text characters, AppleScript readily accepts "text" as a class name synonym for "string." The only time this really comes up is in coercions. Therefore, the following statements yield the same result:

```
(choose file) as string
```

```
(choose file) as text
```

AppleScript, however, is not ambiguous when a script requests the class of a string: it always returns the class name as "string."

Integer and real classes also have a synonym: Number. You would use this synonym primarily in comparison operations, when the distinction between a value being a true integer or true real is of no significance:

```
if myValue is a number then...
```

This way, you don't have to worry that myValue might be a real but you test only for it being an integer (or vice versa).

If you use "number" as the class name for a coercion, AppleScript assigns the value to either the integer or real class, depending on the decimal situation of the value:

```
set myValue to 3 as number
class of myValue
   -- result: integer
```

```
set myValue to 3.0 as number
class of myValue
   -- result: real
```

Next Stop

We've been through the three basic building blocks of a script: commands, objects, and values. From here we can start looking at scripts with a bigger view, such as how scripts make decisions based on values. That's what we'll cover next.

Going with the Flow (Or Not) Control Structures

When you examine yesterday's activities, it may seem as though the day was one long series of events, which started from the instant you came to in the morning until the instant you dropped off at night. In truth, the day doesn't exactly go like that. Upon close examination, the flow of events during the day can be represented in anything but a straight line. A trip to the grocery store—just one of the day's tasks—is a good example of how the flow of events goes this-way-and-that, round-and-round.

Shop Till You Drop

The overall flow of this shopping task takes you from entering the store until you go through the checkout aisle. No sooner do you enter the store than you are faced with your first decision that influences your route: will you need more items than you can carry? If you think there will be too many, then you pick up a basket or extricate a wheeled cart from the snaggle of carts. In other words, you've taken one of two or three paths of action between the front door and the first aisle of the store.

Next, you begin winding your way down the aisles. If you encounter a desired item on a shelf, you pause while picking the item from the shelf. If you have a basket or cart, you place the item in there. When you reach the beginning of one of the aisles, you check whether the categories of items in the aisle match anything on your shopping list. If not, then you skip over to the next aisle, otherwise you work your way down the aisle.

You then pause at the deli counter, and tell the clerk that you'd like some sliced turkey. That instruction applies only to the deli counter clerk, because no one in the produce or bakery departments could possibly help you with your turkey request.

When you later reach a produce bin, you pause. Then you go through a repetition of looking for just the best looking, best feeling peach. You repeat the process—pick up one sample, gently squeeze it, smell it—over and over until you find one that meets your standards. That one goes with the rest of the items you've picked from the shelf, and you move on to the checkout line.

In just this brief foray into a store, the series of motions you made and the results you obtained were influenced by decisions, repetitions, and directing instructions to specific people who could carry out a specific task. If you understand this, then you already understand the nature of AppleScript control structures.

AppleScript Flow Control

Unlike a recorded script, scripts you write rarely flow from top to bottom without some diversion along the way. Such diversions may be needed to direct instructions to a particular application, to provide alternate paths for different results of decisions, and to provide rules to follow while repeating a task. AppleScript provides structures for each of these flow controls: the tell statement; the if-then statement; the repeat statement. We'll spend some time on each.

Tell Statements

You've already seen in dozens of examples thus far how tell statements direct commands to a particular object and/or application. By naming the application in the tell statement, you instruct AppleScript to open the application's dictionary and be ready to use any of the commands or object references available in that dictionary. To compile a script successfully, AppleScript must find all commands and object references in one of the following:

- The dictionary pointed to by the most recent tell statement
- AppleScript's own dictionary
- Any scripting additions buried in the System Folder

Tell statements come in two varieties, the simple and the compound. Their syntaxes are summarized here:

tell *reference* to *statement*

tell *reference*
    [*statement*] ...
end [tell]

You use the simple type when the complete object reference and statement are written as a single statement, as in:

```
tell document 2 of application "Scriptable Text Editor" to print
```

The simple tell statement includes a complete reference to the object directed to carry out a command (print, in this case).

Compound tell statements are more prevalent. The syntax allows a script to establish a default object to which all nested statements are directed. The default object may be as broad as the application down to the tiniest element:

```
tell application "Scriptable Text Editor"
    set font of paragraph 2 of document 1 to "Helvetica"
    set size of paragraph 2 of document 1 to 14
end tell

tell paragraph 2 ¬
    of document 1 of application "Scriptable Text Editor"
    set font to "Helvetica"
    set size to 14
end tell
```

In the first example, the default object is the application. To send multiple commands to the same nested object contained by the application, each statement must include the rest of the reference to the desired paragraph. In the second example, we make the second paragraph the default object, so the two short statements for setting font characteristics automatically apply to that paragraph. In both cases, the compound tell statement ends with the word "end" and, optionally, the word "tell." This instructs AppleScript to sever its ties to the default object designated in the previous tell line.

You can nest tell statements inside one another, as well—even if the objects they point to are in entirely different applications. Here's a skeleton of what such a construction could look like:

```
tell application "SuperWriter"
    (* statements that work in SuperWriter *)
    tell application "SuperSheeter"
        (* statements that work in SuperSheeter *)
    end tell
    (* more statements for SuperWriter *)
end tell
```

The "end tell" line nested inside applies to the nearest preceding tell line—the SuperWriter application in this example. You could accomplish the same results with a longer script, by writing a sequence of tell/end tell statements, as in:

```
tell application "SuperWriter"
    (* statements that work in SuperWriter *)
end tell

tell application "SuperSheeter"
    (* statements that work in SuperSheeter *)
end tell
```

```
tell application "SuperWriter"
   (* more statements for SuperWriter *)
end tell
```

You gain some advantages in compiled size and possibly execution speed by nesting tell statements, however. They also seem more readable when you're following the flow of a script.

It and Me Variables in Tell Statements

AppleScript's vocabulary includes two predefined variable, it and me, which have specific purposes inside tell statements (and elsewhere). The it variable is a shortcut reference to the default object—the object pointed to in the most recent tell statement. By and large, the it variable is optional, but it may improve the readability of your script. Here's an example of this variable in use:

```
tell window 1 of application "Scriptable Text Editor"
   get bounds of it
end tell
   -- result: {1, 39, 485, 362} (for default size window)
```

The statement inside the tell statement could have just as easily read:

```
get bounds
```

because the default object (window 1 of application "Scriptable Text Editor") completes the reference. The it variation, however, makes more sense to someone reading the script for the first time. We also saw this variable's contribution to some variations of the filtered reference form (Chapter 8).

The me variable, on the other hand, points to the script containing the statement, instead of the default object of the surrounding tell statement. For example, if we have a script that defines a bounds property for itself, we may want our script inside a tell statement to get the property from our script, not the property of an object belonging to the default object:

```
property bounds : {0, 0, 0, 0}
tell window 1 of application "Scriptable Text Editor"
   get bounds
end tell
   -- result: {1, 39, 485, 362} (for default size window)
```

Here we still want the bounds property of the default object (window 1). To get the bounds property belonging to the script, we add two little words:

```
property bounds : {0, 0, 0, 0}
tell window 1 of application "Scriptable Text Editor"
   get bounds of me
end tell
   -- result: {0, 0, 0, 0} (script property)
```

AppleScript also allows the alternates:

> get my bounds

and

> tell me to get bounds

In both cases, the me/my variable breaks up the normal flow of the object reference, ignoring the default object, and pointing directly at the script itself.

HyperTalk Alert

While both HyperTalk and AppleScript feature the it and me predefined variables, they are applied very differently in the two languages. Table 10.1 shows commonly confused predefined variables the languages have in common.

Table 10.1 Predefined Variables in HyperTalk and AppleScript

Variable	HyperTalk	AppleScript
it	value returned by get	reference to default object
me	object containing script	scripting containing the statement
result	value returned by some commands and most errors	value returned by get

---

If-Then Constructions

The way AppleScript makes decisions is to test the truth of a statement. If the statement is true, then the script follows one path; if the statement is false, the script follows another path. Whichever path the script follows, it eventually returns to the main path. It's like taking either the high road or low road: both get to Scotland eventually.

Like tell statements, if statements come in two flavors: simple and compound. A simple statement takes place in a single script line in this format:

> if *BooleanExpression* then *statement*

The *statement* parameter is any AppleScript statement. It executes only if the *BooleanExpression* parameter evaluates to true, after which execution continues with the next script line. If the expression evaluates to false, the *statement* parameter is ignored, and execution continues with the next script line.

Understanding Boolean expressions (and operators of all types from the next chapter) helps expand your application of if statements. Any operation that yields a true or false value qualifies as a Boolean expression for the purposes of an if statement. Here are some examples of simple if statements:

```
if x < 3 then beep x

if word 1 of paragraph 4 is "Article" then ¬
    set style of paragraph 4 to bold

if modified of document 1 then save document 1
```

Sometimes, you want a script to take a sidetrip if something is not true. In that case, you can use the Not operator to negate the Boolean expression (i.e., turn a false value into a true one). Here is an example:

```
if not (paragraph 1 of document 1 ¬
    contains "Jimbo") then open file "Jimbo Report"
```

In most cases, however, AppleScript operators have anticipated this need, and provide a number of plain language synonyms for these negatives, such as

```
if paragraph 1 of document 1 doesn't contain ¬
    "Jimbo" then open file "Jimbo Report"
```

Compound if statements are designed to allow multiple statements execute within their confines. The construction also allows for additional Boolean tests to take place together. Here are syntax examples of four common if statement forms:

```
if BooleanExpression [ then ]
    [ statement ] ...
end [ if ]


if BooleanExpression [ then ]
    [ statement ] ...
else
    [ statement ] ...
end [ if ]


if BooleanExpression [ then ]
    [ statement ] ...
else if BooleanExpression [ then ]
    [ statement ] ... ...
end [ if ]


if BooleanExpression [ then ]
    [ statement ] ...
else if BooleanExpression [ then ]
    [ statement ] ... ...
else
    [ statement ] ...
end [ if ]
```

The first form is required whenever more than one statement needs to be executed as a result of the *BooleanExpression* evaluating to true. If you like, you can place a single statement here, instead of creating a long, simple if statement. The then parameter and if parameter after end are optional, but I strongly recommend their use for readability purposes.

In the second form, the script executes one of two possible groups of nested statements. The first group executes if the Boolean expression evaluates to true; the second only if the expression evaluates to false. In other words, execution can't slip through this construction untouched.

Form three is a more elaborate version of the previous form. Its logic is as follows: if the first Boolean expression evaluates to true, then the first nested group of statements executes; if the first Boolean expression evaluates to false, then the second Boolean expression takes control. If it evaluates to true, then the second group of nested statements execute; if the expression evaluates to false, then nothing in the if statement evaluates. It's possible, therefore, that under some conditions (when both Boolean expressions evaluate to false), no statements in the compound if statement execute.

The last form is one more version, which has a final trap in the form of a final else clause. If the first two Boolean expressions are false, then the statements nested under the solo else clause will execute.

You can nest if statements when appropriate. It takes a comparatively complex set of tests and desired results to require nested if statements, but they may be necessary:

```
-- put current date data into a list for convenience
set today to (current date)
set theMonth to month of today
set theYear to year of today
-- start checking month cases
if theMonth is February then
    -- take leap years into account
    if theYear mod 4 = 0 then
        set howMany to 29
    else
        set howMany to 28
    end if
else if {April, June, September, November} contains theMonth then
    set howMany to 30
else -- "all the rest have 31"
    set howMany to 31
end if
display dialog "The current month has " & howMany & " days in it." ¬
    buttons {"OK"} default button 1
```

In this script, which tells you how many days are in the current month (using the U.S. system for date format), notice what happens with the February situation. Because February has two possible outcomes, depending on the year, we have to perform the second test about the year as a separate, nested if statement. An alternate script could have used compound Boolean expressions in the February tests, as in:

```
...
if theMonth is February and theYear mod 4 ≠ 0 then
    set howMany to 28
else if theMonth is February and theYear mod 4 = 0 then
    set howMany to 29
...
```

but the nested version is easier to read, because each nested compound if statement helps the reader focus on the conditions being tested.

This days-of-the-month script is also an example of how compound if statements can replicate Case statements available in other languages. By using a series of else if clauses, a script can define each case and the statements to be executed for each case. Here's another example:

```
display dialog "Please enter A, B, or C:" default answer ""
set answer to text returned of result
if answer is not "" then
    -- here come the cases
    if answer is "A" then
        beep 1 -- or other "A" stuff
    else if answer is "B" then
        beep 2 -- or other "B" stuff
    else if answer is "C" then
        beep 3 -- or other "C" stuff
    else
        display dialog "That wasn't one of the letters." ¬
            buttons {"OK"} default button 1
    end if
else
    display dialog "You didn't enter anything." ¬
        buttons {"OK"} default button 1
end if
```

Notice that each compound if statement must end with an end if statement. The compiler makes sure all ifs are balanced by ends, so when you are writing a complex nested if construction, you can use the Check Syntax feature of Script Editor to perform a pass through the script and point out where things don't work.

Repeat Statements

As demonstrated earlier in an example from real life, we sometimes need to repeat the same operation on a series of things. These operations might be to perform some kind of test on each item to find out which ones meet certain criteria; or to perform the same adjustment to every item in the series. How often or under what conditions we perform those repetitions is the realm of the repeat statement. AppleScript provides a range of statement forms that accommodate a wide variety of repeat conditions:

Type	Description
Repeat	Loops forever, or until a statement tells execution to exit the loop
Repeat Times	Loops a number of times fixed at the beginning of the loop
Repeat Until	Loops forever until a condition is met
Repeat While	Loops only so long as a condition is met
Repeat With	Loops a number of times set either by a counting variable or by the number of items under test

After seeing examples of these different types, you should begin to get a feel for the circumstances recommending each repeat variant in your scripts. It turns out that more than one variety can work for the same loop, and your choice will depend on personal taste and readability of the script.

All repeat statements begin with the word **repeat**, and must have an **end repeat** statement at the end. This **end** statement tells AppleScript where to stop executing statements and start the loop over. The "repeat" word in the end statement is optional, but as with tell and if statements, I strongly urge you to include it to make the script more readable (the reader won't have to guess or look back through the script to discover what's ending).

Repeat

The most basic of repeat constructions is the infinite (or forever) loop. Its syntax is:

```
repeat
    [ statement ] ...
end [ repeat ]
```

Any number of statements can go inside a repeat loop. The reason this is called an infinite loop is that the construction provides nothing to indicate how to get out of it. This would be a mighty boring script segment, since it would sit there doing the same thing over and over until you broke the script (by typing Command-Period or clicking the script editor's Stop button) or restarted the Macintosh.

To provide a way out of the loop, you usually set up an if statement that tests the condition of values being manipulated inside the loop. If the condition is met, then the exit statement forces execution out of the loop at that point.

```
set randomList to { } -- so we can concatenate in loop
repeat
    set randomValue to random number 10
    set randomList to randomList & randomValue
    if randomValue = 5 then exit repeat
end repeat
display dialog "It took " & (count of randomList) & ¬
    " loop(s) to reach 5."
```

This demonstration is a good candidate for the infinite repeat form, because before going into the repeat loop, the script doesn't know how many repetitions it will take. In fact, unless the randomValue variable were initialized prior to the repeat loop, we could not use that identifier as a condition for the repeat while or repeat until forms (because the identifier in the required Boolean expression would not have been defined). Therefore, the only place with enough knowledge to find a way out of the loop is inside the loop. An if statement tests the value of the random number, and escapes the repeat loop when the Boolean test (randomValue = 5) evaluates to true.

Notice something else in this script. Prior to the loop, we initialize a variable as an empty list. Each time through the loop, the list grows by one more item: the most recent random number. After the repeat loop ends, the list still contains all those values, which we use to establish a count of the number of times through the loop. An equally viable method would be to initialize a variable with an integer value of zero, and then add 1 to that variable on each pass. Here's what this variant would look like:

```
set counter to 0
repeat
    set randomValue to random number 10
    set counter to counter + 1
    if randomValue = 5 then exit repeat
end repeat
display dialog "It took " & counter & ¬
    " loop(s) to reach 5."
```

This version might run a hair's breadth faster, because it doesn't have to evaluate the count of items for the display dialog parameter.

Repeat X Times

When a script knows how many times it must execute a repeat loop, the Repeat X Times form is a good one to use. As its name suggests, the leading repeat statement specifies exactly how many times execution loops through the statements nested inside. Syntax for this form is:

repeat *numberOfTimes* [times]
   [*statement*] ...
end [repeat]

The value for the *numberOfTimes* parameter must be an integer. This value can be a hard-wired integer or any expression that evaluates to an integer. Whether you include the optional "times" word is up to you, although it does aid readability. Here is an example that plays with some text in a Scriptable Text Editor document:

```
tell document 1 of application "Scriptable Text Editor"
    activate
    make document
    set selection to "AppleScript is neat!"
    repeat 10 times
        copy space to before paragraph 1
    end repeat
    repeat 10 times
        delete character 1 of paragraph 1
    end repeat
    close saving no
end tell
```

We use the Repeat X Times form, because the script has a specific goal in mind—adding and deleting a fixed number of spaces.

There's nothing preventing a script from breaking out of any repeat loop early with the exit statement. Here's a variation of the earlier random number script that looks for a 5 over 10 loops; if a 5 comes up in fewer than 10 loops, then the script breaks out of the loop:

```
set counter to 0
repeat 10 times
    set randomValue to random number 10
    set counter to counter + 1
    if randomValue = 5 then exit repeat
end repeat
if counter < 10 then
    display dialog "I broke early, because I got a five in " ¬
        & counter & " loops."
else
    display dialog "I never got a five in 10 loops."
end if
```

Because execution continues after the loop, whether the loop ran its course of ten or broke out early, we include a test to handle the value of the counter variable, and produce a message that describes what happened.

Repeat Until

The repeat until form is related to the infinite repeat form, except the repeat statement specifies the condition that needs to be met for the loop to break (without an exit statement). The syntax is:

repeat until *BooleanExpression*
    [*statement*] ...
end [repeat]

The best way to use this form is when your script knows that the Boolean expression is false when the loop starts, and it expects the condition to change as a result of one or more times through the loop. Each time the execution loops back to the top, AppleScript re-evaluates the Boolean expression to see if it is true this time around. If it's true, then execution won't go through another loop; otherwise, it goes one more round.

Since the expression is re-evaluated each time, the statements in the loop must change the value of at least one of the operands in the Boolean expression, preferably working toward a point at which the expression will evaluate to true. Generally, the change would occur after an indefinite number of times—otherwise you could use the Repeat X Times form. We can use a variation of the random number script to demonstrate this form:

```
set counter to 0
set randomValue to 0
repeat until randomValue = 5
    set randomValue to random number 10
    set counter to counter + 1
end repeat
display dialog "I got a five in " & counter & " loop(s)."
```

Notice a big difference over the infinite repeat version. First of all, we initialize the randomValue variable to zero, since it must be defined for us to use it in the Boolean expression of the Repeat Until statement. We go into the loop knowing that the Boolean expression is false to begin with. After that, execution loops on and on—each time, however, the randomValue variable is put to the test of being 5. If it is, then no further execution occurs within the loop.

In some scripts, you'll have values coming in from documents or other sources that only occasionally need adjustment. On the accompanying disk (Handbook Scripts:Chapter 10 folder) are two Repeat Until files that demonstrate this form. Open both the script and the document file (Scriptable Text Editor). The task of this script is to insert ("pad") spaces between the automobile brands and model numbers so that the result can be displayed in a monospaced font, like Courier, in neat columns (perhaps for posting to an on-line service that doesn't have pretty fonts).

The original document appears in Figure 10.1. Here's the script:

```
tell document 1 of application "Scriptable Text Editor"
    repeat with i from 1 to count of paragraphs
        set testWord to word 2 of paragraph i
        set testGraph to paragraph i
        repeat until (checkOffset(testWord, testGraph) of me) = 12
            copy " " to before word 2 of paragraph i
            set testGraph to paragraph i
        end repeat
    end repeat
    set font of every paragraph to "Courier"
end tell


on checkOffset(testWord, testGraph)
    return offset of testWord in testGraph
end checkOffset
```

The script is broken into two parts, because we need AppleScript to do its offset thing with strings in variables—something Scriptable Text Editor can't seem to do (this is actually a subroutine, a technique we'll detail in Chapter 14).

Figure 10.1 The Repeat Until Document file.

The key element for our demonstration is the Repeat Until construction. Its goal is to keep examining the location of the model number in a paragraph of the document, and keep inserting spaces until the second word begins at character location 15. The value for the Boolean expression is the value returned by the checkOffset subroutine, which is nothing more than the integer result of the offset command. Importantly, if the Boolean test returns true before going through the loop (as the first paragraph in this sample does), then nothing in the loop executes for those values: everything is OK the way it is and doesn't need any adjustment.

In a way, you could say that our choice of the Repeat Until construction and the equals (=) operator for our Boolean test was the pessimistic outlook: we assumed that the majority of the tests would fail, and would need the space padding to fix things up. It's not a big deal, since we could have changed the operator and used the more optimistic sounding Repeat While construction.

Repeat While

In contrast to the Repeat Until statement, the Repeat While statement assumes that everything's A-OK in the Boolean test, and the loop should keep going until something upsets the balance. The syntax is:

repeat while *BooleanExpression*
    [*statement*] ...
end [repeat]

As long as the Boolean expression evaluates to true, the loop continues to go round and round.

Often the choice between the Repeat With and Repeat Until forms is the choice of operator in the Boolean expression. We'll make a one-character change in the Repeat Until version of the random number script, and make it a Repeat While version:

```
set counter to 0
set randomValue to 0
repeat while randomValue ≠ 5
    set randomValue to random number 10
    set counter to counter + 1
end repeat
display dialog "I got a five in " & counter & " loop(s)."
```

The difference is all in the point of view. In the Repeat Until version, we say to keep looping until you get a 5; in the Repeat While version, we say to keep looping so long as you don't get a 5. Neither version is better than the other except that positive operators are often more readily understandable by script readers than negative ones.

Repeat With-From-To

AppleScript defines two versions of the Repeat With statement, but their operating methods are so different, I prefer to treat them as two separate repeat varieties. The first one to cover is one I call Repeat With-From-To. Here's its syntax:

repeat with *counterVariable* from *startValue* to *stopValue* ¬
    [by *stepValue*]
        [*statement*] ...
end [repeat]

The purpose of this repeat form is to establish a range of values that will also be used as a counting variable each time through the loop. Let's take an example from the world of the post office. A postal worker has to stuff a group of post office boxes with the latest advertising circular. Of the five hundred boxes at this particular post office, she has a handful of circulars addressed to box numbers 150 through 200. If she were to analyze her actions in AppleScript repeat statement form, they would look like this:

```
repeat with boxNumber from 150 to 200
    move circular addressed to P.O.Box boxNumber¬
        to box boxNumber
end repeat
```

The repeat loop sets itself up by first establishing a range of numbers and as-signing a variable name (boxNumber) that will take on numbers from that range. Because of the repeating nature of this construction, the boxNumber value increments by one each time through the loop. Inside the repeat state-ment is another statement that uses the value of that variable to help it carry out a job. In our postal example, we use the variable twice—to identify an ad-dress and the physical box into which the circular goes. The first time through the loop, the statement evaluates to:

```
move circular addressed to P.O.Box 150 to box 150
```

The second time through the loop, the values increase by one:

```
move circular addressed to P.O.Box 151 to box 151
```

and so on, until the one valued at 200 is performed. Then the repeat loop auto-matically exits, and script execution continues right after the end repeat state-ment (if there is more to execute).

The time to use this repeat form is when your script needs to repeat an operation based on the value of a loop counting variable. Here's an example using Scriptable Text Editor to number paragraphs in a document:

```
tell document 1 of application "Scriptable Text Editor"
    repeat with i from 1 to (count of paragraphs)
        copy (i as string) & ". " to before paragraph i
    end repeat
end tell
```

Notice a couple important points. First, the *stopValue* parameter here is deter-mined by an expression whose value depends entirely on the conditions at the moment—both the *startValue* and *stopValue* parameters can be any expression that evaluates to an integer. Second, we use the letter "i" as the *counterVariable* parameter. You can use any letter or word that would qualify as an AppleScript variable for this job (Chapter 9). Some scripters use letters such as i, n, and x, while in some instances it may make the script more readable if you use a more descriptive word that identifies what the variable represents (e.g., graphCount).

It's also important to note that the variable you use as the *counterVariable* parameter survives past the end repeat statement. Therefore, if your repeat loop contains a test that may exit the loop early, you can later examine the value of *counterVariable* to find out exactly how many times the loop started over.

If your script needs to increment the *counterVariable* by something other than 1 (e.g., the postal worker is doing just the even numbered boxes), then use the optional by *stepValue* parameter. For example, to number every fifth para-graph of a document, you'd modify our earlier examples to read this way:

```
tell document 1 of application "Scriptable Text Editor"
    repeat with i from 1 to (count of paragraphs) by 5
        copy (i as string) & ". " to before paragraph i
    end repeat
end tell
```

Only paragraphs 1, 6, 11, 16, etc. are numbered, because the value of the counting variable jumped by 5 each time the loop executed. The value of the variable i at the end of looping only as high as the variable reached during the last executed loop.

You can also instruct this counting repeat loop to count backwards. Make the startValue larger than the stopValue, and include a negative stepValue parameter:

```
tell document 1 of application "Scriptable Text Editor"
    repeat with i from (count of paragraphs) to 1 by -1
        copy (i as string) & ". " to before paragraph i
    end repeat
end tell
```

This script numbers each paragraph starting with the last one, and works its way down to the first.

Repeat In List

An even more powerful repeat construction is one I call Repeat In List. This one is ideal when a repeat loop needs to work with items in an AppleScript list value class. The syntax is:

```
repeat with loopVariable in list
    [ statement ] ...
end [ repeat ]
```

Unlike the *counterVariable* parameter in the Repeat With-From-To form, the *loopVariable* value is not an integer, but rather a value representing an object from the list. Each time through the loop, *loopVariable* becomes a reference to the next object from the list or record. Some examples are definitely in order.

As a preliminary example, we'll create a simple list of integers, and then use the powers of this construction to add them together:

```
set itemTotal to 0
repeat with oneItem in {10, 20, 30, 40, 50}
    set itemTotal to itemTotal + oneItem
end repeat
itemTotal
    -- result: 150
```

The script first initializes a variable itemTotal to zero, so we can add other integers to it later. At the opening of the repeat loop, we assign references to the successive items of the list to the variable oneItem. Inside the loop, when we perform the arithmetic, we can use the oneItem value for the arithmetic directly. A longer way to write this script (with the Repeat With-From-To form) would be:

```
set itemTotal to 0
set integerList to {10, 20, 30, 40, 50}
repeat with i from 1 to count of integerList
    set itemTotal to itemTotal + (item i of integerList)
end repeat
itemTotal
    -- result: 150
```

Perhaps the biggest difference is that in the Repeat In List form, the list becomes part of the loop construction, whereas in the other method, the repeat parameters concern themselves only with the count and position of items in a predefined list. We end up having to refer to the integerList value more often. The Repeat In List form is compact, with the loopVariable value essentially evaluating to "item 1 of list", "item 2 of list", "item 3 of list"—incrementing by one each time through the list.

As a result, when the items in a list are objects containing properties, your script can access those properties inside a repeat loop with a compact reference:

```
tell document 1 of application "Scriptable Text Editor"
    set letterTotal to 0
    repeat with oneWord in words of paragraph 2
        set letterTotal to letterTotal + (length of oneWord)
    end repeat
end tell
letterTotal
```

When you consider that a lot of data, like the every element reference shown above, comes back as a list, you see how valuable this repeat construction can be in AppleScript. You can place references to groups of objects directly in the repeat loop header, and let the nested statements work with the data directly.

Pay particular attention to the fact that the variable value that seems to represent an item of the list each time through the loop does not truly evaluate to the value of the item, but rather to a reference to the value (the Event Log misleads in this regard). Therefore, if the list consists of three strings, it would be in vain to test whether the loop variable "is" a fixed string—because the script will be comparing a reference class object against a string class object, which will always return false. For such comparisons, it is necessary to coerce the value prior to the test:

```
repeat with oneItem in {"Rob", "Buddy", "Sally"}
    if oneItem as string = "Sally" then -- coercion required
        display dialog "We just reached Sally!"
    end if
end repeat
```

As an added note, contrary to what the *AppleScript Language Guide* (first release) says about this repeat structure, it does not coerce records to lists for use as the *list* parameter. Your script can manually coerce a record to list if necessary (including coercing the list in the repeat statement if you like), but the coercion is not automatic.

Timeout Flow Control

Each time your script sends a command to an application, AppleScript waits up to two minutes for the application to send back a reply (this is part of the Apple event mechanism, which is fortunately hidden from our view). A downside to this is that until the acknowledgment comes back from the program, script execution pauses during this time.

Under normal circumstances, this is no problem, since the application responds within a reasonable time (although some scripters might want to know what "reasonable" means). But there are some things that can bog down the process. For example, if your command is talking to an application running on another Mac, there could be extraordinarily heavy network traffic; or the other machine could be performing a processing intensive task with the very program you're trying to control with your script; or there could be a bug in the program (perish the thought).

Unless told otherwise, AppleScript waits a total of two minutes for an acknowledgment. If nothing comes back (during which time you've been twiddling your thumbs), AppleScript finally reports a timeout error.

There may be circumstances in which you find two minutes isn't enough to guard against a timeout for a particular process that a script is performing. A script object running in the background (Chapter 15) might not care (nor would you) that it's having to wait five minutes for the target application to respond. To lengthen (or shorten) the time a command or series of commands waits for the reply, you can surround those statements with the **with timeout** statement. The syntax is:

```
with timeout [ of ] numberOfSeconds seconds [s]
    [ statement ] ...
end [ timeout ]
```

If you're genuinely concerned about a process timing out to soon and messing up your script, then you should not only extend the timeout time, but also nest the timeout statement inside a try statement so you can more gracefully trap the timeout error:

```
try
    tell application "MagicBase" of machine "Server"
        -- increase to 5 minutes
        with timeout of 300 seconds
            (* time-consuming statements *)
```

```
        end timeout
    end tell
on error errMsg number errNum
    if errNum is -1712 then -- timeout error number
        (* timeout error handling statements*)
    end if
end try
```

It's vital to be on the lookout for timeout bottlenecks, because when a command times out, it not only sends back an error message, but any expected result data won't be there for you. For more information about the try statement and error handling, see Chapter 12.

A script can blow past the timeout issue entirely by requesting that statements be executed without waiting at all. The method involves the ignoring statement, which I've reserved for the next chapter (most applications of this statement involves operators, the subject of the next chapter). This ignoring tactic should be used only in rare circumstances, because your script won't get any feedback about whether the command was ever received by the target application. Nor do any results come back while this ignoring switch is on. Caveat Scriptor!

Other Control Statements

Some other AppleScript constructions affect the flow of a script. Two of them—considering and ignoring—have more influence over the use of operators, so we'll hold that discussion for Chapter 11. Another subject very close to the matter is that of subroutines. I've reserved an entire chapter (Chapter 14) for this powerful aspect of AppleScript.

The remaining control statement to keep in reserve until sufficient applications are available in the area is the with transaction statement. This statement can apply to (primarily) database retrieval applications that support the concept of transactions. From the AppleScript side, placing a series of statements inside a with transaction statement instructs the database application to handle the statements as a kind of single action.

Syntax for this statement is:

with transaction [*sessionID*]
    [*statement*] ...
end transaction

In a typical database application, your script will first open a session, which returns a session ID (to distinguish one session from others that may be open at the same time). That session ID can then be passed as a parameter to the with transaction statement to make sure any nested statements go to the proper transaction. Here's the skeleton of such a series in a fictional application:

```
tell application "Mega Base"
    -- create session and get session ID
    set mySession to make session with data {...}
    -- specify which sessionID
    with transaction mySession
        (* storage/retrieval statements *)
    end transaction
end tell
```

Details about sessions and commands that go inside transactions will accompany applications that offer these facilities. AppleScript's role here is primarily as a facilitator, to makes sure instructions to such an application and transaction object are packaged correctly.

Next Stop

From here we tackle the last large group of words in the AppleScript vocabulary: the operators.

CHAPTER 11

AppleScript Operators

AppleScript is rich in *operators*: words in expressions that perform operations on one or two values to arrive at another value. The values that operators work on are called *operands*. An expression may contain one operand and an operator, or two operands separated by an operator. These formal descriptions sound more complicated than actually working with operators.

Four Operator Types

In an effort to help you readily learn the variety and scope of AppleScript's operators, I've divided them into four categories, some of which have untraditional names—but names that I believe identify their purpose in the language. The four types are:

Type	What They Do
connubial operators	Join two operands together to produce a single value that is a result of a math or other operation on the two.
comparison operators	Compare the values of two operands, deriving a result of either TRUE or FALSE (used extensively as parameters to if-then statements).
containment operators	Determine whether one operand is a part of, or is in a particular position relative to, a second operand.
Boolean operators	Perform Boolean arithmetic on one or two Boolean operands.

233

Much of what operators are all about harkens back to our discussion in Chapter 5 about expression evaluation. By definition, an operator is part of an expression that evaluates to some other value that what the script reads. For example, the expression

2 + 3

shows two integer operands joined by the addition operator. This expression evaluates to 5. It's the operator that provides the instructions for AppleScript to follow in its never-ending pursuit of expression evaluation.

As you will see, it is not uncommon for two operands that look very different in a script to be compared for their equality. AppleScript cares not how the operands read in the script but how their evaluated values compare. Two very dissimilar looking values can, in fact be of identical values. For example, the expression

a = 325

would evaluate to TRUE if the variable named "a" had a 325 integer value assigned to it in an earlier statement in a script.

To help you grasp the range of operators and their requirements quickly, the follow section lists the operators of each type in a table that shows the most vital information: operator syntax, the class of operand values the operator accepts, and the class of the resulting value. Most of these specifications come down to common sense anyway, especially when you look at the plain language wording for the operators.

Connubial Operators

Syntax	Name	Operands	Results
+	Plus	Integer, Real	Integer, Real
−	Minus	Integer, Real	Integer, Real
*	Multiply	Integer, Real	Integer, Real
/	Divide	Integer, Real	Integer, Real
÷ (Option-/)			
div	Integral Division	Integer, Real	Integer
mod	Modulo	Integer, Real	Integer, Real
^	Exponent	Integer, Real	Real
&	Concatenation	All (See below)	List, Record, String
as	Coercion	(See below)	(See below)
[a] ref[erence] [to]	A Reference To	Reference	Reference

Comparison Operators

Syntax	Name	Operands	Results
= is equal[s] [is] equal to	Equal	All	Boolean
≠ (Option-=) is not isn't isn't equal [to] is not equal [to] does not equal doesn't equal	Not equal	All	Boolean
> [is] greater than comes after is not less than or equal [to] isn't less than or equal [to]	Greater than	Date, Integer, Real, String	Boolean
< [is] less than comes before is not greater than or equal [to] isn't greater than or equal [to]	Less than	Date, Integer, Real, String	Boolean
>= ≥ (Option->) [is] greater than or equal [to] is not less than isn't less than does not come before doesn't come before	Greater than or equal to	Date, Integer, Real, String	Boolean
<= ≤ (Option-<) [is] not less than or equal [to] is not greater than isn't greater than does not come after doesn't come after	Less than or equal to	Date, Integer, Real, String	Boolean

Containment Operators

Syntax	Name	Operands	Results
contain[s]	Contains	List, Record, String	Boolean
does not contain doesn't contain	Does not contain	List, Record, String	Boolean
is contained by	Is contained by	List, Record, String	Boolean
is not contained by isn't contained by	Is not contained by	List, Record, String	Boolean
start[s] with begin[s] with	Starts with	List, String	Boolean
end[s] with	Ends with	List, String	Boolean

Boolean Operators

Syntax	Name	Operands	Results
and	And	Boolean	Boolean
or	Or	Boolean	Boolean
not	Not	One Boolean	Boolean

Operators work with a variety of value classes as operands. The specific treatment may vary from class to class, so it's worthwhile discussing how the operators work with each class of values.

Integers, Reals, and Operators

Many operators accept both integers and reals as operands (although some return only a real as a result). In fact, operators such as math operators allow you to mix and match integers and reals in either operand. The value of the result depends on what class is on the left side, and what the result is. Here are examples that show all the possibilities:

```
10 + 10
    -- result: 20 (integer on both sides yields integer)
10 + 10.0
    -- result: 20 (left integer governs, since result is a whole number)
10 + 10.1
    -- result: 20.1 (right real governs, since result must be a real)
```

```
10.0 + 10
  -- result: 20.0 (left real governs)
```

```
10.0 + 10.0
  -- result: 20.0 (real on both sides yields real)
```

For comparison operators, the two operands can be any combination of integer and real values. Their classes are irrelevant, because the operator determines whether the test wins or fails based on the math. Here are some examples:

```
10 = 10
  -- result: true
```

```
10 = 10.0
  -- result: true
```

```
9.9 = 10.0
  -- result: false
```

```
10 > 10
  -- result: false
```

```
10  10
  -- result: true
```

Remember that an operand is any expression that evaluates to the desired value class. Therefore:

```
item 2 of {10, 20, 30} = 20
  -- result: true
```

```
count of {10, 20, 30} = 3
  -- result: true
```

```
49.9 + 50.1 = 100
  -- result: true
```

That includes information from application objects, such as properties and data. As long as you can form the operands into expressions that evaluate to a real or integer class value, you can place them on both sides of a comparison operator.

Strings and Operators

Many operators accept string values as one or both operands. In the connubial group, the most common is the concatenation operator (&). This operator joins the left operand string to the right operand string with no intervening spaces (nor is there a && operator, as there is in HyperTalk, to concatenate and add a space). As a result, if you are joining two words or phrases together, it is important that you take care of any space that may need to go between words. These examples should give you ideas:

```
"Howdy" & "Doody"
   -- result: "HowdyDoody"
```

```
"Howdy" & " Doody"
   -- result: "Howdy Doody"
```

```
"Howdy" & space & "Doody"
   -- result: "Howdy Doody"
```

Use the concatenation operator with any string value, as in:

```
get ((path to extensions) as string) & ¬
   "Scripting Additions:StringLib"
   -- result: "HD:System Folder:Extensions:Scripting Additions:StringLib"
```

If the right operand of a concatenation operator is an integer or real value, AppleScript tries to coerce the value into a string to carry out the concatenation. For example:

```
"Atlanta Olympics " & 1996
   -- result: "Atlanta Olympics 1996"
```

But the weight of a left operand demonstrates itself if you reverse the string and number sides of the operator:

```
1996 & " in Atlanta"
   -- result: {1996, " in Atlanta"}
```

As with most operators that try to coerce right side values, it is the left side that runs the show.

Comparison operators treat strings like a series of lowercase ASCII character values. For two strings to be equal, absolutely every character—punctuation, spaces, tabs, returns, foreign symbols—must be the same in both. Case of letters is irrelevant, since all characters are essentially converted to lowercase for the comparison (unless directed otherwise by **considering** or **ignoring** statements, below).

This reduction to ASCII values helps explain how strings can be checked to determine which comes before or after another. Comparisons are performed character by character from left to right (in Roman languages, at least). The instant a character of the left string is different than the corresponding character in the right string, the operator determines precisely what condition is being checked for, and returns the TRUE or FALSE as needed. If one string is shorter than the other (and matches corresponding characters in the second string), the shorter string is said to come before (or be less than) the longer string. Here are some examples of string comparisons:

```
"Beantown" comes before "Boston"
   -- result: true (some would rather use the "is less than" synonym)
```

```
"MaNcHeStEr" = "Manchester"
   -- result: true (no case sensitivity)
```

```
"123" = "one, two, three"
    -- result: false
```

```
"123" is greater than "one, two, three"
    -- result: false (numerals sort before letters in ASCII)
```

```
"aye" is "eye"
    -- result: false (spelling, not sound, rules)
```

```
"Here and now" < "Here and now."
    -- result: true (note trailing period in second operand)
```

String treatment with containment operators is very straightforward. The conditions must be met like they sound for the result to be TRUE. Similar left-to-right, character-by-character analysis takes place to determine whether one string starts or ends with another or whether one string contains another.

Lists and Operators

The test for equivalency of two lists depends on the evaluated values of the contents of both lists. For example, while

```
{10, 20, "It's me"} = {10, 20, "It's me"}
    -- result: true
```

is obviously true, so is the following:

```
{10.0, 1005, "It's" & " me"} = {10, 20, "It's me"}
    -- result: true
```

Each item in the left operand evaluates to the same value as the corresponding item in the right operand. Such comparisons are performed on an item-by-item basis, so the item orders can't be mixed if you expect a TRUE result. Therefore,

```
{10, 20, "It's me"} = {20, 10, "It's me"}
    -- result: false
```

returns false, because even though both operands have the same items in them, the items are in different orders. The comparison fails the instant it sees that 10 does not equal 20—the first item of both operands.

Containment operators examine corresponding items in lists the same way. For example:

```
{"Odyssey", "by", "John", "Sculley"} starts with "Odyssey"
    -- result: true
```

```
{"Odyssey", "by", "John", "Sculley"} ends with "Sculley"
    -- result: true
```

```
{"Odyssey", "by", "John", "Sculley"} contains "by"
    -- result: true
```

```
{"Odyssey", "by", "John", "Sculley"} contains "by John"
    -- result: false
```

```
{"Odyssey", "by", "John", "Sculley"} contains "Scull"
    -- result: false
```

```
{"Odyssey", "by", "John", "Sculley"} contains {"by","John"}
    -- result: true
```

```
"John" is contained by {"Odyssey", "by", "John", "Sculley"}
    -- result: true
```

A personal note about this last construction: While AppleScript accepts the is contained by operator, some writers (add me to the list) may have a difficult time when reading scripts with this blatantly passive grammar. Spare me the pain by placing the order of operands in your scripts such that you can use the active (contains) version.

Use the concatenation operator to join two lists into a single list. This allows you to fairly simply prepend or append one list to another:

```
{"Two", "lists" } & {"become", "one."}
    -- result: {"Two", "lists", "become", "one."}
```

When the left operand of this operator is a list, you can append items of other classes, because AppleScript turns the right operand into an item of the list (but still bearing its same class as the original):

```
{"She", "loves", "you"} & "yeah yeah yeah"
    -- result: {"She", "loves", "you", "yeah yeah yeah"}
```

```
{"She", "loves", "you"} & "yeah" & "yeah" & "yeah"
    -- result: {"She", "loves", "you", "yeah", "yeah", "yeah"}
```

```
{"As", "easy", "as"} & 3.14159
    -- result: {"As", "easy", "as", 3.14159}
```

As an alternate to the concatenation operator (&), you may also use the beginning and end specifiers to prepend and append to a list, respectively. For example,

```
set theMacs to {"LC", "PowerBook", "Quadra"}
copy "Classic" to beginning of theMacs
theMacs
    -- result: {"Classic", "LC", "PowerBook", "Quadra"}
```

and

```
set theMacs to {"LC", "PowerBook", "Quadra"}
copy "Classic" to beginning of theMacs
copy "Power PC" to end of theMacs
theMacs
    -- result: {"Classic", "LC", "PowerBook", "Quadra", "Power PC"}
```

The same would work for copying another list to the beginning or end of an existing list. While this mechanism would be useful for working with strings in variables, AppleScript does not make that kind of concatenation possible.

If you need to insert an item into a list, the procedure is more complex, because you have to extract the component parts before and after the insertion point, and then use the concatenation operator:

```
set oneList to {"This", "is", "so", "easy"}
set oneList to items 1 thru 2 of oneList & ¬
    "not" & items 3 thru 4 of oneList
    -- result: {"This", "is", "not", "so", "easy"}
```

A lot of AppleScript is tied to lists. The more you know about them, the better your scripts will be.

Records and Operators

Equivalency of records is a bit freer than of lists, because records, by their very nature, are not ordered collections of data, but rather collections of labeled data. The distinction plays a role in determining whether two records are equal.

All that AppleScript cares is that both records on either side of the equivalency operator have the same number of labels, the same label names, and data that evaluates the same. The order of the labels and data is not a factor. Therefore:

```
{name: "Joe", age: 30, weight: 165} = ¬
    {age: 30, name: "Joe", weight: 165}
    -- result: true
```

because the labels and values are the same. For the values, evaluation is again the key:

```
{name:"Joe", age:30, weight:165} = {age:90  3, ¬
    name:{"J", "o", "e"} as string, weight:100 + 65}
    -- result: true
```

As long as the labels are there and the values for each pair of corresponding labels evaluate to the same value, the records are equal. To take this one step further, data extracted from two (equal or unequal) records with the same label and evaluation are also equal:

```
set Joe to {name:"Joe", age:30, weight:165}
set Steve to {age:30, name:"Steve", weight:180}
Joe's age = Steve's age
    -- result: true
```

Containment operators on records have the same freedoms and restrictions as on lists. One record is said to contain another if the smaller record's labels and values can also be found in the first record. Order of labels and values is not a factor.

```
{brand:"Sony", model:"KV-1029", price:"$399"} contains ¬
  {model:"KV-1029", brand:"Sony"}
  -- result: true
```

Both sides of the operator, however, must be a record. AppleScript can't coerce some values into records:

```
{brand:"Sony", model:"KV-1029", price:"$399"} contains "Sony"
  -- result: Error (Can't make "Sony" into a record)
```

If your script must know if a certain value is in a record, but the script can't know the label, you can coerce the script to a list, and then use the operator:

```
({brand:"Sony", model:"KV-1029", price:"$399"} as list) ¬
  contains "Sony"
  -- result: true
```

While you can concatenate records, as in:

```
{lastName:"Doe", firstName:"John"} & {age:21}
  -- result: {lastName:"Doe", firstName:"John", age:21}
```

you have to be careful about combining records with the same labels. Apple-Script discards any field value in the right operand that shares a label with the left operand:

```
{lastName:"Doe", firstName:"John"} & ¬
  {lastName:"Smith", age:21}
  -- result: {lastName:"Doe", firstName:"John", age:21}
```

Booleans and Operators

It's pretty easy to understand Boolean values and things like equivalency operators: each side of the operator must evaluate to TRUE for the expression containing the operator to be TRUE:

```
10 > 5 = "b" comes after "a"
  -- result: true
```

Notice that in this example, each of the operands used an expression to achieve some Boolean value. It's true that 10 is greater than 5; it's also true that "b" comes after "a". Therefore, the overall expression tests the equivalency of a TRUE on one side and a TRUE on the other, yielding a TRUE as a final value. Since so many AppleScript operators evaluate to a Boolean, expect to find operators within things like command parameters that require Boolean values—especially if-then constructions:

```
set John to {lastName:"Doe", firstName:"John", age:21}
if age of John  21 then
  (* statements based on this age group *)
end if
```

Where Booleans can get confusing for some scripters is when you have to use Boolean operators with Boolean values. Let's look first at the simplest Boolean operator, Not. This operator is called a *unary* operator, because it requires only one operand. The Not operator precedes any Boolean value to switch it back to the other value (i.e., from TRUE to FALSE or from FALSE to TRUE). For example:

```
not true
  -- result: false

not (10 > 5)
  -- result: false

not (10 < 5)
  -- result: true

not ("Hard Rock Cafe" ends with "Cafe")
  -- result: false
```

Interestingly, if you were to enter the last example into Script Editor without the parentheses, the compiler rewords the expression to read:

```
"Hard Rock Cafe" does not end with "Cafe"
```

When using the Not operator, it is a good idea to enclose the operand in parentheses. These help the compiler figure out exactly what in the statement you intend to be the operand. It then helps the script reader more fully understand what operand you are reversing.

The And operator joins two Boolean values together to arrive at a logical TRUE or FALSE value based on the results of both operators. This brings up something called a truth table, which helps you visualize how the various operands behave with the And operator:

Left		Right	Result
TRUE	And	TRUE	TRUE
TRUE	And	FALSE	FALSE
FALSE	And	TRUE	FALSE
FALSE	And	FALSE	FALSE

You see that only one condition produces a TRUE result: both operands must evaluate to true. Which side of the And operator a TRUE or FALSE is makes no difference. Here are some simple examples of each possibility:

```
100 > 0 and "z" comes after "a"
  -- result: true

100 > 0 and "a" comes after "z"
  -- result: false

100 < 0 and "z" comes after "a"
  -- result: false
```

```
100< 0 and "a" comes after "z"
   -- result: false
```

In contrast, the Or operator is more lenient about what it evaluates to TRUE. The basis of this operator is that if one or the other (or both) operands is TRUE, then it returns a TRUE. Its truth table looks like this:

Left		Right	Result
TRUE	Or	TRUE	TRUE
TRUE	Or	FALSE	TRUE
FALSE	Or	TRUE	TRUE
FALSE	Or	FALSE	FALSE

Therefore, if a TRUE exists anywhere in the expression, a TRUE is the result. Here are Or operator versions of the previous examples, to show how many more TRUE results we get:

```
100 > 0 or "z" comes after "a"
   -- result: true
```

```
100 > 0 or "a" comes after "z"
   -- result: true
```

```
100 < 0 or "z" comes after "a"
   -- result: true
```

```
100< 0 or "a" comes after "z"
   -- result: false
```

The only way the expression returns false is if both operands evaluate to FALSE.

Coercing Values—The As Operator

Because operators are so "class conscious," it is frequently necessary to change the class of a value to make it work in some comparison or marriage of values by operators. We've already seen that AppleScript at times automatically tries to coerce a value of a right side operand when the left operand governs the situation:

```
"Atlanta Olympics " & 1996 -- string & integer
   -- result: "Atlanta Olympics 1996" (string)
```

```
8 + "45" -- integer plus a string
   -- result: 53 (integer)
```

But the majority of times when you need to change the class of a value, an operator isn't there to help out. Your script may have retrieved a value of one class from a document, but to use that data as a parameter to a command, it must be converted to a different class. Here is an example that fails due to an incorrect value class being passed to the open command:

```
open file (choose file)
   -- result: error
```

This generates an error, because the choose file command returns a value of class alias. The open command expects a file value. To make this statement work, the results of the choose file command need to be coerced to a string, which then becomes a valid parameter to the open file command. AppleScript includes an operator—the As operator—to force coercions. This operator requires two operands: on the left the value to be coerced; on the right the name of the class to which you wish the value coerced. Here's how we would apply the operator to our earlier problem:

```
open file ((choose file) as string)
```

The parentheses are required because it's vital for the results of the choose file command to be coerced to a string before becoming a parameter to the open file command.

You should probably realize by now, however, that not every value class can be coerced to any other value class. Some values simply don't have the right stuff to become another class. Use the following table as a guide to possible coercions:

CoerceFrom	*CoerceTo*	*Example*	*Tips*
Integer	Real	5 → 5.0	
Integer	String	5 → "5"	
Real	Integer	5.0 → 5	Only if real has no fractional part
Real	String	5.1 → "5.1"	
String	Integer	"5" → 5	Only if string represents an integer
String	Real	"5.1" → 5.1	Only if string represents a real
(any value)	Single List	"joe" → {"joe"}	Resulting list is of one value, which may be concatenated with other lists
Single List	(any value)	{"joe"} → "joe"	Resulting value is same class as item in list
List	String	{"Ice","T"} → "IceT"	Depends on text item delimiters
Record	List	{x:1, y:2, z:3} → {1, 2, 3}	Labels are dropped

CoerceFrom	CoerceTo	Example	Tips
Date	String	date "<date>" → "<date>"	One way only
Alias	String	alias "<path>" → "<path>"	One way only

One coercion pair that needs some explanation is the multiple-item list to a string (or text) value class coercion. The results depend on the current settings of the text item delimiters global property.

Consider the following:

```
{2, "Live", "Crew"} as string
    -- result: "2LiveCrew"
```

This result came from the default text item delimiters property (empty). Notice that each item is coerced to a string, and all the strings are concatenated to each other to create one run-on string. But if the property is set to another character, AppleScript inserts that character between items in the list during coercion. Here are some examples:

```
set AppleScript's text item delimiters to space
get {"Now", "is", "the time"} as text
    -- result: "Now is the time"

set AppleScript's text item delimiters to "."
get {"Now", "is", "the time"} as text
    -- result: "Now.is.the time"
```

Notice that the delimiter character goes only between original items, and not within any item (i.e., the two-worded last item, above).

No other coercions are possible with the As operator, but labels for file, alias, application, and script values coerce strings (containing pathnames) just by preceding the string with the label. Thus, in our **open** command example above, the **file** label coerces the string (made by coercing the results from the **choose file** command) to a file to create the proper parameter for the **open** command.

String Comparison Aids

In the many examples you've seen for string comparisons, it has probably become quite evident that except for the case of letters, strings are compared character for character, including spaces between words, hyphens, punctuation, and so on. Your script can, however, alter the way string comparisons are made, allowing for more or less leniency as you decree.

The controlling statements that take care of this are the **considering** and **ignoring** statements. The syntax for these statements is as follows:

considering attribute [, *attribute* ... and *attribute*] ¬
       [but ignoring [, *attribute* ... and *attribute*]]
       [*statement*] ...
   end considering

ignoring *attribute* [, *attribute* ... and *attribute*] ¬
       [but considering [, *attribute* ... and *attribute*]]
       [*statement*] ...
   end ignoring

What's being controlled here is how AppleScript treats the various attributes that all strings have. Here are the string attributes, their normal setting (i.e., if you don't adjust them with these statements), and what they mean:

Attribute	*Default*	*Description*
case	ignores	Distinguishes uppercase from lowercase letters, applying each characters strict ASCII value for comparisons.
white space	considers	Regards spaces between characters as characters to be compared.
diacriticals	considers	Distinguishes characters with diacritical marks (e.g., à, ô, è) from same letters without the marks.
hyphens	considers	Regards hyphens as characters to be compared.
punctuation	considers	Regards punctuation symbols as characters to be compared.

For example, on its own, AppleScript works like this:

```
"howdy" = "HOWDY"
   -- result: true
```

But if you want to know if a string is exactly like another, including uppercase versus lowercase letters, you'd invoke the considering statement as follows:

```
considering case
   "howdy" = "HOWDY"
end considering
   -- result: false
```

You can also combine different attributes with different default behaviors into a single considering or ignoring statement. For example, here is a progression of results from building a complex considering statement:

```
"Chocolate Èclair" = "chocolate eclair"
   -- result: false (diacritical È and e don't match)
```

```
ignoring diacriticals
    "Chocolate Èclair" = "chocolate eclair"
end ignoring
    -- result: true
```

```
ignoring diacriticals but considering case
    "Chocolate Èclair" = "chocolate eclair"
end ignoring
    -- result: false (uppercase and lowercase didn't match)
```

To use these statements reliably, the left operand of a comparison operator inside a considering or ignoring statement should be a value in the script, as opposed to a reference to an application object. In other words, place the string contents of an application object into a variable, and then use that variable as the left operand in a considering or ignoring statement operation.

One other attribute, which we covered in Chapter 10's discussion about Apple event timeouts, is the application responses attribute. Its default behavior is to consider these responses, thus forcing your script to pause while it waits for the target application object to respond back that it received a command. By setting some statements inside an ignoring application responses statement, your script sends the commands and keeps on chugging. You can only do this if you're not expecting any values to come back from the commands, because when your script ignores responses—it really ignores responses.

Operator (and Reference) Precedence

When you begin working with complex expressions that hold a number of operators, it is vital to know in what order AppleScript evaluates those expressions to arrive at its ultimate value. AppleScript assigns different priorities or weights to types of operators in an effort to achieve uniformity in the way it evaluates complex expressions.

In the following expression:

```
4 * 5 + 10
    -- result: 30
```

AppleScript uses its scheme of precedence to perform the multiplication before the addition—regardless of where the operators appear in the statement. Therefore, AppleScript first multiplies 4 by 5, and then adds that result to 10, for a result of 30.

But you can alter precedence by a pair of parentheses. Parentheses, as you'll see in the table below, have the highest precedence, telling AppleScript to evaluate what's inside before doing any other evaluations—even if what's inside is much lower in precedence than other operators in the expression. If we really wanted the earlier expression to add the 10 and 5 together before multiplying that sum by 4, then we would have to force the evaluation of the lower precedence (the addition) ahead of the multiplication:

```
4 * (5 + 10)
    -- result: 60
```

You see that the parentheses had a great impact on the result of this expression. And if your expression contains parentheses inside a set of parentheses, then the innermost parenthetical expression evaluates first, working evaluation outward from there.

AppleScript evaluates expressions according to a strict order of precedence. Since expressions can include references to objects (and how any object may be related to another object), it's valuable to know what gets evaluated first in an expression. This may influence how you use parentheses to control expression evaluation. Table 11.1 lists the precedence order for operators (including containment operators) for AppleScript.

Table 11.1   AppleScript Operator Procedure

Precedence	Operator	Notes
1	( )	From innermost to outermost
2	+ and −	When used with a single value to signify positive or negative
3	s	Object containment (left to right)
4	of in	Object containment (right to left)
5	my its	Object containment (right to left)
6	∧	Exponent (right to left)
7	* / and ÷ div mod	Multiplication and division
8	+ −	Addition and subtraction
9	&	Concatenation
10	as	Value coercion
11	< ≤ > ≥ contains	Comparison operators and their synonyms

Table 11.1   *(continued)*

Precedence	Operator	Notes
12	= ≠	Equality
13	not	Unary Boolean operator
14	and	Boolean operator
15	or	Boolean operator
16	whose	Filter reference
17	reference to	Object reference

Whenever an expression contains more than one operator of the same precedence (possible only with exponent, math, And, and Or operators), AppleScript performs its evaluations from left to right with one exception. Multiple exponent operators in an expression are evaluated from right to left. For example, in the expression:

    4 * 5 * 6

AppleScript proceeds from left to right, first multiplying 4 by 5, then multiplying 20 by 6. But in the expression:

    2^3^4

AppleScript first calculates 3^4 (result: 81.0), and then calculates 2^81.0 to reach an enormous number.

Notice that any math, concatenation, and class coercion is performed prior to any comparison operators. This allows all expressions that can act as operands for these operators to evaluate fully before they are compared.

The key to working with complex expressions—when they're giving you trouble—is to isolate evaluating components, and try them out by themselves if you can. See additional debugging tips in Chapter 13.

Next Stop

Speaking of trouble, the next chapter shows you how to head off potential problems in script by trapping and handling errors efficiently. The test of a good scripter is how bullet-proof a script is; and that is usually a measure of how well errors are anticipated and handled.

CHAPTER 12

Error Checking in Scripts

In the rush to get a script to do what you want, it's hard to resist the temptation to take a "damn the torpedoes, full speed ahead" attitude toward the durability of the code. This is especially true when incorporating user interface elements that allow users to interact with the script. In the real world of using computers, users don't always do what you expect them to do, so your scripts must be on the lookout for potential problems and know how to handle them when they arrive. That's what error checking is all about.

Why We Forget to Error Check

The process of writing a script (or any program in any language) is an intense one. We focus on a problem and the scripted solution with all our might, completely immersed in the flow of the scripts, the statements, the decisions—all those things that eventually make the script work. Something interesting comes of this intensity: we know the script and its inner workings so well, that we don't take into account something going wrong that we didn't encounter ourselves in the script writing process.

An excellent example of this is using the display dialog command to prompt a user to enter some information. The statement may be something like this:

```
display dialog "Enter a number:" default answer ""
```

If the script goes on from here taking the text returned value of the result, such as coercing the number into an integer and applying it to some math or integer parameter of another command, you think nothing of it. After all, the instructions in the dialog explicitly tell the user to enter a number. Moreover, when you use it, you know what happens in the script afterwards, so you wouldn't think of entering anything but a number.

Thinking like that can only send you, the scripter, to your doom.

Here is a list of some of the things a user could do (usually inadvertently) to botch up your perfect script:

1. Click the Cancel button instead of the OK button.
2. Click the OK button without entering a character.
3. Enter a real value when you expect an integer.
4. Enter the text word for a number (e.g., "two").
5. Enter a valid integer, but letting the finger slip to some other non-numeric character an instant before pressing Return.
6. Enter a negative number, when your requirement is for a positive one.
7. Enter gobbledygook to see if the script breaks (this one's intentional).

If you haven't protected your script against these possibilities, most of them could present the user with the embarrassing "Execution Error" alert that AppleScript displays (with a beep) whenever it can't accept the value presented to it in a statement. The alert is embarrassing, because a user views this error as a sure sign of sloppy programming. Your entire script is now suspect.

This is actually an important point about point of view. An inexperienced programmer might consider the problem to be the user's fault because the user didn't follow instructions. But the problem is really the programmer's. Users' expectations are rightfully high. Our job as scripters is to protect the user from making mistakes. The less the user has to think about a script's requirements, the more he or she can think about how the script offers a solution or automation for something that needs doing.

Anticipating Errors

The list above shows the types of errors a scripter should anticipate users making, whether the errors are made intentionally or not. In the case of the display dialog command, the errors break down into three categories:

- Clicking where you don't expect (the Cancel or other button you scripted)
- Entering the wrong kind of information your script needs
- Entering no information

For something like the choose file command, which displays the open file dialog box, even though you can control the kinds of files that appear in the list, there are still a couple of categories of problems:

- Clicking the Cancel button
- Selecting a file that has data unusable by your script

Recall that the choose file command only returns the alias to the file. A succeeding command that opens the file may encounter disk or network problems preventing the open command from working properly—another kind of error to worry about for any command that accesses a mounted volume.

AppleScript Errors

When AppleScript encounters an error while running a script, it gathers several pieces of information. If your script is set up to trap errors, then it can extract this information and perhaps offer some suggestions or alternate routes for the user to take. The way you set up a script to trap an error is to place the statement(s) that could generate an error inside a try compound statement. The formal syntax for this kind of statement is:

```
try
    [ statementToTest ] ...
on error [ errorMessage ] [ number errorNumber ]
    [ from offendingObject ] [ to expectedType ]
    [ partial result resultList ]
    [ global variableID [, variableID ] ... ]
    [ local variableID [, variableID ] ... ]
    [ statementHandllingError ] ...
end [ try | error ]
```

If you anticipate that a command could generate an error, then place the statement containing that command after the try statement. If any errors come back, they'll be trapped by the on error handler that is built into this try statement construction. The handler intercepts the error message that AppleScript normally displays for us in the form of an execution error alert. At the same time, a number of labeled parameters are passed along, which your error handler can assign to variables. In most cases, you will need only two of the parameters: the error message (the text of the error message that would appear in the error alert) and the error number (one of the error IDs).

Here is a simple example of providing error handling for a missing file on a server in Scriptable Text Editor:

```
tell application "Scriptable Text Editor"
    try
        open file "HD:Documents:Master File" of machine "Server"
    on error errMsg number errNum
        if errNum = -1728 then -- can't get the file
            if (list disks) does not contain "Server" then
                display dialog "Mount "Server" and try again."
                    buttons {"Cancel"} default button "Cancel"
            else
                display dialog "I can't find the file "Master File." " &
                    " The file may have been moved or renamed."
                    buttons {"Cancel"} default button "Cancel"
```

```
        end if
    else -- some other error
        display dialog errMsg & " Call the Help Desk."
            buttons {"Cancel"} default button "Cancel"
    end if
 end try
 (* statements to continue processing if file opens *)
end tell
```

All action takes place inside a tell statement directed at Scriptable Text Editor running on the user's machine. Its first task is to open a specific file that always resides on a file server volume. Because we're dealing with an operation that requires the server being mounted, the script must take into account that the user may have forgotten to mount the server or the server is otherwise unavailable. The command to open the file is the statement that goes in the try construction. Should there be any error, execution passes immediately to the on error handler within this try construction.

In the error handler, we assign two of the parameters (the error message text and the error number) to variables, which we use in different circumstances. One of the purposes of an error handler is to help diagnose the problem and offer a solution to the user. Since we know that the kinds of errors will be file related, we can perform some additional testing about the error and provide helpful information. Therefore, our first test is to make sure the error is one we know: the –1728 error (see Table 12.1 at the end of this chapter for error numbers), which signifies AppleScript couldn't get something.

Our first suspect in this case is that the server volume isn't mounted on the users Desktop. We therefore use the list disks scripting addition to find out for sure. If the volume is missing we provide information directing the user how to correct the problem. Otherwise, we suggest that the error has to do with a missing or moved file on the server. The one final possibility is that the error is something we couldn't anticipate, in which case, we supply AppleScript's error message in full, along with information about getting help—since any other error surely indicates a more significant problem.

Pay particular attention to the fact that all display dialog commands that supply error indications to the user have a single Cancel button—not an OK button. This is quite important as far as the script execution flow is concerned. The Cancel button of any dialog (in addition to sending an error command of its own) automatically stops execution of the script if no further error trapping is performed. This is important, because it allows further script statements to appear after the try statement that won't execute once the Cancel button is clicked.

Trapping Cancel Buttons

The display dialog's Cancel button isn't the only one to stop script execution if left untouched. The Cancel button on any file or system-oriented dialog (e.g., choose file, choose folder, new file) works the same way. But there may be times when your script needs to perform some cleanup work as a result of the user clicking the Cancel button—perhaps resetting a script object property (Chapter 15) or advising a user about the consequences of the cancellation.

Your script can trap the user's click of the Cancel button to perform those cleanup tasks. Again, you use the try statement to do it. Clicking the Cancel button generates an error message—but an error message that doesn't trigger the Execution Error alert of AppleScript.

The most surefire way to trap for this is to look for an error number of –128. Here's an example of how you might use this feature:

```
tell application "Scriptable Text Editor"
    try
        open file ((choose file with prompt "Select a file:") as string)
    on error errMsg number errNum
        if errNum = -128 then
            display dialog "You've canceled, so I must stop."
                buttons {"Cancel"} default button 1
        else
            display dialog errMsg & " Call the Help Desk."
                buttons {"Cancel"} default button 1
        end if
    end try
    (* statements to continue processing if file opens *)
end tell
```

In this script's error processing, we look especially for the Cancel button's error number and provide an alert. This alert is for demonstration purposes only: there's no need to tell a user a process has canceled. Instead, the script may want to branch to another subroutine or reset property values. It all depends on what your script is supposed to be doing and what you anticipate the user's expectation would be when clicking the Cancel button of a dialog.

Purposely Generating Errors

AppleScript isn't the only culprit when it comes to generating error messages: you can do it, too. I can think of three excellent reasons why you'd want to generate errors in a script. One would be to help you in writing a script (see Chapter 13 on debugging for more). Another would be to consolidate error handling in a script. A third allows your script to bail out at any point in a script.

To make AppleScript's error alert appear, you send the error command, which has practically the same labeled parameters as the ones indicated in the on error handler syntax. Here's the error command syntax:

error [*errorString*] [number *integer*] [from *objectReference*]¬
    [partial result *resultList*]

The nice feature of this command is that you are in charge of the error message, number, and other parameters. Therefore, you can build your script's own set of error messages and numbers.

When you send the error command, AppleScript displays its Execution Error alert with whatever *errorString* you send along. AppleScript also beeps when that alert appears. With that Execution Error window title, the alert is not altogether friendly for casual users. But when the user clicks the Stop button, script execution stops.

Here's a revised version of the previous script, taking advantage of Apple-Script's error command:

```
tell application "Scriptable Text Editor"
    try
        open file "HD:Documents:Master File" of machine "Server"
    on error errMsg number errNum
        if errNum = -1728 then
            if (list disks) does not contain "HD" then
                error "Mount "HD" and try again."
            else
                error "I can't find the file "Master File." " &
                    " The file may have been moved or renamed."
            end if
        else
            error errMsg & " Call the Help Desk."
        end if
    end try
    (* statements to continue processing *)
end tell
```

For longer scripts, you can even build a separate error subroutine, which consolidates the error handling for multiple try statements scattered throughout the script. The fileLib sample script that is part of the AppleScript Run Time on the accompanying disk provides an excellent example. Several routines in the same script trap errors on their own with the try statement. Commands in the error handler redirect some values to a separate subroutine in the script that is used as a common error display routine for all other subroutines in the script.

Bailing Out of a Script

Even if you don't use a try-error construction, your script can cease execution at any point. For example, a deeply nested if-then decision may leave the user at a point where the best thing to do is provide some friendly message (with an OK button) and halt any further execution. The line immediately after the display dialog command should be:

```
error number -128
```

This is the same message that Cancel buttons in dialogs send. Unless there is a specific trap for this error in your script, AppleScript stops running the script without throwing an execution error alert into the user's face.

Error Numbers and Messages

You will always see negative numbers used for error numbers returned by AppleScript, the System, and scriptable applications. Errors from the same source generally belong to a numeric series. For example, Apple Event errors, which are the most common ones you'll run into, are in the –1700 range; AppleScript errors are in the –2700 range.

The fact that an error that filters back to your script contains both an error number and a plain language message (and sometimes more information) makes it easier to figure out what's happening even when you don't have a reference guide to every error number. While the following suggestion falls under the debugging heading, it's something you can use to help you find out what's happening in a recalcitrant script:

```
try
    (* statement(s) under test *)
on error errMsg number errNum from suspect
    display dialog errMsg & return & errNum
        buttons {"OK"} default button 1
    get suspect
end try
```

This error handler performs triple duty. A display dialog shows you both the full text of the error message, plus the error number (in case you want to build a specific trap for it in your script). Lastly, it gets (for the Result window) a reference to the object that was under consideration when the error occurred. Usually this information is also in the error message, but this extra parameter sometimes carries additional information that can't be displayed as text in a dialog. When the number of statements under test is large, these bits and pieces of information should help you locate the trouble spot more quickly.

Although the above error handler makes a complete listing of errors somewhat redundant, below are lists of the more common error numbers and their messages:

Table 12.1 Common Error Numbers and Their Messages

System Errors

–43	File *name* not found.
–108	Out of memory.
–128	User canceled.
–192	A resource wasn't found.

Table 12.1 *(continued)*

System Errors	
–904	Not enough system memory to connect to remote application.
–906	Remote application isn't running.
–915	Can't find remote machine.
–30720	Invalid date and time *string*.
Apple Event Errors	
–1700	Can't make *expression* into a *className*.
–1701	Some parameter is missing for *commandName*.
–1708	*Reference* doesn't understand the *commandName* message.
–1712	AppleEvent timed out.
–1719	Can't get *reference*. Invalid index.
–1723	Can't get *expression*. Access not allowed.
–1728	Can't get *reference*.
AppleScript Errors	
–2701	Can't divide *number* by zero.
–2753	The variable *variableName* is not defined.

Most of these errors—especially Apple Event and AppleScript errors—should be used as guides for debugging purposes and should not appear or even need to be handled in a script you hand to someone else to use.

Which leads us to the next chapter to cover debugging techniques for Apple-Script.

CHAPTER 13

Debugging Scripts

Through version 1.1, AppleScript's Script Editor doesn't include a debugger in the traditional sense of the word. If you've programmed in other languages or environments (even HyperCard 2.x), you probably have the experience of being able to step through program execution statement by statement. Other tools then allow you to examine the values of variables at each step, helping you spot where data isn't in the form you expected when you wrote the program.

Debugging is a critical part of the AppleScript script writing process, but we're restricted to using a few comparatively crude tools: the Result window, the Event log, and the display dialog scripting addition. Without the help of third-party script editors (Chapter 32) we cannot step through a script to observe variable values, but we can use the Script Editor's tools at any point to get a reading of a value in either of these venues.

The goal of this chapter is to present some suggestions about how to work through problems you encounter while assembling a script. As more scripters get into the act, additional tips and tricks are bound to spread across the scripting universe. But these should get you started.

Script Editor Setup

As you work on a script, you should have some additional Script Editor windows open to help in the process. After the script window you're writing in, the most important window is the Result window. You should open that window each time you start up Script Editor. My preference is to place it in the upper right corner of the screen.

The script window is often best placed hugging the lower right corner of the window for a couple of reasons. First, it allows you to see at least part of the Result window. Second, it leaves room to view documents opened by applications you're scripting (if any). Then, while you test your script and it modifies the contents of documents, you can keep at least a partial view on both the script and the document being modified.

You should also be prepared to open up one or two other smaller script windows in the same vicinity as the main script window. As your script grows, you will want to test isolated commands and expression evaluation away from the main script. If your script is working with a scriptable application, one of the extra script windows (which can remain untitled and unsaved unless you want to save some fragment for the next scripting session) should have a tell statement set up to accept commands directed at an application. This prevents you from having to write a tell statement to the application over and over again to check evaluation of things like object references and values returned from application-specific commands.

The third script window is one you use to test statements and expression evaluations that are not performed by a scriptable application, but by Apple-Script. You must exercise care when isolating statements or fragments like these: if they appear in your script anywhere nested within a tell statement, you should isolate them in the script window you use for testing application-specific statements: even though the application and AppleScript may have statements and objects in common (e.g., character, word, paragraph), the application may treat certain operations differently (or not support them as fully as Apple-Script).

One more window, the Event Log, isn't needed unless you're doing some debugging as described later in this chapter. I generally set it up as a shallow window at the bottom of the monitor.

As you can see, serious script writing can get pretty window-intensive. Larger monitors are certainly preferred so you can reduce the amount of overlapping or hidden windows. And perhaps the ideal scenario is a dual monitor setup, with the larger monitor devoted to the Script Editor windows.

Compile and Execution Errors

No sooner do you start writing a script than you must recognize the difference between a compile-time error and an execution error. They're quite different, and require different debugging tactics.

Unless you're writing an enormous script on a slow Macintosh, you should have Script Editor check the syntax of any completed thought. By that I mean constructions such as if-thens, repeats, try statements, nested tell statements, considering and ignoring statements—any structure that requires an end statement.

You can even check the syntax before completely filling in these kinds of balanced structures. Whenever I start such a structure, I immediately enter the end statement, as in:

```
repeat with eachItem of longList

end repeat
```

In other words, I type the opening statement, type a couple of returns, and then enter the **end** statement. I'm also likely to press the Enter key to perform a syntax check on the outer structure. By knowing that the outer frame works, I can start filling in the space inside the complex statement. I can then check the syntax every few statements if I want confirmation that I'm handling complex object references or command parameters properly.

You know when an error is a compile-time error when the Syntax Error alert appears (Figure 13.1). Script Editor highlights the word, expression, or statement that is causing the compiler grief—although the problem may be in an earlier line. When you click the Cancel button, the script will not have reformatted itself in the pretty printing.

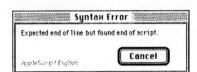

Figure 13.1 A syntax error alert.

The compiler doesn't syntax check application objects to the extent you might expect. For example, if an object property requires a list value, the compiler doesn't check for that possibility. Therefore, the syntax checker would pass setting a bounds property of a window (which usually requires a list of four integer values) to a single integer. Only when the script runs does the application protest, signaling that the data is of the wrong type (integer instead of a list value class).

Saving an uncompilable script is sometimes necessary when you are mired in a problem, but need to quit Script Editor. Trying to save a script as a compiled script (the default choice) forces Script Editor to compile the script. If compilation fails, a special alert appears telling you that you can only save as a text file (Figure 13.2). Clicking the Save button then brings you to the Save As dialog for Script Editor. The only choice available in the dialog's popup menu is Text. When you reopen the file later, any pretty printing that may have been in part of the script is gone.

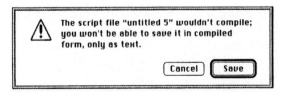

Figure 13.2 Saving an uncompilable script must be done as text only.

Of course, the only kind of errors you could get during a syntax checking moment are compile-time errors. But if you instruct a newly modified script to run, it first compiles, and then runs. You'll know which kind of error you get by looking at the error alert. An Execution Error alert is one that comes about while actually running the script (Figure 13.3). It means that the script passed the syntax check, but something about the values involved while running the script caused it to break.

Figure 13.3 An execution error alert.

Using the Result Window

As we've demonstrated hundreds of times in examples throughout this book, the Result window shows the value of the last expression to execute in a script. You can use that behavior to your benefit when you isolate a statement or short series of statements, and you're having trouble with one of the values therein. Similarly, while a script is under construction, you can find the value of the last executable expression in the script, whether it's nested in a compound statement or at the end of the script. It's not unusual to append to a script a variable whose contents you want to view in the Result window after the script runs.

While the result window shows the value of only one expression, you can gang up two or more expressions into a list, which becomes the single expression displayed in the result window. Here's an example:

```
display dialog "Enter your last name:" default answer ""
set userName to text returned of result
display dialog "Enter your ID number:" default answer ""
set userID to text returned of result
{userName, userID}
  -- result: {"Danny", "345"}
```

The Result window shows the evaluation of whatever expression is in the last statement.

Display Dialog

Prior to the advent of the Event Log in version 1.1, it was common practice to use display dialog as a debugging tool to show the contents of intermediate values. This command is somewhat risky, however, if you're not sure of the classes of values you want to examine. Remember that the display dialog requires a string as an argument about what appears in the dialog. Most numbers automatically coerce to strings, so this method works for that kind of data. But if the value you need to inspect happens to be a list, record, or data, your debugging is compounded by the fact that the display dialog command will generate an execution error of its own, complaining about the wrong class (type) of parameter.

Event Log Window

AppleScript 1.1 still doesn't have the kind of interactive debugging support that allows you to step through scripts (while they execute) and view intermediate values of variables, but Script Editor does provide another feedback mechanism for scripters: the *event log*. The event log appears in a Script Editor window that displays the messages being sent to applications outside of AppleScript (i.e., other applications and scripting additions), as well as the resulting data that comes back from a number of commands. The event log can therefore assist in run-time debugging.

To turn on the event log, choose Open Event Log from the Controls menu. The Event Log window appears initially near the bottom of your screen (Figure 13.4). Two checkboxes let you decide which items you want to appear in the window as a script runs. The settings for viewing both events and results are the most informative.

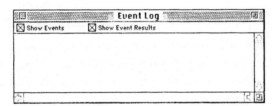

Figure 13.4 The Event Log window as it first appears.

Once the Event Log window is open, any script you run in Script Editor will have its events written to the log. Consider the following script:

```
display dialog "Enter a number between 1 and 10:" default answer ""
set userValue to (text returned of result) as real
if (userValue < 1) or (userValue > 10) then
    display dialog "That value is out of range." buttons {"OK"} default button 1
else
    display dialog "Thanks for playing." buttons {"OK"} default button 1
end if
```

Figure 13.5 shows the log created while running the script and entering a "5" in response to the prompt. The most important item to notice about the log is that only events that go outside AppleScript appear in the log. For this script, that means the Display Dialog events, which go to the scripting addition. All internal machinations, such as setting the values of variables or operations involved with conditional control structures (if-thens, repeats), do not appear in the log. If the event returns data of any kind (such as the record that comes back from the Display Dialog scripting addition command), the value appears in the log indented and signaled by an arrow (-->).

Figure 13.5 The window shows all returned values.

A primary value of the event log is that it displays the precise contents of data passed as parameters with events and the returned values. For example, if a script assembles command parameters from various sources as variables, you can use the event log to examine the true content of parameters as they are being sent to the target application. In the following script:

```
set sysPath to (path to system folder as text) & "System"
set sysModDate to (modification date of (info for alias sysPath)) as text
display dialog "Your System was last touched on " & sysModDate & "."
```

we extract the modification date of the System file, coerce it to a string, and then insert it as a piece of the parameter sent to the display dialog command. Figure 13.6 shows the event log for this script. The log shows all the transactions between the script and various scripting additions (path to, info for, display dialog). All variable setting, record-field extraction, coercion, and concatenation is performed within AppleScript, so those items don't appear in the log. But the display dialog command's parameter is shown in the log exactly as it is sent to the display dialog scripting addition.

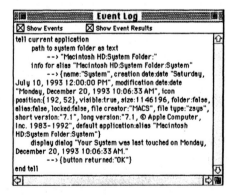

Figure 13.6 Event Log for a script that calls scripting additions.

Event Log Commands

The event log, itself, provides three commands that let you control the log during script execution: start log, stop log, log *<expression>*. Unless instructed otherwise, the event log automatically displays events and results whenever the Event Log window is open (there is no hidden event log). Therefore, if you need to view only a portion of a script in the log, you can turn the log on and off from within the script (logging slows the execution speed of a script, so for a long script, you may want to log only a small part).

Let's say in the system modification date script, above, we only want to see the display dialog command and its parameter. We can disable the event log at the beginning of the script and turn it back on when needed, as in:

```
stop log
set sysPath to (path to system folder as text) & "System"
set sysModDate to (modification date of (info for alias sysPath)) as text
start log
display dialog "Your system was last touched on " & sysModDate & "."
```

Figure 13.7 shows the resulting Event Log window. Only the display dialog event and its result are logged. You may insert stop log and start log commands in as many places as you like within a script. Importantly, the start log command has no effect if the Event Log window is not open—the command does not open the window.

Figure 13.7 Only commands that call
scripting additions or other
applications appear in the log.

The third logging command, log *<expression>*, lets you record the value of variables into the event log. The log command inserts a line into the log (in the form of a comment); the line may be anything you pass as a parameter to the log command. The log command also momentarily overrides the stop log command, so you may insert log commands inside an otherwise locked area.

In the System modification date script, above, we can use the log command to view the contents of just the sysModDate variable before sending it as part of the display dialog command:

```
stop log
set sysPath to (path to system folder as text) & "System"
set sysModDate to (modification date of (info for alias sysPath)) as text
log sysModDate
```

```
start log
display dialog "Your system was last touched on " & sysModDate & "."
```

Figure 13.8 Using the Event Log to show only the lines you want to investigate.

Figure 13.8 shows the contents of the variable value as the first line of the log, because the log is still off at that point. You are not limited to using variables as parameters to the log command. Any string expression will also do, including concatenated strings, as in

```
log "The sysModDate variable is: " & sysModDate
```

This command presents an event log entry that looks like this:

```
(*The sysModDate variable is: Friday, November 19, 1993 9:03:37 AM*)
```

Importantly, the log command displays values of other classes. Therefore, if a variable contains things like a date object or a reference to a file or alias object, the Log coerces the value to a string for review purposes. But be careful not to assume that the actual value in the script is also a string.

As one more example, we use the log command inside a repeat loop to show the values of random values:

```
stop log
set counter to 0
set randomValue to 0
repeat while randomValue ≠ 5
    set randomValue to random number 10
    set counter to counter + 1
    log "Loop " & counter & " = random value of " & randomValue
end repeat
display dialog "I got a five in " & counter & " loop(s)."
```

Figure 13.9 shows a typical event log for this script, demonstrating how we can view the values of multiple variables with a single log command. Other uses include inserting log commands at various junctures of a complex if-then construction, to log when and with what values script execution passed through those points.

Until a full debugger is built into AppleScript, the event log is about the best debugging tool that Script Editor has to offer. Third-party editors (Chapter 32) offer additional debugging tools, which serious scripters should consider.

Figure 13.9 Viewing multiple variable
values in single log statements.

Beeps

They're crude debugging tools, but in lieu of a real debugger, system beeps can help you determine if execution is taking a desired path. For example, in an if-then construction, a **beep** command placed in one of the execution pathways can tell you if execution is actually going that way: run the script and listen for the beep. Use only one beep per test, because you need to be scientific about locating bugs: test for one identifiable thing at a time.

If you have a scripting addition that plays different system sounds, you might consider calling different sounds in different spots of your script. I recommend this only to scripters with good ears.

Beeps also help in repeat loops. For example, if you suspect that a repeat loop is exiting earlier than you planned, place a **beep** command as the first line inside the loop. Run the script and count the beep sounds as they play. The number of beeps tells you how many times the loop started executing—somewhere in that last loop, a condition was met that let the loop exit.

Try Statements

As detailed in the previous chapter, the try statement and error handler is an equally valuable debugging tool. The error message conveyed to you by Apple-Script contains potentially useful information that can help you spot the problem with your script execution.

"Commenting Out" Lines

If you go on a tear, and write many lines of script without checking them along the way—it's a temptation sometimes when you're working through a complex logic sequence—you may discover that you get some compile errors early in the script. If you want to see if part of the script compiles properly or check the value of a result, you need a way to tell AppleScript to ignore one or more lines of script.

Rather than cut the following lines away, and paste them into another script window as a holding cell, it's more convenient to comment out the lines you don't want to compile or execute. If you're commenting just a line or two, the double-hyphen at the beginning of the line is a quick way to get them out of the line of fire.

But for larger segments, it's even quicker to surround the group with the (*...*) pair of comment symbols. Insert the (* (left parenthesis, asterisk) at the beginning of the line that is to be taken out; insert the *) (asterisk, right parenthesis) at the end of the group.

```
tell application "Scriptable Text Editor"
    set windowCount to count of windows
    if windowCount = 0 then
        display dialog "There are no open windows to arrange." ¬
            buttons {"Phooey"} default button 1
    else
        (*activate
        set nextWindowBounds to {1, 39, 481, 305}
        repeat with i from 1 to windowCount
            set bounds of window i to nextWindowBounds
            move window i to front
            repeat with j from 1 to 4
                set item j of nextWindowBounds to (¬
                    item j of nextWindowBounds) + 20
            end repeat
        end repeat*)
    end if
end tell
```

In the example above, I commented out the entire else statement to make sure the first part of the if-then-else statement works. As you fix bugs, you can move the starting symbol down the script, testing each line or couple of lines as needed. Some third-party editors (Chapter 32) simplify the process of commenting and uncommenting groups of statements.

A Debugging Demonstration

Let me demonstrate a typical debugging sequence, using a number of the techniques described above. The script's purpose was to work with the Bill of Rights Scriptable Text Editor document (Chapter 8), setting the Article paragraphs to bold. While this could be accomplished in a number of ways, I chose the filtered reference. I figured I could have Scriptable Text Editor bold all paragraphs whose first word was "Article."

Part 1: Quick-and-Dirty

My first attempt in a rush was the following:

```
tell application "Scriptable Text Editor"
    set style of paragraphs whose first word = "article" to bold
end tell
```

The script compiled without complaint. But an execution error said: "Scriptable Text Editor got an error: Some data was the wrong type." and the middle line of the script was highlighted.

I backed up a bit to see if perhaps I wasn't setting the style correctly. So I modified the script to set the style of just the first paragraph:

```
tell application "Scriptable Text Editor"
    set style of paragraph 1 to bold
end tell
```

This also compiled, but came up with a different execution error: "Scriptable Text Editor got an error: Can't get paragraph 1. Access not allowed." and the same center line was highlighted. What this was telling me is that the reference to paragraph 1 was not sufficient to accomplish the task. Had I written a try statement around this and asked to view the offending object, the problem would have been more readily identifiable:

```
tell application "Scriptable Text Editor"
    try
        set style of paragraph 1 to bold
    on error from whatObject
        get whatObject -- to the result window
    end try
end tell
    -- result: paragraph 1 of application "Scriptable Text Editor"
```

I had committed the sin of writing an incomplete reference. In Scriptable Text Editor, paragraphs are elements of documents, not the application. I needed to add a reference to the document to complete the reference.

So back I went:

```
tell document 1 of application "Scriptable Text Editor"
    set style of paragraph 1 to bold
end tell
```

Success! This script compiled and worked. The first paragraph of the STE document was, in fact, changed to boldface.

Part 2: Getting Granular

Time to try the filtered reference again, now that more global issues have been solved:

```
tell document 1 of application "Scriptable Text Editor"
    set style of paragraphs whose first word = "article" to bold
end tell
```

Compilation ran fine again, but not execution. This time the error read: "Scriptable Text Editor got an error: Can't set word 1 to bold."

This was puzzling. Certainly word 1 must be a valid object, I thought. I isolated a single instance of this to test the case. In a separate script window, I entered:

```
tell document 1 of application "Scriptable Text Editor"
    word 1 of paragraph 1
end tell
```

and the Result window showed, as I had hoped:

```
-- result: "Article"
```

So what do you mean when you say you can't set word 1 to bold? I attacked the problem from a different angle: let's see what the every paragraph reference looks like. Perhaps I can see why a word 1 reference doesn't work. Again, in a separate script window I entered:

```
tell document 1 of application "Scriptable Text Editor"
    paragraphs
end tell
```

The result came back as a list, which was predicted, since I was asking for multiple objects. The beginning of the data looked like this:

```
-- result: {"ARTICLE I", "Congress shall make no law respecting
an establishment of religion, or prohibiting the free exercise
thereof; or abridging the freedom of speech, or of the press; or the
right of the people peaceably to assemble, and to petition the
government for a redress of grievances.", "", "ARTICLE II", "A
well regulated militia, being necessary to the security of a free
state, the right of the people to keep and bear arms, shall not be
infringed.", "", "ARTICLE III",...}
```

Each paragraph's text is its own string item in the list, also as I would expect. Then I noticed something in the third item: an empty string item. That item is the blank line between articles. They occur predictably after each article's text body. Paragraph 3, for one, had no words in it, and yet my script was trying to do something to word 1 of it. Was that the problem?

To test that hypothesis, I tried this isolated example:

```
tell document 1 of application "Scriptable Text Editor"
    word 1 of paragraph 3
end tell
```

When I ran this script, I hit paydirt in the form of another error message: "Scriptable Text Editor got an error: Can't get word 1 of paragraph 3 of document 1. Invalid index." Similar symptom, but this time with more information (and experience) to back it up. I learned something about Scriptable Text Editor's behavior at the same time: an object with an indexed reference must exist, or STE thinks you're trying to pull a fast one (instead of just ignoring the call).

It took awhile, but I finally knew why my filtered reference wasn't going to work as is. What I had to do was come up with a way to make the script not choke on a reference to the first word.

Part 3: Rethink

I figured that an additional test was required in the filtered reference, one that checked whether the paragraph was empty. Since I knew that I could use the it variable to refer back to an object to the left of the filter reference keywords (whose and where), my first attempt was this:

```
tell document 1 of application "Scriptable Text Editor"
    set style of paragraphs whose first word = "article" ¬
    and where it ≠ "" to bold
end tell
```

Unfortunately, this didn't even compile. The compiler highlighted the word "where" and said it expected an expression. Aha! I was using multiple whose/where keywords when apparently just one is needed, as long as each operand of the Boolean And expression is, itself, an expression. I removed the "where," and created something not very grammatical, but I'd give it a try:

```
tell document 1 of application "Scriptable Text Editor"
    set style of paragraphs whose first word = "article" ¬
    and it ≠ "" to bold
end tell
```

This compiled OK, but the execution error was the same old one about being unable to set word 1 to bold. This was before I learned (and this problem helped me learn) that in expressions joined by Boolean operators (And in this case), AppleScript evaluates the left operand expression first and applies it; if the execution fails, then the right operand isn't even given a chance. That also meant that if the left operand failed gracefully, then the right wouldn't get caught trying to do something it shouldn't. Therefore, I reversed the order of the Boolean operands:

```
tell document 1 of application "Scriptable Text Editor"
    set style of paragraphs whose it ≠ "" and ¬
        first word = "article" to bold
end tell
```

Equally ungrammatical, but AppleScript–syntactically correct, this version performed the task I had hoped for. It ignored paragraphs (it) that were empty, and didn't even try to find out word 1 of such paragraphs.

Part 4: Clean It Up

The last step wasn't so much debugging as finding a more English grammatical way to express this filtered statement. I used the alternate keyword, which made all the difference in the world:

```
tell document 1 of application "Scriptable Text Editor"
    set style of paragraphs where it ≠ "" and ¬
        first word = "article" to bold
end tell
```

I could even add some parentheses to aid readability:

```
tell document 1 of application "Scriptable Text Editor"
    set style of paragraphs where (it ≠ "" and ¬
        first word = "article") to bold
end tell
```

The parentheses help a reader recognize that the arguments for the filtered reference extend across the line break and also reinforces that fact that this is a Boolean operation.

Lessons Learned

It may seem like a long road to solve a problem, but this is not atypical of the methodologies you will use when errors come up that you don't readily understand. There were a few important lessons from this demonstration:

1. Object references are number 1.
2. Expression evaluation is also number 1.
3. Things in a new application don't always work the way you expect them.
4. Isolate problems to their narrowest expressions, and check their contents.
5. Error messages don't always tell the complete story, so you have to sometimes figure out what they're really telling you.

Nothing replaces a well-integrated debugging system for a programming language, but until we have that for AppleScript, we'll have to improvise with the kind of techniques shown in this chapter.

Next Stop

In the next chapter, we up the power ante by describing AppleScript subroutines and script libraries.

CHAPTER 14

Using Subroutines, Handlers, and Script Libraries

While some programmers might say that designing and using subroutines is an art, it is truly a skill any active AppleScript scripter can develop. The more you can think of your scripts in terms of subroutines, the more likely you'll be able to reuse chunks of code from one scripting task to another. Over time, you should be able to build libraries of routines that you can either copy and paste into a script, or load directly into a script as it runs. This chapter tries to help you think in terms of subroutines and libraries.

Subroutines and Scripts

For the most part, your script starts execution at the beginning, and runs through the end in a linear, statement-by-statement fashion. Even conditionals—if-then and repeat loop constructions—are part of this linear flow if you take one giant step back and view your script as a single running entity.

But you may well encounter scripts that seem to repeat the same sequence of steps in more than one place. I'm not talking about stuff inside a repeat loop, which you intentionally repeat, but rather a few steps you need several times. For example, perhaps your script retrieves some values from a document or table in several places, and you either must check the type of value it is or must perform some kind of unit conversion (e.g., meters to feet) for your script math to work correctly.

There is no particular "strike you down from the heavens" penalty for repeating this kind of code in a script. Yes, the script will be somewhat larger in file size, because the compiler isn't designed with artificial intelligence to see the patterns you've created. But as a scripter, you have genuine intelligence, which allows you to see those patterns. Such patterns are a dead giveaway for the possibility of a subroutine.

In place of repetitive code should be a single statement that calls a subroutine. At its most basic level, such a call would look like any AppleScript command. When script execution reaches this call, execution detours to the subroutine code, which is in the same script. Execution continues through the subroutine until it finishes, at which point execution returns to the main script, resuming with the statement immediately following the subroutine call.

HyperTalk Alert

AppleScript subroutines behave very much like user-defined commands in HyperTalk. In fact, except for the way parameters are formatted, you could easily mistake one for the other. The major difference, however, is that AppleScript doesn't provide a separate mechanism that replicates a HyperTalk user-defined function. In AppleScript, any subroutine can return a value to the statement that called the subroutine.

Subroutine Concerns

Designing a subroutine entails two interrelated concerns: the constructions of the subroutine and the statement that calls the subroutine. In most cases, a script needs to pass some data to the subroutine, and the subroutine returns some information back to the script. As in the hypothetical example of a unit conversion subroutine, your script needs to send the raw value to the subroutine; the subroutine returns the converted value (or perhaps an error if the value was of the wrong type). But when you think about it, the idea of issuing a command and getting some kind of result back is no different from most AppleScript or application commands. You already know how to handle information coming back from such a call.

You can spot a subroutine in any script, because it begins with the word "on" or "to" and, like any AppleScript compound statement, ends with the word "end" (and, optionally, the name of the subroutine). If you've scripted in HyperTalk, you know this kind of construction by the name *handler*. It's the same in AppleScript. And, as in HyperTalk, a handler traps a message (command) bearing the same name.

What may seem confusing at first, however, is that a script does not execute a subroutine unless the subroutine is called. In other words, the "rule" that a script executes from top to bottom has an exception. Thus, the executing script statements and subroutines can coexist in the same script file with no problem.

Let's look at a simple subroutine that calculates the circumference of a circle of any diameter:

```
on circumference(diameter)
    if {real, integer} contains class of diameter then
        return (diameter * 3.14159)
    else
        return ""
    end if
end circumference
```

The name of this subroutine is circumference, a good choice, since its name also gives a clue about what it does. The subroutine expects to be passed a value for the diameter to be calculated. In the form shown here (there is another form as well), the parameter is labeled with a plain language variable, diameter (any variable identifier, including old standby "x" could be used). Since this subroutine may be called from any source, including user input, it checks to make sure the parameter is something that can be multiplied, before any attempt to do so. I've also combined the action of calculating the diameter (by multiplying it by pi) with the statement that sends the results back to the calling command. This return statement is what does it.

In the script that calls this subroutine would be the command name, along with a value to be calculated set in parentheses:

```
circumference(12)
    -- result: 37.69908
```

In practice, the command may be part of a get command or other statement requiring the calculated value. Here are some possibilities:

```
get circumference(12)
set circum to circumference(12)
display dialog "The circumference of 12\" is: " & circumference(12) & "\"."
```

Values passed to subroutines as parameters observe the same kind of expression evaluation behavior as you've seen with other commands. The following examples are the same:

```
circumference(12)
circumference(6+6)
circumference(x) -- where x is a variable containing 12
circumference(text returned of ¬
    (display dialog "Enter a number 12:" default answer 12)¬
    as real)
```

You see, it's just like any command. A subroutine is a way to extend the command vocabulary of a script—and it's all scripter-definable.

Subroutine Scope

One other concern not mentioned above affects subroutine calls made inside tell statements. As described at length in Chapter 10, the tell statement directs all commands nested inside it to the application (or script object) named at the head of the tell statement. The problem is that if you call a subroutine inside a tell statement, the subroutine call first goes to the application (or script) that is the default object. The application, however, won't have your subroutine's command in its dictionary, and will send back an error saying that the application doesn't understand that command.

To force AppleScript to send the command directly to the current script, rather than to the default object, the subroutine call must refer to the script. The syntax for that is to add the words of me after the call or my (or tell me to) before the call: the script tells AppleScript to send the message to the current script. Here is how this might appear in a TableServer table that contains a value to be calculated for a circumference (assuming the circumference subroutine is also located in this script file):

```
tell application "TableServer"
    make table with properties {name:"Geometry", ColCount:2}
    set name of column 1 to "Diameter"
    set name of column 2 to "Circumference"
    repeat with i from 1 to 12
        make row at table "Geometry" with data {i, circumference(i) of me}
    end repeat
    close table "Geometry" saving yes
end tell
```

This script builds a new two-column table. The left column, named Diameter, is filled with the values 1 through 12, using the index value (i) of the repeat loop. In the cell to the right of each diameter value is the circumference value (passing the same index value as a parameter). Notice that we add the words of me to direct this command to the current script. We could also have made that line to read:

```
make row at table "Geometry" with data {i, my circumference(i)}
```

which would read a little better. Had we not included this direction, we'd get the execution error message shown in Figure 14.1.

Subroutine Definitions—Two Types

AppleScript gives us two quite different ways to define a subroutine. The differences are primarily concerned with the ways a subroutine handles parameters passed to it. One version is called a *positional parameter* type; the other is the *labeled parameter* type.

Figure 14.1 Error received
without directing a subroutine
call to its own script.

Positional parameters are best for those subroutines that have only one or two parameters or as a way to begin testing a subroutine. Eventually, you should progress to the labeled parameter style, since it reads much better and offers a great deal of flexibility in the calls you make to the subroutine.

We'll start our discussion of subroutine definitions with the positional parameter type, which is the kind we used in the circumference example.

Positional Parameter Subroutines

As its name implies, the positional parameter style of subroutine places great importance on the position, or order, of parameters in a series of parameters. Parameters are placed in a comma-delimited series within a set of parentheses following the subroutine name. The formal syntax is:

on | to *subroutineName* ([*parameter*] [, *parameter*] ...)
    [global *variableID* [, *variableID*] ...]
    [local *variableID* [, *variableID*] ...]
    [*statement*] ...
end [*subroutineName*]

For now, ignore the global and local variable parts of the definition. We'll cover them in a separate section later in this chapter.

Every subroutine begins with either "on" or "to." Your choice depends solely on which one reads best. Often, the "to" preposition sounds good with a *subroutineName* parameter that is a verb. It's like saying "to do such and such, perform the enclosed statements." While all parameters are shown to be optional (and you can have plenty of them), the enclosing parentheses are not. Therefore, even if the subroutine accepts no parameters, the subroutine definition would have an empty set of parentheses, as in:

```
to doSomethingGreat( )
   (* statements that do something great *)
end doSomethingGreat
```

If you forget to enter them into Script Editor, the compiler puts them there for you.

Parameters are variable identifiers that you can use in the enclosed statements of the subroutine. We did this in the circumference subroutine:

```
on circumference(diameter)
    if {real, integer} contains class of diameter then
        return (diameter * 3.14159)
    end if
end circumference
```

where "diameter" is used twice for its value. AppleScript places no limits on the parameter variable. Your subroutine can modify its value and return that modified value, if you like.

Here is a more complex subroutine, which takes a single parameter—the best application of a positional parameter subroutine. This subroutine accepts strings, and removes any blank lines between paragraphs:

```
to stripBlanks(textIn)
    set textIn to paragraphs of textIn
    set newText to ""
    repeat with testGraph in textIn
        if (count of testGraph) > 0 then
            if newText is "" then
                set newText to newText & testGraph
            else
                set newText to newText & return & testGraph
            end if
        end if
    end repeat
    return newText
end stripBlanks
```

In this subroutine, the first thing we do is convert the incoming string to a list of paragraphs, which will assist in evaluation later down the script. We then initialize a string variable, because we'll be concatenating things to it in the repeat loop—we need something there, even if it is blank, to append a string to it.

With the incoming data now in a list, we can use the Repeat In a List form of repeat loop to see if there are any characters in each paragraph. If a paragraph shows any signs of character life, we append it to the newText variable (placing a return between paragraphs such that the last paragraph does not end with a return). Paragraphs of length zero are passed over. Finally, the newly assembled string (without blank lines) is returned to the calling statement.

This example is interesting because it can be called from within a tell statement directed at something like Scriptable Text Editor. Yet, because the subroutine is not in the tell statement, it is using AppleScript's text and item parsing, not Scriptable Text Editor's. In fact, the subroutine doesn't know or care where the source string came from or goes to, once its blank lines are stripped.

A very important point to remember about positional parameter subroutines is that when you pass multiple parameters, the values you pass must be in the same position as the receiving parameter variables in the subroutine. Here is a subroutine that expects two values:

```
on checkVolumes(startupDisk, volCount)
    set allVolumes to list disks
    if startupDisk is item 1 of allVolumes and ¬
      (count of allVolumes) = volCount then
        return true
    else
        return false
    end if
end checkVolumes
```

In this case, the first parameter is a string containing a name of a startup disk volume; the second parameter is an integer of the number of volumes expected to be on the Desktop. The calling statement would look something like this:

```
checkVolumes("HD120",2)
```

Because the parameters are positional, the "HD120" will be assigned to the startupDisk parameter at the subroutine, just as the integer 2 will be assigned to the volCount variable. If you reverse the positions of the parameters in the subroutine call, the wrong values will be assigned to the variables, and you'll have execution errors from here to next Sunday.

Equally important with positional parameters is that all parameters must be specified in a subroutine call, even if their values are to be empty. We've just seen what a valid call would be. If we wanted to pass empty values, we'd have to send empty strings or, for the integer, a zero:

```
checkVolumes("",2)
```

```
checkVolumes("HD120",0)
```

```
checkVolumes("",0)
```

None of the following would be accepted:

```
checkVolumes("HD120",)
```

```
checkVolumes(,)
```

```
checkVolumes(,2)
```

In fact, if you try to compile the first two of these last three, the compiler won't even accept them, because it expects an expression after the comma; for the last one, the compiler compiles the parameters to one, dooming the subroutine call to execution error.

Positional Parameter Subroutine Call

We've just been exploring the call that makes a subroutine jump into action. The formal syntax definition is:

subroutineName ([*parameterValue*] [, *parameterValue*] ...)

The *subroutineName* must be the same as that of the subroutine you're calling. Case isn't a factor, but spelling is. Subroutine names can be only one word.

As with the subroutine it calls, the call must have a set of parentheses, even if no parameters are being passed. All parameter values must be in a comma-delimited series within the parentheses. Remember that it is the value that gets passed, not the variable name that may be carrying that value. This means that in the subroutine, you can reassign that value to the same or different variable name for use within the subroutine (see below about variable scope of subroutines).

Labeled Parameter Subroutines

While possibly intimidating at first glance, labeled parameter subroutines are truly the way to go for all but the simplest parameter passing. They provide far greater flexibility in design and execution than positional parameter subroutines. They also offer some shortcuts when one or more parameters are Boolean values—things like switches that tell the subroutine what options may be in force each time through the script.

To get the hard part out of the way, here's the formal syntax definition for a labeled parameter subroutine:

on | to *subroutineName* [[of | in] *directParameter*] ¬
    [*subroutineParamLabel parameter*] ... ¬
    [given *labelName:parameter* [, *labelName:parameter*] ...]
    [global *variableID* [, *variableID*] ...]
    [local *variableID* [, *variableID*] ...]
    [*statement*] ...
end [*subroutineName*]

Again, we'll defer discussion about the global and local variables to a later section in this chapter.

A *directParameter* is essentially an unlabeled parameter. Like all parameters in this definition, it is a variable identifier which receives the value passed to it by the calling routine. While the of and in words are optional (and help readability), the only other restriction about the *directParameter* is that it must be the first parameter after the *subroutineName*. If you think about the display dialog command, it has a similar setup, with a direct parameter (the string that goes into the dialog message) plus a bunch of optional, labeled parameters:

    display dialog "Here's the direct parameter string."

The next parameter grouping in this definition (*subroutineParamLabel* parameter) is a bit complex at first. A *subroutineParamLabel* is one of 21 predefined labels (all in the form of prepositional phrases). You must use one per parameter and only one of each type per subroutine. Here is the list of labels:

above	for
against	from
apart from	instead of
around	into
aside from	on
at	onto
below	out of
beneath	over
beside	through
between	thru
by	under

The purpose of all these prepositional phrases is to let you make readable, meaningful commands to your subroutines. For example, this is how we could make the checkVolumes subroutine example from earlier in this chapter more understandable by utilizing two of these special parameter labels:

```
to checkVolumes against startupDisk for volCount
    set allVolumes to list disks
    if startupDisk is item 1 of allVolumes and ¬
        (count of allVolumes) = volCount then
        return true
    else
        return false
    end if
end checkVolumes
```

At the calling end, the statement must also name those labels:

```
checkVolumes against "HD120" for 2
```

As with other labeled parameters you've seen with various commands, labeled subroutine parameters can be placed in any order. It's the labels that tell AppleScript what values to assign to which parameters in the subroutine. Therefore, the call to the checkVolumes subroutine could also be:

```
checkVolumes for 2 against "HD120"
```

In both cases, the "HD120" string will be assigned to the startupDisk variable in the subroutine, because the "against" label makes that connection; similarly for the "2" integer and the volCount variable attached to the "for" label. Because each subroutine's parameters and their interrelationships present a unique set, you can use these labels to make those relationships clearer to the user than just a bland list of values (as with positional parameters).

But if those predefined labels aren't sufficient for your needs, you can add your own labels. The "given" keyword must precede one or more custom labels and their variable identifiers. Here's yet another version of the checkVolumes subroutine, this time demonstrating how a custom parameter label may be best of all for this situation:

```
to checkVolumes against startupDisk given volumeCount:volCount
    set allVolumes to list disks
    if startupDisk is item 1 of allVolumes and ¬
        (count of allVolumes) = volCount then
            return true
    else
        return false
    end if
end checkVolumes
```

This definition specifies a custom label, volumeCount, but the same volCount variable identifier as the other forms. The call to this style would look like this:

```
checkVolumes against "DannyBook" given volumeCount:2
```

Definitions and calls allow for multiple custom labels after the given, each one separated by a comma. For example:

```
to checkVolumes given disk:startupDisk, volumeCount:volCount
    ...
end checkVolumes
```

which would be called by:

```
checkVolumes given disk:"HD120", volumeCount:2
```

As you can see, it's possible to create any mixture of direct, predefined labeled, and custom labeled parameters in a subroutine definition. Use whatever makes the most grammatical sense to you. Don't be afraid to use something awkward while under construction and then change it later on. Just be sure to make the same change to the statement that calls the subroutine.

Caution: If you are creating a labeled parameter subroutine that has only one parameter, AppleScript requires that the preposition for that single parameter be anything except of. This is due to the ambiguity caused by object containment syntax, which makes liberal use of this preposition.

Labeled Parameter Subroutine Call

We've already seen a variety of labeled parameter subroutine calls in the previous section. But such calls have further powers to simplify the passing of parameters consisting of Boolean values. To understand this, let's look at the formal definition of these calls:

```
subroutineName [ [ of | in ] directParameter ] ¬
    [ subroutineParamLabel parameterValue ] ... ¬
    [ given labelName:parameter [, labelName:parameter ] ... ] ¬
    [ with labelForTrueParam ¬
    [, labelForTrueParam, ... and labelForTrueParam ] ] ¬
    [ without labelForFalseParam ¬
    [, labelForFalseParam , ... and labelForFalseParam ] ]
```

Everything is the same through the given types of parameters. That means that this form adheres to the same predefined labels as well as allowing custom labels to match the ones in the subroutine definition.

But if the subroutine has one or more labeled parameters whose values are Booleans (TRUE or FALSE), then you can pass those Boolean values by simply listing the parameter labels in the with and without clauses. Any label following the with preposition is passed a TRUE value from the calling statement; any label following the without preposition is passed a FALSE value.

As an example, I've created a subroutine that checks for the class of any value. To take data into the subroutine, it has one direct parameter (the value to be tested) and four labeled parameters, each representing a class. The subroutine uses these labeled parameters as switches to know which test(s) to perform on the value being passed in. Here is the subroutine:

```
on classCheck of valueIn given stringClass:testString, ¬
    numberClasses:testNumbers, listClass:testList, ¬
    recordClass:testRecord

    if testString then
        set stringResult to (class of valueIn is string)
    else
        set stringResult to true
    end if

    if testNumbers then
        set numbersResult to ({real, integer} contains class of valueIn)
    else
        set numbersResult to true
    end if

    if testList then
        set listResult to (class of valueIn is list)
    else
        set listResult to true
    end if

    if testRecord then
        set recordResult to (class of valueIn is record)
    else
        set recordResult to true
    end if

    return stringResult and numbersResult and listResult ¬
        and recordResult
end classCheck
```

As the subroutine runs, it performs a test of the value against any of the four classes whose labeled parameter comes in as TRUE. Each test, itself, returns a false value only if the test is requested and it fails. The final Boolean expression (in the return statement) calculates the combined Boolean values of all four possible tests; if any one fails, a FALSE value returns to the calling statement.

The real demonstration point of this subroutine is the way it's called. The long-winded way would be something like this:

```
classCheck of 100 given stringClass:true, ¬
    numberClasses:true, listClass:false, recordClass:false
```

But we can pass those TRUEs and FALSEs by incorporating them into with and without clauses:

```
classCheck of 100 with stringClass and numberClasses ¬
    without listClass and recordClass
```

The subroutine assigns TRUE to testString and testNumbers, while assigning FALSE to testList and testRecord. It's a kind of shorthand in the calling statement that addresses just the labels. While the form makes the statement appear in more natural language, it does force the script reader to mentally perform the assignation.

One final point about labeled subroutine calls: while the order of the parameters (except for the direct parameter) can be willy-nilly, every parameter defined in the subroutine must be in the call as well. Failure to have a label-for-label match results in an execution error.

Subroutine Variables

In the formal definitions for both types of subroutines, you saw references to parameters labeled as global and local variables. The reason they are mentioned in subroutine definitions is that variable behavior becomes somewhat skewed by subroutines.

Until now, we were comfortable with the fact that a local variable defined anywhere in a script made that variable available to any statement below it in the script. As it turns out, subroutines are like little protected enclaves within a script: unless directed otherwise, a variable defined outside a subroutine is not alive inside the subroutine; conversely, any variable defined in a subroutine dies after the subroutine executes. Let's look at some examples to explain:

First, we'll define a variable as a string outside a subroutine and assign an integer to a variable with the same name inside the subroutine:

```
set myValue to "Gumby"
on varTest( )
    set myValue to 25
    return myValue
end varTest
```

```
varTest( )
  -- result: 25
myValue
  -- result: "Gumby"
```

We reused a variable name inside a subroutine. If it weren't for the subroutine, reassigning the variable to an integer would have simply replaced the string with the integer. But since the integer assignation was inside the subroutine, the outer variable goes untouched.

To make the same variable apply to both inside and outside the subroutine, we use the **global** statement inside the subroutine:

```
set myValue to "Gumby"
on varTest( )
  global myValue
  set myValue to 25
  return myValue
end varTest
varTest( )
  -- result: 25
myValue
  -- result: 25
```

The **global** statement tells the subroutine to use the myValue variable from outside (if it's there). Therefore, in this construction, the **set** command actually replaces the string with the integer. After the subroutine ends, the global-ness of the variable persists: there is only one myValue variable in this entire script. If the variable had not been declared prior to the subroutine, it would have been initialized within the subroutine and its existence and value would extend after the subroutine.

As you saw, there was no need in the first example to declare a local variable within the subroutine: its default behavior made any new variable a local variable. But that changes when a script property has been defined in the same script. A script property is like an object's property: a value that is stored with the script object (see Chapter 15 for more about script objects and their properties). The point is, however, that a script property is very global in scope by its nature. For example:

```
property myValue:"Gumby"
on varTest( )
  set myValue to 25
  return myValue
end varTest
varTest( )
  -- result: 25
myValue
  -- result: 25
```

In other words, the global-ness of a property pervades even subroutines. Here, the **set** command is actually adjusting the value of the script property, changing it from a string to an integer.

To prevent this while using the same variable identifier as a property (probably not a good idea, anyway), you must declare a local variable in the subroutine:

```
property myValue:"Gumby"
on varTest( )
   local myValue
   set myValue to 25
   return myValue
end varTest
varTest( )
   -- result: 25
myValue
   -- result: "Gumby"
```

The local declaration keeps the property of the same name out of the subroutine altogether. Once the subroutine ends, the local variable and its value are discarded, leaving the field open for the property to reign once again.

Recursion

AppleScript allows subroutines to call themselves: a process known as *recursion*. The legendary factorial calculation offers a good example:

```
on factorial(n)
   if n > 0 then
      return n * (factorial(n - 1))
   else
      return 1
   end if
end factorial
```

As AppleScript performs this subroutine round and round, it essentially nests the intermediate values for evaluation after the last time through. Be sure to test recursive subroutines carefully, because it is easy to overpower the limits of memory (specifically, the stack that tracks all the pending operations) if you're not careful. In Chapter 20, we apply recursion to another real-world application that could give you some scripting ideas.

Turning Subroutines into Libraries

Everything we've said about subroutines up to this point implied that subroutines exist in the same scripts as the statements that call them. There's nothing wrong with this, except that once you've defined some generic subroutines, there are more efficient ways to get their powers into multiple scripts without copying and pasting them into those scripts. You can make a subroutine (or better yet, a collection of related subroutines) into a *script library*.

A script library is nothing more than a subroutine that has been saved as a compiled script (either editable or run-only). To bring the power of a script library into another script, you use the load script command. Once loaded, your script talks to the library as if it were another application (via a tell statement) and as if its handlers were commands belonging to that application.

In the Handbook Script:Chapter 14 folder is a library of subroutines for performing some paragraph sorting and blank line stripping from big blocks of text. The four subroutines are:

    on sortLines of textIn given sortOrder:s

sorts lines (paragraphs) of text in either "ascending" or "descending" order.

    to stripBlanks(textIn)

strips away blank lines between paragraphs. It can be used by itself, and is called by sortLines in its work.

    on classCheck of valueIn given stringClass:testString, ¬
        numberClasses:testNumbers, listClass:testList, ¬
        recordClass:testRecord

tests a value against a series of classes specified as arguments—called by other routines in the library.

    on listToParagraph of newLines given sortOrder:s

reconverts lists of paragraphs to return-delimited text, according to "ascending" or "descending" sorting order—called by other routines in the library.

This library is saved as "paragraphLib." Most libraries have "Lib" (rhymes with jibe) at the ends of their file names to help us distinguish a library from an ordinary script.

A library consists strictly of subroutines, and perhaps some properties. There is no other executing script in a library, because it doesn't run like a script. Other scripts call the subroutines into action (which may call other subroutines in the library), but there are no other freestanding statements to execute.

Storing Libraries

Since a script must load a library by its pathname, things can get pretty tricky if you plan to hand over the script and library to other users. Your script can't possibly know the eventual pathname to files. While your script could ask the user the first time (and store the path as a property), there is another method that works correctly the first time: insist that the library file be stored in the Scripting Additions folder inside the Extensions folder. Your library will share the company of any scripting additions on that user's Macintosh. In fact, copy paragraphLib from the Handbook Scripts:Chapter 14 folder to the Scripting Additions folder now to experiment with the following scripts.

The benefit here is that your script can use the **path to** command to determine the path to the Extensions folder. It's a simple task to append the rest of the path to your library. For example, to get the path to paragraphLib in Scripting Additions, use the following statements:

```
get (path to extensions as string) & ¬
   "Scripting Additions:paragraphLib"
set graphLib to load script file result
```

or combine the two statements as:

```
set graphLib to load script file ((path to extensions as string) & ¬
   "Scripting Additions:paragraphLib")
```

Loading the script object assigns the script object to the variable graph Lib. Your script can now grab some text and have the library sort it. Try it yourself with the script below. First load a list of months, numbers, whatever into the frontmost document of Scriptable Text Editor. Then enter and run the following script:

```
get (path to extensions as string) & ¬
   "Scripting Additions:paragraphLib"
set graphLib to load script file result
set theText to text of ¬
   (document 1 of application "Scriptable Text Editor")
tell graphLib
   get sortLines of theText given sortOrder:"ascending"
end tell
   -- result: (sorted list)
```

By loading that script as a script object, we've put the power of the dozens of lines of code into this script without the enormous overhead those lines would add to this script. In the tell statement, we talk to the script object and send it a command as if it were a full-fledged application. In fact, if the library had properties, we could get and set its properties just as we do for an application object.

Open the paragraphLib script with Script Editor, and study it for the many examples of subroutine definitions and calls. You'll find a smorgasbord of subroutine and parameter styles, each one tailored to the kind of data and calls it expects.

Handlers in Attachable Applications

Although we don't have much to play with in the AppleScript-attachable arena just yet, AppleScript does have a mechanism that allows you to write handlers that get stored in an application's object. For example, let's say that an application allowed you to attach a script to a document object (the program would have a script editor for writing script that belong to that object). You could write handlers for that object that respond to commands that object gets from other scripts (perhaps from a script you wrote with Script Editor, or a script that came from an entirely different application).

The formal definition of this kind of handler is nearly identical to the labeled parameter subroutine, with the exception of the predefined labels:

```
on | to commandName [ [ of ] directParameter ] ¬
    [ [ given ] paramLabel: parameter [, paramLabel: parameter ] ... ]
    [ global variableID [, variableID ] ... ]
    [ local variableID [, variableID ] ... ]
    [ statement ] ...
end [ commandName ]
```

Command handlers can be written to respond not only to user-defined commands, but also to the application's commands. In other words, if you want the object to perform some special processing in lieu of a regular command, the command handler would trap the command before it reaches the application dictionary.

If this syntax, and that of the labeled parameter subroutine looks familiar from an earlier chapter, you're correct. The error handler in a try statement is merely a predefined variation of this labeled parameter subroutine. In the error handler's case, the labels are predefined. You can assign global and local variables in exactly the same way as you may need for any subroutine. The same rules apply about the lack of variable persistence into and out of an error handler as for any subroutine.

Next Stop

In the next chapter, we take the final leap, creating script objects that can become droplet applications and agents.

CHAPTER 15

Script Properties, Objects, and Agents

This chapter assumes that you have a good grasp of all that has come before. If this book were used in an AppleScript classroom course, this chapter would be part of the advanced topics section. While the material may be complex, the rewards for working your way through can be high. We start with a detailed look at script properties, which some might regard as super variables. Then we look at script objects, which build on your exposure to subroutines. Finally, we see how we can make script objects into agents—little helpers running in the background for us to alert us to things happening behind the scenes.

Script Properties

While the subject of script properties could have been covered in Chapter 9's discussion of variables, I feel it makes more sense here, because properties are even more useful in script objects, which we'll cover later. Properties are also useful in subroutines.

Application objects, as we saw earlier, have properties, whose values we can view (and sometimes modify). These were the properties like bounds of a window or the value of a cell. Pretty straightforward AppleScript stuff.

But you can also assign one or more properties to a script. The formal syntax for doing this is:

property | prop *propertyLabel: initialValue*

PropertyLabel is the name for the property (just like "bounds" is the name of one window property), whereas *initialValue* is the value the script assigns to the property when the script is initialized (more on that in a moment). This property statement can go anywhere in a script, and the property label and its value may be accessed in any statement after this declaration.

With one exception (discussed later), property declarations are made at the outermost level of a script (i.e., not nested in any tell statement or subroutine). In this form, a property behaves like an ultra-global variable. We saw evidence of this in the last chapter, where a global property's value was available and modifiable inside even the normally exclusive domain of the subroutine. Recall this example:

```
property myValue:"Gumby"
on varTest( )
    set myValue to 25
    return myValue
end varTest
varTest( )
    -- result: 25
myValue
    -- result: 25
```

While the property, myValue, was initially set to a string value, it was modified within the subroutine and stayed that way after the subroutine ended.

Property "Persistence" in Compiled Scripts

Notice that I said a property's initial value is assigned to a property when the script containing the declaration initializes. That implies that the value can change, which it can. But how long the property maintains its modified value, and under what circumstances the value persists from session to session is a squirrely subject. Let's take it one step at a time.

1. Start by creating a demonstration script that has a property named "beanCount," whose goal is to maintain a count of the number of times the script runs:

```
property beanCount:0
set beanCount to beanCount + 1
display dialog "Since the last initialization, this script has run " & ¬
    beanCount & " time(s)."
```

When you first compile this script, it sets the value of beanCount to zero. The first time you run the script, the value of beanCount increases by 1, and shows itself that way in the dialog. Click the Run button again, and the value increases to 2.

2. Add a blank line to the end of the script and click the Check Syntax button to re-compile the script. Run the script, and you see the value has reset itself. This is good in a way, since it means each time you modify a script, it resets property values, so you can begin testing from the same point each time.

3. Run the script until the dialog says you've run it 5 times.

4. Save the script as a compiled script, with the name "Bean Counter" *Saving the script saves the current value of the property with it.*

5. Close the script window.

6. Re-open the Bean Counter script in Script Editor.

7. Do not make any changes to the script, but click the Run button. The message indicates with its new count of 6 that the script did, in fact, remember its last setting when it was saved.

8. Run the script a few more times until the counter reaches 10.

   Now comes the tricky, not particularly intuitive, part. Notice that the File menu does not offer a Save option. Does that mean that the script is automatically saving the value of the accesses property for us behind the scenes? There's only one way to find out.

9. Close the script window. There is no prompt for saving changes.

10. Reopen the Bean Counter script, and, without making any changes to the script, run it. Lo and behold, the changes made in our previous excurions were not saved. The value of beanCount was the same as when we saved the script originally. The only way to update the value in the saved version of the file would be to use the Save As file menu option, and overwrite the previous version.

This example was with a script that you open and run in Script Editor. When you save a script as an application, things get more interesting (and useful).

Property "Persistence" in Script Applications

We'll now see that when a script is turned into an application, properties do persist from one running to the next, even when the script application quits in between. We may as well use the script we've been working with, since it demonstrates the point.

1. Add a blank line to the end of the Bean Counter script, and re-compile. This resets the property to zero.

2. Choose Save As from the File menu, but this time, select Application as the type. Overwrite the previous compiled version.

3. Close the Bean Counter script window in Script Editor.

4. Switch to the Finder, and locate the Bean Counter application you just created.

5. Double-click the app. The dialog tells you this is the first time it's running since initialization. When you click OK or Cancel, the script ends, and the appliation quits.

6. Double-click the app again. The dialog now reveals that the beanCounter property has, in fact, incremented by one, and is stored with the application when it closes.

7. Repeat Step 6 as often as you like. The property value indeed persists.

If you re-open the script in Script Editor, you'll find that the beanCounter property value is whatever it was at the last running. Even though the script is saved as an application, running it from Script Editor won't make the property persist: it will increment when you run it in Script Editor, but go back to its last saved value when you close the script.

These are valuable lessons, because the persistence of properties is a tricky concept. Another method of achieving data persistence is to save property data in an application document, and reload the data from the document when running the script. TableServer, because it is windowless and nicely structured for tabular data, could be a useful tool for this method.

We'll come back to properties again once we cover the basics of script objects.

Script Objects

You aren't limited to using objects defined in applications or AppleScript, itself. You can create your own objects—objects whose names, properties, and execution behaviors are entirely under your control. A script object may be part of a larger script or a script unto itself.

Unless you've worked with object-oriented systems before, the concept of script objects may be hard to grasp at first. Often, the hard part is making the jump from a series of AppleScript statements to a tangible object. In truth, script objects are artificial entities. In some ways they remind me of make-believe friends children concoct in their imaginations.

Let's create one of these imaginary friends. He's named Mac. His behavior is limited to responding to one command: telling us the version of System software running on the machine. Mac is smart enough to take in the name of the person who is asking, and make that name part of the response. Mac also has a property, which tracks the name of the last person to ask for System software version information. Here is the definition of Mac as a script object:

```
script Mac
    property lastPerson : ""
    to saySystemVersion to someone
        set lastPerson to someone
        get short version of (¬
            info for file (((path to system folder) as string) & "System"))
        return someone & ", I am currently running System " & result & "."
    end saySystemVersion
end script
```

To get Mac to respond, we must send a command it understands (saySystem-Version) with whatever parameter it expects (someone's name). In the same script, for instance, we can issue this command:

```
tell Mac to saySystemVersion to "Patrick"
    -- result: "Patrick, I am currently running System 7.1."
```

Notice the use of the tell statement. This is just like directing a command to an application. We can use the syntax talking directly to the script object by name when the object and calling statement are in the same script (we'll see what differences are required if the script object is in a separate script object file later).

Mac also has the lastPerson property, just like the one we used in an earlier example. To access this property, we use the same kind of reference as a property of an application object:

```
get lastPerson of Mac
    -- result: "Patrick" (after running the above call)
```

We can then combine accesses to commands and properties in a script that talks to Mac:

```
display dialog "Please enter your name:" default answer ""
if text returned of result ≠ "" then
    set someone to text returned of result
    if lastPerson of Mac = someone then
        display dialog "What, you again?"
    else
        tell Mac to saySystemVersion to someone
        display dialog result
    end if
end if
```

If you want this script object to always start out with the lastPerson property set to empty, you must save it after compiling the script. Saving after running the script, will save the current value of lastPerson (as we demonstrated earlier). As long as the script stays open, the lastPerson property will continue to change with each new name applied to the script. When you close the script, the property reverts back to its saved (empty) state. Just to reinforce a point, however, if you save the script *as an application*, and run it from the Finder, the property will remember the last name even after the script application quits.

The formal syntax description of a script object is as follows:

```
script [ scriptObjectVariable ]
    [ property | prop propertyLabel: initialValue ] ...
    [ handlerDefinition ] ...
    [ statement ] ...
end [ script ]
```

The ellipsis (...) after each type of placeholder indicates that you can define any number of those kinds of items. Therefore, you can have multiple properties and/or handler definitions in a script object. In the example about Mac, we've seen how all these elements work, except for the statement placeholder. For that, we should talk more about running script objects.

Running Script Objects

To best understand the variety of responses to the Run Script command, start with the following script object, saved as a compiled script named "Mac":

```
script Mac
   property lastPerson : ""
   to saySystemVersion to someone
      set lastPerson to someone
      get short version of (¬
         info for file (((path to system folder) as string) & "System"))
      return someone & ", I am currently running System " & result & "."
   end saySystemVersion
   display dialog "Mac just ran." -- added this line for demonstration
end script

display dialog "Please enter your name:" default answer ""
if text returned of result ≠ "" then
   set someone to text returned of result
   if lastPerson of Mac = someone then
      display dialog "What, you again?"
   else
      tell Mac to saySystemVersion to someone
      display dialog result
   end if
end if
```

When you run this script manually in Script Editor, AppleScript is doing the same as sending the Run command to this script. A script's default behavior in such cases is to execute every executable line in the script. In this case, nothing in the upper script object definition runs until it is called by the statements in the lower group. Since only the saySystemVersion handler is called, the freestanding statement (display dialog "Mac just ran.") does not execute when the Run command is sent to the script as a whole.

Now open a new, small script window, and enter the following script, which sends the Run command to the script file:

```
run script file "Mac"
```

When you run this script, it sends a single Run command to the script file (which can be open or closed). This is just like clicking the Run button for the Mac script in Script Editor.

If you run this little script multiple times, you'll notice something else that proves a point about properties: the value of the lastPerson property doesn't change. That's because each run command initializes the script object—an action that automatically resets properties defined in a compiled script. Of course, you may design a script that just performs something on its own, and you don't have to worry about updating properties. In such a case, this run script construction suits you fine.

Load and Run

Now modify the small script to perform the following:

```
repeat 3 times
    run script file "Mac"
end repeat
```

Even if you enter the same name each of the three times, Mac doesn't remember the last person's name, because the run script command keeps initializing the object each time through the repeat loop. If, however, you want to let the script run while keeping the lastPerson variable up to date, you must first load the script into a variable, and then work with the script object:

```
set MacScript to load script file "mac"
repeat 3 times
    run MacScript
end repeat
```

When you run this script and enter the same name each time, you get the "What, you again?" alert after the second attempt, because the run command (instead of a run script command) is sent repeatedly to an open script object. Only when you run this smaller script again, which re-loads a copy of the saved Mac script object, does the lastPerson value start from empty again.

In case you want the script object to remember the last value of the property, you can summon the powers of the store script scripting addition. The command, however, requires a pathname to the stored file, so you might have to modify your script a bit to get that information. Here's one way to do it:

```
set scriptPath to choose file "Select the "Mac" script file:" ¬
    of type "osas"
set MacScript to load script file (scriptPath as string)
repeat 3 times
    run MacScript
end repeat
store script MacScript in scriptPath replacing yes
```

The last command stores the current state of the script object as modified during the repeat loop, replacing the original version that contained the empty property.

Now, what about the statement in the Mac script object definition that's supposed to display a dialog that says it's running? This line (and any other statements not part of a handler definition within the script object) executes only when the object—not the script—receives a run command. Therefore, to see that line execute, we'd have to modify our calling script as follows:

```
set MacScript to load script file "mac"
tell Mac of MacScript to run
```

In other words, we first load a copy of the entire script into a variable (MacScript), and then direct the run command to the script object, Mac. None of the handlers in Mac execute, because they haven't been called. Nor do the statements below the script object execute, because the run command was directed to the Mac object, not the entire script.

If your head is still swimming, re-read this section. It does make sense in light of AppleScript's manner of directing commands to specific objects.

Advanced Object-Oriented Techniques

AppleScript provides facilities for inheritance and delegation among script objects. Using some of the script objects in earlier examples, we'll explore these concepts.

Inheritance

A script object may inherit the properties and commands of another script by establishing a special *parent* property. A parent property, whose formal syntax is:

```
property | prop parent: scriptObjectVariable
```

tells AppleScript that a script object shares everything that the parent has. A script object containing a parent property is called a *child*. A child can have only one parent, whereas a parent may have any number of children (the parent has no designation in its script signifying that it is a parent—all the work stems from the child's declaration of a parent property).

If we start with our Mac script object:

```
script Mac
    property lastPerson : ""
    to saySystemVersion to someone
        set lastPerson to someone
        get short version of (¬
            info for file (((path to system folder) as string) & "System"))
        return someone & ", I am currently running System " & result & "."
    end saySystemVersion
    display dialog "Mac just ran."
end script
```

we can create another object that is a child of Mac. That script object we'll call "computer," and looks like this:

```
script computer
    property parent: Mac
end script
```

Any command or property request we send to the computer object is carried out by the Mac object. It's as if the computer object were:

```
script computer
    property lastPerson : ""
    to saySystemVersion to someone
        set lastPerson to someone
        get short version of (¬
            info for file (((path to system folder) as string) & "System"))
        return someone & ", I am currently running System " & result & "."
    end saySystemVersion
    display dialog "Mac just ran."
end script
```

Therefore, if the calling statement reads:

```
tell computer to saySystemVersion to "Joe"
    -- result: "Joe, I am currently running System 7.1."
```

the reply comes from the handler in Mac, because computer hands it off to its parent.

The advantage to this mechanism is that the computer object can now have some of its own properties and handlers in addition to those of the Mac object, but computer doesn't have to replicate any of Mac's items. By declaring the parent property, the child has added all that functionality to itself.

It also means that if the child needs a slight variation of a handler or property that is contained in the parent, the child's script can intercept the command before it reaches the parent. For example:

```
script computer
    property parent : Mac
    to saySystemVersion to someone
        get short version of (¬
            info for file (((path to system folder) as string) & "System"))
        return "Hey, bub, it's " & result & "."
    end saySystemVersion
    display dialog "Mac just ran."
end script
```

With this version, if we say:

```
tell computer to saySystemVersion to "Joe"
    -- result: "Hey, bub, 7.1."
```

the command is caught by the handler in computer.

Delegation

A child can not only intercept commands that would otherwise make their way to the parent, but the child can trap a command under some circumstances and let it pass to the parent under others. For this to work, the child's version of the handler must contain a **continue** statement.

The formal defintion of the continue statement is:

continue *commandName parameterList*

where the parameters are the command and parameters required by that command's handler in the parent. All parameters must be in the same form as the handler (i.e., matching positional parameters or labeled parameters as the case may be). We can look at an example from the same Mac/computer parent/child relationship from above. In this case, we modify the child so that it delegates the saySystemVersion command to the parent if the name of the user is Mike (after all, it could be Mike Spindler, and we want the script objects to be polite); anyone else gets the rude version from the child:

```
script computer
    property parent : Mac
    to saySystemVersion to someone
        if {"Mike", "Michael"} contains someone then
            continue saySystemVersion to someone
        else
            get short version of (¬
                info for file (((path to system folder) as string) & "System"))
            return "Hey, bub, it's " & result & "."
        end if
    end saySystemVersion
    display dialog "Mac just ran."
end script
```

The call then goes out:

```
tell computer to saySystemVersion to "Joe"
    -- result: "Hey, bub, 7.1."
```

or

```
tell computer to saySystemVersion to "Mike"
    -- result: "Mike,I am currently running System 7.1."
```

Notice that we didn't have to make any changes to the parent. It's all in the child. We can even be more subversive by slightly altering the parameters delegated to the parent:

```
script computer
    property parent : Mac
    to saySystemVersion to someone
        if {"Mike", "Michael"} contains someone then
            continue saySystemVersion to "Michael"
        else
            get short version of (¬
                info for file (((path to system folder) as string) & "System"))
            return "Hey, bub, it's " & result & "."
        end if
    end saySystemVersion
    display dialog "Mac just ran."
end script
```

Instead of continuing with either "Mike" or "Michael," we pass along only "Michael," no matter which version is entered in the call. Therefore:

```
tell computer to saySystemVersion to "Mike"
    -- result: "Michael,I am currently running System 7.1."
```

Creating Droplets

A droplet is an informal term for any application that runs when you drag and drop one or more Finder items (files and folders) onto the application's own icon. In some ways, a droplet behaves like an agent (described more fully below), because by dropping an item onto you script application, you essentially hand off control to the application, and let it do whatever it is programmed to do.

What makes a script application (i.e., a script saved as an application) a droplet is an **on open** handler in the script. The act of dropping a Finder item on a droplet causes the Macintosh to send an open message to the droplet. It is encumbant upon your application to have an **on open** handler that traps the open message.

When Script Editor saves a script as an application, the icon it assigns to the script is shown in Figure 15.1a. But if Script Editor detects an **on open** handler in the script, it assigns a different icon, as shown in Figure 15.1b. The difference is in the down arrow on the icon, indicating that the application is designed as a droplet. Of course, it's up to your script to do something with the information that comes with the open message (a list of files or folders).

(a)   (b)

Figure 15.1 Regular script application
icon (a) and droplet icon (b).

To demonstrate, below is the script listing for the application Show Creator & Type. The script application file is in the Handbook Scripts:Chapter 15 folder. This application lets you drag any number of files or folders to it, and it displays back (one at a time) the four-character creator and file type signatures that the Finder uses. This can be a helpful tool for scripters who need to find out the file type for a choose file dialog parameter under construction.

Here's the script:

```
-- dropping a file(s) on a script application
-- sends an open command along with a list
-- of aliases for the dragged file(s). This
-- handler executes upon the drop.
on open fileList
    -- work through each file dragged with repeat in list form
    repeat with oneFile in fileList
        -- info for command in file commands addition
        set allInfo to info for oneFile
        -- set Boolean
        set isFolder to allInfo's folder
        -- call subroutine to extract name of file or folder
        set fileName to nameFromPath of (oneFile as string) ¬
        given isFolder:isFolder
        if fileName is not "" then
            -- assemble and display appropriate messages
            if isFolder then
                display dialog """ & fileName & "" is a folder." ¬
                    buttons {"Okeedokee"} default button 1
            else
                set details to return & "Creator: " & ¬
                    allInfo's file creator & return & ¬
                    "File Type: " & allInfo's file type
                display dialog "Info for "" & fileName & "":" & details ¬
                    buttons {"Thanks"} default button 1
            end if
        end if
    end repeat
end open

-- subroutine to extract file or folder name
-- from a complete path name. Uses isFolder
-- labeled parameter and variable as Boolean switch.
on nameFromPath of thePath given isFolder:isFolder
    if thePath = "" then return ""
    -- save current settings
    set oldDelims to AppleScript's text item delimiters
    -- we need colons to take apart the path
```

```
        set AppleScript's text item delimiters to ":"
        if isFolder then
            -- don't want the last colon
            set fileName to text item -2 of thePath
        else
            -- no colon text item to worry about
            set fileName to text item -1 of thePath
        end if
        -- restore prior settings
        set AppleScript's text item delimiters to oldDelims
        return fileName
    end nameFromPath
```

The script consists of an **on open** handler, where most of the action is, plus a subroutine, which extracts the file or folder name from each pathname supplied to the on open handler. Notice that the parameters that went with the open message is a list of alias references. The first thing we do is establish a repeat loop to work through each item in the list (in case there are multiple items). Then we use the info for command (scripting addition) to separate the folders from the files. We need this information to properly extract the name of the item (we have to parse differently for paths to folders, which contain a final colon). At the same time, the command returns the creator and file type in separate records, which we save for later assembly in the report back to the user. Before displaying the results, we assemble it into a multiple-lined string, which we then pass to display dialog. A sample readout of an Excel 4.0 file appears in Figure 15.2.

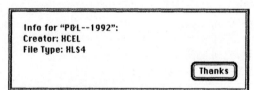

Info for "P&L--1992":
Creator: HCEL
File Type: HLS4
[Thanks]

Figure 15.2 Example dialog produced by
Show Creator & Type droplet.

We save this script as an application. Checking the "Never Show Startup Screen" checkbox is optional in the Save dialog, because droplets don't show splash boxes when they run by having something dropped on them. If you double-click the application, the splash box appears, unless you had checked that checkbox.

To run the application, simply drag any Finder object to the droplet icon. The application zooms open like any application, showing its name in the menubar briefly. After a few seconds, a dialog displays the findings of the open handler. When you click the dialog's button, the application then quits.

You can assign properties to these applications, and their values (if updated in the course of running) will be saved to the application. For example, you could record behind the scenes how many times a particular shared script application was used on the network by creating a counter property that increments each time the script opens (put the incrementer into the open handler).

Script applications are powerful uses for AppleScript. Consult the Sample Scripts folder from the AppleScript Run Time. It contains a number of other examples of script applications and droplets, some of which invoke the powers of the finderLib library to perform tasks such as file reconciliation between two folders.

Agents

The idea of software agents, while not new, hasn't seen much in the way of practical applications as yet. One vision, presented in John Sculley's notion of a Knowledge Navigator box, is portrayed by a computer-generated face and voice, which (who?) performs all kinds of tasks for the computer's owner: taking phone messages; passing along messages to other people; digging up research data and analyzing it for the human.

A lot of that is still out in the future, but the concept of agents is practicable today. AppleScript is one tool that lets everyday Mac users (well, at least those who can grasp AppleScript) create special-purpose agents who work in the background for the user. In the Sample Scripts folder of the Run Time are some examples of agents that monitor changes to a folder, alerting you if something was added (perhaps for a shared folder on a network, and you're awaiting delivery of a file from a co-worker).

Reminder Alarm Agent

To demonstrate how to create an agent out of an AppleScript script application, I've written an elementary daily reminder application. Its purpose is to beep and display a message at any number of pre-set times during the day. These aren't appointment reminders, per se, unless you have a standing appointment at the same time every day. These are best thought of as reminders for things you may forget to do every day, such as check your e-mail, listen to the radio for a specific stock market report, or take medication.

This application screams for a user interface, and in Chapter 31 I'll show you a fancy version of this agent built with FaceSpan. But to keep things simple for the demonstration, we use Scriptable Text Editor as a permanent repository for alarm times and messages. While we could store it all in a script property, using Scriptable Text Editor gives you easier access to editing and testing various values.

The data file format is simple. Each line of the document is a single entry consisting of three or more AppleScript words. The first word is the time's numbers; the second word is the AM or PM designation (this example is obviously scripted for U.S. time formats, but could be modified for others). Remaining words in each line comprise the message that is to be displayed when the alarm reminder goes off. Figure 15.3 shows an Alarm Data document with sample data in it.

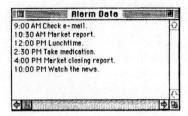

Figure 15.3 Alarm data
document.

You can study the script in more detail for data parsing and assembly, but I want to highlight the elements that make this script an agent, and let it run in the background. Here's the script:

```
property alarmList : { }
on run
    tell application "Scriptable Text Editor"
        open file "Alarm Data"
        set alarmData to contents of document 1
        close window "Alarm Data"
    end tell
    repeat with i from 1 to number of paragraphs of alarmData
        set oldDelims to AppleScript's text item delimiters
        set AppleScript's text item delimiters to {space}
        set oneEntry to {{" ", " "}}
        set item 1 of item 1 of oneEntry to ¬
        date ((text items 1 thru 2 of paragraph i of alarmData) as string)
        set item 2 of item 1 of oneEntry to ¬
        (text items 3 thru -1 of paragraph i of alarmData) as string
        set AppleScript's text item delimiters to oldDelims
        set alarmList to alarmList & oneEntry
    end repeat
    repeat until alarmList = { } or ¬
        item 1 of item 1 of alarmList > (current date)
        set alarmList to rest of alarmList
    end repeat
    if alarmList = { } then
        display dialog "All alarm times have passed for today." ¬
            buttons {"Bye"} default button "Bye"
        quit
    end if
    alarmList
end run

on idle
    if alarmList ≠ { } then
```

```
            if item 1 of item 1 of alarmList  (current date) then
                activate me
                display dialog item 2 of item 1 of alarmList ¬
                    buttons {"OK"} default button "OK"
                set alarmList to rest of alarmList
                return 0
            end if
        else
            quit
        end if
        return 5
    end idle

    on quit
        set alarmList to { }
        continue quit
    end quit
```

The script consists of a single property and three handlers. AlarmList is the property that stores the current list of pending alarms. This value is set in the run handler.

The Run Handler

When you double-click this script application (or place an alias to it into the Startup Items folder and restart your Mac), the script receives a Run message. Inside this handler, the script opens the Alarm Data document with Scriptable Text Editor to yank out a copy of the data.

Cycling through the paragraphs of the data, the script assembles a list of lists (thus the complex-looking parsing going on here). Given the sample data shown in Figure 15.3, this is what the data would look like if all records are in alarmList:

```
{{date "Friday, July 2, 1993 9:00:00 AM", "Check e-mail."}, {date "Friday, July 2,
1993 10:30:00 AM", "Market report."}, {date "Friday, July 2, 1993 12:00:00 PM",
"Lunchtime."}, {date "Friday, July 2, 1993 2:30:00 PM", "Take medication."},
{date
"Friday, July 2, 1993 4:00:00 PM", "Market closing report."}}
```

When dealing with dates and times, as this script does, you must be careful about the way date values are treated. While our data file specifies only times, AppleScript inserts any missing data when coercing the data to a date value. If you supply a time only, AppleScript supplements it with the current date. This happens to work great for this application, but it may trip up some other application you work on.

In assembling the alarm list, this application assumes the data is already in chronological order. In a real alarm application, there would be a user interface to enter alarms at any date and time in the future, plus a sorting mechanism to place the data in chronological order. Part of the list assembly procedure is to test whether the list has anything left in it—perhaps the user starts the application late in the day. Rather than occupy RAM (although only 200K for a script application) for nothing pending, we alert the user that all alarms have passed for today, and send a quit message, which I'll get to in a moment.

We've seen run handlers in other script applications earlier in this chapter, but normally this means that the script runs and then automatically quits when it finishes. To prevent that automatic quitting, you must save this kind of agent script application with the Stay Open checkbox checked in the Save File dialog box. Opening an appliation saved this way makes it go through its run handler (if it has one), but then the application stays open, showing itself in the Application menu, and presenting stripped-down File and Edit menus when it is the active application.

Idle Handler

Now, we must make sure our script checks the system clock against the top item in the alarmList. To trigger that check, our script includes an idle handler, which intercepts the idle message that every Stay Open script application receives from the system. This idle message is similar in many ways to the Hyper-Card idle message, although the message is sent only to script applications, not scripts running in Script Editor. The major difference, however, is that we need to be more concerned about sapping the Mac's system cycles with script applications.

Most agents you create don't need to perform their tasks once every fraction of a second, as they would if they responded to every idle message. You'd notice a slowdown in overall machine performance in most cases, too. A special version of the Return statement inside an idle handler sends a special instruction to the System, advising it how long to wait before sending this particular script application an idle message.

In our script, we set the timer to 5 seconds (the integer after the return statement indicates how many seconds until the next idle message is sent to the application). That means for our application, the timer could be as much as 4.9 seconds slow. How accurate you need an application like this is up to you, but keep system degradation in mind if you shorten the interval.

Inside the idle handler, we compare the current time against the first item (the time) of the first item (entire alarm item) of the alarm list. If the current time is later, then we activate the script application so it takes precedence over whatever else is going on at the moment, and displays the alarm message. We also send an immediate return message for a couple reasons. If another item is set to the same time, you want it to appear immediately after dismissing the alert for the first item, instead of waiting 5 seconds. Also, since we quit the application when the last alarm has rung for the day, you want that to happen immediately, as well.

Quit Handler

In both the run and idle handlers, we issue a quit command. This is actually the same quit command that the application gets if the user chooses Quit from the File menu (or shuts down the Mac). We have a quit handler in this script to reset the alarmList property to empty before the application quits. This way, we know the property will be empty the next time the user starts the application. If we didn't need any special processing when the script quits, we could omit this handler.

Notice, however, that the quit handler also contains a Continue statement. If we didn't have this statement here, the quit message would never reach the application. Therefore, if you have a quit handler, be sure to let the message continue.

Script Objects and Networked Computers

AppleScript does not provide a built-in mechanism that allows one user to run a script on another user's Mac across a network. There are excellent security reasons for this, predominantly preventing pranksters from screwing with other users' machines without their knowledge. But many network adminstrators do need to run scripts on other Macs to assist in network maintenance and software site licensing requirements. It is possible, fortunately, to run scripts on other Macs, but it requires that a small script application always be running on the other Macs.

At the heart of this setup is a small script, called Network Script Runner (located in the Handbook Scripts:Chapter 15 folder). This script app is nothing more than the following script:

```
on networkRun(myScript)
    return (run script (myScript))
end networkRun
```

The application is saved as a stay-open application, and it requires no user interface. If the script being run on the remote Mac returns any values, then those values are passed back to the administrator's script that called Network Script Runner. Ideally, this application should startup on every networked Mac whenever the Mac starts up (an alias in the Startup Items folder does the trick). On each Macintosh, Program Linking should be turned on, and this program's Program Linking (via the Sharing menu item in the File menu) also turned on. For security's sake, program linking should be password protected so that only the authorized network administrator(s) can access this program.

To run a script on another Mac, the adminstrator uses the following script structure:

```
set myProgram to (choose application with prompt ¬
    "Locate "Network Script Runner" on the desired Mac.")
tell myProgram
```

```
        networkRun(runThisScript)
    end tell

    -- here's the script object
    script runThisScript
        (* script statements to run on remote Macs, such as... *)
        tell application "Scriptable Text Editor"
            activate
            make new document
            copy "Howdy" to end of document 1
            -- show how to get data back
            count character of document 1
        end tell
    end script
```

How this all operates is that the network administrator sends a script object to the remote Mac, which then runs that script object. By creating a script object consisting of any script statements that the remote Mac is equipped to perform on its own (i.e., has AppleScript and all necessary scripting additions or applications installed there), the adminstrator can have free reign over the remote Mac.

The administrator script, above, is set to show the program linking dialog each time. But any such script could be modified with hardwired paths to the Network Script Runner application on any Mac in any zone of the network. What can't be automated via AppleScript by itself is the password request screen that appears the first time the adminstrator links to the program in any given session. Even though the volume containing the remote program does not have to be mounted on the administrator's desktop, the program link request still generates a program linking password request. You might consider PreFab Player (Chapter 32) or QuicKeys as a method to automate this part of the transaction if you want such operations to run completely unattended.

Summary

This chapter is chock full of three-pocket-protector-level techniques and applications for AppleScript. While simple scripting is fun and productive, the promise of creating standalone applications that integrate the best programming you can do with the powers of scriptable applications should stimulate your imagination. In Part III, we'll look at some real-world applications as well. I hope that you begin to explore applications for script objects and agents, and bring the future to your Macintosh.

PART III

Putting AppleScript to Work

CHAPTER 16

Scripting Finder Operations with FinderLib

Prior to the general release of the scriptable Finder with System 7.5, Apple-Script came with a supplementary file—called finderLib—which provided early scripters with a modest amount of Finder scripting. FinderLib is a library of routines that any script could use to control some Finder operations. Because it was used by a number of scripters and may still be used by those who have yet to upgrade to System 7.5 (or later), this chapter covers Finder-level scripting with finderLib. If you have the scriptable Finder, you should use that instead, and consult Chapter 17 for details.

What FinderLib Does

The library is a run-only (i.e., not editable) script object. If you've followed directions earlier in this book, then you've already moved the file to the Scripting Additions folder inside the Extensions folder. If you haven't done this, then you can find finderLib in the Scripting the Finder folder, which came with earlier releases of the AppleScript runtime software.

FinderLib contains 18 handlers, most of which are dedicated to Finder operations; the rest provide utility functions for extracting components of path names and other practical functions. Details for all of these functions are contained in the Scriptable Text Editor file, named Scripting the Finder. Before performing any finderLib operations on your own, you should study this file. I won't be repeating its contents here, although I will point out some special information that may not be obvious from the documentation.

Here, then, are the Finder functions that finderLib provides AppleScript scripters and their corresponding manual functions:

copyFiles from *fileList* to *destinationFolder* with | without warning
Dragging selected file(s) from one folder to another

duplicateFiles at *fileList*
Selecting file(s), and choosing Duplicate from the File menu

moveFiles from *fileList* to *destinationFolder* with | without warning
Dragging selected file(s) from one folder to another with Option key

putAwayFiles at *fileList*
Selecting file(s), and choosing Put Away from the File menu

moveFilesToTrash at *fileList*
Dragging selected file(s) to the Trash

emptyTrash( )
Choosing Empty Trash from the Special menu

openFiles at *fileList*
Selecting file(s), and choosing Open from the File menu

printFile at *fileList*
Selecting one file, and choosing Print from the File menu

makeAliases at *fileList*
Selecting file(s), and choosing Make Alias from the File menu

selectFiles at *fileList*
Selecting file(s) within a folder or root level

restartMac( )
Choosing Restart from the Special menu

sleepMac( )
Choosing Sleep from the Special menu (portable Macs only)

shutDownMac( )
Choosing Shut Down from the Special menu

checkFile (*pathname*)
Returns a valid alias class file name for any file name (or list of file names)

fileContainer from *pathName*
Returns the path to the folder containing a specified file or folder

fileName from *pathName* with | without trailingColon
Returns just the file name from an alias reference

diskName from *pathName*
Returns just the volume name from an alias reference

listFiles at *destinationFolder*
Returns list of pathnames to each file in a specific folder

Obvious omissions include commands to rename a file and create a folder. There is no access to control panels. The Chooser might be high on some scripters' wish lists, especially a command that allows connecting to a server via AppleShare or File Sharing.

Loading FinderLib into Scripts

Before your script can take advantage of any of these commands, you must load finderLib as a script object into your script (Chapter 14). You have two ways to load the script, each method offering its own set of advantages and disadvantages. One way is to load the script permanently as a property of your script; the other is to have your script load finderLib from the disk as the script runs.

Loading as Property

By setting a property of your script to the finderLib script object, you essentially copy the finderLib code into your script. To accomplish this, your script would need to begin with something like the following:

```
property finderLib: ""
if class of finderLib ≠ script then
    set finderLib to load script (choose file with prompt¬
        "Where is "finderLib"?" of type "osas")
end if
```

This script fragment checks to see what class the finderLib property is. If it isn't a script object (because the script has just been initialized), then it asks the user to locate the finderLib file. Assuming that the user has located finderLib, the script assigns the script object to the finderLib property of your script.

When you run this script once and save it as either a compiled script or application (and don't recompile it again later), the property will maintain the finderLib script object. In fact, the library code becomes part of your saved script. Therefore, if the user doesn't have finderLib on his or her Macintosh, it doesn't matter—your script has it already. The property will forever be a script class, and the user won't ever be asked to locate the finderLib file.

That's the primary advantage of this method. Your script becomes a self-contained entity, requiring that the user have only the requisite extension that allows AppleScript to run. Additionally, your script doesn't have to hit the disk to load the finderLib object. Execution is significantly faster.

The disadvantage, however, is that this storage of the finderLib object in your script adds approximately 20K to the size of your script. That means that the finderLib code could be residing in several script applications on your or your user's hard disk. It doesn't take too many of these scripts to start adding up to big numbers of redundant code.

Dynamically Loading FinderLib

An alternate is to load finderLib when the script runs each time. To simplify this method, it helps to install finderLib in a fixed location on each user's Mac. The Scripting Additions folder is an excellent place for script libraries. This allows you to hard-wire the load script command as follows:

```
set finderLib to load script (alias ((path to ¬
    extensions as string) & "Scripting Additions:finderLib"))
```

by using the path to command to get most of the path to finderLib.

One potential downside to this strictly hard-wired method is that it takes your script some time to access finderLib and load it into your script. Another is that you cannot count on the user always installing software the way you intend.

While this hard-wired method may work fine for the things you write for yourself (you know better than to move finderLib), you have to fortify your script to accommodate less obedient users. Here is another version, adapted from the suggestion in the finderLib documentation that can handle most situations:

```
property finderLibAlias : ""
repeat
    try
        set finderLib to load script finderLibAlias
        exit repeat
    on error
        set finderLibAlias to (choose file with prompt ¬
            "Where is "finderLib"?" of type "osas")
    end try
end repeat
```

This script declares a property that isn't a script object, but rather just an alias reference to the script library file. The statement that loads the script is in a try statement for a couple of reasons. First, if this script is run from the Script Editor, the value of finderLibAlias may be empty (the first time it runs), so the load script command will produce an error. Similarly, if this script is saved as an application, the property may contain an invalid path name to the finderLib file on someone else's Mac, also resulting in an error. In either case, the on error handler traps the error and asks the user to located finderLib. Because this is all inside a repeat loop, the next time through, the load script command should work, and the repeat loop exits.

While this method is efficient on the disk space score (a single copy of finderLib is shared by as many scripts as you need), it means that execution may be slow each time the script runs. Your choice between the two major methods, therefore, is predominantly a choice between speed (the persistent script object property) and size (the dynamically loaded version).

Telling FinderLib

As discussed in Chapter 14, loading a script object is only part of the task required to access a library's commands. Your script must treat a script object like any application, issuing a tell statement to direct any further statements to the object. Therefore, after any of the load script examples, above, your script then needs the following construct:

```
tell finderLib
    (* statements to finderLib*)
end tell
```

For simple statements, you can also send commands in a single tell statement, as in

```
tell finderLib to emptyTrash( )
```

I recommend this form for the occasional call to a finderLib command.

FinderLib Command Parameters

As defined in the *Scripting the Finder* document, there are only three possible kinds of parameters that a finderLib command requires. For those that require no parameters, your script must still call them with empty parentheses, as in the emptyTrash( ) command above.

Depending on the command, the parameters may be one or more of the following:

pathName

fileList

destinationFolder

FinderLib accepts as valid pathnames any of the following: an alias reference; a file reference; or a string containing the path for any Finder object (file, folder, disk volume). Internally, finderLib summons its own checkFile subroutine to do its best to convert the parameter to an alias—which the rest of the command requires internally. The following examples would qualify as valid *pathName* parameters for finderLib:

```
"HD:Documents:Correspondence:Letter to Joe 9/11/93"

file "HD:Documents:Correspondence:Letter to Joe 9/11/93"

alias "HD:Documents:Correspondence:Letter to Joe 9/11/93"
```

The key ingredient, obviously, is a pathname to the file or folder, regardless of its class (string, file, or alias).

A *fileList* parameter must be in the form of a list class value. Each item in the list must be one of the valid pathname forms (string, file, or alias types), and each item can be of a different class, if necessary. Internally, finderLib applies the checkFile subroutine to each item before passing the values onto the command to handle whatever operation is the provenance of that command. Here is an example incorporating string and alias class items in a single list class value:

```
{"HD:Documents:Memo Template", alias "HD:Documents:Letter Template"}
```

If you are passing a single file item to a *fileList* parameter, you can leave the reference in a plain string, alias, or file reference, and let finderLib handle the coercion to a list form for you. You can also pass a single item in a list, as in:

```
{"HD:Documents:Correspondence:Letter to Joe 9/11/93"}
```

You can pass the contents of an entire folder as a parameter by using one of finderLib's commands to get a list of files in the format that can be passed to another command as a valid *fileList*. The listFiles command produces a list of pathnames for all files within a given folder (this command differs significantly from the list files command in the File Commands scripting addition, because the latter returns just the item names, not their paths). Here's how this would look as a parameter to the selectFiles command:

```
selectFiles at (listFiles at "HD:Documents:Correspondence:")
```

The parentheses aren't required, but do help in readability, showing more clearly that the parameter is yet another command.

To fill the requirement for the *destinationFolder* parameter, the value must be a valid pathname to a folder, meaning that there must be a trailing colon. You can hard-wire the parameters, or use some other finderLib commands (fileContainer and diskName) to extract folder paths. Here are some examples:

```
"HD:Documents:Correspondence:"

alias "HD:Documents:Correspondence:"

fileContainer "HD:Documents:Correspondence:Letter to Joe 9/11/93"

diskName "HD:Documents:Correspondence:Letter to Joe 9/11/93"
```

Don't forget that you also have the path to scripting addition command available for passing a path to one of the special folders:

```
path to extensions
```

This command returns an alias, which is a valid class for the *destinationFolder* parameter.

Trash Minder

To demonstrate some of these commands and their possibilities, this section describes a script application, called Trash Minder. I've designed it to empty the Trash once per hour and when I shut down the Mac. For this to work right, Trash Minder is best started up with the Mac (place an alias to it in the Startup Items folder). Here is the script:

```
-- TrashMinder from "Danny Goodman's AppleScript Handbook"
-- by Danny Goodman
-- Published by Random House
-- ©1993 Danny Goodman. All rights reserved.
```

```
-- Saved as a Stay-Open script application.

-- Persistently stores alias to finderLib after first search
property finderLibAlias : ""
-- Holds finderLib as object while script runs, as needed
-- by run and quit handlers. Emptied on quit to keep
-- this script file to a small size.
property finderLib : ""

-- executes upon startup to load finderLib
on run
    repeat
        try
            set finderLib to load script finderLibAlias
            exit repeat
        on error
            set finderLibAlias to (choose file with prompt ¬
                "Where is "finderLib"?" of type "osas")
        end try
    end repeat
end run

-- Empties Trash every 3600 seconds (1 hour)
on idle
    tell finderLib to emptyTrash( )
    return 3600
end idle

-- Final empty on quit; clear finderLib object
-- so it doesn't get stored in this script;
-- let quit message continue to actually quit this
-- application.
on quit
    tell finderLib to emptyTrash( )
    set finderLib to ""
    continue quit
end quit
```

This is a simple, yet powerful script that creates an agent to mind our Trash for us. The comments take up more space than the AppleScript code.

Three handlers take care of everything the script needs. A run handler makes sure the finderLib library is loaded when the script starts up. The finderLib script object must go into a property because we need the property's global-ness for the idle and quit handlers to access the object. The idle handler makes a simple in-line statement to finderLib to empty the Trash, and then tells the System not to bother coming back to this application for an hour. All idle handlers, like this one, execute one time immediately after the run handler. Feel free to adjust this value up or down if you want the Trash emptied less or more often.

In the quit handler, we again empty the Trash before closing up shop. We also empty the finderLib property. Failure to do so would save the script object to the file, bloating the file by about 20K of the same code already in the finderLib file. The continue message is also vital, since without it, the application never gets the quit message that removes it from memory. In fact, you'd be almost irrevocably stuck in this little program, because no matter how many times you choose Quit from its File menu, the quit message never reaches the part of the application that actually quits.

By the way, if you should find yourself accidentally in this situation (because you forgot to include a continue quit statement), hold down the Shift key and choose Quit from the File menu. This bypasses the script's quit handler.

Alias Maker

We'll use the other library loading method in another script application that puts finderLib to work. The purpose of this droplet is best defined by a scenario. A user likes to keep aliases to the most active files and folders in a couple folders out on the Desktop. The contents of those folders change a lot as projects come and go. This droplet sits in each of those active folders, and creates aliases in its own folder level of whatever files and folders are dragged to it. If the user views the root level in a text view, all relevant files and folders—no matter how nested or from what folders they come from—can be selected and dragged to this droplet at once.

Here's the script:

```
-- Alias Maker from "Danny Goodman's AppleScript Handbook"
-- by Danny Goodman
-- Published by Random House
-- ©1993 Danny Goodman. All rights reserved.

-- Saved as a script application.

-- Persistently stores finderLib after first search
property finderLib : ""

on open fileList
   if class of finderLib ≠ script then
      set finderLib to load script (alias ((path to ¬
         extensions as string) & "Scripting Additions:finderLib"))
   end if
   -- get path for Alias Maker, whose container
   -- is the eventual container of the new aliases
   set myPath to path to frontmost application

   tell finderLib
      -- use finderLib's command to get precise container path
      set myPath to (fileContainer from myPath) as string
      -- work through each dragged item
```

```
        repeat with oneFile in fileList
            -- first create the alias
            makeAliases at oneFile
            -- disassemble name to take care of possible folder names
            set theItemName to fileName from oneFile without trailingColon
            set thePathName to fileContainer from oneFile
            -- watch out for long file names, which get truncated,
            -- and reassemble with proper length
            if my (count of theItemName) > 25 then
                set oneFile to thePathName & ¬
                    (characters 1 thru 25 of theItemName)
            else
                set oneFile to thePathName & theItemName
            end if
            -- move each alias file to Alias Maker's folder
            moveFiles from (oneFile & " alias") to ¬
                myPath without warning
        end repeat
    end tell
end open
```

To make this script application a droplet, we need an **open** handler, which signals Script Editor to save the script with the droplet icon and behavior. Statements in the **open** handler execute whenever a Desktop item is dragged to the script.

The first task is to make sure the script library is loaded. We set this one up to load finderLib and keep it stored in the finderLib property. Next, we'll eventually need to know the path to the folder containing the droplet, so we use the **path to** scripting addition to get the path before doing anything else in the Finder.

We then loop through each of the items in the list of files and/or folders passed as a parameter to the **open** handler. For each one we use finderLib's **makeAliases** command to create an alias at the same level as the original. Before we move the alias file to the same folder as the droplet, however, we take apart the full path name, dividing it into its two components (path and name). This allows us to check the length of the name by itself. If the name is over 25 characters long, then the Finder truncates the file name before appending the word "alias" to the file name. If we detect that the original file name is longer than 25 characters, we truncate the name ourselves here, because we'll be adding the "alias" part of the name in a moment to move the file. Otherwise, we just reassemble the path and name as it was originally. Finally, we move the alias file to the location of the droplet.

In case you're wondering how I knew about the long file name business, I can tell you it didn't cross my mind when I started designing this script. It was only during testing a prototype that errors came back signaling that the parameter being sent to the **moveFiles** command was not the true name of the alias. I then went back to the Finder and tried manually creating aliases for long-named files to understand the Finder's behavior. Testing like this is another way you, as a scripter, can try to *anticipate* problems users may encounter with your applications. In this case, the design of the script changed significantly as a result of this discovery. But that iterative process is also common in application design.

Scripting the Scriptable Finder

Included with System 7.5 is not only AppleScript run time software but also an extension that makes the Finder scriptable via any OSA scripting language. The extension, named Finder Scripting Extension, is required, and is where the dictionary is located.

The Finder as an Application

It's easy to overlook the fact that the Finder is an application that runs on the Macintosh. With the Finder automatically presenting the desktop every time you start a Macintosh (at least those Macs that don't have simpler user interfaces installed), the tendency is to equate the Finder with the Macintosh operating system. But the Finder is the file management interface that we use to organize files and folders stored on disks and other volumes. It is this same file management facility that we script with the scriptable Finder. To direct script statements to the Finder, we use a common tell statement that summons the Finder application, as in:

```
tell application "Finder"
    (* statements for Finder to execute *)
end tell
```

By the same token, it is important to understand that the Finder is a distinct application from other system-related things we use, such as control panels and desk accessory applications. Therefore, a scriptable Finder does not automatically make control panels or desk accessories scriptable. Until each specific item is created as a scriptable entity (only the Views and Users & Groups control panels are scriptable at this time), we have to rely on other methods (e.g., PreFab Player, described in Chapter 32, or keyboard macro utilities such as QuicKeys or Tempo) to automate procedures that involve such items.

Finder Object Model

While we'll get into the details of the Finder's object model later in this chapter, it should be comforting to know early on that the object model implementation for the scriptable Finder is a good one. By and large, the objects you work with in scripts are the same ones you normally work with by clicking and dragging around the desktop. Objects, such as disks, files, and folders, have rich sets of properties that help your scripts find out or set virtually anything that the typically conservative Apple engineers feel is safe to twiddle with.

One characteristic that will strike home early is that objects store lots of information about themselves that you don't think about in a graphical environment—but information that is essential to control them via a text-based scripting language. Moreover, that information can often be viewed and (when allowed) modified even when the item is not in view on the desktop—changing the name of a deeply nested folder, for instance. For, while there are many commands and objects related to visible things on the desktop, for the most part items do not have to be visible or open for scripts to work on their properties. This is certainly different from the way we manually work with Finder items. Therefore, it is possible, as an example, to script a different size and location of a window that opens when you manually open a folder, without having the window open to make those changes.

Recording Scripts

The Finder is recordable, so you can manually go through a procedure once and let the Script Editor record the steps for execution the next time. As with any recordable application, the Finder's recording capability is a good way to learn its preferred way of working with objects. Recorded scripts, however, operate in a brute force manner. They look for objects by name in the same containers they were in during the recording of the script. If the items move or their names change, then the pre-recorded script probably won't work again.

What you will also probably realize after trying to record a script to automate some procedure you manually perform on a regular basis is that recorded scripts don't take into account any of the intelligence that you bring to the procedure. For example, you may automatically know after a day's operation which folders contain items you'd like backed up. A recorded script will work only on the folders you select on a given day. Instead, you'd probably like the script to figure out if the folder's contents have been modified since the last backup. Or, you may wish to add comments to the Get Info dialog window for all items within a folder, regardless their quantity or name. These kinds of operations are certainly scriptable, but not recordable.

Object Orientation

More so than any other scriptable application you're likely to see in the near future, the Finder's object model is fashioned along lines that reveal a strong object oriented programming heritage. By this I mean that a number of object types have the same properties as objects with more "global" scope. For example, an Item is one of the most global objects. A Finder item, which can be visually represented in the Finder by an icon, has a set list of properties, such as its creation date, the name of disk on which it is located, its icon, its name, and so on—things that all such items have in common. But specific kinds of items have *additional* properties that pertain only to them. A file is one kind of item, while a container is another kind of item. Each one has properties unique to its object class: a file, on the one hand, has a creator type (a four-character code that identifies the application that generated the file), a switch for whether the file is a stationery pad or not, and so on; a container, on the other hand, has a particular kind of view (icon, name, size, kind, etc.) attributed to it, a switch about whether items in any of the outline views are expanded, and so on.

When you look up an object in the scriptable Finder's dictionary, you see only the properties that are unique to that specific object. Unfortunately, there is no indication in the dictionary entry as to what other object properties are inherited from the next object up the hierarchy (the parent object). Since some objects inherit properties through multiple levels of objects, it is virtually impossible to derive from the dictionary alone a list of all properties for a given object.

To help you visualize the relationships of various objects, Figures 17.1 through 17.3 present tree diagrams of every object defined by the Finder's object model. To see what properties apply to any object, follow the connecting line up the hierarchy. Each object the line meets contains properties that also apply to the objects lower in the hierarchy.

In Figure 17.1, we focus on the entities we typically see in the Finder as file, folder, and disk volume icons. The parent of them all is the Item object. Following the left-hand branch, we come to the File object, which is a special kind of item. Below the File object are seven even more specific types of file objects, some of which have additional properties unique to themselves. Even though several objects have no additional properties, their existence helps define what a particular file may be. For instance, the following three statements yield the same information:

```
size of font file "Times" of suitcase "Times" of folder "Fonts" ¬
    of folder "System Folder" of startup disk

size of file "Times" of suitcase "Times" of folder "Fonts" ¬
    of folder "System Folder" of startup disk

size of item "Times" of suitcase "Times" of folder "Fonts" ¬
    of folder "System Folder" of startup disk
```

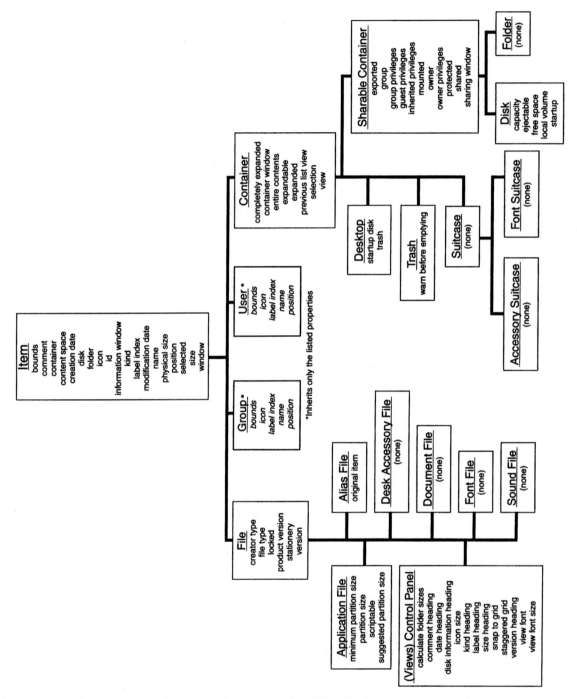

Figure 17.1 Item object hierarchy of the Finder.

This is so because the size property is inherited by the font file by virtue of it being a child of the File object and a grandchild of the Item object (where the size property is defined). But if you try to refer to the font file as a different kind of file, as in

size of **sound file** "Times" of suitcase "Times" of folder "Fonts" ¬
of folder "System Folder" of startup disk

the Finder returns an execution error, because it doesn't recognize the Times file as a valid sound file.

This behavior might lead you to want to use the parent object reference—Item in this case—at all times. You can, in fact, do that, even when a property is unique to a descendent object. For instance, the following three statements are all valid:

original item of **alias file** "My File Alias" of startup disk

original item of **file** "My File Alias" of startup disk

original item of **item** "My File Alias" of startup disk

Even though the original item property is unique to Alias File objects, any of the parent or grandparent object references work as well.

Let's follow the right-hand branch of Figure 17.1 to examine the concept of containers. As its name implies, a Container object is one that can hold one or more other objects. Therefore we can ask the Finder to give us the contents of a container, since the values will be other Finder items (some of which may also be containers). The Finder won't yield the contents of a file—only the file's application can do that. But you see that suitcases are obvious containers. Similarly, the Desktop and Trash are unique objects of their own (not folder objects, as you may have come to think in other AppleScript pathname constructions).

The Finder has a separate branch of container for Sharable Container objects. These are items that can be set up for availability on a File Sharing network. Most of the properties of such objects are the ones normally set in the window when you choose Sharing from the Finder's File menu. Under this category are the Disk and Folder objects—familiar objects we see on the Desktop. While a Disk object has some additional properties for itself, a Folder object inherits all the properties of a Sharable Container, Container, and Item.

Two object classes derived from the Item class have to do with the Users & Groups control panel. As can happen in an object oriented environment, such as this, a child object can be designed to inherit only some of the parent's properties. Such is the case with the User and Group objects, whose properties are limited to a handful of Item properties. They also have additional specific behavior in that these objects can be referred to only when the Users & Groups control panel is open. The same is *not* true for the properties associated with the Views control panel, whose settings are available even when that control panel is closed.

Figure 17.2 shows the hierarchy of Content Space objects. These objects are concerned primarily with visible things in Finder windows. In addition to container (i.e., disk and folder) windows, a Content Space object may also be the window you see when you choose Get Info for an item, the window you see when you choose Sharing from the Finder's File menu, and the Status window (e.g., during a file copy operation).

There is intentional overlap with a number of properties in the Content Space and Item object hierarchies. The reason is that your scripts are given the flexibility to retrieve or set properties of an object via the direct approach (to the Item object) or recreating the method of manual setting in windows. For example, both of the following statements achieve the same result:

```
modification date of folder "Documents" of startup disk

modification date of information window "Documents Info"
```

Notice the differences between the two statements, however. In the first, we are retrieving the modification date of a folder item whose complete reference (folder "Documents" of startup disk) we supply; in the second, we refer to a value displayed in the folder's Get Info window, whose name consists of the item's name and the word "Info." For the latter construction to work at all, however, the information window for that item must already be open (either manu-

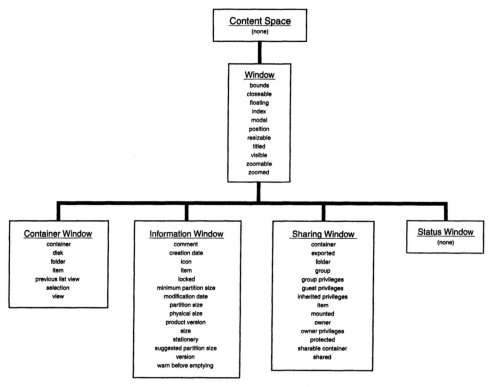

Figure 17.2 Content space object hierarchy of the Finder.

ally or by script), although not necessarily active. Hence my assertion earlier that Content Space object references deal with visible things in Finder windows.

Figure 17.3 shows a potpourri of other objects and their properties. Process objects may be a new concept to you. A process is essentially a running program whose name appears in the Application menu (although in early versions of scriptable Finder, the Finder itself doesn't register as a process, which it should for consistency's sake). While a Process object appears to share a number of properties with its corresponding Application File and Information Window objects, the fact that the program is running makes most of the Process objects read-only. Thus, you can change the minimum partition size property of a non-running application via its Application File object reference; you can do the same via the program's Information Window, provided the Get Info window is open on the Desktop; but, you can only retrieve the minimum partition size of a Process object, because the Finder doesn't change this value while a program is running.

The Application object, which refers to the Finder itself, contains a number of properties that refer to specific locations in a volume. For example, if a command refers to a file in the extensions folder, the extensions folder property of the Finder application supplies the appropriate reference for the necessary parameter. Therefore, instead of having to hardwire the reference to the extensions folder like this:

```
get version of item "Apple CD-ROM" of folder "Extensions" ¬
    of folder "System Folder" of startup disk
```

you can use the property as a shortcut:

```
get version of item "Apple CD-ROM" of extensions folder
```

The Finder's extensions folder property returns the reference needed for the Get command.

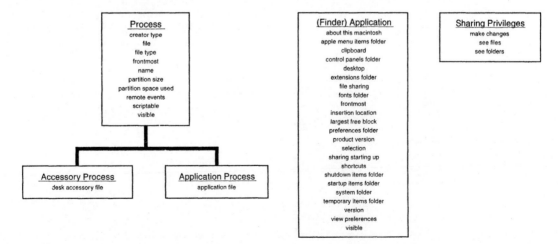

Figure 17.3 Miscellaneous object hierarchy of the Finder.

About Pathnames and References

If you've written scripts with file-related scripting additions, finderLib (Chapter 16), or other Finder-related scripting additions (e.g., Jon's Commands or the GTQ OSAXen, Chapter 33), it may take a bit of getting used to Finder's way of referring to its items in AppleScript. The Finder prefers a different way of referring to its items in a script. Colon-delimited pathnames can be used under some circumstances, but the preferred method of referring to items is a more plain-language description of the container hierarchy for an item. Let's look at some examples.

In commands outside of scriptable Finder (e.g., choose folder, choose file scripting additions), file and alias references that include complete pathnames are the standard. For example, if in response to the choose folder command, we select the Alarm Clock desk accessory, the value returned by the scripting addition would be:

```
alias "Macintosh HD:System Folder:Apple Menu Items:Alarm Clock"
```

But scriptable Finder's preferred method of describing that object is the following:

```
file "Alarm Clock" of folder "Apple Menu Items" of folder "System Folder" of startup disk
```

Rather than use a solid pathname, the Finder states the location of the Alarm Clock file in terms of its container hierarchy: in the Apple Menu Items folder, which is in the System Folder, which is on the startup disk volume.

To the credit of the scriptable Finder, it can use either version of the object descriptor for most commands. For example, the following two Finder commands accomplish the same end:

```
open alias "Macintosh HD:System Folder:Apple Menu Items:Alarm Clock"
```

```
open file "Alarm Clock" of folder "Apple Menu Items" ¬
    of folder "System Folder" of startup disk
```

This interoperability is essential, because your scripts will still use the original scripting additions for some user interface commands (e.g., choose file), and the data returned by these scripting additions will have to work with scriptable Finder.

Things do get tricky, however, with some commands and certain special containers, such as the desktop. For instance, with finderLib, you could cite the startup disk, the Desktop, and the Trash as the destination for a file copying command by their pathnames (with trailing colon, since they are designated folders), such as

```
copyFiles from alias "Macintosh HD:Letters:" to ¬
    alias "Macintosh HD:Desktop Folder:"
```

Scriptable Finder, however, won't accept alias references to non-intuitive, hidden folders such as the Desktop Folder, Trash, and the startup volume as destination containers. Even the Finder object class "folder" doesn't help here. For example, the statement

```
copy folder "Macintosh HD:Letters" to ¬
    folder "Macintosh HD:Desktop Folder:"
```

produces an error around the Desktop Folder alias object. That's because these kinds of hidden folders aren't legitimate folder objects in the Finder's eye. Instead, they are special container objects of their own, especially the desktop and trash. Therefore, Finder's preferred method of writing the previous statement is:

```
copy folder "Macintosh HD:Letters" to desktop
```

If you must use pathname notation, however, you must look a bit deeper into the object hierarchy of the Finder. While the Desktop Folder is not a true folder in the Finder's eye, it is still a Container—another class of object of Finder. The Finder will recognize a container object by its pathname. Thus, to use the pathname notation for the Desktop Folder with Finder, you turn the pathname into a container object:

```
copy folder "Macintosh HD:Letters" to ¬
    container "Macintosh HD:Desktop Folder:"
```

As shown in Figure 17.1, the Item object has even greater scope. An item can be a container (folder, disk) or a file (document, application, alias file). When you can't predict what kind of item will be processed by a Finder command (e.g., a user can drop a folder or file onto a droplet), the item object reference will allow the Finder to recognize the pathname reference without difficulty:

```
copy folder "Macintosh HD:Letters" to ¬
    item "Macintosh HD:Desktop Folder:"
```

With so many other parts of AppleScript dealing with pathnames, these tips on accommodating them fully within the scriptable Finder should prove valuable to you as you familiarize yourself with the depth of the Finder's object model.

Default Value Classes

Every object class returns some kind of information when it is the object of a get command. For example, in the following script,

```
tell application "Finder"
    get windows
end tell
```

the Finder returns a list of references to all windows currently open on the desktop, such as this:

```
-- result: {window of startup disk of application "Finder", window ¬
    of folder "Applications" of startup disk of application "Finder"}
```

The most common returned value is a reference that best fits the situation. In the case of the windows values, above, the Finder provides a list of references to physical windows. But consider this script:

```
tell application "Finder"
   processes
end tell
   -- result: {application "Script Editor", application "Microsoft Word", ¬
      application "MacDraw Pro", application "Alarm Clock"}
```

Here, the references are to running applications, not the locations of their files on your disk. These kinds of references, for instance, can be used as parameters to other commands. Here is an example of a brute force script that quits all open applications—except the Finder and Script Editor:

```
tell application "Finder"
   set theApps to processes whose name ≠"Script Editor"
end tell
repeat with oneApp in theApps
   activate -- in case of Save Changes dialog
   tell oneApp to quit
end repeat
```

In this example, once we set theApps variable to a list of running processes, we can use that list as data for the ensuing repeat loop.

When specifying the plural object class in these situations, the order of the references returned in the list depends on the nature of the object. In the case processes, for instance, the returned list is based on their launching order, rather than the alphabetical order in which they appear in the Application menu. Windows, on the other hand, are listed according to their layered position on the Desktop, with the frontmost window appearing first in the list. Contents of a window are listed in the order in which they appear either in the current list view order (by name, size, kind, etc.) or, if the view is now by icon or small icon, the last list view order selected for that window (that's what the previous list view property of a window is all about).

Support for "Whose" Clauses (Filtered References)

The scriptable Finder is very good at interpreting whose clauses to help scripts select items that meet certain criteria (see Chapter 8's discussion about filtered references for a refresher course on whose clauses). While downright sluggish compared to System 7.5's Find desk accessory (which, unfortunately, is not scriptable), the Finder's whose clause support does alleviate what would otherwise be cumbersome and very time-consuming iterations through containers to locate specific items.

An example we'll flesh out later in this chapter is a statement that returns a list of references to every item within a folder that has been modified since 12:00 am on January 2, 1995:

```
every item of folder "Documents"of startup disk ¬
   whose modification date > date "1/2/95"
```

Upon compilation, the date object changes to:

```
date "Monday, January 2, 1995 12:00:00 AM"
```

The statement returns a list of all items (files and containers) that qualify. To limit the returned list to only files generated by applications, you can change the object reference to every document file, rather than every item. Still, be careful of one aspect of this construction: the folder reference looks no further than the first level contents. Therefore, the above statement returns a list of only those qualifying items whose immediate container is the Documents folder. To get the nested contents of a container, you must summon a property of a container: entire contents, as in:

```
every item of entire contents of folder "Documents" of ¬
    startup disk whose modification date > date "1/2/95"
```

Searching through the entire contents of a heavily loaded container, however, is slow and often appears to be hanging up the machine because there is no feedback about processing (or you may have to extend the timeout for the statement). Therefore, it may be prudent to divide a big job among several containers. For example, instead of copying all newly updated files from a giant Documents folder to a backup disk in one swipe:

```
copy every document file of entire contents of ¬
    folder "Documents" of startup disk ¬
    whose modification date > date "1/2/95" to disk "Backup"
```

you should spread the task among multiple copy statements:

```
copy every document file of entire contents of folder ¬
    "Correspondence" of folder "Documents" of startup disk ¬
    whose modification date > date "1/2/95" to disk "Backup"
copy every document file of entire contents of folder "Invoices" ¬
    of folder "Documents" of startup disk ¬
    whose modification date > date "1/2/95" to disk "Backup"
```

At least you'll observe some disk activity between statements to calm your nerves.

Scriptable Finder Commands

Let's now examine the commands we can use with the Finder. As is common with a number of scripting dictionaries attached to applications, the one with the Finder contains a few items in the Standard Suite that are of little or no value to a scripter. We'll focus here on the commands that you use to script Finder objects.

One valuable piece of knowledge about Finder commands to keep in mind is that a vast majority of them return a result of some kind (these command results are different from the default values of objects, discussed earlier in this chapter). Most typically, the result is the reference to the scripted object after the command has acted on the object. For example, moving a file from one folder to another with the move command yields a result of the reference to the file in its new location, as in

```
tell application "Finder"
    move file "Letter File" of startup disk to folder "Correspondence" of ¬
        folder "Documents" of startup disk
end tell
    -- result: file "Letter File" of folder "Correspondence" ¬
    of folder "Documents" of startup disk of application "Finder"
```

Why this feature is so important is that your script may perform several actions on a particular item, such as moving it, renaming it, and so on. After each command, you need the proper reference of the item to carry out the next command. If a command works on multiple items (e.g., copying to a backup disk several items selected by a whose clause), the Finder returns a list of new references for all the items. Therefore, if you want to move the Letter File item from the previous example, and then rename it, here's what the script would look like:

```
tell application "Finder"
    set myFile to (move file "Letter File" of startup disk to folder "Correspondence" of ¬
        folder "Documents" of startup disk)
    set name of myFile to "Letter to Joe"
end tell
    -- result: (empty)
```

The move command returns its result (the reference to the moved file) into the variable myFile. In the second statement, the script sets the name property of the item referred to by the contents of the myFile variable. Unfortunately, setting the name property does not return the desired value in this case, so if we want to do more with this item, we could either keep track of the reference manually, or use another method of working with the item:

```
tell application "Finder"
    set myFile to (move file "Letter File" of startup disk ¬
        to folder "Correspondence" of ¬
        folder "Documents" of startup disk)
    set myFolder to folder of myFile -- get new enclosing folder
    set name of myFile to "Letter to Joe"
    -- now assemble new reference
    set myFile to file "Letter to Joe" of myFolder
end tell
    -- result: file "Letter to Joe" of folder "Correspondence" ¬
    of folder "Documents" of startup disk of application "Finder"
```

With that understanding, we now proceed to the individual commands.

clean up [all | *itemReference* [by *propertyLabel*]]

The clean up command mimics and sometimes supplements the Clean Up command in the Finder's special menu. To use this command on individual items or everything in a container, the container window must be open on the Desktop, and the view must be by either Icon or Small Icon.

The clean up all variation works only with items on the Desktop (i.e., nothing in any open windows). Items are set in the grid pattern according to their name, and the Trash icon is placed in its default position at the lower right corner of the screen.

This command lets you specify individual items within a window or the entire contents of one or more windows. Here are some examples:

```
clean up windows -- all open windows

clean up {window "Documents",window "Applications"}

clean up file "Letter to Joe" of window "Documents"
```

Notice that you don't have to supply a full reference to a window for this command: it looks for an open window by the supplied name, regardless of its nested location within the disk organization.

When the itemReference parameter is a container window, then you can further specify the order the icons should be arranged starting at the top left corner of the window, and working across and down. The propertyLabel parameter accepts any of the following properties:

name	version
size	comment
modification date	

In other words, you can script the arrangement of icons according to any of these properties—something you can't do manually except by detailed manual labor. For example, to arrange items in the startup disk's window by name, the command would be:

```
clean up window of startup disk by name
```

Failure to include a propertyLabel parameter causes the Finder to align objects to their nearest grid location, rather than zipping them all to the top of the window.

close *objectReference*

The Finder allows a script to close any window that may be open on the Desktop (but not the Desktop, itself). You may supply either a complete reference to the container whose window you want closed, or, more simply, just the name of the window. Therefore, the following statements accomplish the same end:

```
close folder "AppleScript™ Utilities" of folder "Development" ¬
    of startup disk

close window "AppleScript™ Utilities"
```

A script that wishes to close a window should exercise care prior to issuing the close command. If the window is not open, the script will get an execution error, disrupting the flow of the script. It is wise to test for the existence of the window prior to issuing the close command (as well as many other commands in the Finder that assume the existence of an object). Here is a script fragment that demonstrates how this is done:

```
set myWind to a reference to window "AppleScript™ Utilities"
if myWind exists then close myWind
```

The first line creates a variable that holds a reference class object (a standard, though infrequently used, AppleScript object) to the window under scrutiny. We must use the reference class here rather than just setting the variable to the window object, because the compiler won't compile the script if that window isn't open (the compiler tries to resolve the window reference against the real thing on the Desktop). After that, we can use the variable to see whether the window exists and close the window if it does exist.

When more than one window with the same name is open at the same time, the close command automatically closes all windows bearing that name. To limit the close to a particular window of the same name, use either the folder reference or the window reference to the folder as a parameter to the close command:

```
close folder "New Stuff" of folder "Development" of startup disk
```

```
close window of folder "New Stuff" of folder "Development" of startup disk
```

Either one of these constructions closes a very specific window connected to a particular folder.

computer *gestaltSelector* [has *valueToTest*]

Your scripts can peek into the innards of the Macintosh running the Finder to determine a variety of configuration attributes. The gestaltSelector parameter of the computer command determines what hardware attribute you wish to know about. While *Inside Macintosh:Operating System Utilities* (Addison-Wesley) goes into great detail about the Gestalt Manager, the scriptable Finder provides some shortcuts to the gestaltSelector parameter. You may supply any of the following constants:

CPU	operating system
FPU	sound system
MMU	memory available
hardware	memory installed

Unfortunately for the unsuspecting scripter, the Finder returns code numbers for most of these properties (although memory comes back as an integer of bytes). For example, the CPU parameter returns the following values:

0	*unknown microprocessor*
1	*68000*
2	*68010*
3	*68020*
4	*68030*
5	*68040*

Similarly, the FPU values are:

0	*no FPU installed*
1	*68881 FPU*
2	*68882 FPU*
3	*built into 68040*

In addition to the constants provided by the scriptable Finder, you can also use the four-character Gestalt codes that programmers use. For instance, to retrieve the identifying number of the Macintosh model, you use the gestalt-MachineType code, which is "mach" (all lowercase). A statement that checks for whether the current machine is a Quadra 840 AV (code 78) would be:

```
if computer "mach" has 78 then
   -- do stuff that works on this machine
end if
```

Some of these codes have two or three characters and spaces to pad to four characters total. Since the parameter to the computer command must be four characters, be sure to include the space(s):

```
computer "kbd "
   -- result: 12 (PowerBook ADB keyboard)
```

The returned value of the computer command is always an integer (one of the codes). The optional second parameter lets you supply a code to test, in which case the command returns a Boolean, depending on the result of the comparison.

In general, this command should be used only by experienced programmers who understand the implications of the Gestalt Manager.

copy *expression* to | into *objectReference*
put *expression* to | into *objectReference*

Finder's copy command extends the powers of AppleScript's basic copy command. When the parameters evaluate to appropriate kinds of Finder object references, the Finder performs the type of item copy operations you'd expect from the Finder (i.e., the equivalent of Option-dragging an item from one container to another). For example, if the expression parameter is any of the Item class objects and the *objectReference* parameter is a container or container window, then the Finder indeed makes a copy of the designated item in the container. For example:

```
tell application "Finder"
   copy item "Letter to Natalie" of startup disk to desktop
end tell
   -- result: file "Letter to Natalie" of application "Finder"
```

Notice that the Finder's item copying routine returns a reference to the new item. When copying an item, the destination must be a valid container or open container window. If you can't predict ahead of time what kinds of objects your script will be copying to (i.e., a disk one time, a folder the next, the desktop after that), use one of the more global references (Item or Container) to accommodate all comers:

```
tell application "Finder"
   set destination to (choose folder with prompt ¬
      "Select a target folder:") as text -- strip alias reference
   copy document file "Howdy" of startup disk to container destination
end tell
   -- result: file "Howdy" of application "Finder"
```

In this instance, the choose folder command returns an alias reference which would fail as an argument to the Finder for locations such as the desktop. But by first coercing the reference to text, we can turn it into a container reference in the copy statement, satisfying the Finder's requirement for a valid container as the second parameter.

You may include any number of items in the first parameter, provided they're gathered in an AppleScript list. The items can be of all different specific kinds, and may be in as many different locations as there are items. Only one container may be specified as the objectReference parameter, however.

Copying an item object to a variable causes the reference to the item to be copied to the variable, as in:

```
tell application "Finder"
   copy item "Howdy" of startup disk to myItem
end tell
myItem
   -- result: file "Howdy" of startup disk of application "Finder"
```

This happens because the default value returned by an object is always its reference. Thus, that's the value that gets copied to the variable.

You can also use the copy command to set properties of objects. For example:

```
tell application "Finder"
   copy "Joe's Letter" to name of item "Howdy" of startup disk
end tell
   -- result: (none)
```

Without any Finder item copying activity, however, the copy command here returns no values, as just demonstrated.

The Finder is perhaps the first scriptable application to recognize the heritage of HyperCard's language, HyperTalk, and its famous put command.

Therefore, if you feel more comfortable using the put command (with the into preposition, as it's used in HyperTalk), you may do so. Upon compilation, however, the Finder converts the statement to the copy syntax.

count (of) [each | every] *className* [(in | of) *objectReference*]
number of *className* [(in | of) *objectReference*]

To obtain the number of any particular kind of object inside a container or container window, use the count command (or its number synonym). If the *objectReference* is an item class (or any of its container class children), the container does not need to be opened for the count command to do its job. But any container window must be opened to use a reference to the window.

The count command is also a good learning tool for the different classes of item objects. While I don't know the makeup of your desktop or startup disk, enter each of the following commands inside a tell statement directed to the Finder, and notice the numbers that come back in the result window:

    count of items of desktop

    count of files of desktop

    count of alias files of desktop

    count of containers of desktop

    count of disks of desktop

    count of folders of desktop

The desktop object is not counted as one of its own items. It is actually an item of the application, so the following statement produces a count of one higher than count of items of desktop:

    count of items -- *of application "Finder"*

In all the above examples, I've used the plural class name of each class. This is in lieu of the more verbose method of specifying "each" or "every" before the class name. If you choose to use those adjectives, then you may use only the singular form of the class name.

data size of *objectReference* [as *className*]

Adapted from the standard suite of Apple events, the data size command has little value for Finder objects. This is primarily because the command operates on the default value returned by the object named in the *objectReference* parameter—usually a reference class value. To obtain the number of bytes the item occupies on a disk (i.e., the number of bytes you'd see in the object's Get Info dialog), extract the size property of the item instead.

Some properties of items do have data sizes that may be of value to a script. For example, one way to see if an item has a comment in its Get Info window is to get the data size of the comment, as in

```
data size of comment of file "Letter to Joe" of startup disk
    -- result: 0 if no comment
```

Requesting the data size of an item's icon returns roughly the sum of sizes in bytes of all icon resources in that icon's family.

delete *itemReference*

The delete command performs via a script the same action as dragging one or more items to the Trash. For the *objectReference* parameter, you may specify a reference to a single item or an AppleScript list of items. Windows or container windows are not valid objects for this command—only file and container items (but not the desktop or trash). Some examples are:

```
delete file "Joe's Letter" of folder "Documents" of startup disk

delete {folder "Empty Folder" of startup disk, ¬
    document file "Untitled" of startup disk}
```

Remember that this command merely moves the item to the Trash. Use the empty command to finish the job.

duplicate *objectReference* [to *locationReference*] ¬
[replacing (conflicts | existing items)]

If you don't specify a *locationReference* parameter to the duplicate command, the action is identical to that of the Duplicate command in the Finder's File menu: it generates a duplicate of the selected item(s) in the same container as the original, appending the word "copy" to the name(s) of the copies:

```
tell application "Finder"
    duplicate file "Joe's Letter" of startup disk
end tell
    -- result: file "Joe's Letter copy" of startup disk of application "Finder"
```

That would make the duplicate command with a *locationReference* parameter to appear to behave identically to the copy command. But chances are you'd rather use the duplicate command because of the optional extra parameters that instruct the Finder to automatically "overwrite" any existing item with the name of the copy (whether it be in the same container as the original or another container). There are actually many ways to specify that an item's copy should "overwrite" an item with the same name:

```
replacing conflicts
replacing existing items
with replacing
replacing true
```

In keeping with Apple's tendency to safe scripting, the replacing parameter doesn't completely overwrite the previous file. Instead, the Finder moves the earlier version to the Trash.

Failing to specify the replacing parameter causes different results depending on the location. If the location is the same container as the original, the Finder increments the name (e.g., file "Joe's Letter copy 2" of startup disk of application "Finder"). But in another container, the script will get an execution error, rather than something like a safe alert box prompting the user about the conflict. To avoid the execution error, your script will have to pre-check for the existence of the object, as in

```
tell application "Finder"
    if file "Howdy" of desktop exists then
        display dialog ¬
            "Replace existing file with the same name?" ¬
            buttons {"Cancel", "OK"} default button "OK"
            -- clicking "Cancel" stops script execution
    end if
    duplicate file "Howdy" of startup disk to desktop replacing conflicts
end tell
```

As intimated in the first example for this command, the duplicate command returns a reference to the duplicate item. This allows you to continue processing the new item, such as changing its properties.

eject [*diskReference*]

The eject command behaves just as the Finder's Eject menu command. You may specify one or more (in a list) references to volumes currently mounted on your Desktop as parameters to the eject command.

For the command to succeed, the ejectable property of the disk must be true. Therefore it would be wise to check for this property prior to ejecting any volume:

```
if ejectable of disk "Backup" then eject disk "Backup"
    -- result: disk "Backup" of application "Finder"
```

But just as the Finder's manual Eject command leaves a dimmed image of the disk on the Desktop, so does the scripted eject command. To both eject the disk and remove the icon (or just remove a dimmed icon), use the put away command (below).

empty [*trashReference*]

A *trashReference* is nothing more than a way the Finder knows about the Trash—the easiest being the word "trash," itself:

```
empty trash
```

```
empty the trash
```

The scripted version of this command (similar to the Empty Trash command of the Special menu), does not warn the user about emptying the Trash, regardless of the setting of the Warn Before Emptying property/checkbox of the Trash object.

If you are writing an extensive script that summons the powers of multiple applications, feel free to slip in the short one-line statement

```
tell application "Finder" to empty trash
```

anytime you feel the Trash may contain unneeded items.

erase *diskReference*

Devious folks might have twisted ideas about the chaos they could create on a network of shared disks, but the **erase** command is benign when it comes to shared disks mounted on your desktop or even your own startup disk. If the response to the manual action of selecting a disk and choosing Erase Disk from the Special menu results in an error alert of some kind, the scriptable Finder simply ignores the scripted equivalent.

Only when the *diskReference* parameter points to a mounted disk volume that is reformattable from the Finder does it carry out the command. And even then, the erasure requires human intervention to make selections in the dialog box (although they could be scripted with PreFab Player or QuicKeys). You may specify one or more (in a list) references to disk(s) for erasure. The command returns the reference to the disk(s) you erased or attempted to erase (in the case of a disallowed erasure).

exists *objectReference*
objectReference exists

Because so many of the Finder's commands fail if their objects are not to be found, you will find yourself using the **exists** command (it reads best in the second version) often. The command, which accepts any Finder object except Sharing Privileges as a parameter, returns a single Boolean value regardless of the number of objects listed as its parameter. Therefore, if you should check for the existence of three items, and one does not exist, then the returned value is false—the command uses AND logic to calculate its returned value.

As Boolean values, the results of an **exists** command come in handy as switches for if-then constructions:

```
if file "Apple Photo Access" of extensions folder exists then
( * do stuff that requires this extension *)
else
   display dialog ¬
      "Sorry. Cannot continue. Install "Apple Photo Access" extension." ¬
         buttons {"Cancel"}
end if
```

When you don't check for the existence of an object and try to issue a command to a non-existent object, the execution error that comes back may be a bit misleading. For example, the following statement:

```
size of file "Foo" of startup disk
```

results in an execution error that states

```
Finder got an error: Can't get size of file "Foo" of startup disk.
```

When you read this message, and by the fact that the word "size" is highlighted in the script, your first thought may be that you're trying to get the wrong property. In fact, your script can't get that property because the file doesn't exist. Unfortunately, the error message makes it sound as though the file exists, but the rest of the request is in error. Therefore, whenever you receive an execution error like this in Finder, your first suspect should be the object reference, rather than the command.

[get] *objectReference* [as *className*]

The Finder's version of the get command operates very much like AppleScript's own version. As usual, the get command name is optional. The following two statements yield the same result:

```
get folder "Documents" of startup disk
folder "Documents" of startup disk
    -- result: folder "Documents" of startup disk of application "Finder"
```

When the objectReference is a Finder object, the resulting value is the complete reference to the object. But you may also specify a property of an object, such as:

```
modification date of document file "1994 P&L" ¬
    of folder "Financial" of startup disk

original item of alias file "Reminder" of startup items folder

frontmost of process "Microsoft Word"
```

Property values come back in whatever class they belong, such as Boolean (true or false), date, list of coordinate points, and strings, to name a few. Some values can be coerced by adding the optional as parameter. Interestingly, the Finder's get command does a bit more processing on some coercions. Date objects coerced as text, for instance, comes back in an abbreviated date format, which AppleScript 1.1's own current date scripting addition doesn't do:

```
modification date of folder "Documents" of startup disk as string
    -- result: "Fri, Aug 12, 1994, 11:27 AM"
```

If you specify multiple objects (or plural classnames) as the *objectReference* parameter, the Finder returns a list of items, as in

```
folders of startup disk
    -- result: {folder "Development" of startup disk of application "Finder", ¬
        folder "Applications" of startup disk of application "Finder", ¬
        folder "Documents" of startup disk of application "Finder", ¬
        folder "System Folder" of startup disk of application "Finder"}

frontmost of processes
    -- result: {false, false, true, false}
```

In this last example, we got a list of the frontmost property settings for all processes currently returned by the Finder. Only one can be true, but the values by themselves don't tell a script very much. By combining this get statement with a whose clause, however, a script can determine the frontmost application:

```
every process whose frontmost is true
    -- result: application "Script Editor"
```

We know now that a single application will fit the bill, and this is the way we can get the details about it.

make [new] *className* [at *containerReference*] ¬
[with properties {*propertyLabel:propertyValue* ¬
[, *propertyLabel:propertyValue*] ... }] ¬
[to | with data *objectReference*]

Creating new Finder items is the job of the **make** command. The only classes of objects that the Finder can make are:

accessory suitcase

alias file

file

folder

group

user

In all cases, the new item that is created has no real data in it. For example, creating a file simply generates an empty SimpleText text file; a folder is obviously empty. For the most part, your scripts will use this command to generate alias files and folders, as well as users and groups for file sharing applications. For generating new text files or accessory suitcases, you are better served by scripting applications that perform those jobs.

By specifying a *containerReference* parameter, you can direct the Finder to put the new item in a container of your choice. Without any data for this parameter, the new item is placed on the Desktop, and assigned a name consisting of the word "untitled" and the name of the object class:

```
make new accessory suitcase
    -- result: suitcase "untitled suitcase" of application "Finder"

make folder
    -- result: folder "untitled folder" of application "Finder"
```

Of course, you have to be somewhat smart about specifying the kind of container as the destination: you can't create a new folder inside a font suitcase, for instance. But you can do it to other mounted disk volumes, and even the Trash (but why would you want to do that?).

At the same time you create a new item, you can set one or more of its properties by passing arguments along with the **with properties** parameter. The most common property to set is the name. For example, to create a new folder in the startup disk level whose name is "Today's Files" and set to be a sharable folder, the statement would be:

make folder in startup disk with properties {name:"Today's Files", shared:true}
    -- result: folder "Today's Files" of startup disk of application "Finder"

Not only is the folder icon property named after the statement, but the icon has changed to a sharable folder (Figure 17.4).

Today's Files

Figure 17.4 **A folder created as a sharable folder.**

Creating an alias to an item exhibits slightly different behavior with regard to otherwise optional parameters. If no *containerReference* parameter is supplied, then the Finder creates the alias in the same container as the original (as if choose Make Alias from the File menu), appending the word "alias" to the file name. Therefore, you should always specify a destination for the alias (unless you want to leave it with the original). Moreover, you must always include the last parameter: a valid reference to the original item of the new alias. For example, the following statement creates an alias on the Desktop to the Scripting Additions folder:

make new alias file at desktop to folder "Scripting Additions" of extensions folder
    -- result: file "Scripting Additions" of application "Finder"

Notice two things about this: first, the word "new" is required when making a new alias file; and second, when the destination is other than the original item's container, Finder does not add the word "alias" to the item's name. You may still, of course, pass along a new name property to rename the alias entirely:

make new alias file at apple menu items folder to application file ¬
        "Microsoft Word" of folder "Applications" of startup disk ¬
        with properties {name:"Word Processing"}

From this statement, a new entry, named "Word Processing," appears in the Apple menu to launch Microsoft Word. Notice here, too, that I've changed the order of the parameters. Since these are the equivalent of labeled parameters (Chapter 14), they can be placed in any order that reads best.

The only other caution about the **make** command is that the optional word, "new," must be omitted if you are creating a new text file. The statement

make new file

conflicts with the new file scripting addition. Therefore,

make file

is the accepted syntax.

move *objectReference* to *containerReference* ¬

   [replacing conflicts | existing items]

Unlike the copy command, the move command changes the location of a given item on the disk (provided the destination is on the same volume as the original location). The *objectReference* must be any valid Item class object—something other than the Trash that can be represented on the Desktop as an icon. This command has nothing to do with repositioning windows (see bounds property of window class objects, below).

Because your script may move an item to a container that already has an item by that name, you can specify that the command replace any existing item that has the same name. Any of the following synonyms for the replacing parameter are valid:

```
replacing conflicts
replacing existing items
replacing true
with replacing
```

But this can be risky if you're not sure that the item you're about to replace is just another copy or generation of the same kind of file. It is possible, for instance to replace a folder you need with a file of the same name.

Fortunately, the replacing parameter merely places the replaced item into the Trash. But it is better to write your script to test first for the existence of an item with the same name, and get the user's explicit permission to overwrite. See the similar discussion in the copy command, above.

Be aware that if the destination container is on another disk than the original, the move command automatically switches to a copy command in its behavior. This is, after all, how the Mac behaves when you drag an item to another disk volume. If the intention is to truly move the item, then your script must specifically delete the original. Here's an example that archives yesterday's correspondence files to a new folder on the archival server volume:

```
set todayZeroHour to date (date string of (current date))
set yesterdaysDate to date string of ((todayZeroHour) - (1 * days))
set newFolderName to yesterdaysDate

tell application "Finder"
    if disk "Archive " exists then
        make new folder at disk "Archive " with properties {name:newFolderName}
        move (every document file in folder "Letters" of startup disk ¬
            whose modification date < todayZeroHour) to folder ¬
            newFolderName of disk "Archive "
        delete (every document file in folder "Letters" of startup disk ¬
            whose modification date < todayZeroHour)
        empty trash -- or not if you want to play it safe
    else
        display dialog "Mount the Archive server and run this script again."
```

```
        end if
    end tell
```

You could also use the copy command in place of the move command in the above script, since the actions of both commands across disk volumes are identical.

open *objectReference* [using *applicationReference*]

The behavior of the open command varies widely with the type of object your script specifies as the *objectReference*. The only objects that don't respond to the open command are the Finder application, desktop, sharing privileges, and status window. Here is a synopsis of how the open command affects various classes of objects:

file classes For a document file, launches the application associated with the file and loads the file (the same as double-clicking the file in the Finder). Specify the using parameter to alter the application that opens the file. For an application file, starts the application.

container classes Opens the window to the container on the screen (the same as double-clicking a disk, folder, suitcase, or Trash in the Finder).

process classes Brings the process to the front of the screen (except the Finder, which is not recognized as a process in early versions of the scriptable Finder). This is similar to an activate command sent to an application (how you bring the Finder to the front), but the process does not need to be scriptable to respond to the open process command.

user and group classes When the Users & Groups control panel window is open, reveals the settings windows associated with those items.

Another kind of object that we haven't spent much time talking about yet is the selection object, defined as part of the Standard Suite. You see references to the selection often in scripts you record, because scriptable Finder interprets a double-click of an item as the two-step process of clicking once to select the item, and choosing Open from the File menu. Therefore, a recorded script might say something like this:

```
select item "Documents" of startup disk
open selection
```

while a purely scripted version might consolidate the operation as the following:

```
open folder "Documents" of startup disk
```

Feel free to write scripts with selection objects if you like, but proficient scripters will try to streamline their scripts with as few statements as possible.

To open multiple items with one statement, the *objectReference* parameter may be a list of items (of mixed classes, if you like), but you may also send the open command to the contents of a container. You must, however, follow a specific syntax:

> open every item of *containerReference*

The plural class name for an item is not valid in this context.

print *objectReference*

The print command can act on the same kinds of objects you can select for printing via the Print command in the Finder's File menu. An object reference that is a document file will launch the document's application and print the document from there. Conversely, you can print the contents of any container (window or desktop).

While you cannot specify an alternate application to print from the Finder, you can instead use the open command on a document file with an application that recognizes that file type, and script a print command for that application (provided the application is scriptable).

To print a series of items, place references to those items in a list. But to print the contents of a container (e.g., a folder containing a number of document files), the syntax must be very specific:

> print every item of *containerReference*

The plural class name for items of the container is not accepted.

put away *objectReference*

Like a few other Finder commands, the put away command's actions vary with the type of object—as the Put Away command in the File menu does. For disk objects, the command unmounts the volume (including ejecting ejectable disks). Any folder or file on the desktop is put away into the startup disk container. And for an item in the Trash, the put away command restores the item to the container from which it was moved to the Trash. Restoring items from the Trash can be accomplished in numerous ways. In addition to naming the item's reference by name,

> put away item "Anderson Invoice" of trash

you can also refer to items by number or use any other applicable reference, such as the following:

> put away item 1 of trash

> put away every item of trash

> put away document files of trash

As in the manual Finder, the command does not affect windows, which must be closed to be removed from the Desktop.

quit

The Finder's quit command is independent of quit commands you might send to quit other applications. In the following statement,

> tell application "Finder" to quit

you instruct the Finder to shut itself down as a process. Doing so causes all Desktop items (icons, windows, etc.) to disappear. Version 1.1 of AppleScript won't let you script the relaunching of the Finder—you must close all other running processes, at which time the Finder automatically relaunches. In later versions, you should be able to use AppleScript's launch command to restart the Finder or direct a tell statement to the Finder application.

restart
shut down
sleep

These three commands, which carry no parameters, are the scripted equivalent of the same commands in the Finder's Special menu. Restarting and shutting down the computer via script still cause the Mac to ask users about saving changed documents in running applications. To prevent these interruptions, you script should close down all processes prior to issuing either the restart or shut down commands.

Only PowerBooks computers respond to the sleep command. While a Power-Books sleeps, all processes are maintained in suspended animation, so no scripts run (in case you want to script the machine to come on at a certain time).

reveal *objectReference*

The reveal command is a helpful aid when you need to work with objects in their container windows. By specifying a reference to any nested item, you can instruct the Finder to open the window containing that item. At the same time, the reveal command selects the object, making it available for opening:

```
reveal folder "March 1995" of folder "Correspondence" ¬
    of folder "Documents" of startup disk
open selection
```

The above script first opens the Correspondence window on the Desktop and selects the March 1995 folder. The open statement in the next line, opens the folder to reveal its contents. Remember, then, that the goal of the reveal command is to select a nested object. A reference to the selected object comes back as the result, allowing your script to perform additional actions on that item.

When the *objectReference* parameter is an alias class item, the command reveals the alias file. But you can also script Finder to reveal the original item of the alias, as in:

```
reveal original item of item "Word Processing" ¬
    of apple menu items folder
    -- result: file "Microsoft Word" of folder "Applications" ¬
        of startup disk of application "Finder"
```

There is no real magic to this construction: getting the original item of an alias returns a valid object reference, which then becomes the parameter to the reveal command.

While the **reveal** command can accept multiple object references (in a list), only the last item(s) from the same container in the list will be selected. Any other windows that were opened while revealing the previous items will stay open, but no item will be selected in them.

select *objectReference*

The **select** command's behavior is in some ways similar to that of the **reveal** command. The primary distinction is that for the **select** command to actually highlight an object (as if clicking once on the item), the container window for that item must already be open. While the desktop is always open (as long as Finder is running), other folders or disks will have to be opened prior to selecting one or more items in the containing window.

Whose clauses work nicely with the **select** command. For example, to select all folders on the startup disk whose modification date is after 12:00 am today, the script would be:

```
set todayZeroHour to date (date string of (current date))
select every folder of startup disk whose modification date > todayZeroHour
```

The command then returns a list of all selected items, from which I can perform further processing, such as copying to a backup disk. Moreover, all selected items become part of the selection object, which responds to many commands, such as

```
move selection to disk "Archive"
```

An important tip to remember is that sometimes your scripts need to de-select an item prior to further operations. For example, there is a quirk in the **duplicate** command, which leaves not only the newly made duplicate item selected, but its name is also selected in the window. If your script then sets the name of the duplicate item to something new, the Finder accepts the change, but doesn't truly change the name of the item. To accomplish the name change, your script must first de-select the new item. The best way to de-select an item is to select nothing with a **select** command followed by no parameters. This lone command leaves the Finder in a state with no items selected.

set *objectReference* to *expression*

The Finder's **set** command behaves just as AppleScript's built-in command. By and large, you use the command to set properties of objects to appropriate values, as in

```
set name of folder "untitled folder" of startup disk to "Databases"

set shared of disk "Macintosh HD" to true

set bounds of window "Applications" to {47, 53, 303, 407}

set frontmost of process "FileMaker Pro" to true
```

When the first parameter is not a valid Finder object or other reserved word, AppleScript treats the word as a variable, into which goes the value of the expression parameter.

Sometimes it may not be clear from the dictionary as to the format or type of value a particular property requires. The best way to figure this out is to use AppleScript to get the current value of the desired property from an existing object. The resulting value will be formatted in the class the property expects (e.g., date, rectangle coordinates, object reference, string, or Boolean).

shut down (see restart)

sleep (see restart)

sort *referenceList* by *propertyLabel*

Unlike many of the commands in the Finder suite, the sort command does not make any changes to the contents of any window or other container. Despite the action-sounding name of this command, it merely returns a list of items sorted according to the desired property.

One key to using this command successfully is knowing how to fulfill the *referenceList* parameter. Any single object will do, but there's no point sorting a single object. Better yet is either a hard-wired list of items or items of a container. There is a distinction between a container and its items for this parameter. Consider the following:

```
sort startup disk by modification date
     -- result: startup disk of application "Finder"
```

Since we specified a single item (even though it is a container), the command returned the single item. But by asking for a particular kind of item of the container, we get what we want:

```
sort items of startup disk by modification date
     -- result: (references to all items with the most recent first)
```

You are free to be as specific as you like, retrieving only document files or only folders whose sharing property is true:

```
sort (folders of startup disk whose shared is true) by name
```

The second key to working with the sort command is figuring out which properties can be used as the *propertyLabel* parameter. Virtually every series of objects can be sorted by the common properties (name, creation and modification dates, kind), but a number of properties don't work with this command. For example, no Boolean property can be used as a sort key.

Also, the order in which items come back depends on the type of data. Lists of strings or references are alphabetical; dates come back with the most recent first; some numeric properties, such as label index, come back in descending order. If sorting order is important to the successful running of your script, be sure to run some tests on known objects to make sure the items come back in the order you expected.

If you want to change the sorting order for items displayed in a window, adjust the view property of an open window.

update *objectReference*

As you work with scriptable Finder, you will probably notice that some actions that take place in a script don't appear to happen instantaneously on the disk, particularly in processing-intensive scripts. The Finder performs the screen updating when some free processing cycles are available to the system.

If you'd rather not wait for those updates to occur, you can force the Finder to update container windows of your choice, either singly or any grouping, such as

```
update startup disk
```

```
update {folder "Documents" of startup disk, folder "Applications" of startup disk, ¬
    desktop}
```

Remember that updating applies only to the visual appearance of items in windows. Items are updated internally the instant a command is carried out.

Finder Objects and Properties

The dictionary for Finder Scripting Extension is one of the better ones, given the limitations of the format. A majority of the property descriptions for objects are self-explanatory. I will focus here on supplementary information for various properties. Remember to check Figures 17.1 through 17.3 to see how various objects may be related to others and what properties they inherit from their parents.

Accessory Process

You can obtain the file reference of any running desk accessory process via the desk accessory file property:

```
desk accessory file of accessory process "Alarm Clock"
    -- result: file "Alarm Clock" of folder "Apple Menu Items" ¬
        of folder "System Folder" of startup disk of application "Finder"
```

The process name must be the same as it appears in the Application menu, and the process must be running at the time you seek information about it.

Accessory Suitcase

An accessory suitcase is a special purpose container that can hold one or more desk accessory files. While suitcase containers act like virtually any kind of Finder container, you cannot script many actions for their contents. Nor do suitcase contents respond to commands that most other items do (see desk accessory file and font file descriptions, below for more details).

Alias File

Because of the syntactical confusion about alias references in other AppleScript commands and scripting additions, it should be comforting to know that a

Finder alias file is the kind of alias file you see as an icon with italicized name in any Finder container window. It's original item property (read-only) provides the reference of the item to which the alias file is an alias.

Application

The Finder's sole application object is the Finder, itself—the object of any tell statement directed to the Finder. A majority of the properties of the Finder application are handy references to containers your scripts may need to access from time to time—things like extensions folder, preferences folder, apple menu items folder, desktop, and trash.

The about this Macintosh property goes deeper into the running processes than the processes command does. The returned value includes any process that shows up taking memory in the About This Macintosh dialog box:

```
about this macintosh
    -- result: {process "HyperCard" of application "Finder", ¬
        process "Microsoft Word" of application "Finder", ¬
        process "QuicKeys™ Toolbox" of application "Finder", ¬
        process "Reminder Agent" of application "Finder", ¬
        process "Script Editor" of application "Finder", ¬
        process "System Software" of about this macintosh of application "Finder"}
```

Notice the System Software process. This represents the system and Finder running beneath all applications. Like any process, you can obtain various pieces of information about it:

```
partition size of process "System Software" of about this macintosh
    -- result: 4678074 (your figure will vary)
```

Another potentially useful property is largest free block, which tells you the amount of RAM available for loading an application (the same value as is in the About This Macintosh dialog). Since you can obtain the various partition sizes of application files, you can check for sufficient space prior to attempting a program launch:

```
tell application "Finder"
    if (largest free block) > partition size ¬
        of application file "Microsoft Excel" of folder "Applications" ¬
            of startup disk then
        tell application "Microsoft Excel" to launch
    else
        display dialog "Not enough memory to run Excel the way you like."
    end if
end tell
```

It's true that the Finder also evaluates the RAM situation upon any attempt to run an application, but you may prefer to have control over the process in a script.

File sharing is another place you can use Finder properties to make sure things are setup the way you want. For instance, a script can turn on file sharing. But the process of starting file sharing is not instantaneous, so if your script must both turn on file sharing and perform some actions relying on file sharing being on, you can hold up the script while sharing is starting up:

```
set file sharing to true
repeat until not (sharing starting up)
end repeat
(* more statements to do file sharing stuff*)
```

The repeat loop will actually slow down the startup process (since the script is grabbing some processor cycles that would otherwise be devoted to starting file sharing), but failure to wait for sharing to be on will cause script execution errors.

Finally, the visible property doesn't remove everything from view, as you might think. It's behavior is the same as choosing Hide Finder from the Application menu: all windows are hidden, but Desktop icons stay visible. To completely hide the Desktop, you must quit the Finder (but see cautions in the quit command description, above).

Application File

Unlike plain old AppleScript commands to applications (e.g., launch), which usually do not require a pathname for the program, any Finder command directed to an application file object must have the full reference as part of the object specifier. Therefore, while you can

```
launch "Microsoft Excel"
```

without a pathname, you must do the following to read a property of an application file:

```
get scriptable of application file "Microsoft Excel" ¬
    of folder "Applications" of startup disk
```

Because an application file is a child of the file class and a grandchild of the item class, you may use either of those two object class identifiers for application files if you like.

The scriptable property can be misleading if you're not careful. An application is scriptable in the Finder's eyes if it can respond to the four basic Apple events (known in AppleScript as Open, Run, Print, and Quit). This does not mean that the program is OSA-scriptable. A number of programs were made "System 7 Savvy" a couple of years ago, which indicate they respond to the core Apple events. OSA scripting came along further down the road, and at the moment, the Finder doesn't give us a clue as to the OSA scriptability of any application or process.

Via a script, you can change the two memory partition sizes that are user modifiable in an application's Get Info dialog box: Minimum size and Preferred size. The corresponding properties are minimum partition size and partition size. The Get Info dialog displays all memory values in kilobytes. Since each kilobyte is actually 1024 bytes, you have to do some arithmetic to calculate how your script should set the byte count of an application. For example, if you want the minimum partition to be 750K, you must set the value to 750 * 1024 bytes—768000:

```
set minimum partition size of application file "SuperWhiz™ " ¬
    of folder "Applications" of startup disk to 768000
```

Here's a handy script you save as an application to create a droplet that automatically adjusts the memory partitions of all programs dropped on it to 1200K:

```
on open fileList
    set newMinRAM to 1024 * 1200
    set newprefram to 1024 * 1200
    tell application "Finder"
        repeat with oneFile in fileList
            if kind of item (oneFile as text) is "application program" then
                set minimum partition size of ¬
                    application file (oneFile as text) to newMinRAM
                set partition size of ¬
                    application file (oneFile as text) to newprefram
            end if
        end repeat
    end tell
end open
```

This kind of droplet could come in handy for those who create HyperCard or FaceSpan standalone applications, and want a quick way to set the partitions after each build.

Application Process

These application processes are the ones that were launched as applications (not desk accessories) and show up in the Application menu, and whose references can be obtained by getting the Finder's processes. The lone property of this object class, application file, reveals the full reference to the application file that launched the process.

Container

We've seen that a container can be any item that holds other items. Opening a container displays a window of its contents. Most of the properties that are unique to containers have to do with its visual appearance when its window is open—things like whether its list view is completely expanded, what item are selected, and so on.

The view property, analogous to choices in the Finder's View menu, consists of an integer corresponding to a table of view possibilities:

Integer	View by
0	small icon
1	icon
2	name
3	modification date
4	size
5	kind
6	comment
7	label index
8	version

As an alternate, the words in the righthand column are also constants that you may substitute for the integer. But for comparison values, use the integers. In other words, this statement works:

```
if view of startup disk is 1 then beep
```

while the following generates an error:

```
if view of startup is icon then beep
```

The Finder does not recognize these constant values in comparison operations.

Related to the list view is the previous list view property. Stored as any integer value between 2 and 8, this property remembers the most recent outline view style chosen for the window's contents. The Finder keeps this information for all containers, and uses it for establishing the order of items returned by other commands.

Some of the expanded view properties are tricky. In particular, the expandable property is a Boolean value that indicates whether the container can be expanded *within the window of its containing window*—which must be open and in an outline view for the expanded property to be set to true. In other words, these properties are meant to help you expand or close up the expanded view of a folder you see in a list view. For example, consider the startup disk container, which starts out as an icon view, and we want to expand the view of the Documents folder that is in the startup disk:

```
tell application "Finder"
    if not (expandable of folder "Documents" of startup disk) then
        set view of container of folder "Documents" of startup disk to 2
    end if
    set expanded of folder "Documents" of startup disk to true
end tell
```

Our first test is whether the Documents folder can be expanded. If it's not, that means that the startup disk container is in one of its icon views, and must be changed to an outline view (we choose number 2, view by name). Notice how we use the container property of the Documents folder to obtain the proper reference to the container of the Documents folder. Finally, we set the expanded property of the Documents folder, which means that the folder is expanded within the startup disk's list view.

One other property to be careful with is the entire contents property. It returns a list of references for absolutely every item in this container, drilling down through all nested levels of containers therein. For large containers (disks, startup disk, high-level folders), this can be a time-consuming task. You will hear disk activity at first, and then perhaps no activity for some time. You may think that the Mac has frozen, when in fact, it is still processing. Trying to display the results of the entire contents of a large container will more than likely outrun the 20,000 character limit of the Result window. Nor does limiting the result with whose clauses speed the effort—the Finder must still retrieve every item for the whose clause to test the designated property. Getting this property, incidentally, does not time out AppleScript—I've seen it go more than 10 minutes on a hard disk volume with 250MB of data on it (and that was with a Quadra 840AV processing power).

Container Window

Properties unique to a container window are similar to those of a container, since the two objects describe much the same kind of stuff.

Content Space

A Finder content space is any location that can hold information, usually in a window, but also including the Desktop. This is not limited to container windows. As the parent class of all windows, the content space includes information windows, status windows, and the sharing window. A content space parent object has no properties—they're all defined by the special-purpose content spaces of the children objects.

Control Panel

All the properties denoted in the dictionary for the control panel object are actually properties for only one control panel: Views. In other words, scriptable Finder has given us a scriptable control panel here (along with Users & Groups, which has its own objects), but this is the only one that affects how the Macintosh behaves. The properties correspond to settings within the Views control panel, most of which are simple Boolean settings.

The icon size property is an integer from zero to two, corresponding to the large, medium, and small icon size, respectively. And the view font property is an integer representing the ID of the font used to display text in various views. To set this property, you must know ahead of time what the ID for the desired font is.

References to a control panel object must include its name and container, as in:

```
set calculate folder sizes of control panel "Views" ¬
    of control panels folder to true
```

Equally important, the control panel must be open to get or set any properties. Therefore, if your script adjusts settings in the Views control panel, users of your script will see the changes made in the panel, itself.

Desk Accessory File

While a desk accessory file is a descendant of the File and Item classes, it is not a full member of the family when the file is located inside a suitcase. Only when such a file is free and clear of a suitcase may you duplicate, move, copy, and delete it. Unfortunately, once a desk accessory file is in a suitcase, you cannot script a way to get it out—in fact Finder's script recording ignores anything you do inside a suitcase window.

Desktop-Object

This is the formal name for the object known to your scripts simply as "desktop." While descended from the Container object, it inherits only the following properties from all containers: container window, entire contents, previous list view, selection, and view. Not all of these, however, are settable (e.g., the view is always set to icon). For the most part, you will use the desktop as a destination container for various commands, as in

    make new alias file to control panels folder at desktop

Disk

The disk object is one of the Finder's most nested objects, inheriting properties from the Item, Container, and Sharable Container classes, while adding several unique properties of its own. A disk object is any volume that is mounted on the Desktop. This includes hard disks, floppy disks, removable mass storage, networked file servers, and shared volumes on a network.

If you have multiple disks mounted on your Desktop, you can use whose clauses to help identify disks that meet certain criteria for a command:

    put away (every disk whose ejectable is true)

This statement unmounts every ejectable volume located on the Desktop.

Document File

One of the most common file class objects, a document file is a file that is generated by an application. It inherits its properties about such things as file type and creator from its parent File class; many more properties come from the Item class.

If your script must know the name of the folder holding a file, be careful about which property you summon. For example, this statement

    get folder of document file "Sample Text" of startup disk

yields an execution error, because the container of a document file on the startup disk is not a folder, but a disk. The safest method is to specify a container reference, as in

```
get container of document file "Sample Text" of startup disk
    -- result: startup disk of application "Finder"
```

That way, no matter what kind of container it is, the script will work and return a valid reference for further processing.

File

A file object encompasses document files, application files, and several others (see Figure 17.1). Properties unique to files include the creator type and file type—four-character codes that are normally hidden from view of users, but help the Finder know what kind of icon to show in icon view windows. It's dangerous to set these two properties unless you are very familiar with the implications of those settings. Still, you can set a bunch of text files to launch your favorite word processor by changing the creator. Here's the script for a droplet (save it as an application) that changes any SimpleText file to a Microsoft Word text file:

```
on open fileList
    tell application "Finder"
        repeat with i in fileList
            set filePath to i as string
            if file type of file filePath is "TEXT" then
                set creator type of file filePath to "MSWD"
            end if
        end repeat
    end tell
end open
```

Folder

A Finder folder is merely a special-purpose container with no extra properties of its own. Still, the folder designation in a reference becomes meaningful if you try to claim another type of container (e.g., startup disk, desktop, trash) is a folder. Even though other AppleScript commands and scripting additions indicate that locations such as the desktop and trash are folders in their eyes, they are most definitely not folders in the Finder's scripting eyes. If your script can't predict what kind of container a user might choose (say, from a choose folder dialog), then use the container object reference rather than the folder reference.

Font File

As with the desk accessory file, a font file is a full citizen of the Item and File object hierarchy, only so long as the font file is outside of a font suitcase. Whenever a font file is inside a suitcase, you cannot script it to respond to numerous important commands, such as copying, moving, deleting, or duplicating.

Font Suitcase

A font suitcase is a typical Finder container, except that it can hold only font files. You can move, copy, and delete font suitcases, which may come in handy if you want your script to shift fonts in or out of the Fonts folder for a particular operation. But quite often, a font suitcase can contain multiple related fonts (e.g., several fonts that are good for fax documents). You cannot remove by script individual font files from a font suitcase—only the entire suitcase.

References to font suitcases located in the Fonts folder must include the full reference

```
font suitcase "Onyx" of fonts folder
```

but the Fonts folder doesn't have to be open to perform scriptable operations on font suitcases.

Group
User

Related to only the Users & Groups control panel, a group is an object that defines a named collection of multiple users for file sharing. Unfortunately, a group object is specified more as a file rather than a container, even though in real life it feels more like a container (of user icons). Therefore, while you can create new groups with the make command, you cannot assign users to or remove users from any group while under script control. You can, however, find out what users are assigned to any group:

```
contents of group "Accounting" of control panel "Users & Groups" ¬
    of control panels folder.
```

This yields a list of references to users (as items) in that group (which makes a group seem like a container).

The user object is scriptable with about the same lack of flexibility as a group. For example, you can create a new user, but there are no properties to set that replicate the checkboxes inside a user's specification window (e.g., allow program linking).

Information Window

Properties of the information window object correspond one-for-one with items you can view and/or change in an item's Get Info dialog window. In many cases, the properties you work with in this window can be retrieved or set directly on the object without having to open the Get Info window or make the longer reference to the window. The following two statements have the same result:

```
physical size of information window of folder "Documents" of startup disk
physical size of folder "Documents" of startup disk
    -- result: 55476224
```

Unlike some other window objects in the Finder, the information window does not need to be open to massage it, provided you use the full reference. If the Get Info window is open, and you want to refer to the window as is, then you must name it correctly, with the item name plus the word "Info."

The most efficient way to work with information window–specific properties, however, is via a full reference (which is derived from the information window property of any Item class object). As an example, the following script opens the information window of any folder on the startup disk that is larger than 25MB (in case we want to see what the jumbo folders are on the disk):

```
open (information window of folders ¬
    of startup disk whose physical size > 25600000)
    -- result: {information window of folder "Development" ¬
        of startup disk of application "Finder", information window ¬
        of folder "Documents" of startup disk of application "Finder", ¬
        information window of folder "System Folder" of startup disk ¬
        of application "Finder", information window of folder "Applications" ¬
        of startup disk of application "Finder"}
```

But other visual window properties that are inherited from the Window class object (e.g., bounds, index, titled, etc.) can be manipulated only when the window is open. You may reference such windows in any of the ways demonstrated here:

```
bounds of information window of folder "Documents" of startup disk
bounds of information window "Documents Info"
bounds of window "Documents Info"
    -- result: {8, 46, 250, 263}
```

Which style you use will often depend on what information is available as a result of other commands in a script.

Item

The Finder item is the granddaddy of object classes for most of what you script in the Finder. Whenever a script will act upon any of the possible item class children, it's safest to use the item class reference for the item. For example, here's a script that creates aliases on the Desktop for whatever kind of item is in a folder called "Important Stuff":

```
make new alias at desktop ¬
    to every item of folder "Important Stuff" of startup disk
```

The command will be carried out no matter what kind of item is in the folder (as desired). Had we filled the last parameter with "every file" or "every container," the script would halt with an execution error if it encountered an item of a class not covered by the one named.

The item class' properties form the foundation for every file and container object you use. Because most of the properties are explained sufficiently well in the dictionary, I'll focus on a few that need a bit more information.

You see bounds properties attached to a number of objects, including windows. The value for a bounds property is a list of four integers, representing the coordinate points for any visual artifact of the object. Measurements are in pixels from the top and left edges of the startup screen of your Mac (monitor number 1 for multiple monitor setups). The first two integers specify the coordinates of the top left point of the object; the second two specify the bottom right point. The order of integers is as follows: {left, top, right, bottom}.

Icons also have specific restrictions upon their size. Full-size icons must measure 32 pixels square, while small icons (including those in list views of windows) measure 16 pixels square. Finder will not allow your script to set the bounds of a pixel to a size other than the one allowed for a particular view type.

With respect to the size of an item, the Finder defines two properties: physical size and size. The first is often a larger number than the second, because it represents how much space on the disk the file occupies. How much overage there is depends on the size of the disk volume, because larger volumes have larger sector sizes—not every byte of a sector is necessarily used by the file or container. The plain size property, on the other hand, is the actual size of the item in bytes (in the Get Info window, it's the value in parentheses in the Size field).

As indicated by its position in the hierarchy of Figure 17.1, it's a good idea to be fully aware of the properties of the item class, since they're also available to all more specific items below (except for Group and User objects).

Process

The Finder process object is a parent class, which encompasses application and desk accessory processes—programs of one type or another that occupy RAM and, presumably, do some work. While a process seems to share a number of properties with application files, most of the properties are read-only while the program runs as a process.

The same caveat about the scriptable property for an application file applies to a process as well. Scriptability in these cases merely means that the process can respond to the core Apple events, but not necessarily OSA scripting commands.

Also, as noted earlier, in the first versions of the scriptable Finder the Finder itself does not show up as a process when your script asks for a list of every process, even though it shows up in the Application menu. This should be corrected in later versions.

Sharable Container
Sharing Privileges
Sharing Window

Properties associated with these three object classes concern themselves with file sharing settings and the status of shared objects (folders and disks). For instance, a script can make a container available for sharing on a network; it can distinguish between containers on a Desktop that are part of the user's machine or are on the screen by virtue of file sharing; it can establish which users or groups can access an item it shares on the network.

Because so many of the properties here reflect settings of a sharing dialog, Figure 17.5 shows a sample dialog and callouts of the equivalent properties. What may not be clear from the illustration, however, are the settings for group, guest, and owner privileges. Each of these has three settings, which are of class sharing privileges. For example, to turn off the make changes checkbox of the group privileges, the syntax would be:

```
set make changes of group privileges of startup disk to false
```

This assumes, of course, that the startup disk is set for sharing. Also, the sharing window does not need to be open to make these kinds of adjustments, unless the target of the command is the Sharing Window, itself.

To help you get a feel for a number of the key properties of these objects, the following script performs a sequence of steps to turn sharing on for a folder named "Sales Stats" with some special settings: no guest access; setting only a group named "Sales Office" to have password read-only access to files on the disk. Here's the script:

```
tell application "Finder"
    set shared of folder "Sales Stats" of startup disk to true
    set owner of folder "Sales Stats" of startup disk to "Danny Goodman"
    set group of folder "Sales Stats" of startup disk to "Sales Office"
    set see files of owner privileges of folder "Sales Stats" of startup disk to true
    set see folders of owner privileges of folder "Sales Stats" of startup disk to true
    set make changes of owner privileges of folder "Sales Stats" of startup disk to true
    set see files of group privileges of folder "Sales Stats" of startup disk to true
end tell
```

The behavior of sharing settings under script control is a bit different from setting items in the window manually. Of primary importance is that if you set the shared property of a container to true, all checkboxes for owner, users/groups, and guests are unchecked. Therefore, your script must specifically turn on all settings you want checked.

Among elements of file sharing that are missing are transparent methods of mounting servers from other locations—doing so without having to go through the password dialog. It is unlikely that the security-conscious folks at Apple will ever build this facility into the scriptable Finder. But a volume mounting OSAX

shared

owner

group

protected

owner privileges

group privileges

guest privileges

Figure 17.5 Sharing dialog and scriptable properties.

is provided on the companion disk (and described in Chapter 33) to help out. QuicKeys 3.0 provides a similar facility.

Sound File

A sound file is any file that contains sound resources of types that the system recognizes (including those that you can record from the Sound control panel). Unfortunately for scripters, sounds are normally stored as items in the System's suitcase. As you've seen for other items in suitcases (desk accessories and fonts), such items don't respond to most file-oriented commands.

This is especially problematical for scripters, because the Finder does play a sound file with the **open** command, as long as the sound file is outside of a suitcase. And since a script cannot copy or duplicate an item from a suitcase, you must prepare copies of system sound files and store them elsewhere on the disk for your scripts to play. For example, by manually making a copy of the Sosumi sound file from the System onto the startup disk, the following script line gets the Finder to play the sound:

```
open sound file "Sosumi" of startup disk
```

As a result, you might consider finding a convenient, known place for a Sounds folder somewhere in your System Folder, and maintain copies of desired sounds there. If you intend to give your script to others, you must also either include the sound files (if licensing and copyright allow) and have the user install them in the proper folder (but not the System suitcase).

Status Window

Finder status windows are the small windows that appear during lengthy Finder processes, such as copying a large number of files, or emptying a loaded Trash container. As full-class window objects, status windows would show up in lists of all windows that were gathered while such status windows were showing. Since most of the operations that trigger status windows these days pre-empt further script processing, there is little need to worry about these windows. But as the Macintosh operating system becomes more multitasking, we may want a script to check for the existence of a particular status window before processing the next statement.

Suitcase

The suitcase object is the parent class of both the font suitcase and accessory suitcase, meaning that the suitcase class identifier will work for either one, while the more specific identifiers must match the class of suitcase in the object reference. All suitcases inherit the properties of Item and Container class objects, adding none of their own. Suitcase references, like any other item, must include all containers leading to the suitcase object, as in

    suitcase "Times Roman" of fonts folder

Trash-Object

This is the formal name for the Finder's Trash, although our scripts call it simply trash. The trash-object has one unique property among containers: warn before emptying. This is the same Boolean property that is set with the checkbox of the same name in the Trash's Get Info dialog. This setting, however, does not affect the empty trash command, which empties without warning.

User (see Group)

Window

The Finder's window object is an important object because it defines properties for every kind of window. Among the properties are those that let you determine (but not change) whether a window is a floating palette or modal window—although at this point in the Finder's development, those instances rarely if ever occur at a stage that a script could check them.

Of all the properties two are concerned with coordinate settings of what is called the content region of a window. The content region is the space within a window that is not occupied by the titlebar or scrollbars—where actual content appears.

Windows can be referred to by name (pathnames aren't needed, because the Finder checks for a match against all open windows in the Finder process), but also by index number. The window with an index of 1,

    window 1

is the frontmost window in the Finder. As the layers move further away from the front, the index value of the window increases. Accessing windows by index is risky, because the instant another window comes to the front, the index values of all windows shift.

You can, however, find out whether a particular window is in front. An unlisted property of a content space object is the name property. Therefore, you can use this statement:

```
name of window 1
    -- result: "Macintosh HD"
```

to see if the front window is the one you desire to be in front. You can also arrange the order of open windows by setting the index property of each one to the desired level. If you do this, however, be sure you start by specifying the lowest numbered windows first, so as not to get other windows out of order.

Scriptable Finder Versions of Applications

In Chapter 16, I presented two Finder-related applications. One minded the Trash, while the other created alias files of anything dropped onto the script application. In this chapter, you can see how having the scriptable Finder makes these applications even easier to create, since you don't have to worry about finding or loading finderLib.

Here's all that is needed for the TrashMinder application:

```
-- TrashMinder 2.0 from "Danny Goodman's AppleScript Handbook"
-- by Danny Goodman
-- ©1994 Danny Goodman. All rights reserved.

-- Saved as Stay-Open script application.

-- Empties Trash every 3600 seconds (1 hour)
on idle
    tell application "Finder" to empty trash
    return 3600
end idle

-- Do one final empty when this app quits (on shutdown)
on quit
    tell application "Finder" to empty trash
    continue quit
end quit
```

This simple application is also the foundation for any kind of procedure you want to have your Finder perform on a regular basis during the day.

The Alias Maker droplet also gains a great deal of simplicity by using scriptable Finder in place of finderLib:

```
-- Alias Maker 2.0 from "Danny Goodman's AppleScript Handbook"
-- by Danny Goodman
-- ©1994 Danny Goodman. All rights reserved.

-- Saved as script application.

on open fileList
```

```
tell application "Finder"
    -- get path for Alias Maker, whose container
    -- is the eventual container of the new alias(es)
    set myPath to container of application file of process "Alias Maker"
    -- work through each dragged item
    repeat with oneFile in fileList
        -- create the alias
        make new alias to oneFile at myPath
    end repeat
end tell
end open
```

The scriptable Finder version works many times faster than the finderLib version, because it can do more work with fewer commands.

More Examples

System 7.5 installs a number of prewritten Finder scripts inside the AppleScript folder. Among the samples is a background agent that watches a shared folder for any changes, and alerts you when something has been added, removed, or modified. You can open these scripts to examine how they work. Make copies of them to modify on your own.

Finder scripting is a lot of fun. If your imagination starts running away with itself, that's a good sign you've been bitten by the scripting bug (but I hope not buggy scripts!).

CHAPTER 18

Scripting the Scriptable Text Editor

As you may have recognized in other discussions in this book, the distinctions between scripting with AppleScript's vocabulary and that of applications such as Scriptable Text Editor can blur. A lot of this has to do with the fact that AppleScript defines a number of the same kinds of objects as defined in Scriptable Text Editor—notably portions of text, such as paragraphs, words, and characters. This might mislead a beginner into thinking that AppleScript, itself, contains the vocabulary to deal with a lot of different kinds of data. As you'll learn in the next chapter, however, such is not the case.

AppleScript provides default definitions for text objects primarily for the convenience of parsing text returned from other commands (e.g., the path names that come from many Finder-related commands) and reassembling text to pass as parameters to other commands. But when inside a tell statement directed at a text-oriented program, such as Scriptable Text Editor, the object definitions for that program take precedence over AppleScript's definitions. By and large, the definitions are the same, but occasionally, such as text item elements and delimiters, their behaviors can diverge. The point is, therefore, to not take for granted any similarities between objects and properties in AppleScript and an application—or between similar applications for that matter.

Since you can retrieve the complete dictionary for Scriptable Text Editor via the Script Editor, I won't be repeating that information here. You may want to print the dictionary for further study if you like. What I'll be doing here, however, is pointing out some information and suggestions that aren't obvious in the dictionary listing.

Commands

I'll start with the commands defined in Scriptable Text Editor. It's important to show the syntax definition in a form consistent with others in this book (which may vary slightly from the form in the dictionary view) to help you understand some of the parameters.

close *directParameter* [saving in *file*] [saving yes | no | ask]

The only kinds of objects you can close in Scriptable Text Editor are documents and windows (which, as you'll soon see, are interchangeable anyway). Any valid window or document reference (usually named or indexed references) work. If you specify no more parameters, the default behavior would be the same as if you manually clicked the close box in the window: you would get an alert asking if you want to save changes.

Two optional parameters are dangerously close in their labels, distinguished by a single preposition (in). Use the saving in *file* parameter when you want to save a document for the first time or if you want to save a copy with a different name (or pathname). The file parameter must be a file reference (e.g., file "HD:Correspondence:Letter to Fred") for the script to compile.

Once a document has been saved, you can then use the other parameter, saving yes, to quietly save any changes to the document when it closes. To quietly discard all changes (such as when you use a document window as a workbench for string manipulation before yanking the data out for transfer to another application or document), specify saving no.

copy [*expression* [to *variableOrReference*]]

The copy command gets an overhaul inside Scriptable Text Editor. In addition to its AppleScript behavior for copying data into another variable or location, this version allows some copying to the Clipboard if the parameters are handled correctly.

First of all, if no parameters are specified—notice they're all optional here— then Scriptable Text Editor copies whatever is selected to the Clipboard. The application must be the active application (use the activate command) for any Clipboard-based operation to work properly. Optionally, you don't have to select text to be copied to the Clipboard, if you include an object reference as the first parameter. For example:

    copy paragraph 1 of document 1

copies the text of the paragraph to the Clipboard. For this to work, the direct parameter must be a reference to a single object that can be copied (e.g., paragraph, word, or character—but not plural or filtered references). You cannot copy a variable value to the Clipboard.

By including the second parameter, you tell the command to forget about the Clipboard, and copy the value of the first parameter to the second parameter, whether it be a variable or a reference to another location in the same or other document. In the following example, the script copies the first word of a paragraph to a variable value:

    copy word 1 of document 1 to firstWord

whereas, the following script copies the same word to the end of the document:

    copy word 1 of document 1 to end of document 1

When both parameters are included, the copy command returns a value of the reference to the data in its copied location. Otherwise, no result comes back.

count [of] *directParameter* [each *className*]

By and large, the count command in Scriptable Text Editor works the same as the AppleScript version. The tricky part, however, is when you use it to determine the count of a range of elements. Different range reference forms give you different results, so you must test this command against a representative sampling of the data you expect to count.

For example, if you start with the document shown in Figure 18.1, and you want to get a count of all words in paragraphs one and two, you might be tempted to use either of the following commands interchangeably:

    count of words from paragraph 1 to paragraph 2
    count of words of paragraph 1 thru 2

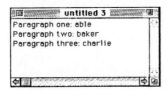

Figure 18.1 Sample
document.

The problem is, you'll get vastly different results. What you must pay attention to is how the references evaluate before they are counted. Let's follow each one to see what happens.

    tell document 1 of application "Scriptable Text Editor"
        count of words from paragraph 1 to paragraph 2
    end tell
        -- result: {1, 1, 1, 1, 1, 1}

Here's why:

    tell document 1 of application "Scriptable Text Editor"
        words from paragraph 1 to paragraph 2
    end tell
        -- result: {"Paragraph", "one:", "able", "Paragraph", "two:", "baker"}

In this case, the count command is telling you how many words there are in each item of the data returned by the reference. This was probably unexpected. To get the actual word count from this range format, you have to resort to the unseemly statement:

```
count of (count of words from paragraph 1 to paragraph 2)
```

But if we look at the other method of range reference we get an equally odd result:

```
tell document 1 of application "Scriptable Text Editor"
    count of words of paragraphs 1 thru 2
end tell
    -- result: {3, 3}
```

In this case, the expression words of paragraphs 1 thru 2 produces a list of lists:

```
-- result:{{"Paragraph", "one:", "able"}, {"Paragraph", "two:", "baker"}}
```

and the count command dutifully returns the count of words within each item of the outer list.

A more grammatical way of getting a word count is to assemble a different set of objects. For example, if we employ Scriptable Text Editor's text object and a range reference,

```
text from paragraph 1 to paragraph 2 of document 1
```

we receive the actual string, and the paragraph-ness of the source material is diluted. If we then get the words from that string, as in

```
words of (text from paragraph 1 to paragraph 2 of document 1)
```

we're back to a single list of words derived from the string. A count of that gives us the desired results:

```
tell document 1 of application "Scriptable Text Editor"
    count of words of (text from paragraph 1 to paragraph 2)
end tell
    -- result: 6
```

I've said it before, and I'll say it again, expression evaluation (including reference evaluation) is Number One.

cut [*directParameter*]

If no parameter is specified, then Scriptable Text Editor removes whatever is selected from the document and copies it to the Clipboard. Optionally, you don't have to select text to be cut, if you include an object reference as the first parameter. For example:

```
cut paragraph 1 of document 1
```

cuts the text from the paragraph and copies it to the Clipboard. For this to work, the direct parameter must be a reference to a single object that can be cut (e.g., paragraph, word, or character—but not plural or filtered references).

data size *of directParameter* [*as className*]

While related in a way to the length property of an object, the data size command should be used with extreme care. First of all, the command returns an integer or list of integers representing a byte count of the data, depending on the nature of the *directParameter* reference. For a single object (e.g., data size of word 3), the value is a single integer; for a range of objects, the returned value is a list of integer, each item in the list containing the data size for each object.

The data size in bytes, however, also includes a four-byte class identifier (which you don't see in the data). To avoid this extra four-bytes from getting into your formula, you can coerce the value with an extra parameter. For example if the first word of a document is "This," here are two methods of employing the data size command:

```
data size of word 1
   -- result: 8

data size of word 1 as string
   -- result: 4
```

For most operations involving the character length of text, the length property or count command are better suited.

delete *directParameter*

This command permanently deletes whatever text is referred to in the direct parameter. Notice that this command works only on application objects, not contents of variables within a script (even if it is within a tell statement directed to Scriptable Text Editor). As you can tell from these examples:

```
delete last paragraph

delete words 4 thru 6

delete words from word 1 to word 2

delete the selection

delete text from word 3 to word 5 of paragraph 4
```

you can specify single objects or ranges of objects. Be aware, however, that when you delete a word, none of the spaces surrounding the word are deleted with the word. In fact, if you delete a range of words, none of the spaces between words within the range are deleted, either. To delete a range of words, including their spaces, delete the text object specified by a range reference (see the last example, above).

duplicate *directParameter* [*to reference*]

When you specify all parameters to the duplicate command, the results are the same as the copy command when copying one chunk of information to another location. The primary difference, however, is that if you don't specify a destination parameter, then the duplicate command places a copy of the original immediately after the original in the text. Also, like the copy command, duplicate works only with single objects, not ranges or plural objects, unless the range is part of a text object specification, as in

```
tell document 1 of application "Scriptable Text Editor"
    duplicate (text from word 1 to word 2 of paragraph 4) to end
end tell
```

exists *directParameter*
directParameter exists

The exists command is one of the more helpful ones (found in many applications) that lets your script determine if a particular object exists before your next statement tries to do something to it. The direct parameter must refer to a valid reference to an object (or range of objects). This command returns a Boolean value as a result, and is therefore commonly used as if it were a unary operator in if-then and repeat constructions:

```
tell application "Scriptable Text Editor"
    if not (window 1 exists) then
        make new window
    end if
end tell
```

Unfortunately, there is no negative synonym for the exists command (e.g., window 1 doesn't exist), so you may have to fashion statements with the Not operator to come up with the desired logic.

[get] *directParameter* [as *className*]

This get command works like AppleScript's. The formal definition includes an optional as className parameter, which coerces the value as it goes into the result variable. AppleScript also achieves the same result by appending an as operator to the get statement. It's a one-step convenience you should remember, since you don't need an extra statement to coerce the value for another use later.

make [new] *className* [at *location*] [with data *dataValue*] ¬
[with properties ¬
{*propertyName*: *propertyValue*,...,*propertyName*: *propertyValue*}]

The make command is one of the more powerful ones in Scriptable Text Editor, provided you understand its intricacies (and its bugs). The purpose of this command is to generate new objects—documents, paragraphs, words, or characters. We've already seen in the script recording session in Chapter 3 how the make new document statement works. You can direct the new document window to be placed at the beginning or end of the queue of windows.

Text objects require data (even empty data, if necessary, to quash weird behavior that inserts the word "quill"—Scriptable Text Editor's original code name—as the default data). Interestingly, when you make a new word or paragraph, Scriptable Text Editor inserts the proper spaces or return characters to keep the new object distinct from its neighbors. For example, if we start with the document shown in Figure 18.2a, and issue the following script:

```
tell document 1 of application "Scriptable Text Editor"
    make new word at end of word 1 of paragraph 1 ¬
        with data "number"
end tell
```

the document is modified as shown in Figure 18.2b, which shows spaces on either side of the new number. I could also have made the new word at beginning of word 2, but if the statement had read:

```
make new word at word 2 of paragraph 1 with data "number"
```

the make command would have *replaced* word 2 with the new word. Therefore, be careful to use relative references when you mean them.

The same goes for inserting paragraphs. If the script makes a new paragraph at some location, Scriptable Text Editor places a return before and after the new data, creating what the script asked for: a new paragraph.

You can use this technique to insert spaces or carriage returns at any location. The most reliable way is to make the new object at the end of an object, and pass an empty data value, as in:

```
repeat 2
    make new paragraph at end of paragraph 3 with data ""
end repeat
```

This fragment inserts blank lines after paragraph 3. Whatever data you pass, it must be appropriate for the object you're creating. In our case here, any string or number that can be coerced to a string will work.

The command also allows your script to set properties of the new object at the same time it creates the object. An optional parameter, with properties, lets your script supply a record of property labels and values. Of course, the properties must be among the properties that Scriptable Text Editor defines for

Figure 18.2 Adding a new word.

the object you're creating. For example, you can create a new document window and set its bounds property at the same time:

```
tell application "Scriptable Text Editor"
    make new document at beginning ¬
        with properties {bounds:{50, 50, 300, 300}}
end tell
```

For text, you may want to set multiple properties, as in:

```
tell document 1 of application "Scriptable Text Editor"
    make new paragraph at beginning with data "Introduction" ¬
        with properties {size:24, style:bold, font:"Palatino"}
end tell
```

which sets three properties of the new text. As with any labeled parameters, the properties can be in any order, and only those you want to set need to be included.

move *directParameter* to *relativeReference*

The move command works with single objects only (i.e., not ranges or plural objects), and moves the data to another location in a document. The destination is any relative reference, so it could even be a location in another open Scriptable Text Editor document. The key is that the references to both the source and destination need to be complete:

```
tell application "Scriptable Text Editor"
    move paragraph 1 of document "Bill of Rights" to ¬
        end of document "Article Numbers"
end tell
```

Only the exact data referred to in the direct parameter is taken for the ride—no word or paragraph delimiters come along, unless they're included in a **text from** *range* object. Test your application thoroughly to make sure you are getting the desired results.

open *fileReference*

While the open command is a common one in AppleScript, when an application, such as Scriptable Text Editor, defines it for itself, the program puts its own spin on the command's behavior. For example, if the open command is directed to Scriptable Text Editor, then only files it can open are valid parameters. Scriptable Text Editor can open files it created and any other file saved as a text-only file (file type TEXT). For example:

```
tell application "Scriptable Text Editor"
    open file "HD:System Folder:Control Panels:PowerBook"
end tell
```

generates an error indicating that Scriptable Text Editor cannot open a file of that type.

If a file is already open when a script tries to open it, Scriptable Text Editor does not open a second copy. The command is essentially ignored.

paste *directParameter*

As simple as this command looks, it does require additional stuff to make it work as desired. As in the manual world, a script must either select text for replacement by what's in the Clipboard, or set the text insertion pointer someplace. Therefore, in AppleScript, you must select either a chunk of text or an insertion point (that invisible space between characters) at some location before issuing the paste command. See the discussion about the **select** command and the insertion point object later in this chapter.

As an alternative to pre-selecting the paste location, you may specify the spot as a parameter to the **paste** command. For example, to replace the second paragraph of a document with the contents of the Clipboard, the script would be:

```
tell application "Scriptable Text Editor"
    activate -- required for all Clipboard activity
    paste paragraph 2 of document 1
end tell
```

It reads funny, because we're actually pasting *into* the specified object.

print *directParameter*

The print command works only on the following Scriptable Text Editor objects: files, documents, and windows (the two last objects being largely identical anyway). A file or alias reference may be used for files, as in:

```
print file "HD:Correspondence:Letter to Fran"
```

For documents and windows, the parameter is any valid reference that points to an open document. That means you can use the indexed reference (e.g., window 2) or name reference (e.g., document "Bill of Rights"). The command also accommodates multiple items of mixed classes in a list, as in:

```
print {document "Bill of Rights", window 2, ¬
    file "HD:Correspondence:Letter to Fran"}
```

Each print command presents the Print dialog box for user entry of further settings, such as multiple copies. Therefore, by placing multiple files in a list, the script produces a single dialog to cover all documents. Moreover, Scriptable Text Editor doesn't appear to store its Page Setup attributes with each document, so you may not be able to script one document out of many to print landscape, while the rest print portrait.

quit [saving yes | no | ask]

> This is pretty standard stuff. If you don't specify the saving parameter, the default behavior is **saving ask**, which presents an alert to the user asking to save changes to each modified document that is open at the time.

revert *directParameter*

> Just like the Revert menu command, this AppleScript command restores a document (or window) object to the state that was last saved to disk. Unlike the menu command, however, the scripted version does not present an alert asking the user for confirmation. It's assumed that if your script is calling it, you know what you want (and the user should accept it). The parameter for this command can be any document or window reference, as in
>
> > revert document "Bill of Rights"
>
> and only a single object can be reverted with each call to this command.

save *directParameter* [in *fileReference*] [as text]

> This is the command you use to save a new or existing document. The direct parameter must be a reference to an open document or window (and only one per **save** command). If the file already exists on the disk, and you just want to save an updated version, then you don't need any further parameters.
>
> But if you want to save the document in another location or with another file name, or if the document hasn't been saved yet, you can specify a file name parameter, as in:
>
> > save document 1 in file "HD:Correspondence:Memo to Frank"
>
> Omitting a file name parameter on an untitled window, produces the unwanted result of saving the document to a file named "untitled x," where x is the number of the untitled window in the window's titlebar. Be careful with saving a new document to include a file name parameter.
>
> You can also elect to save the document as a plain text file that can be opened by lots of other programs. Append the **as text** parameter to take care of that job. Be forewarned, however, that any text styles, fonts, and sizes are lost when saving a document as text.

select *directParameter*

> Since a lot of other commands can work with text selections (a selection is an object), the **select** commands is an important one in Scriptable Text Editor. It allows a script to select any text object—insertion point, character, word, paragraph, or text—of a document. Selecting a range of text requires a specific range reference form.

When a script selects an object, it performs the same action as if you had manually selected the object with the mouse. Activating the program after issuing the **select** command, you see the object selected. It is now ready for copying, pasting, or replacing.

To insert text at a point without replacing any text, you use the **select** command to select an insertion point, as in:

```
select insertion point after word 3 of paragraph 2
```

This action is the same as clicking the text cursor at the point to plant the physical text insertion pointer. For example, if you start with the document in Figure 18.3a, and then run this script:

```
tell document 1 of application "Scriptable Text Editor"
    select insertion point before word 2
    set selection to "number "
end tell
```

the document changes to what appears in Figure 18.3b. The script selects the point immediately before the second word, and then sets that point to some new text—just like typing it there manually.

Selecting a range of text in a document requires selecting the text object of a range reference, as in:

```
tell application "Scriptable Text Editor"
    select (text from word 20 to word 45) of document 1
end tell
```

You must use this text from *range* form, and not text of words 20 thru 45, which generates an error indicating multiple objects. This is a critical fine point for selecting a range of text. Fortunately, you can even mix the classes of objects in the range reference, as in:

```
tell application "Scriptable Text Editor"
    select (text from word 20 to paragraph 4) of document 1
end tell
```

which selects all text starting with word 20 of the document to the last character of paragraph 4.

(a)   (b)

Figure 18.3 Inserting a word via an insertion point.

To perform the same as selecting the entire contents of a document, use the following construction:

```
select text of document 1
```

AppleScript and Scriptable Text Editor also accept the word **contents** for text.

When the object of the **select** command is a document or window, the command brings the referenced object to the front, as if clicking on it with the mouse. If the window is already at the front, nothing bad happens to your script.

set *directParameter* to *value*

We saw earlier in the book how AppleScript's own **set** command is used primarily as a way to assign values to variables or properties. In Scriptable Text Editor, the command assumes added powers of being able to assign a value to an existing text object. For example:

```
set paragraph 1 to "Introduction"
```

replaces whatever paragraph 1 of the document was with the new word. That goes for other kinds of text objects as well, as in:

```
tell document 1 of application "Scriptable Text Editor"
    select insertion point before word 2
    set selection to "number "
end tell
```

where the **set** command replaces a selection object with a string value. In all cases, the value being assigned to the text object must be a string or other class that can be automatically coerced to a string (e.g., no lists or records).

Objects

We now switch from the command side to the object side. Again, I'll only supplement here what you can find in Scriptable Text Editor's own dictionary. The important parts about an object's definition are the properties. While the elements become important in determining the hierarchy of containers (e.g., character contained by a word contained by a paragraph, etc.), the listings of elements often contain information that is of value to Scriptable Text Editor's internal workings, but are either not accessible or are not relevant to scripts you write.

Application

Applicable commands: **open, print, quit, run.**

A few of the properties of an application require some explanation.

You can get the contents of the application's clipboard property (which, when you switch out to another application, becomes the system Clipboard), but you must be careful with this. The data in the Clipboard is not simple text. For example, if you copy the first paragraph of the Bill of Rights document to the Clipboard, here's what AppleScript sees in the Clipboard:

```
{Error! Cannot open data source., ¬
    "ARTICLE I", paragraph 1 of document 1 of ¬
    application "Scriptable Text Editor", "ARTICLE I"}
```

Yikes! This actually contains a lot of information that is helpful when the data is pasted into another document, but it's probably more than you bargained for if you just wanted to find the text that was copied. You can, however, get the clipboard property of the application coerced to two valuable classes:

```
clipboard as string
    -- result: "ARTICLE I"
```

```
clipboard as reference
    -- result: paragraph 1 of document 1 of application "Scriptable Text Editor"
```

In theory, you can also set the contents of the Clipboard, but the data must be in the same form that you see above for its full data set, not just some string.

Scriptable Text Editor has its own text item delimiters property, which is independent of AppleScript's global text item delimiters property. The confusion that reigns supreme here, however, is tied to the text item object of Scriptable Text Editor. The text item delimiters property of the application (which is fixed as a comma) determines how Scriptable Text Editor defines each text item object. See the discussion, below, about the text item object for more about the distinction between this object and AppleScript's, and why you can mix the two within a script directed at Scriptable Text Editor.

The other property worth noting is the selection property. It contains a complete reference to whatever text is selected in the document, usually by character count. That means you can use this property as a parameter for commands that allow such things, such as cut, copy, and move, as in:

```
move the selection to end of document 1
```

As an alternate to the select command, you can also set the selection property to a valid reference. Therefore, the two statements

```
select paragraph 1 of document 1
set selection to paragraph 1 of document
```

perform the same actions.

Character

Applicable commands: copy, count, cut, data size, delete, duplicate, exists, get, make, move, select, set.

The dictionary's list of elements for the character object is misleading, because you can truly work only with the text element of any character or series of characters, although this element gets you nothing more than the characters themselves:

```
characters 1 thru 7 of document 1
   -- result: {"A", "R", "T", "I", "C", "L", "E"}
text of characters 1 thru 7 of document 1
   -- result: {"A", "R", "T", "I", "C", "L", "E"}
```

To get the actual string of characters, use the text object defined by a range of characters:

```
text from character 1 to character 7 of document 1
   -- result: "ARTICLE"
```

Other properties are straightforward except for the style and uniform styles properties, which are also available in other objects. I'll take the time here to explain what these properties are all about.

Starting with the style property, let's use the first character of the Bill of Rights document as a workbench. If we get

```
style of character 1 of document 1
   -- result:{class:text style info, on styles:{plain}, ¬
      off styles:{bold, italic, underline, outline, shadow}}
```

the resulting record looks complex, but it tells us a lot about the style characteristics of the character (or other text object we may have selected). The first field listing the class is always the same for this data, and we can generally ignore it. The other two fields, on styles and off styles, tell us which font styles are on and off, respectively. For example, if we manually change the first character to be bold and underlined, the style property of character 1 would be

```
{class:text style info, on styles:{bold, underline}, ¬
   off styles:{italic, outline, shadow}}
```

In other words, the bold and underline styles are both on for that character, while all others are off. The record always shows all possible enhanced styles, and in which category they fall.

But unlike other records, your script cannot access the values directly. Instead, you can see if the style property of a text object contains a certain style, as in:

```
if style of word 1 contains {bold,italic} then
   set style of word 1 to plain
end if
```

The governing style for any text object is the style of first character of the object, even if the real style should vary among characters elsewhere within that chunk of text. And that brings us to the second property, uniform styles.

For any chunk of text, there may be styles that are on for all characters and off for all characters; other styles may be on or off depending on the character. The uniform styles property reveals in the same kind of on styles/off styles record which styles are valid—uniform—for the entire text object. For example, in the word

<u>AppleScript</u>

all characters are bold, and some are underlined. The uniform properties of this word in Scriptable Text Editor would be:

```
{class:text style info, on styles:{bold}, off styles:{italic, outline, shadow}}
```

Notice that the one style that is both on and off at various characters—underline—isn't listed in either category. By deduction you figure out which styles are variable. The true value of the uniform styles property is that you can determine if an entire chunk of text is set to a particular style:

```
if uniform styles of word 1 contains {bold} then
    set style of word 1 to plain
end if
```

Setting a chunk of text to a particular style also takes some care. While you can use the long-winded version of the record as a parameter to the set command (it's still long-winded even if you leave out the class field, as you're allowed), as in,

```
set style of paragraph 1 to ¬
    {on styles:{italic}, off styles:{bold, underline, outline, shadow}}
```

you can also use a shortcut, if you use it carefully. The shortcut allows you to pass along only the style(s) you want on, as in:

```
set style of paragraph 1 to {italic}
```

(you don't have to put a single parameter in a list if you don't want to, but it's good practice to remind you that multiple settings require a list form). The potential problem here, however, is that this does not turn off any other styles that may affect the text object. For example, if a paragraph is already bold, and we set its style to italic, then the result is a paragraph in bold, italic. Sending the long parameter solves the problem, as does an intermediate setting to plain before resetting to another style or combination of styles.

This whole system may seem complex at first, but get used to it. Expect to see this system to be in any program that supports user-settable font-styles.

Window/Document

Applicable commands: close, copy, count, delete, duplicate, exists, get, make, move, print, revert, save, select, set.

As mentioned earlier, window and document objects are interchangeable: you can't have one without the other, and each ends up having the same elements and properties. And what a list of properties they have. Most are read-only, and define visible properties of the document window.

The bounds property is a bit unusual, unless you've done some other Macintosh programming before. The property contains coordinate points for the location of the document area of a window (exclusive of titlebar and scrollbars). While the value is a list of four values, they represent two points on your screen. Your screen's coordinates start at 0,0 at the upper left corner of the screen. The left value of a point represents the horizontal (y) distance from zero. Therefore, the point 100,0 is 100 pixels to the right of zero at the very top edge of the screen.

If the bounds property of a document window is the list {50,50,350,350}, it means that the top left corner of the document area (below the titlebar) of that window is at point 50,50 on you screen, and the lower right corner is at point 350,350 on your screen. The visible area would be exactly 300 by 300 pixels square.

To move a window on the screen, you set the bounds property, feeding it a list of all four coordinates. While other programming languages may let you adjust the location of the window by just setting its position property (the upper left corner), Scriptable Text Editor doesn't give us that ability (the position property is read-only). Therefore, if we want to move the window and keep it at its same size, we must adjust all four coordinates before setting the bounds property of the document window.

File

Applicable commands: open, print.

The file object comes into play in only a few instances, as you can see from the list of commands that address this object. While it may be easy to confuse a document and file, AppleScript regards them as very distinct objects, with no shared behavior or properties. A file is merely a place name on a disk, whereas a document is the information stored in that place.

Insertion Point

Applicable commands: copy, count, data size, exists, get, set.

An insertion point is a strange text object, when you first meet it. It is a text object of zero length, and exists between characters (or between a character and either the beginning or end of a document). Don't confuse the insertion point with the insertion pointer. There is only one insertion pointer—that flashing bar you locate between characters; there are as many insertion points in a document as there are slivers of zero-length space between characters. Therefore, insertion point 1 is the space between the beginning of a document and the first character; insertion point 2 is the slot between characters 1 and 2; and so on.

The insertion point object bears many of the same properties of other text objects, especially font and style characteristics. The reason for this is that you can set the characteristics prior to inserting text at that point—text that will assume the font and style properties of the insertion point. For example:

```
tell document 1 of application "Scriptable Text Editor"
    set style of insertion point before paragraph 4 to shadow
    set selection to before paragraph 4
    set selection to "howdy "
end tell
```

Here we set the style of the point immediately before paragraph 4. Then we set the insertion pointer to that spot by selecting it. In the final set command, we replace the zero-length insertion point with a word. In the process, the new word assumes the font and style properties of the insertion point it replaces.

As you might guess, the insertion point object is pretty important in text-oriented scripting, even if AppleScript allows you to omit the explicit reference to it in many circumstances. For instance, the statement

```
copy "Fred" to insertion point before paragraph 4
```

can also be stated more succinctly by

```
copy "Fred" to before paragraph 4
```

Scriptable Text Editor understands the shorter version to mean copying to the insertion point before the paragraph.

Finally, while the number of commands that the object understands is lengthy, the need for ever calling some of them is remote to nil. For instance, as long as the reference to any insertion point is valid, it always exists. There also isn't much need to copy an insertion point, since there's nothing to it, and anywhere you copy it already has one.

Paragraph

Applicable commands: copy, count, cut, data size, delete, exists, get, make, move, select, set.

The paragraph object is pretty straightforward in Scriptable Text Editor. Its definition is the same as that of AppleScript, plus several properties, which we've already discussed in relation to other text objects. The length and offset properties can come in handy when you need to calculate the character locations of the beginning and end of a paragraph. The offset property tells you how many characters into the document the paragraph object starts. Add the length of that (minus one), and you have the offset of the last character as well.

Selection

Applicable commands: copy, count, cut, data size, delete, duplicate, exists, get, make, move, set.

A selection object consists of whatever text is currently selected in a document, defined in a range reference of the largest text objects it can determine (words if the selection starts at the beginning of one word and stops at the end of another; otherwise a character count). If no characters are selected, then the selection is the reference to the location of the text insertion pointer. A document always has a selection, even if it is just an insertion point. For example, if the first two words of the second paragraph of the Bill of Rights document are selected, the selection is:

(text from word 3 to word 4) of document 1 of application "Scriptable Text Editor"

But if we select up to—but not including—the last character of the second word, the selection object is defined as:

(text from character 11 to character 23) ¬
    of document 1 of application "Scriptable Text Editor"

And if we position the text insertion pointer just before the last character of that second word, the selection object comes back as:

insertion point after character 23 ¬
    of document 1 of application "Scriptable Text Editor"

Use of the selection object is primarily as a text object to be copied from or to. While you can set the selection object to some range of text, you can accomplish the same with the **select** command.

Text

Applicable commands: copy, count, cut, data size, delete, duplicate, exists, get, make, move, select, set.

Scriptable Text Editor defines the text object as a series of one or more contiguous characters. A single text object can contain a range of other objects—very helpful when you need to pass a range to a command that works only with single objects (e.g., move).

Here is how you can change a range reference of paragraphs into a single text object:

get text from paragraph 1 to paragraph 3 of document 1

This returns the actual text string of the range indicated in the boundary parameters, and not a list of words or paragraphs. In fact, all carriage returns between paragraphs are preserved, which would not be the case in:

get paragraphs 1 thru 3 of document 1 as string

or

get text of paragraphs 1 thru 3 of document 1

each of which returns its own peculiar data and class, but not the one that is an exact copy of the text you see in the document. This takes some getting used to, so be prepared to stumble the first few times you attempt to work with the text object.

Text Item

Applicable commands: copy, count, cut, data size, delete, duplicate, exists, get, make, move, select, set.

A text item object is reliant on the (fixed) comma text item delimiter property of the Scriptable Text Editor application. It is distinct from items of a list and AppleScript's text item objects. A Scriptable Text Editor text item object is part of a document, and not valid for anything in a variable within a script—that's what AppleScript's text items are for. Therefore, you can mix references to AppleScript's text item delimiters and text items with those of Scriptable Text Editor within a tell statement directed that the program. AppleScript's property and object definition applies to text you work with in variables.

A text item is any chunk of text between commas (or between the beginning and a comma; or between a command and the end). Each text item within a designated chunk of text has an index, and the number of text items depends on the number of commas within that chunk.

To demonstrate the differences between Scriptable Text Editor's and AppleScript's text item objects, consider the following script:

```
tell application "Scriptable Text Editor"
    -- STE's text item object
    set STEFirstItem to text item 1 of document 1
    -- put text into variable for AS's text item object
    get text of document 1
    set ASFirstItem to text item 1 of result
end tell
{STEFirstItem, ASFirstItem}
    -- result: {"able", "able, baker, charlie, dog."}
```

Notice that the Scriptable Text Editor text item object of a document is defined by the comma; AppleScript applies its own text item delimiters property (default of { }), and regards the entire variable value as a text item. We would have to change AppleScript's property to {","} for the results to be the same.

Text Style Info

Applicable commands: copy, data size, exists, get, set—all indirectly.

This object is the object that specifies the font style info (on styles and off styles) of a text object. You don't call this object directly, but do touch it (behind the scenes) when you get and set the style of any text object. This object is listed in the dictionary for the sake of completeness, but only tends to confuse newcomers as being an object you access like any other object.

Word

Applicable commands: copy, count, cut, data size, delete, duplicate, exists, get, make, move, select, set.

Properties of word objects are the same as paragraph objects. The length and offset properties can be as useful when working with words as they are for paragraphs. The same text style behavior also applies to words.

Applied Scriptable Text Editor

In Chapter 3, we recorded a script that combined five files into one. Now that we've learned more about AppleScript and Scriptable Text Editor, it's time to revisit that script, and revise it for more elegance and efficiency. You can refer to the original listing in Chapter 3 or view it from the script application file in the Handbook Script:Chapter 03 folder.

The most obvious point to acknowledge is that this is a repetitive operation in itself. Except for the names of the files, the copying and pasting into the final document are the same for each of them. That should be a signal for condensation into some kind of repeat loop.

Another potential problem for the script, especially if you hand it over to inexperienced Macintosh users, is that it relies heavily on the contributors placing their revised snippets in precisely the folder originally designed. When you recorded the script, the path names to those places were hard-wired. But if a hard disk name should change, then the path names are no longer valid, and the script breaks. We can build in protection for that, and, via script properties, make sure that any changes that occur get recorded to the script so the consolidator won't have to go hunting around volumes for the files the next time.

Here's the revised script for version 2.0 of SW License Consolidator:

```
property fileNames : {"0. Introduction", "1. License", "2. Restrictions", ¬
    "3. Warranty", "4.General"}
property pathNames : {"", "", "", "", ""}
property consolidatedFile : ""
tell application "Scriptable Text Editor"
    activate
    make new document at beginning
    -- work our way through each of the files
    repeat with i from 1 to count of fileNames
        -- set up a repeat loop that recursively tries opening
        -- one of the stored path names. If the open fails, then
        -- the error handler prompts the user to locate the file,
        -- and sets the value of the property for the next time
        repeat
            try
                open file (item i of pathNames)
```

```
                   -- open worked, so let's get out of repeat loop
                   exit repeat
               on error
                   choose file of type "QUIL" ¬
                       with prompt "Locate the file "" & item i of fileNames & "":"
                   set item i of pathNames to (result as string)
                   -- now we can loop around and try again
               end try
           end repeat
           -- grab the entire opened document, including styles
           set oneChunk to contents of document 1 as styled text
           close document 1 saving no
           -- append it to new document
           copy oneChunk to end of document 1
       end repeat
       try
           save document 1 in file consolidatedFile
       on error
           -- only if consolidatedFile property is empty
           -- or previous volume no longer exists.
           -- save it to the root
           set consolidatedFile to (path to startup disk as string) & "Software License"
           save document 1 in file consolidatedFile
       end try
   end tell
```

The behavior of script properties comes in handy for this application. By storing the names to the individual files as a list in a property, it simplifies making changes to the file names, or modifying this script to work on a different set of files. The pathNames property will, after the first time through the script, store the complete pathnames to each of the files. We must initialize it as a list of five empty strings, because we need to address each item by number when we store information there for the first time. If the list were completely empty, AppleScript would squawk if we tried to set item 1 to some value. The last property is the path to the saved consolidated file. This could be hard-wired with a value, if you like.

The heart of the script is a large repeat loop, which cycles through each of the component files. A nested repeat loop sets up a try statement to open each of the files stored in the pathNames property. If the file opens successfully, then execution exits out of the repeat loop; otherwise, it goes to the error handler. There, the user is prompted to locate a specific file, and the corresponding item in the pathName property is set (when saved as a script application, the new settings will automatically be stored with the script so it won't have to go through this error routine unless the path is no longer valid). The repeat loop goes around again to try the open file command.

I've modified how the script gets the data from the component files into the main document. Instead of copying and pasting (which takes a bit more time due to screen updates for the selection process), the new script copies the contents of each component as styled text (to preserve any font settings), closes the component, and then copies the value to the end of the consolidated document.

Once all five components are in the document, we use one more try statement to make sure we save the file properly. The method here of trying a save to a pathname and then catching any error is a variation of the one used above for opening. Instead of putting everything in a repeat loop, the error handler sets the property value and performs the save itself, rather than sending execution around to let the earlier save command do the job. I've shown both methods for the sake of demonstration. You may prefer one over the other for your own scripts.

While both the recorded and revised versions of this script accomplish the same task, the second version has a number of advantages. The most important is that the new version anticipates potential problems that someone running the script may have (e.g., a missing or renamed volume or folder), and provides a mechanism to let the user fix the script without even knowing it. Anticipating user problems is a big part of programming of any kind. I hope this example demonstrates how your scripts can head off support problems before they ever happen.

Another advantage to this second method is that for the convenience of the scripter—but to no detriment of the user—the script is easier to maintain and modify. There is less code to deal with, and most of what would need attention is at the top in the script properties. Scripts should not only make the user's life easier, but the scripter can make the scripter's life easier as well.

More Scripting Examples

For now, I refer you to the handful of Scriptable Text Editor scripts in the Sample Scripts folder. They provide a few examples of manipulating text in such documents. In Chapter 20, we'll come back to Scriptable Text Editor as I demonstrate scripts that integrate this program with both scriptable Finder and TableServer in some practical scenarios.

CHAPTER 19

Scripting TableServer

While a lot of what's built into AppleScript seems to promote scripting of text-based applications, the majority of applications you'll be scripting will more than likely be table-based. Spreadsheet and database programs, plus client-server query tools present the majority of their data in tables: columns and rows. As an excellent introduction to working with tables, this book comes with Table-Server, designed by Chang Laboratories, Inc.

TableServer is probably unlike other programs you've used before. First of all, it was designed from scratch to be a scriptable application. One of its goals was to support the Apple event table suite in as pure a form as possible. Second, it doesn't display its data in windows. In fact the program is entirely windowless. The goal was to provide more of a scriptable table engine than a user application. Much of what you learn about scripting tables with TableServer will apply to learning how to script other table-based applications.

What's a Table?

If you've ever used a spreadsheet program, then you have a good visualization of a table. A TableServer table is an ordered collection of information, organized into *rows* and *columns*. TableServer accommodates tables up to 40 columns wide, and as many rows as fits into TableServer's application memory. Each intersection of a row and column is a specific *cell*. Each row and column has both an indexed number (starting with 1 at the upper left corner) and a name. To get or set data in any cell, you specify a cell address by its cell number or name, along a specific row.

For ease of accessing cells by this coordinate system, TableServer's default behavior is to assign the values of the top row of cells and the left column of cells to be names of columns and rows. Let's look at an example. Consider the table shown below:

Element	Symbol	Atomic Number	Atomic Weight
Actinium	Ac	89	227.0278
Aluminum	Al	13	26.98154
Americium	Am	95	243.0614
Antimony	Sb	51	121.75
Argon	Ar	18	39.948
Arsenic	As	33	74.9216
Astatine	At	85	209.987

Unless scripted to behave otherwise, a TableServer table assumes column names based on values of the cells in the first row (Element, Symbol, etc.); it also assigns names to each row based on values of cells in the first column (Element, Actinium, Aluminum, etc.). This simplifies access to any given cell, because the reference to a cell sounds very much like plain language. Therefore, if you want to get the contents of the cell representing the atomic number of argon, the AppleScript statement would be:

```
value of cell "Atomic Number" of row "Argon"
    -- result: 18
```

I think you can see how this naming scheme makes data lookups very easy and readable in a script. Don't, however, confuse TableServer with the functions of a fully powered database program. TableServer doesn't sort data, search, or include formulas for cells. A table is a very simple data array, and TableServer provides the facilities to a add and delete rows of data, access values of one or more cells, replace data in existing cells.

TableServer Table Files

There is no magic to the disk files created by TableServer. They're simply TEXT files (with object property information stored as resources in the file). Each row is a tab-delimited paragraph of text, with tabs separating data in columns. This grants us a couple benefits.

First, we can create tables in a window by manually entering data in any text processing or spreadsheet program, and saving the document as a text-only file. Just make sure to type a Tab between columns of data (the data doesn't have to line up in the document, but there must be only one Tab between columns of data) and return characters between rows of data (including one final return at the end of the last row). It also means that you can use optical character reading software and a scanner to transfer large printed tables to a TableServer table.

When you create a table in this manner, you should run the following script to then save the newly created table with TableServer. The purpose of this is to change the creator signature of the file so it is represented by the Finder as a TableServer file. Once the file is saved with the TableServer creator, you won't be bothered by a request to save a plain table each time your script closes it. Here's the script (in the Chapter 19 folder under the name "TableServer Saver") that lets you open the text-only file, and save it as a TableServer table file:

```
set newFile to (choose file of type "TEXT" ¬
    with prompt "Locate the table to convert:") as string
tell application "TableServer"
    open file newFile
    close table 1 saving in file newFile saving yes
end tell
```

The second advantage of having a table in TEXT format is that while you're learning how to use TableServer, you can open a table in something like Scriptable Text Editor to see how the table is structured. You cannot, however, watch a table change dynamically this way—it's not a viewer to a table.

Working with Tables

Like any document, a table must be opened before you do anything with it. Tables assume the names of their file names (not their pathnames), and you should refer to tables primarily via their names. When you're finished with a table, you should close it. If you don't, the table will stay open as long as Table-Server stays open, even if your script ends. Therefore, here's the basic structure you should observe:

```
tell application "TableServer"
    if not (table tableName) exists then
        open file fileReference
    end if
    (* do your thing with the table tableName*)
    close table tableName
end tell
```

The reason you want to perform the test for an existing table is that the open file command produces an error if you try to open a table that is already open. Since your script may be interrupted by an error—thus preventing the closure of the table from a previous test—the table may already be open. The construction, above, covers all bases.

Complete references in TableServer include a reference to the table, just as Scriptable Text Editor references include the document. If you should omit the table reference in a command, TableServer defaults to the "topmost" table—table 1. But since it is not easy to know which tables may be open at any time or which one is table 1, your script could get into trouble not specifying a named table.

Commands

Let's run through TableServer's commands to supplement the information that is in the dictionary. Additional information may be found in the TableServer Docs files, which you can view or print with Scriptable Text Editor.

close tableRef [saving in *fileReference*] [saving yes | no | ask]

>After working with any table, you should immediately close it so the table doesn't hang around. If possible, refer to the table by name (rather than number), as in

>```
>close table "Presidents"
>```

>```
>close table "Statistics" saving in "HD:Documents:Statistics"
>```

>```
>close table "Statistics" saving yes
>```

>You don't have to worry about any of the saving parameters unless your script has modified the table. And you only need to specify the **saving in** parameter under one of two conditions: you're saving the table for the first time as a Table-Server document; or you want to save the current state of the table with a new file name. In the script earlier in this chapter, we used all parameters to save a table imported from a text-only file created with another program. The final saving parameter lets you specify whether the file should be automatically saved when the document closes (**saving yes**), should not be saved (**saving no**), or should let the user figure out if the file should be saved (**saving ask**).

count [of] *objectReference* [each *className*]

>The count command is most helpful in determining the number of tables open at any moment, as well as the number of columns or rows within a table. Because TableServer considers a cell to represent a column, the count of cells equals the number columns. To determine the actual number of cell intersections, multiply the number of rows by the number of columns.

>While TableServer supports the each *className* parameter, it's more efficient to go straight for the count of the object you want. For example, the following two statements achieve the same result:

>```
>count of table 1 each row
>```

>```
>count of rows of table 1
>```

>with the second version being both more direct and much easier to read.

delete *objectReference*

>TableServer lets you delete either a single row or an entire table:

>```
>delete row 5 of table "Disk Library"
>```

>```
>delete table "Statistics"
>```

>Range references for multiple rows are not supported; nor can you delete a column of data (a table's column count is fixed at creation time). Deleting a table performs the same action as closing a table without saving it—the file is not deleted, only the table from TableServer's memory.

exists *objectReference*
objectReference **exists**

Whenever your script is unsure about a particular table, row, or column being available for a command, it's best to test for its existence. Failure to do so will cause an execution error if the object is missing when called in a statement. We do that in our skeleton structure of how to use tables—testing for the existence of a table before opening it.

You can pass a list of objects for the objectReference parameter, as in:

```
set validity to exists rows {"Arsenic","Aluminum","Barium"}
    -- result: {true, true, false}
```

You can then find out in one operation whether any item is missing:

```
if {true, true, false} contains false then
    (* statements to take care of missing stuff *)
end if
```

Repeating through the items in the returned value, your script could also determine which item(s) is missing.

[get] *reference* [as *className*]

The result of this command is the data that comes back from whatever the reference parameter calls for. As with AppleScript's own get command, the command name is optional. More than likely, you'll be using copy or set to transfer a copy of data to a variable.

Knowledge about TableServer object references is the most important factor in this command (and copy and set). The most important point to bear in mind when getting data from cells, rows, and columns, is that unless you request a specific property of any of those objects, the returned value is a complete data record for the object—something your script probably doesn't want.

Nine times out of ten, your script will want the value property of a cell or row of cells. Let's compare the difference between a cell object and the value of a cell object. If we use the Periodic Table table displayed earlier in this chapter as an example, we'll get both a particular cell and the value of that cell:

```
cell "symbol" of row "argon" of table 1
    -- result: {class:cell, name:"Symbol", «property data→:"Ar"}
```

```
value of cell "symbol" of row "argon" of table 1
    -- result: "Ar"
```

The possibilities for types of data you can get from a table are many, but to simplify matters, I've prepared a series of kinds of data you're most likely to want from a table, and an example of syntax that gets that data. In the Chapter 19 folder of scripts from this book is a table named "States." The table is four columns wide (the state name, the year it entered the Union, its postal code abbreviation, and its capital). I'll use that table here for examples of statements and results. I encourage you to try the examples yourself, and watch for the results in the Result window. Copy the file to the same folder as TableServer, and work within the following construction:

```
tell application "TableServer"
    if not (table "States" exists) then
        open file "States"
    end if
    set returnedValue to (* statement to test *)
    close table "States"
end tell
returnedValue
```

In the result values shown below, tab characters are illustrated by a right arrow symbol (➔), although these symbols don't appear in the Result window.

To get: names of all open tables:

```
name of every table
    -- result: {"States"}
```

To get: the entire table contents as a tab- and return-delimited chunk of data:

```
table "States" as text
    -- result: State➔  Entered Union➔  Abbreviation➔Capital
        Alabama➔ 1819➔  AL➔ Montgomery
        Alaska➔   1959➔  AK➔ Juneau
        Arizona➔  1912➔  AZ➔ Phoenix
        ...
        Wyoming➔1890➔   WY➔Cheyenne
        "
```

(Note the return character delimiter at the end to delimit the last row of data.)

To get: the entire table's contents as a list of lists (i.e., each row being its own list):

```
Value of every cell of every row of table "States"
    -- result: {{"State", "Entered Union", "Abbreviation", "Capital"}, ¬
        {"Alabama", "1819", "AL", "Montgomery"}, ..., ¬
        {"Wyoming", "1890", "WY", "Cheyenne"}}
```

To get: the value of a single cell:

```
Value of cell 4 of row 12 of table "States"
    -- result: "Honolulu"
```

```
Value of cell "Capital" of row "Hawaii" of table "States"
    -- result: "Honolulu"
```

To get: values of every cell in a row as a list:

```
Value of cells of row "Hawaii" of table "States"
    -- result: {"Hawaii", "1959", "HI", "Honolulu"}
```

To get: values of every cell in a row as tab-delimited text:

Value of cells of row "Hawaii" of table "States" as string
  -- result: "Hawaii→ 1959→ HI→ Honolulu"

To get: values of every cell in a column as a list:

Value of cell "Capital" of every row of table "States"
  -- result: {"Capital", "Montgomery", "Juneau",..., "Cheyenne"}

To get: names of every column as a list:

name of every column of table "States"
  -- result: {"State", "Entered Union", "Abbreviation", "Capital"}

To get: names of every column as tab-delimited text:

name of every column of table "States" as string
  -- result: "State→ Entered Union→ Abbreviation→ Capital"

To get: names of every row:

name of every row of table "States"
  -- result: {"State", "Alabama", "Alaska", ..., "Wyoming"}

You may notice that you cannot obtain information from multiple columns (e.g., name of every row) in tab-delimited text form. If you try to coerce the result to a string, the string contains no delimiters (tabs or spaces) between items in their string form. If you need to work with elements from a column of data, then use the more efficient method of parsing the list class value.

make [new] table [with properties *record*] [with data *values*]
make [new] row[s] at table *tableReference* with data *values*

Let's work with new tables first. While in general it's easier to create tables in another format, there's nothing preventing a script from creating a table from existing data derived from other sources (e.g., a spreadsheet cell range, downloaded mainframe data, etc.). As long as the data is fed to the table in the proper format, TableServer couldn't care less. Moreover, you can create a table with the barest minimum of specifications (a name and column count), and then use the make rows command to fill in the data later.

Making a table does not do anything to the table to preserve it on the disk. You must do that with a close or save command separately. Until then, however, the table you make lives in TableServer, and you can work with it just as with any table. In fact, you may prefer to use a TableServer table as a convenient scratchpad for data that eventually goes into another application.

While the definition for the make table command indicates that there are two optional parameters, at least one of the parameters must be present to create the table. And if the parameter is the with properties parameter, then you must pass along a value for the colCount property of a table. This is because a table must be created with a fixed number of columns (between 1 and 40). There is no such thing as an empty table. Actually, the best minimum parameter to send is both a column count and a name, since you want to refer to the table by name immediately:

```
make table with properties {name: "Statistics", colCount: 6}
```

Unlike creating a new document in a lot of applications, a new table doesn't appear "in front of" the rest. For example, if one table is already open, and your script makes a new one, the new table becomes table 2 (at least until table 1 closes). That's why assigning a name is so important to keeping multiple tables straight.

To pass data straight to a table while you create it, the values parameter needs to be data in a format commensurate with the construction of the table you wish to create. Data must be in either list or record form. Lists are perhaps the easiest to work with if you're hard-wiring the data (i.e., not obtaining it from another source). If you supply a single level list, then the data is interpreted as being cells of a single row:

```
make new table with properties {name:"Stoneage Stars"} ¬
    with data {"Fred", "Barney", "Wilma", "Betty"}
table "Stoneage Stars" as string
    -- result: "Fred➜ Barney➜ Wilma➜ Betty
    "
```

To supply multiple rows of data, you must provide a list of lists:

```
make new table with properties {name:"Television Families"} ¬
    with data {{"TV Husband", "TV Wife"}, ¬
    {"Fred", "Wilma"}, {"Barney", "Betty"}}
table "Television Families" as string
    -- result: "TV Husband➜   TV Wife
        Fred➜   Wilma
        Barney➜   Betty
    "
```

Once a table is created (and open), you can add more rows of data to it with the make rows command. You must specify a table (preferably by name) and the data that goes into the row. Rules for new row data follow those of creating rows of data in a new table. For example, in the last script fragment, we created a table named "Television Families." To add a single row, we would use the following statement:

```
make row at table "Television Families" with data {"Ozzie", "Harriett"}
table "Television Families" as text
    -- result: "TV Husband➜   TV Wife
        Fred➜   Wilma
        Barney➜   Betty
        Ozzie➜ Harriett
    "
```

Or we can add multiple rows with a list of lists, as in:

```
make rows at table "Television Families" ¬
   with data {{"Ward", "June"}, {"Homer", "Marge"}}
table "Television Families" as text
   -- result: "TV Husband→   TV Wife
      Fred→   Wilma
      Barney→   Betty
      Ozzie→ Harriett
      Ward→  June
      Homer→   Marge
      "
```

Another type of data you can use to create a new table or add rows is another TableServer table. This is how you can join two tables together as one. Schematically, it would go like this:

```
copy table 1 to tableA
copy table 2 to tableB
make table with properties {name:"Bigger Table"}¬
   with data tableA
make rows at table "Bigger Table" ¬
   with data tableB
```

But you cannot use this method to extract one table and hope to use that data directly to build a table with more or fewer columns, because a table object includes the column count as a read-only property.

open [file] *fileName* | *fileList*

TableServer is more lenient with the open command than Scriptable Text Editor, in that you can omit the word "file" from the parameters. Also—and this is one great feature—you can pass a list of table file names as a list to have TableServer open multiple tables with one statement, as in

```
open {"States","Countries"}
```

As with any file command, the more specific the file name (i.e., providing a complete pathname) the better things will be. Without a pathname, TableServer looks only in its own folder for a match. If none is found, your script receives an execution error.

quit [saving yes | no | ask]

TableServer's quit command operates like most. The default behavior is for TableServer to ask the user about saving changes to any modified tables. Because TableServer doesn't take up a lot of RAM (you can crank it down to less than 100K if you don't have lots of big tables open at once), you might consider leaving it open a lot. If you have many scripts that access tables, this will save time in script execution, since the script won't have to wait for TableServer to load. On the other hand, because the program runs without windows—and therefore gives an impression of being somewhere between an application and a background task—you may elect to quit TableServer at the end of any script that uses it.

save *tableReference* [in *fileName*]

Use this version of saving only if you want to save an intermediate copy of a table in your script before closing it (where the **close** command allows you to save the file at the same time). You must specify which table you mean to save, preferably by name. Specify a *fileName* parameter only if the table has not yet been saved to disk or you wish to save the table with a different name or path.

set *objectReference* to *values*

TableServer provides much flexibility in how you plug data into cells with the **set** command. Perhaps the best way to describe the many possibilities is to provide a list of scenarios and typical commands you can give to accomplish specific data-stuffing tasks. To carry this out best (and let you try each one), you should create a three-column table, which we'll call "TV Families." Before trying any of the **set** commands, create the table with the following script:

```
tell application "TableServer"
    make table with properties {name:"TV Families", ColCount:3}
    repeat 5
        make row at table "TV Families" with data {"","",""}
    end repeat
end tell
```

Now you can substitute the **make table** command line and repeat statement with the following two-line fragments to view how the **set** command works its mysterious ways. In the result values shown below, tab characters are illustrated by a right arrow symbol (➜), although these symbols don't appear in the Result window.

To set a value in a single cell:

```
set cell 1 of row 1 of table "TV Families" to "Dad"
table "TV Families" as string
```

```
-- result:    "Dad ➜      ➜
              ➜      ➜      ➜
              ➜      ➜      ➜
              ➜      ➜      ➜
              ➜      ➜      ➜
              "
```

To set values of multiple cells within a row:

```
set cell {2, 3} of row 1 of table "TV Families" to {"Mom", "Kids"}
table "TV Families" as string
```
    -- result: *"Dad   Mom   Kids*

→	→	→
→	→	→
→	→	→
→	→	→

        "

To set values of multiple, non-contiguous cells within a row:

```
set cell {1, 3} of row 2 of table "TV Families" to {"Ozzie", "Rick & Dave"}
table "TV Families" as string
```
    -- result: *"Dad   Mom   Kids*

Ozzie	→	*Rick & Dave*
→	→	→
→	→	→
→	→	→

        "

To set values of an entire row:

```
set row 3 of table "TV Families" to {"Rob", "Laura", "Richie"}
table "TV Families" as string
```
    -- result: *"Dad   Mom   Kids*

Ozzie	→	*Rick & Dave*
Rob	*Laura*	*Richie*
→	→	→
→	→	→

        "

To set values of all cells of a row to the same value:

```
set row 2 of table "TV Families" to ""
table "TV Families" as string
```
    -- result: *"Dad   Mom   Kids*

→	→	→
Rob	*Laura*	*Richie*
→	→	→
→	→	→

        "

To set values of all cells in a column to the same value:

```
set cell 2 of every row of table "TV Families" to ""
table "TV Families" as string
```
    -- result: *"Dad   →   Kids*

→	→	→
Rob	→	*Richie*
→	→	→
→	→	→

        "

To set values of all cells in a table to the same value:

```
set table "TV Families" to ""
table "TV Families" as string
    -- result:    " →        →        →
                   →        →        →
                   →        →        →
                   →        →        →
                   →        →        →
                   "
```

In addition to feeding multiple cells within a row a list of values, you can also supply a tab-delimited sequence or a record, but the number of tabbed items or labeled fields must match the column arrangement of the table.

Objects

Now we'll examine the objects that TableServer defines. Their dictionary definitions are relatively straightforward, although some of the properties listed there are of interest to TableServer's internal workings, and cannot be accessed (for reading or writing) by a script.

The most important part of working with TableServer objects is recognizing the reference forms that each supports. Support tends to be on the simple side, which makes learning easier, but you may try some of the more elaborate references you learned from Scriptable Text Editor (like filtered reference forms) only to be disappointed that they are not in TableServer. You may, however, have a chance to work with them and table objects in other table-based applications.

Table

Applicable commands: close, count, delete, exists, get, make, open, save, set.

Reference forms: Table references are generally made by index number (risky, as described earlier), name, and property references.

Among the properties, the colCount is an interesting one, because it is not modifiable on the fly, but is one of the properties you can set when you create a new table with the make command. You may wish to check the modified property before closing a table (in case the script makes it possible to modify the table), and based on that finding, save the table quietly (i.e., without bothering the user with a save changes alert).

An important property to be aware of is rowNames. The title of this property may be misleading, because the value is actually an integer, signifying which column number is used by the table to assign names to rows. The default value is 1, which means that the name of any row is the value of its first cell. But if you adjust the rowNames property of the table, then another column's values can assume that role. This could come in handy if you're importing data from another table, and the second or third column has values that best distinguish one row's data from the rest.

Row

Applicable commands: count, delete, exists, get, make, set.

Reference forms: Index, name, plural, property.

As explained earlier, each row has a name, which is determined by the value of a cell in the column designated as the naming column (set with the table's rowNames property). While you cannot change the name property of a row, if you change the value of the cell that controls the row's name, then the row's name obviously changes as well. The cell list property is used internally by TableServer.

Cell

Applicable commands: count, exists, get, set.

Reference forms: Index, name, plural, property.

Cells are the heart of tables, because they contain the data your scripts manipulate. A cell's name is the name of the column (the value of the topmost cell in the column). When you need a cell's data, you must get the value property of the cell. And a cell's address is always an intersection of the cell (column) reference and row reference, as in:

```
cell 3 of row 6
cell "Capital" of row "Vermont"
```

Cells may contain up to 256 characters each, and store only string data. Therefore, only strings and classes that can be readily coerced to strings (integers and reals) can be stored in TableServer cells. Dates, aliases, and the like, must be coerced to strings before being placed into a cell.

Column

Applicable commands: count, exists, get, set.

Reference forms: index, name, plural, property.

A script's ability to work with a column is not as free as with a row. You cannot add columns to an existing table. And, while you can obtain the value of every cell in a row, you cannot do the same for every cell in a specific column (unless you do so by asking for cell x of every row). But, like rows, columns assume their names by the values of the first (top) cells in the columns. The name always comes from the first row of cells, and cannot be adjusted to another row.

Application

Applicable commands: quit.

Reference forms: name, property.

The application object features two read-only properties. One is its name, TableServer, which must be the ultimate target of any command. You can also check the version of the copy you have:

```
get version of application "TableServer"
    -- result: "1.0d1"
```

Table Data Caution

If you plan to access a table's data by column and row names, you must be careful about duplicate names. The Presidents table is a good example. If a script performs the following:

```
get cell "Vice President" of row "Grover Cleveland"
    -- result: "Thomas A. Hendricks"
```

the only data you'll be able to retrieve is the data from Cleveland's first term of office. His two terms had another president, Benjamin Harrison, in between. Cleveland's two terms are listed separately, two rows apart. As long as the reference to the row is by name, only the first one will ever be accessed. The same is true for columns that may have the same name, in which case, only the leftmost column will be accessed.

This may have implications on the kind of data you store in TableServer tables. A definite prerequisite is that the data in the column you use to signify row names be unique for each row. Ditto for the data in the first row for column names.

Applied TableServer

In the rest of this chapter, I'll present two applications for TableServer to demonstrate how to script it. The first application is in a simple quiz program, which accesses the States table located in the Handbook Script:Chapter 19 folder. The second demonstrates how to use AppleScript as a relational glue between two related tables.

State Capitals Quiz

The first example is a simple script that works with a four-column table consisting of data about each of the 50 United States. The States table consists of four columns: State, Entered Union, Abbreviation, and Capital. I've provided these extra columns for you to experiment with a medium-sized table.

Here is the script that interacts with the user and accesses the table:

```
tell application "TableServer"
    if not (table "States" exists) then
        open file "States"
    end if
```

```
repeat
    set i to random number from 2 to 51
    set capital to Value of cell "Capital" of row i
    display dialog "Enter the capital of " & ¬
        Value of cell 1 of row i & ":" default answer ""
    if text returned of result is capital then
        display dialog "That is correct!"
    else
        display dialog "Sorry, the correct answer is: " & ¬
            capital & "."
    end if
end repeat
close table "States"
end tell
```

The quiz script assigns a random number between 2 and 51 (the first row of the table consists of column names, so we don't want that data to appear in our quiz) to the variable i. We use that variable to pre-load the value of the Capital cell of that variable row, and then ask the user to enter the capital of that row's state (Figure 19.1). We compare the text entered by the user against the pre-loaded data. If it matches, the user is congratulated; otherwise we show the correct answer. All of this is inside a repeat loop, so that the user can continue through the quiz until he or she clicks one of the dialogs' Cancel buttons. Finally, we close the table when finished.

If this were to be handed out as a learning aid, there are a number of improvements that can be scripted without too much difficulty—and would be a good exercise of your newly found scripting expertise. For example, the randomness does not guarantee that every state will be picked within 50 tries, nor that a correct answer removes a state from the pool. I would want to include a tracking scheme that records which states were answered correctly, and make sure that within the same session, the quiz doesn't ask that state again; incorrect states would be thrown back in the running, to give the user a chance to prove what he or she has learned.

Another extrapolation would be to include some scoring mechanism, so multiple students could enter their names, and have their scores recorded as persistent properties or in another table. In fact, if the data were placed into a table, you could then bring that table into an Excel spreadsheet for further

Figure 19.1 Entry dialog for State Capitals quiz.

analysis. If you've written or used any other simple quiz-like programs before, then I'm sure you can think of other ways to extend the functionality of this application.

Relational Table Lookup

The next demonstration shows you how to create relational table lookups with AppleScript. At the core of this demonstration is the Presidents table, which we met in Chapter 6. In the second column of this table are abbreviations for the party to which the each president belonged. A second table, Political Parties, consists of two columns: the first contains the abbreviations found in the Presidents table; the second contains the full name of the parties.

In this script, the user is asked to enter a president's name. After making sure the name, as entered by the user is in the table, it looks up the party abbreviation, which then becomes a row name for the long version lookup in Political Parties. Here's the script:

```
tell application "TableServer"
    if not (table "Presidents" exists) then
        open file "Presidents"
    end if
    if not (table "Political Parties" exists) then
        open file "Political Parties"
    end if
    display dialog "Enter the full name of a President:" ¬
        default answer "George Washington"
    set president to text returned of result
    if not (row president of table "Presidents" exists) then
        display dialog "Can't find a president by that name."
    else
        set partyAbbrev to Value of cell "Party" ¬
            of row president of table "Presidents"
        set party to Value of cell 2 of row partyAbbrev of table "Political Parties"
        display dialog president & " belonged to the " & party & ¬
            " party."
    end if
    close table "Presidents"
    close table "Political Parties"
end tell
```

There are no special tricks in this kind of lookup, but you must be careful that each command goes to the desired table. The supreme advantage of named tables shines through in this example, since you don't want to rely on indexed tables here.

In the next chapter, I'll show you some ways of integrating the three applications we've spent time with: Finder, Scriptable Text Editor, and TableServer.

CHAPTER 20

Integrating Applications with AppleScript

In this chapter, we'll explore another aspect of AppleScript that has great potential: integrating applications or application modules. As mentioned in the Introduction, the Macintosh operating system and document architecture appears to be moving in the direction of compound documents that rely on any number of preprogrammed modules to work with each other. AppleScript and OSA-scripting will be the glue that makes those modules communicate with the document and with each other.

We can get a preview of what that will be like, and demonstrate further scripting techniques in the three script applications in this chapter. Each one blends two scriptable applications to produce meaningful work. I've designed two of them to work as droplets, and one as a regular double-clickable script application.

Three Applications

The first droplet, called Folder->Tables, produces a table (i.e., tab-delimited text file) of the contents of any folder dropped onto it. In the table are useful bits of information, such as version, size, and last modification date. When someone asks you for the contents of your Extensions or Control Panels folders to track down some incompatibility, these tables will be most helpful. This script uses the scriptable Finder and TableServer, although the resulting table can be opened in any spreadsheet, imported into a database, or viewed with any word processor.

Also Finder-related is Pretty Folder Directory, a droplet that blends the powers of scriptable Finder and Scriptable Text Editor. Drop a folder on this application, and it produces a nicely formatted listing of the contents of the folder, including the nested contents of all folders contained therein. As an added convenience, when a file contains a version number, we include that with the file's name in the listing. The script is, of course, highly modifiable to let you determine the font and style characteristics of folders and files in the listing.

Rounding out the collection is Mail Merger, a script application that brings together TableServer and Scriptable Text Editor. While Scriptable Text Editor doesn't have any mail merging powers built in, a script and a table of data (which could be derived from any database) give it those powers. While it's unlikely you'd use this combination yourself, when other commercial word processing programs offer mail merging, you can see how AppleScript can give a program powers it doesn't have on its own.

All three of these scripts and sample files are in the Handbook Scripts:Chapter 20 folder of the companion disk materials. Drag this folder's contents to the same level as TableServer and Scriptable Text Editor. You should run each one before reading the sections below about how they work inside. While the scripts in this chapter are longer than the ones we've seen elsewhere in the book, they are representative of the kinds of advanced scripts you can expect to write. Scripts may be longer, but the spirit of scripting is to try to do as much as possible in as few lines as possible.

One important note about the script listings in this book. Long lines (or lines of deeply nested statements) have been divided to fit the margins of the book page. When you view the actual scripts in Script Editor, you will sometimes find lines broken differently. Some of this is due to Script Editor's idiosyncrasies in dividing long and nested lines. I personally don't care for some of its tactics, but we cannot override such things in this editor.

Folder->Table

Combining the facilities of scriptable Finder and TableServer, Folder->Table is a droplet that invites you to drop any folder on it. When you do, it creates a Table-Server table of its contents. Figure 20.1 shows the partial results of dropping my Extensions folder on this application, and then opening the table in Excel.

	Name	Version	Kind	Size	Last Modified
1					
2	QuicKeys™ Toolbox	3	system extension	110K	Tue, Aug 10, 1993, 12:00 AM
3	◻Disinfectant INIT	3.3	system extension	8K	Tue, Nov 9, 1993, 9:37 AM
4	720K Floppy Disk Formatter	1	system extension	40K	Tue, Jun 29, 1993, 4:00 PM
5	Apple CD-ROM	4.0.2	system extension	25K	Mon, Nov 23, 1992, 12:00 PM
6	Apple Modem Tool	1.5	communications tool	170K	Tue, Aug 31, 1993, 12:00 PM
7	Apple Photo Access	1.0.2	system extension	185K	Mon, Nov 23, 1992, 5:00 PM
8	AppleScript™	1.1	system extension	298K	Wed, Dec 8, 1993, 1:00 PM
9	AppleShare	7.1	Chooser extension	75K	Mon, Aug 17, 1992, 12:00 PM
10	AppleTalk ADSP Tool	1.0.1	communications tool	36K	Wed, Jul 14, 1993, 12:00 PM
11	AppleTalk ImageWriter	7.0.1	Chooser extension	51K	Wed, Mar 4, 1992, 12:00 PM
12	Apple® Event Manager	1.0.2	system extension	39K	Wed, Aug 18, 1993, 12:00 PM
13	Audio CD Access	4.0.2	system extension	10K	Mon, Nov 23, 1992, 12:00 PM
14	CD Remote INIT	1.3	system extension	11K	Mon, Nov 23, 1992, 12:00 PM
15	Express Modem Tool	1.1.2	communications tool	52K	Wed, Aug 4, 1993, 12:00 PM

Contents-Extensions

Figure 20.1 An example of the results of dropping a folder on Folder->Table, as viewed in Microsoft Excel.

Here is the script for Folder->Table:

```
on open folderPath
    -- error check for multiple files
    if (count of folderPath) > 1 then
        display dialog ¬
            "Please drop only one folder at a time." buttons {"OK"} default button "OK"
        error number -128
    else
        set folderPath to item 1 of folderPath
    end if

    -- error check to for folder only
    tell application "Finder"
        if kind of folderPath ≠ "folder" then
            display dialog ¬
                "Please drop a folder only." buttons {"OK"} default button "OK"
            error number -128
        end if

        -- assign Finder-derived values to variables for later
        set folderName to name of item (folderPath as string)
        set tableName to "Contents-" & folderName
        set folderList to contents of item folderPath
    end tell

    tell application "TableServer"
        -- create table and assign first row's data/column names
        make new table with properties {name:tableName} ¬
            with data {"Name", "Version", "Kind", "Size", "Last Modified"}
        -- cycle through each item in the folder
        repeat with eachItem in folderList
            -- first get detailed data from Finder
            tell application "Finder"
                set itemName to name of eachItem
                -- see if there's a version for the item
                try
                    set itemVers to version of eachItem
                on error
                    -- if not, set value to empty
                    set itemVers to ""
                end try
                set itemType to kind of eachItem
                set itemSize to ((round ((size of eachItem) / 1024) ¬
                    rounding up) as string) & "K"
                set itemModDate to (modification date of eachItem) as string
            end tell
            -- enter data into new row of table
```

```
            make row at table tableName with data ¬
                {{itemName, itemVers, itemType, itemSize, itemModDate}}
        end repeat
        -- close and save table
        close table tableName ¬
            saving in file ((folderPath as string) & ":" & tableName) saving yes
    end tell
end open
```

Initial Error Checking

The whole script is written as one on open handler, which automatically makes the script turn into a droplet when it is saved as an application. Since a user could conceivably drop any kind of item on this droplet (or any number of things), the first thing the script does before processing any data is to check the validity of what has been dropped on it. The Apple event open message that arrives at the droplet also brings along as parameters a list of aliases of file(s) dropped on the application.

The first if-then construction checks to see how many items are in the list. For the condition in which multiple items appear in the parameter, we alert the user to the problem, and bail out of the script with the error statement that simply quits the script application. If there is just one item, then we extract it from the list class object that came along with the open message

In the second if-then construction, the script uses the Finder to see if the item dropped onto the droplet is a folder. Since the app works only with folders, we reject here anything that isn't a folder, again bailing out quietly with the error statement.

If execution has survived the if-then constructions, then we know we're ready to get to work on the folder. Before we do that, however, we use some of Finder's scripting routines to set some variables we'll need later, including the folder's name by itself and the list of items in the folder. It's slightly more efficient to put the list of items into a variable and work with them later from the variable, than going through a repeat loop that calls the Finder each time.

Switch to TableServer

The stage is set now for our table-building task. We use the window-less Table-Server to build our table file. First we create a new table, whose name was determined earlier, since it includes the name of the folder. While in the process of creating the table, we send it the first row of data, which not only lets us assign the names of the columns, but it sets the all-important colCount property of the table at the same time. For this program, I've elected to extract the version number, item kind, size, and last modified date for inclusion in the table. Each of these pieces of information is a property of almost every kind of Finder item. I also felt that I would rather see the version number immediately following the file name (if the file has a version resource).

The bulk of the work occurs in the repeat loop, which uses the compact style to cycle through each item of the list, folderList. After gathering the properties of an item we create a new row in the table with the items filled in. For those cells that don't have any data (e.g., the version of a folder), we insert an empty string as the value. TableServer has no problem with that.

Once the script has been through all the items in the folder, it closes the table, saving it to a file with the same name that identifies it as the contents of a specific folder.

Additional Ideas

Even though TableServer doesn't provide a mechanism to view a table's contents directly, it is efficient in letting us build tables. Whether we save the TableServer table as is, or copy the table into another table-based application, such as a spreadsheet, depends entirely on your scriptable software and what you intend to do with the information. TableServer is efficient as even an invisible intermediary for tabular data, which you can then transfer *en masse* to another application for further massage.

Pretty Folder Directory

Beauty is in the eye of the beholder, so your idea of "pretty" may differ from mine. Still, the script in this application produces a Scriptable Text Editor document that contains, in outline form, the complete contents of any folder that is dropped onto it. The "pretty" part comes from the fact that you can specify font, size, and styles independently for folder and file names. As delivered, the script bolds folder names, and keeps file names in plain font. Figure 20.2 shows a sample of the document produced with my System folder.

The script for Pretty Folder Directory follows:

```
property indentOffset : 0

on open folderPath
    -- error check for only single file
    if (count of folderPath) > 1 then
        display dialog ¬
            "Please drop only one folder at a time." buttons {"OK"} default button "OK"
        error number -128
    else
        set folderPath to item 1 of folderPath
    end if

    -- error check for folder only
    tell application "Finder"
        if kind of folderPath ≠ "folder" then
            display dialog ¬
```

Figure 20.2 An example of the results of the
Pretty Folder Directory script.

```
            "Please drop a folder only." buttons {"OK"} default button "OK"
        error number -128
    end if
end tell

tell application "Scriptable Text Editor"
    activate
    make new document at beginning
    -- create document header to suit your whims
    tell document 1
        copy "Contents of "" & folderPath & """ to end
        set size of last paragraph to 14
        set style of last paragraph to {bold, underline}
        copy return & "Reported on: " & (current date) as string to end
        set size of last paragraph to 14
        set style of last paragraph to plain
        copy return & return to end
        set size of last paragraph to 10
    end tell
end tell

-- preset indentOffset property to the let subroutine
-- know that a nested folder pathname is the starting
-- point for calculating indented sub-items
set oldDelims to AppleScript's text item delimiters
set AppleScript's text item delimiters to ":"
```

```
        set indentOffset to (count of text items of (folderPath as string)) - 1
        set AppleScript's text item delimiters to oldDelims
        -- convert folderPath value to scriptable FinderSpeak
        tell application "Finder" to set folderPath to folder folderPath
        -- call subroutine to do the real work
        my (extractContents from folderPath)
        -- clean up
        set indentOffset to 0
end open

-- a recursive subroutine, which calls itself for
-- each nested layer within the main folder
to extractContents from folderPath
    tell application "Finder"
            -- how many tabs for folder item (first one is "")
            set indentString to (setIndent for folderPath) of me
            tell document 1 of application "Scriptable Text Editor"
                copy return & indentString & (name of folderPath) to end
                -- anything executing here is a folder, so we bold it
                set style of last paragraph to bold
            end tell
            -- now get contents of the folder
            set folderContents to (contents of folderPath)
            -- if there's something inside, then we dig deeper
            if folderContents ≠ {} then
                -- we cycle through each item in the folder
                repeat with i from 1 to count of folderContents
                    -- if it's another folder, then we recurse
                    if kind of item i of folderContents is "folder" then
                        extractContents of me from (item i of folderContents)
                    else
                        -- otherwise, put plain file name into document
                        set itemName to (name of (item i of folderContents))
                        set indentString to (setIndent for item i of folderContents) of me
                        -- we extract the short version property of the file
                        try
                            set theVersion to version of item i of folderContents
                            set theVersion to " (" & (theVersion as string) & ")"
                        on error
                            set theVersion to ""
                        end try
                        tell document 1 of application "Scriptable Text Editor"
                            copy return & indentString & itemName ¬
                                & theVersion to end
                            -- file names are plain style
                            set style of last paragraph to plain
```

```
                    end tell
                end if
            end repeat
        end if
    end tell
end extractContents

-- returns a string of tabs (if any) to help
-- pad the front of items nested in the folder.
-- requires the full pathname of one item
to setIndent for itemName
    set returnedVal to ""
    -- coerce to string
    set itemName to itemName as string
    -- do AppleScript's text item delimiters number on it
    set oldDelims to AppleScript's text item delimiters
    set AppleScript's text item delimiters to ":"
    -- folders have extra colons, which throws off indentCount
    -- so we special-case folders
    if last character of itemName is ":" then
        set indentCount to ((count of text items of itemName) - indentOffset) - 1
    else
        set indentCount to ((count of text items of itemName) - indentOffset)
    end if
    -- reset the ol' global property
    set AppleScript's text item delimiters to oldDelims
    if indentCount > 0 then
        -- build up tabs based on indentCount
        repeat indentCount times
            set returnedVal to returnedVal & tab
        end repeat
    end if
    -- send string back
    return returnedVal
end setIndent
```

Initial Error Checking

This script, written as a droplet, contains a few handlers to help divide the work of this script into manageable segments. We use one property which is defined as such because we need its values within multiple instances of a handler (see below). By initializing the value in the open handler, it is ready for us wherever we need the value throughout the rest of the script.

Since this droplet, like Folder->Table, requires a folder be dropped on it, the script begins with exactly the same error checking as the other application. Refer to its description for details if you need them.

Get the Document Started

In the succeeding tell statement, directed at Scriptable Text Editor, we create a new document, and insert the header information. While the formatting I've put into this script is rather simple, and doesn't summon any other fonts, this is the place to modify the script for the document's title and line that indicates what date and time the report was made. At the end of the header, we insert a couple returns and set the font size to 10 for subsequent additions.

The IndentOffset

This application provided a couple challenges for compact design. One was the fact that I wanted each level of a nested item to be indented one more tab character than the next higher level item—just like an outline. The method I finally settled on was to use the number of file/folder items in a pathname (i.e., items separated by colons) as a measuring device. Since the depth of an item is immediately apparent from its pathname, the script could use those items as indentation counters.

But for that to work properly, I had to worry about the folder dropped on the script that was already nested. In other words, even a folder such as the Extensions folder would need to start its items in the document at the left margin, even though its pathname shows the folder to be three levels deep (HD:System Folder:Extension). What the script had to do, then, was to establish an offset value that would equalize any folder so that the outermost folder (i.e., the one dropped on the script) would appear in the document with an offset of zero tabs.

With that long explanation, the next several lines of the script, which temporarily change AppleScript's text item delimiters to a colon, find out and store how many levels deep the dropped folder is. The reason the value is decreased by one is that folder names have a trailing colon, which needs to be ignored in our calculations. The indentOffset value is a property, which we'll be able to use in a subsequent handler.

Recursion to the Rescue

The second major challenge for this script was handling the cases in which folders may go many levels deep. The brute-force way would have been to create an obnoxious series of nested if-then statements to handle the folder that contained yet another folder, and so on. The problem with such an approach is that there is no way to accurately predict how many levels deep a user could have things stored in a folder. And producing an application like this that abruptly stops when it reaches a certain level is unacceptable.

Instead, I came up with the idea to make the process of writing data out to the Scriptable Text Editor document a recursive process. Before jumping into the code, let's look at what I mean by recursive.

Assume there is a Folder A, which contains Folder B, which, in turn, contains Folder C. Each of these folders also contains one or more files. If we design the script right, it can begin processing Folder A, placing its name at the left margin, and its files tabbed in one level. But when it encounters Folder B in the listing, the most efficient method would be for Folder B's contents to be handled exactly the same way Folder A's contents were handled—and with the same code. The same goes for the script when, while processing Folder B's contents, it encounters Folder C. Another call to the very script that handles Folder B would take care of Folder C and its contents.

The mental model I have of this is like a spiral, winding ever deeper around a single axis. Other times when I think of this, an Escher print appears in my head, so don't worry if you can't picture recursion right away. Eventually, however, the tight winding of the spiral unwinds. Processing reaches a kind of bottom, and any items held in suspended animation get picked up and processed. It's pretty cool, and fortunately AppleScript allows us to control our recursive destinies.

Recursive Code

All of this recursion takes place in the extractContents subroutine. Its lone parameter is the Finder description of a folder whose contents need reporting. For the first time through, this is the folder that was dropped on the script; in subsequent, recursive calls, the folder will be one nested inside.

The first task is to report the folder to the Scriptable Text Editor document. To make up the line that gets written to the document, we also summon the setIndent subroutine, which returns the number of tab characters required for any level of item (it uses the indentOffset property we set in the open handler). We simply append the folder name to the end of the Scriptable Text Editor document, and set its style to bold (you may choose some other text formatting).

Now comes the fun part.

Finished with the folder, we look to see if there is anything inside (with the help of Finder's contents property of a folder). If so, we start cycling through each item. The first thing we check for is whether an item is another, nested folder. If it is, then we recurse—calling the same extractContents subroutine we're already in, but this time passing the nested folder as the parameter. While this goes on, any files that are still at the same level as the nested folder are automatically stored in a holding pen for processing later, once the recursion is finished. This recursion can go on until the script application runs out of memory storing all the pending operations (of course, you can adjust it with the Get Info dialog in the Finder).

For items that have a version property, we retrieve and format the information for the file, and append it to the file name. Then we append the file name to the end of the Scriptable Text Editor document, setting the font style to plain (or whatever you want).

Sound Simple?

Once this kind of processing is explained, it makes sense, and even sounds simple. But coming up with a solution like this takes experience. And lots of debugging. Also, Script Editor didn't provide as much help as a scripter would like in figuring out when parentheses would help it compile or execute a statement. When there is doubt about how AppleScript may evaluate a complex expression (including those involving data returned from commands), it doesn't hurt to slap an extra pair of parentheses to make the expression clearer. The more help you give AppleScript, the more likely your scripts will run with less debugging.

Mail Merger

Our last application integrator script gives mail merging capabilities to Scriptable Text Editor. For this application to work, it makes a couple assumptions. First, the data is kept in a TableServer file (or any tab-delimited one that can be opened by TableServer), and the first row of cells in the table contains the column names for the table.

These column names are the ones that must appear in the Scriptable Text Editor template document (inside angle brackets). This is actually the way most word processors, such as Microsoft Word work. In other words, where you want the Company field from the table to appear in the letter, you type

```
<Company>
```

Because this script uses AppleScript's offset scripting addition to locate these placeholders, the placeholders and column names must match cases, as well. In the merging process, the placeholder is replaced by data from the table. Figure 20.3 shows the Form Letter Template file that is in the Handbook Scripts:Chapter 20 folder. Use this file and the Addresses table to run your trials for the Mail Merger script.

The script for Mail Merger is as follows:

```
on run
    doMerge("")
end run

-- written to accommodate files passed by open handler
-- of a droplet
to doMerge(fileList)
    -- get file paths for template and table
    set bothFiles to loadFiles(fileList)
    set templateFile to item 1 of bothFiles
    set tableFile to item 2 of bothFiles
    -- extract just file names for document names
    tell application "Finder"
        set templateName to name of item templateFile
```

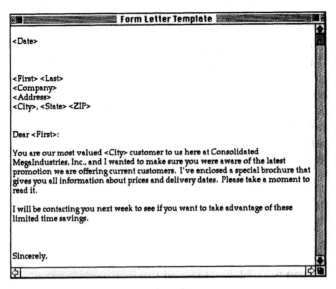

Form Letter Template

```
<Date>



<First> <Last>
<Company>
<Address>
<City>, <State> <ZIP>


Dear <First>:

You are our most valued <City> customer to us here at Consolidated
MegaIndustries, Inc., and I wanted to make sure you were aware of the latest
promotion we are offering current customers. I've enclosed a special brochure that
gives you all information about prices and delivery dates. Please take a moment to
read it.

I will be contacting you next week to see if you want to take advantage of these
limited time savings.


Sincerely,
```

Figure 20.3   Form Letter Template.

```applescript
        set tableName to name of item tableFile
    end tell

    -- open table and set variables from data in table.
    -- we'll use fieldNames to access cells in each row
    -- and to look for placeholders in the template.
    -- maxRecords is the number of times we'll go thru (-1)
    tell application "TableServer"
        if not (exists table tableName) then open tableFile
        set fieldNames to ¬
            name of every column of table tableName & "Date"
        set maxRecords to (count of rows of table tableName) - 1
    end tell

    tell application "Scriptable Text Editor"
        activate
        open file templateFile
        -- cycle through each record (except labeled first one)
        repeat with i from 2 to maxRecords
            -- check for placeholder of each field name
            repeat with j from 1 to count of fieldNames
                -- keep going in case more than one per field
                repeat
                    set theDoc to contents of document 1
                    set oneField to item j of fieldNames
                    -- find offset of placeholder
                    -- via script's subroutine
```

```
            tell me to set itemOffset to ¬
                (calcOffset of ("<" & oneField & ">") ¬
                    given larger:theDoc)
            -- if no more placeholders, then onto next one
            if itemOffset = 0 then exit repeat
            -- special case for <Date> placeholder
            if oneField is "Date" then
                copy text from word 2 to word 4 of ¬
                    ((current date) as string) to ¬
                        text from character itemOffset to ¬
                            character (itemOffset + ¬
                                (length of "<Date>") - 1) ¬
                                    of document 1
            else
                -- get table's cell value...
                tell application "TableServer" to ¬
                    get Value of cell oneField of row i ¬
                        of table tableName
                -- ...and put it into placeholder's spot
                copy result to text from character ¬
                    itemOffset to character (itemOffset + ¬
                        (length of oneField) + 1) ¬
                            of document 1
            end if
          end repeat
        end repeat
        -- un-comment next line to print
        -- print document 1
        -- restore original for next round
        revert document 1
      end repeat
  -- tidy up
  close document 1
  end tell
  tell application "TableServer" to close table tableName
end doMerge

to loadFiles(fileList)
    -- fill template file
    set templateFile to (choose file of type "QUIL" ¬
        with prompt "Select a template file:") as string
    -- fill table file
    set tableFile to (choose file of type "TEXT" ¬
        with prompt "Select a table to merge:")
    if file creator of (info for tableFile) ≠ "tTB7" then
        display dialog "That file is not a TableServer document."
```

```
        error number -128
    else
        set tableFile to tableFile as string
    end if
    return (templateFile as list) & tableFile as list
end loadFiles

-- must keep offset command outside of STE
to calcOffset of smaller given larger:larger
    return offset of smaller in larger
end calcOffset
```

Structure

I set up this script to work as a double-clickable application, but not a droplet. I'll say more about the droplet possibilities later. The script consists of a short run handler, which calls the main handler that performs the merge. That doMerge handler, in turn, calls two other smaller handlers for special purposes.

It was important to design this script in a generalizable fashion, so that any table and any placeholders could work, as long as they matched. In other words, rather than hard-wire the script to handle, say, correspondence and a specific name-and-address table, I wanted the script to work with other kinds of documents and tables. Only the method of entering placeholders in the text would be a constant. Moreover, the script had to handle tables that may have more columns of data than the Scriptable Text Editor document template calls for. This script handles all that nicely.

Loading Variables

It's a good idea to assign values to pervasive variable at the top of a script. It makes the script more easily maintainable, and lets a reader get a good idea of what values are important throughout the script. Don't worry about catching all the important variables the first time through the design. You'll probably revisit the issue multiple times in the process. But assigning variables early is like a carpenter loading a tool belt with all the right tools before climbing to the roof (although scripters usually work with a net).

For this script, the initial variables are all file related. We call the loadFiles subroutine to put our two file pathnames into an organized list. The parameter (fileList) being passed here is in anticipation of adapting this script to accommodate a droplet design, in which case, the file(s) dropped on the script would be passed to loadFiles (see below). In any case, for his simpler version, load-Files queries the user to pick out the template and table files in turn. It even performs a bit of a check on the table, making sure it is a TableServer file.

Back in the doMerge handler, we take apart the names, assigning each to its own variable for ease of access and readability. We also have the scriptable Finder get just the file names from the paths—we'll definitely need the table's name for working with the table object safely by name.

Get Placeholder Names

In the next batch of statements, we instruct TableServer to get the names of all the rows in the table. We will actually merge from the point of view of the table, rather than the document, letting the column names drive our repetitions through the document. Therefore, the fieldNames variable, containing a list of all of the table's columns becomes a pivotal piece of data for this script. Because merged documents may contain dates in addition to table data, we append the Date field to the list (we'll have to handle its data separately later, but the overhead for that extra handling will be less than if we set up a separate merge facility just for the date placeholder). Equally important is the number of records we need to cycle through (maxRecords).

Merging

The hard work comes in the tell statement to Scriptable Text Editor. Things get hairy in here, because we must occasionally make calls to other handlers in the script as well as TableServer. We also go three deep into repeat statements to cycle through all the relevant data.

After opening the template file, we start one of the repeat loops, which initializes a counting variable (i). The counting variable will increment from 2 (the second row of the table, which is where the actual data begins) to the total number of rows in the table. In other words, the outermost repeat loop gradually works its way down the table.

For each row of data, we begin working our way across the columns. We set another counting variable (j) to help us keep track of which column we're working with. Because it's possible that a document may contain more than one instance of a column placeholder (as our sample document does), we start yet another repeat, so that each instance of every column is covered. This innermost repeat loop is set up as an infinite loop, which the script breaks out of when there are no more instances of a placeholder for a given column.

To prepare for the actual merge, we must find where the placeholder for a column's data is located in the document. The script grabs the most recent contents of the document and the name of the column (including the placeholder-identifying angle brackets)—passing both as parameters to the calcOffset subroutine in this script. Scriptable Text Editor doesn't like the offset scripting addition command, so we must isolate its call outside the tell statement. In any case, the returned value is an index to the character in the document where the placeholder begins (or zero if the placeholder is not in the document). When the value is zero, it means that there are no more instances of that placeholder, and the innermost repeat loop can exit—execution picks up in the next outer repeat loop with the next column/placeholder.

Next, when we're ready to replace the placeholder with the data, is where we handle the special case for the <Date> placeholder. For this example script, we use current date's formatting, which, admittedly, doesn't work for all international date systems (so we might have used one of the date OSAXes from the GTQ collection on the companion disk, described in Chapter 33). We copy the relevant parts of the current date data to the text of the document as defined by character offset (starting with the offset value, and ending with the character at the end of the placeholder).

For table data, the process is nearly the same, except we send a message to TableServer to extract the data from the cell and row coordinates specified by the variable values for each time through the loop. The script inserts the data into the template document the same way it does for dates.

Ready for Next Time

When all placeholders have been covered, the script can print the document. In the sample file and script listing, the print command is commented out. If you want to see the printouts, open the script with Script Editor and remove the comment symbol before the print command. Also between repeat loops for each row of data, the script sends the revert command to Scriptable Text Editor. It is vital that the document and placeholders be returned to the original state for the next row of data.

At the very end of the script, we close up the files we used.

Additional Ideas

As mentioned earlier, you can enhance this script so that it works as a droplet. The file loading process would need some care in design, but would be a good exercise. For example, you would have to anticipate that users may drop the wrong kinds of files onto the script. Therefore, the loadFiles subroutine would need some beefing up to investigate files dropped on the script, place correct file(s) in the right order for the returned values, and even prompting the user for one or both missing files.

Integrating with Other Applications

I believe it has been important for this volume so far to focus on the scriptable applications that are on the companion disk and, in the case of Finder, on your System (7.5). That way I know you have those applications, and can learn from them. Some of the examples for which we used TableServer can be adapted to other table-based scriptable applications, such as Microsoft Excel and FileMaker Pro.

As you will see in the next part of this book, other scriptable applications have much more power in their data handling abilities. Mastering those applications, and working their power into customized solutions will become an important part of your AppleScript work.

PART IV

Third-Party Scriptable Applications

CHAPTER 21

Scripting Third-Party Applications

The remainder of this book is dedicated to features of numerous commercial scriptable applications. It is unfortunate that learning how to script one application in a product category doesn't necessarily prepare you for scripting other products in the same category. Therefore, a script you write for Scriptable Text Editor may not run in WordPerfect, and definitely won't run in Claris MacWrite Pro. Each of these products has defined a different way of working with objects (when it supports objects), and has a different set of commands. Still, there are similarities in the way you approach any scriptable application to learn its features and quirks. That is the focus of this chapter.

Knowing the Program

I can't emphasize enough how important it is to be very familiar with an application you intend to script. By this I don't necessarily mean the scriptable part of the program, but rather the way users normally interact with the program and data stored in its documents. Very often, a program has a lexicon of its own to denote parts of documents or processes. These words are then often carried over to the OSA-scripting commands and objects that are defined in the product's scripting dictionary.

From some of the experimentation you did with TableServer in Chapter 19, you may think that all databases have just the kinds of objects and commands defined by this "pure implementation" of the Table Suite. But if you then apply what you know about TableServer to FileMaker Pro, you soon discover that FileMaker has some terminology of its own that plays an important role in scripting. For instance, FileMaker databases allow their designers to create multiple layouts (views) to the same database. Sample databases provided with the product (like Contacts and Projects) were designed with almost a dozen different layouts each. Not all database fields are represented on each layout, while some layouts have fields that are unique to them (e.g., they calculate summary values based on other fields). In any case, the importance of this knowledge is that the name of the layout becomes a key part of a cell's reference—something you didn't have to worry about in a simpler database, such as TableServer.

As another example, Excel 5 defines an object called the Workbook, which may contain numerous worksheets. If you don't understand how Excel workbooks work when manually using the program, you will have great difficulty managing multiple worksheets or multiple workbook files under AppleScript. Each of these objects must be part of references to data entry or retrieval cells if you have any hope of transferring information to the desired locations in the Excel document files.

The basic recommendation, therefore, is to be well acquainted with the depths of a product you intend to script before you begin scripting. If you must risk scripting a new product in a hurry, then it will definitely be worth your time to sit through whatever tutorial comes along with the program. It should acquaint you with at least the basic terminology of the program, which you may then recognize in the scripting dictionary.

Approaching a New Program

Because every program's OSA scripting is different, it takes a bit of exploration to become familiar with scripting possibilities for the program. To that end, I've assembled a sequence of questions for which I seek answers each time I start to fiddle with a new scriptable application.

Is the Program Recordable?

As mentioned elsewhere in this book, script recording is a two-edged sword. On the one hand it lets someone who doesn't know much about scripting or the scripting of a particular application automate a manual process easily. But the downside is that such scripts can't be very smart—they can't make decisions or repeat operations in a truly iterative way (in a repeat loop).

Script recording, however, is still a good way to learn some of the basics about a program's objects. Turn on the recorder from the script editor, switch to the program, and perform several common operations, such as creating a new document, entering some data, copying and pasting data from within the document, opening a sample file, and saving a test file. Then examine the script and look especially for object references about the document and the data you entered.

Not every program's recorded scripts provide the precise scripting verbiage you would use in truly scripted actions—even though what the recorder captures will work fine. The difference is that very often the recorder captures actions in a rudimentary way as it watches what you do. For example, instead of a typical script action of blasting a number into a cell, the recorded method may show the cell being physically selected first, and the entry going into the selection. Yes, this works, and you may continue to replicate the recorded syntax in your own scripts, but such a method is slower and more verbose than a comparable action performed solely by scripting.

Does the Application Support the Object Model?

Once I determine the recordability of a product, the next task is to inspect the scripting dictionary to see if it supports the Object Model. It's easy to see if the program's designers have defined objects for the dictionary, because as you scroll through the left column of dictionary words, objects appear in italics. At this point of my perusal, I'm not concerned about the specifics—just the fact that a product includes objects in its dictionary is generally a positive sign.

I am often suspicious, however, if the dictionary indicates support only for the Core and Standard Apple event suites. This suspicion comes from a few examples of products that show standard object support in the dictionary, yet the objects are of little or no value to the product (e.g., text objects in a graphics program, and nothing else). A better situation, however, is when the dictionary includes one or more additional suites, either of a generic nature (e.g., the Text Suite) or specific to the program.

In any case, object definitions usually indicate that the commands defined for the program will be in line with commands you may know from other programs—which brings us to the next question.

Does It Support an Object Model You Know?

Just because a program has defined objects, even in specific event suites, doesn't mean that the objects behave the same way as the same kind of objects do in other programs. For example, two table-based applications might define a cell object, but the way your scripts must refer to these cells in each program could vary significantly: one may prefer to point to the cell as cell x of row y; another may prefer a format for the cell reference as cell "RxCy," where the "R" stands for "row," and the "C" for "column." Unfortunately, you can't always tell this from the dictionary (see about getting stuff into and out of a document, below). But you can examine an object's defintion and see if it has the same kind of properties you know for similar objects in other programs you know.

As much as I would like to see all programs of a category maintain a common denominator of object and command definitions, I don't recommend shunning a program because its dictionary is foreign to you. More important is whether the program does what you need, and whether the tasks you wish to automate can be scripted. The fact that a dictionary may bear new definitions and formats only means that there will be some extra learning time involved prior to successfully scripting the application.

How Extensive Is the Dictionary?

In virtually every example I've seen of a large scripting dictionary, the programming team has given significant thought to the scripting implementation. Among the largest dictionaries I've seen are those for QuarkXpress, HyperCard 2.2, and Excel 5. Scrolling through the commands and objects of these dictionaries in the Script Editor seems to go on for miles. These three programs are admittedly quite deep in their own right, yet their designers supplied access to a great deal of that depth so that scripters won't have to resort to calling scripts in the programs' own languages.

Does the Program Support "Whose" Clauses?

One of the most valuable constructions in the AppleScript syntax is the filtered reference (Chapter 8), otherwise known as whose clauses. A whose clause allows a script to ask a program to work on a number of objects that meet certain criteria, such as all records of a database whose State field is "TX." When an application supports whose clauses, it can save lines and lines of scripting or figuring out how to make the program select objects by its own mechanism (e.g., a Find command).

The dictionary may reveal whether the programs will respond to whose clauses. When viewing the details of container objects (documents, windows, etc.), a list of elements will usually indicate how those elements may be addressed. If the listing includes items available by "satisfying a test," then the authors have likely implemented at least some level of whose clauses.

If a program supports whose clauses, it is mostly likely to be on common objects that have numerous properties—documents, paragraphs, records, and so on. To verify whose clause support, first create a document in the application that has known data and settings that you can test for. Make sure that the contents of at least two objects have something in common.

Next, make sure the program responds to the every element reference (a prerequisite for filtered references) by getting a property of all items in the document. Sometimes merely naming the object returns the object's contents, as in

    every paragraph of document 1 -- *Scriptable Text Editor*

    every record -- *FileMaker Pro*

    every item of startup disk -- *Finder*

Other times, you may need to specifically request the value of the object to see understandable data, as in

    Value of every Cell of Range "R1C1:R10C10" -- *Microsoft Excel*

In this last example, we limited the excursion to a range of 100 cells, since getting every cell of a worksheet is time consuming and overruns the ability of the Result window to show the results.

Once you know that the every element reference works, it's time to try a filtered reference by adding a valid whose clause. A whose clause must focus on a property that certain objects have in common, such as contents, text format, or any other property setting. Here are examples that build on the ones above:

-- *Scriptable Text Editor*
every paragraph of document 1 whose contents contains "Fred"

-- *FileMaker Pro*
every record whose cell "State" contains "CA"

-- *Finder*
every item of startup disk whose kind is "folder"

-- *Microsoft Excel*
Value of every Cell of Range "R1C1:R10C10" whose font is "Geneva"

Of all the tests, above, only the one for Excel fails, meaning that it is unlikely you'll be able to use whose clauses in Excel. Indeed, the dictionary entries for elements bears this out, because none are listed as satisfying a test. Knowing that a particular program does not support whose clauses is valuable knowledge early on, so you won't waste time trying to write them later and wondering what the problem is with your script.

How Do You Get Stuff Out of a Document?

A vital operation for many scripting tasks is retrieval of information from a document. Retrieving information generally entails the ever-popular get command, so the true focus is on accurate ways of referring to objects and their information.

To the conscientious scripter, the dictionary information listed as elements of objects often contains valuable information (if the developer has been so kind as to provide that information). For example, look at the listing of elements for the Scriptable Text Editor document object:

Elements:

character by numeric index, before/after another element, as a range of elements, satisfying a test

insertion point before/after another element

paragraph by numeric index, before/after another element, as a range of elements, satisfying a test

text as a range of elements

text item by numeric index, before/after another element, as a range of elements, satisfying a test

word by numeric index, before/after another element, as a range of elements, satisfying a test

The description after each object name indicates the kinds of references your scripts can use for the object. A character, for example, can be signified by its character count, by its location relative to another object, by a range reference, and a filtered reference ("satisfying a test"). Therefore, any of the following references would be valid:

character 35 -- *index (character count) value of 35*

character after word 3

characters 10 thru 20

every character whose style is plain

In contrast, the insertion point object has only one kind of reference: a reference to a position relative to another object:

insertion point before character 1

As further examples, here are the element descriptions for a document object in Scriptable Text Editor:

document by numeric index, by name, as a range of elements, satisfying a test

A different reference type—by name—is listed here. Therefore, we can refer to a document by number (the frontmost document being number 1), its name, to multiple documents within a range of documents, or those satisfying a whose clause (based on a property of a document object).

Some program's objects, however, still don't give you enough information about addressing them from a script. Excel is a particularly good example. First of all, if you come from any other table-based environment, you think of the cell as the basic information object. Excel, however, utilizes the range object as the primary object for data access, even if the range is of a single cell. Not only that, but the syntax for ranges is different from that which you tend to use (and which Excel, itself uses by default) when working with ranges in formulas. For example, if you manually type a formula into cell A4 to sum the three cells above it, the formula reads

=SUM(A1:A3)

with "A1:A3" representing the range of cells starting at A1. In scripting, however, ranges must be specified in their RaCb:RcCd nomenclature. There is no indication of this in the dictionary, but you do get a hint of this by inspecting scripts you record. But the point is that the dictionary definition for the Range object lists only the "name" reference, which in Excel's instance means either a name previously defined for the range or by its RaCb:RcCd format. Therefore, the range object consisting of the three cells described above would be:

Range "R1C1:R3C1"

As you can see, it may take a combination of experimentation and script recording to find out how a program refers to its basic objects.

What we're really interested in, however, is the data that is contained in those objects—that's what we're scripting about, anyway. Once you can successfully refer to a data object, it's time to see what the default reference returns. In other words, enter the equivalent of a **get** statement that points to an object holding some kind of known data (i.e., data you've entered into a sample document). In many programs, the default reference returns the contents of the object. For example:

```
paragraph 1 of document 1 -- Scriptable Text Editor

record 1 -- FileMaker Pro

cell 1 of record 1 -- FileMaker Pro

folder 1 of startup disk -- Finder
```

All of these return data in a form that is perfectly natural: a Scriptable Text Editor string; a tab-delimited record for FileMaker Pro; a string of a cell's contents from FileMaker Pro; and a reference to the first folder in sorting order of the startup disk in the Finder.

But not every default reference returns just the object's value. Consider TableServer's default returned value for the first cell of the "Presidents" table demonstrated in Chapter 6:

```
tell application "TableServer"
  cell 1 of row 1
end tell
    -- result: {class:Cell, Name:"President", «class data»:"George Washington"}
```

Instead of the contents, we get a record listing a few properties of the object. To get the contents of the cell, we have to look deeper into the dictionary, where we see a property of a cell defined as:

Value 'ctxt'—the content of the cell

It turns out that the value property (or other property name incorporating the word "value") is a common way to extract the data from an object whose default reference doesn't return its data. For TableServer, then, the data extraction would be:

```
tell application "TableServer"
  value of cell 1 of row 1
end tell
    -- result: "George Washington"
```

FileMaker Pro actually can return data with both types of references:

```
every Cell of Record 1

cellValue of every Cell of Record 1
```

Both forms return an AppleScript list, with each cell's value a string item within the list.

How You Get Stuff Into a Document?

The effort you exert in learning how to retrieve information from a scriptable application's document goes a long way into helping you enter information into documents. Primary concerns are selecting the desired command, knowing how to refer to objects that are to receive the information, and formatting the information you're about to insert into the document.

On the command side of things, it's a relatively short list of possibilities, depending on the object and the program. The most common commands for entering new information are:

```
set
copy
make
create
```

This list is deceiving, because the first two are identical in their action (just different in the order of their parameters), and the generally speaking, a program will support one of the last two, but rarely both. You cannot, however, assume that programs supporting the make or create commands define them in the same manner, so it's a good idea to check the dictionary for parameters in each program.

Setting (or copying) data involves doing so to an existing object or insertion point, depending on the kind of document you're working with. For example, text processing documents that support the Object Model let you set any potential text cursor location (insertion point) to some new text value. The following script places the text "Howdy" at the beginning of the document:

```
tell document 1 of application "Scriptable Text Editor"
    set insertion point 1 to "Howdy"
end tell
```

Even more commonly in text processing documents is to put text at a location named by relative reference:

```
copy "Howdy" to beginning

copy "The End" to end

copy ", however," to after word 3 of paragraph 3

set after word 3 of paragraph 3 to ", however," -- awkward reading
```

For some other kinds of documents, you use similar set or copy constructions directed at an object (although probably not with relative references). Also, an application may define its own set command for the sake of its internal clarity (i.e., to distinguish the command from a standard set command). For example, one way to plug a value into a FileMaker Pro cell is as follows:

```
tell application "FileMaker Pro"
    Set Data of Cell "State" to "OH"
end tell
```

FileMaker's variation of the set command is set data. The above command puts text into a specific cell of the current record showing in the database window (whether or not the application is active).

But when an application's default reference for its objects does not yield the contents of the object (when retrieving we have to get the value or cellValue of the object), a script must set the value property for that object. Therefore, in Excel, to insert a number into a spreadsheet cell, the construction would be like this:

```
set value of Range "R4C5" to 5959
```

It is vital to know the format of data your script needs to insert into a document. For example, setting the value of three consecutive fields of a database will undoubtedly require that the data for each field be separated in some fashion. To know how best to format the data, retrieve some sample data of a similar range first. In TableServer, for instance, if we retrieve the value of all cells of a row, we get a list:

```
tell application "TableServer"
    Value of cells of row 1
end tell
    -- result: {"George Washington", "F", "John Adams"}
```

Therefore to set the value of those cells to different values, the script must format the data the same way:

```
tell application "TableServer"
    set Value of cells of row 1 to {"George Washington", "Federalist", "John Adams'
end tell
```

Another method of entering data into a document is, when appropriate, to create a new object and assign data to that new object at the same time. That's where the make or create commands come in. Sending the commands without any additional parameters generally creates a new, blank object. But to send some data along, you should check the dictionary entry of the make or create commands for with data and/or with properties labeled parameters. In addition, there may be a parameter that lets you specify where in the document the new object should go (usually with an at parameter label). Let's take these parameters one at a time to see how they work.

The with data parameter is the key one, since the data you pass as this parameter is the data that generally goes into the new object. The format of the data must be in the same format as you'd extract from that object. For instance, you can instruct Scriptable Text Editor to create a new paragraph at the current text insertion point with the words "New Paragraph" in it:

```
tell application "Scriptable Text Editor"
    make new paragraph with data "New Paragraph"
end tell
```

This action inserts the proper carriage return(s) to make the data stand as its own separate paragraph object. A FileMaker Pro record, on the other hand, expects its data to be either in a tab-delimited string, or in a list, as in:

```
Create New Record With Data "General Magic" & tab & ¬
   "Atkinson" & tab & "Bill" & tab & "Chief Scientist"
```

```
Create New Record ¬
   with Data {"General Magic","Atkinson","Bill","Chief Scientist"}
```

Data for each cell is in the same order as the fields in the layout.

FileMaker is a bit more lenient than other programs, because if you retrieve the record, it comes back as a list, making you expect the program would accept only a list of data. In fact, unless you experiment to find out about other possibilities, you probably wouldn't know to use them.

The with properties parameter can let you pass additional information about the object you're creating. Any settable property of the object can be adjusted as it's being created. For example, in TableServer, we saw that you can create a table by supplying information about its number of columns and other data:

```
make table with properties {name:"TV Families",ColCount:3}
```

Properties passed this way are generally expected in this AppleScript record format, each record clearly specifying the properties and their corresponding values. You can elect to set only those properties that you wish at creation time. In a text processing program, for instance, you may wish to set some font properties, as in:

```
make new paragraph with data "New Paragraph" ¬
   with properties {font:"Courier", size:24, style:bold}
```

A final parameter (optional in some programs, required in others) specifies where the object is to go. Failure to indicate the location usually places the new object at whatever location would receive keystrokes or a new object from the program's New menu (when the menu item applies to content items). But the at parameter lets your script control the insertion spot. Relative references almost always work, such as:

```
at end
```

```
at beginning
```

```
after <object>
```

```
before <object>
```

Appending a new object to the end of the document (or as the last record of a database) requires the at end variation. In most cases, creating a new object like this inserts the new object, perhaps disturbing only the sequence of existing objects. But be sure to test this out on known data first: some variations might overwrite the object before which or after which the new object is to go (most likely a bug in the scriptable program).

As you can see, the make and create commands can be rather powerful constructions, depending on the program's support for them.

How Do You Massage Stuff Inside a Document?

As you dig more deeply into scripting data within a document, you get further away from any commonality that scriptable applications may share. In the majority of cases, each program defines a number of commands and objects that are unique to itself, causing scripters to have to learn the scripting vocabulary and idiosyncracies of each scriptable application. In succeeding chapters, you will see numerous examples of working with specific applications. In this section, however, we'll discuss what few trends can be deduced from scripting implementations in today's apps.

Of course, the category of pseudo-scriptable applications—the ones that expect you to do serious scripting in the program's own scripting or macro language—have a lot in common. In addition for support of just a handful of common commands and objects (if that much), they usually contain scripting dictionary definitions for two essential commands:

do script

evaluate

The first command, **do script**, runs a script or macro written in the program's own language. Somewhere in the architecture of the language is a way to assign a name to the script (it may appear in a customizable menu, for instance). That name becomes the parameter for the **do script** command. You must run tests on calling these macros with the **do script** command, because processes that take a long time may require the AppleScript timeout setting be adjusted upward to accommodate the macro's execution.

Occasionally, a macro will supply or return some data, much like a function does. In such cases, the value comes back as the result of the **evaluate** command. Again, the parameter for the command is most likely the name of an internal macro or script in the program's own language. To capture the value, assign the result to a variable in your own script, such as

set returnedValue to evaluate "ProgramMacro"

You must also exercise care in the format of the returned value. If you are accustomed to receiving AppleScript list objects or records for multiple-piece data, it's more than likely that the program's internal scripting language doesn't return data in those formats. Therefore, check carefully for the format of the data, and write AppleScript code to get it the way you want it.

For true object scripting within a document, it is important to keep accurate track of the objects you're working with. In the case of the scriptable Finder, for example, we saw that virtually every command returns the reference to the object just manipulated, so you can perform another task on that object with the comfort that you have its most recent and accurate reference. Not all programs are that friendly, so as you begin working on a script that controls objects in documents, I suggest you activate the program during script construction so you can see the process taking place—and perhaps see where or why something doesn't work as you expected. In many cases, the problem is one of context: the object you want to work on isn't available or has a new reference as a result of a previous action.

The vast differences in working with the specifics of scriptable applications causes difficulty when trying to get help from other people who know Apple-Script (in case you're either intimidated by or disappointed with the product support from the program publisher). Unless your colleagues have had direct experience with the very program you're stuck in, it's unlikely that they'll be able to help you with specific questions. But if you belong to one of the on-line services that have forums for scripting (Chapter 30), there's a good chance someone will have experience with all but the most off-beat applications.

Moving onto Applications

One word I wish to add prior to the chapters about specific applications. Scripting is a very custom process. The more support for scripting a program supplies, the more diverse the applications its scripting users will find for the program. It is therefore impossible to anticipate every question or application you are likely to have about the applications from the rest of this book that you script. My goal in the remaining chapters is to provide you with enough clues to the general behavior of a program's scripting environment to help you uncover solutions to your thorniest problems. I believe it's important to see lots of examples for the most common tasks, so that they'll provide pointers to syntax and other constructions that will get you to a successful script.

CHAPTER **22**

FileMaker Pro

Version

2.1v3

Recordable

No.

Object Model Support

Good support for entering, retrieving, and manipulating data within existing databases. Not intended for scripted creation of databases.

Supports Whose Clauses

Yes, but see below.

Important Application Concepts

Of the three key concepts you should keep in mind while scripting FileMaker Pro, the most important is the distinction between the database and the layout. Bear in mind that layouts are merely views to whatever fields are appropriate for the layout. Not every layout contains every field of the database. In fact, it is possible that the entire collection of fields may not appear in any layout. Despite this, your scripts have access to data in any field, regardless of the layout currently displayed in FileMaker. What your script accesses are cells of records, as in

cell "Person Responsible" of Record 4

437

If you wish to view a particular layout while a script manipulates a database, your script is free to do so.

Layouts come into play when your script relies on the selection of fields that are viewed through a layout. For example, if a database has two different data entry layouts (as many of the Claris sample databases do), retrieving a record of one layout gets data only from the fields visible in that layout:

Record 3 of Layout 1

Record 3 of Layout 2 -- *different fields*

If you don't specify a layout, FileMaker assumes you mean the layout that is currently showing in the database window.

Unfortunately, there is an anomaly that returns unexpected information when trying to establish field information about the underlying database (i.e., the one with all the fields). While your script can establish the correct number of fields in the database by querying the database object for this information, you cannot get the names or other properties (including values) for the fields:

count of every field of database 1
    -- *result: (* correct number of fields in the database. *)*

name of every Field of Database 1
    -- *result: (* names of fields belonging only to layout 1 *)*

Fortunately, there is a hidden workaround: a special Layout number zero. This layout, while not counted as one of the database's official layouts, returns the desired information about the database's fields:

name of every Field of Layout 0
    -- *result: (* names of fields in the database *)*

You can use this same construction to get a record consisting of every field of a particular record:

Record 10 of Layout 0

The second important object distinction to understand about FileMaker is that between a field and a cell. To FileMaker, a property of a field is a property that applies to every instance of that field, in all records of the database. For instance, if you set the value of a field,

tell application "FileMaker Pro"
    copy "magazine ad" to Field "Referral Type" of Layout 1
end tell

then that field in all records will assume that same data. FileMaker won't accept an attempt to address a field object of a specific record, because there can be no record-specific field. To set the data of a field for only a single record, you must address the target object as a cell of a particular record (of a particular layout)

```
tell application "FileMaker Pro"
    copy "word-of-mouth" to Cell "Referral Type" of Record 3 of Layout 1
end tell
```

Even though in this instance we enter a value into a cell of a particular record of a particular layout, FileMaker behaves just as if we had manually entered the data into the field, meaning that the data for that cell will appear in all layouts that contain that field, each time we view Record 3.

The last key concept is that of selected records. Whenever a database is displaying a subset of the entire database, your scripts can access only the records "showing." To restore access to the entire collection, use the **show every record** statement, which performs the same action as the Find All item in FileMaker's Select menu.

Scripting Overview

FileMaker Pro's scripting has gone through a number of revisions and bug fixes, so some items that may have worked one way in previous versions (e.g., getting tab-delimited records from some data retrieval syntaxes when everything should have been AppleScript lists) won't work in the latest version. Be that as it may, FileMaker's implementation has evolved into a relatively straightforward environment within the friendly confines of retrieving, insertings, and massaging data. Since you cannot make changes to the graphical appearance of items in a FileMaker layout via scripting, regard FileMaker as a scriptable database engine.

Because some syntax constructions yield unexpected results (e.g., retrieving data from sorted records, below), it is important to test your scripts on known sample data in a database you create. Manually modify the database (sort, select, etc.), and make sure your scripts provide the results you expect under all circumstances.

FileMaker Pro has its own scripting language (of sorts). You can call File-Maker scripts from an AppleScript script (use the **do script** command) if that helps leverage your scripting. Moreover, you can put AppleScript scripts into the Scripts menu to make your scripts appear to be a part of the database. To accomplish this, write and test your script using Script Editor (or equivalent). Then save the script as a standalone application. In FileMaker, follow these steps:

1. Choose ScriptMaker... from the Scripts menu.
2. Enter a name for your script as you'd like it to appear in the Scripts menu.
3. Click the Create button.
4. Click the Clear All button.
5. Scroll to the bottom of the lefthand list of functions.
6. Click on Send Apple Event [].

7. Click the Move button.

8. Click the Specify button.

9. In the dialog, select Open Application from the event popup.

10. Select the standalone script you saved earlier.

11. Click all Save, OK, and Done buttons to clear all the dialogs.

The script item now appears in your menu. It is important to make sure your script works from anywhere within the database. That means that it must name layouts and fields so that the commands work regardless of the layout or record the user is viewing when summoning the script from the menu.

Retrieving Information

The scripts in this section (available on the companion disk) demonstrate ways to extract information from a FileMaker Pro database. While FileMaker Pro defines get data commands and cellValue cell properties, neither are required to retrieve information from elements of a database.

The first script focuses on extracting object names and information from known locations in a database. The second provides examples of extracting information from a database via whose clauses. Both scripts require the Contacts sample database (which comes with FileMaker) be open in FileMaker Pro. The best way to observe the results of each form is to run the script with the Script Editor Event Log window open. If you should ever receive an error that says "Object not found," it usually means that you have specified an object that is not available based on the currently selected records (e.g., Record 8 when only two records are currently showing), or the object is not available in the current layout.

```
-- FileMaker Retrieve - 1
tell application "FileMaker Pro"
    Show every Record -- make sure we start out at same place

    -- names of all fields in database
    Name of every Field of Layout 0

    -- names of fields from specific layout
    Name of every Field of Layout "Fax Cover Sheet"

    -- names of layouts
    Name of every Layout

    ----------------------

    -- data from field of all records
    Field "Contact Last"

    -- data from single cell of record of current layout
    Cell "Contact Last" of Record 2

    -- data from single cell using optional cellValue property
    cellValue of Cell "Contact Last" of Record 2
```

```
                         -- data from entire record of whole database
                         Record 2 of Layout 0

                         -- data from entire record through a given layout
                         Record 2 of Layout "Fax Cover Sheet"

                         ---------------------

                         -- a range of cells from a record
                         Cells 1 thru 3 of first Record

                         -- a cell from a range of records
                         Cell "Main Number" of Records 3 thru 6

                 end tell

                 -- FileMaker Retrieve - 2
                 tell application "FileMaker Pro"
                         Show every Record -- make sure we start out at same place

                         -- data from entire database (list of lists)
                         every Record of Layout 0

                         -- data of entire database through a layout view (list of lists)
                         every Record of Layout "Envelope"

                         -----------------

                         -- whose clauses
                         every Record whose Cell "State" is "MA"

                         every Record of Layout "Envelope" whose Cell "State" is "MA"

                         Cell "Company Name" of (every Record whose Cell "State" is "CA"¬
                                 and Cell "Contact Type" is "Bus.")

                 end tell
```

In the next script, we examine how to retrieve counts of various objects.

```
                 -- FileMaker Counts
                 tell application "FileMaker Pro"
                         Show every Record
                         -- number of records in database
                         Count of Records of Database "Copy of Contacts"

                         -- number of currently "found" records
                         Count of Records

                         -- number of fields in database
                         Count of Fields of Layout 0

                         -- number of fields in a layout
                         Count of Fields of Layout "Envelope"

                         -- does NOT return valid information
                         Count (every Record whose Cell "State" is "CA")
                         -- instead, show every qualifying record,
```

```
            -- then count "found" records
            Show (every Record whose Cell "State" is "CA")
            Count of Records

            -- restore selected records to all
            Show every Record
        end tell
```

Inserting New Information

As with most scriptable applications, FileMaker Pro allows new information to be put into a database document by setting the data of an existing record and by creating new objects (and passing properties along for the ride). In the dictionary, FileMaker defines the Set Data command, which is optional. You may use the standard AppleScript Set or Copy commands to move information into objects.

Because the commands in the script modify the contents of the Contacts database, you may prefer to open a copy of the database for executing these statements—leaving the original intact for exploration later.

```
    -- FileMaker Insert
    tell application "FileMaker Pro"
        activate -- so you can watch
        -- insert/modify data in single cell of a record
        set Cell "Referral Type" of Record 3 to "magazine"

        -- insert/modify data in same cell of ALL records,
        -- in this case, setting the value of a radio button
        set Field "Holiday Card" to "Yes"

        -- inserting stepped values
        repeat with x from 1 to Count every Record
            set Cell "Contact Code" of Record x to "AS" & x
        end repeat

        -- insert in non-contiguous cells of a record
        set {Cell "Zip" of Record 3, Cell "Other Zip" of Record 3} ¬
            to {"12340", "12340"}

        -- insert values into select cells of a record
        set Record 3 to {"Widgets 'R Us", "Henry", "Widget", "", "808-555-9000"}

        -- setting multiple values of a checkbox field
        set Cell "Contact Type" of Record 3 of Layout 1 ¬
            to "Pers." & return & "Trade"

        -- insert multiple-lined text
        set Cell "Notes" of Record 3 to "Son:Kevin" & return & ¬
            "XMAS card 1994"
```

```
-- create new record and stuff first fields with data
Create New Record With Data {"Apple Computer, Inc.", ¬
    "David", "Nagel", "Wearer of Many Hats", "408-996-1010"}

-- clone record, replace some items, and make new record
set oneRecord to Record 3 of Layout 1
set item 2 of oneRecord to "Dorothy"
set item 3 of oneRecord to "Adams"
Create New Record of Layout 1 With Data oneRecord
end tell
```

Massaging Information in a Document

One item to be aware of is how FileMaker Pro treats sorted records. If you choose to have FileMaker sort records, you must exercise care in the way you extract the sorted data. If you're not careful, you'll get data in the unsorted order.

First, here are examples of sorting statements:

```
-- sort layout by a single field
Sort Layout 1 By Field "State"

-- sort layout by multiple fields
Sort Layout 1 By {Field "State", Field "Contact Last"}

-- sort layout in alternate order
Sort Layout 1 By Field "Zip" In Order Descending
```

Once the database is sorted the way you want, here are examples of data retrieval statements that yield data in the sorted order:

```
field 1

every record

fields 2 thru 4

cell "Contact Last" of last record
```

The following example unexpectedly returns data in the unsorted order:

```
cell 1 of every record
```

Therefore, be sure to test your sorts and data retrieval syntax for accuracy.

You can execute menu commands from a script via the do menu command. The syntax description in the dictionary is not complete, because you must name a menu item as well as its menu, as in:

```
do menu menu item "Delete Found Set" of menu "Edit"
```

In case your script may be used by FileMaker Pro users with other language versions, you can also substitute the menu item and menu numbers. Menu 1 is the Apple menu, and menu item numbers start with number one from the top of the menu.

Electing to execute some menu items, however, will eliminate the benefit of automating a process. Those menus that lead to dialog items (the ones followed by the ellipsis character—Option-colon) will display their respective dialog boxes, and wait for user input. If FileMaker is not the active application, the FileMaker icon will flash in the Application menu in the menubar.

More powerful, however, is executing FileMaker scripts from your AppleScript script. The **do script** command requires just the complete name of the existing script in the database. For example, in Contacts is a script that sorts the records by state, and displays them in a list in layout 5. That script, named List by Area, can be called from a script this way:

```
do script "List by Area"
```

Because you can specify that a FileMaker script perform actions without displaying associated dialog boxes, a mixture of FileMaker and AppleScript scripts can accommodate some processes that can't be done without user input, such as printing. To set up such a FileMaker script, use ScriptMaker (in the Scripts menu) to create a new macro that goes to the desired layout and prints without a dialog box (Figure 22.1). You don't have to put this script in the Scripts menu, since it is generally invisible to everyone except your script. Then, your AppleScript script can do something like this to select a desired range of records, and print accordingly:

```
tell application "FileMaker Pro"
    activate
    Show (every Record whose Cell "State" is "CA")
    Do Script "Print List"
end tell
```

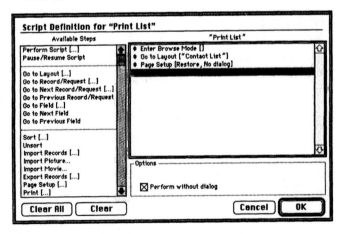

Figure 22.1 Setting up a macro to print.

In this manner, you can automate FileMaker processes that AppleScript doesn't have the power to do, yet to the user, the automation appears seamless. Also, if you encounter an existing database that has buttons that trigger FileMaker scripts, look inside the button in Layout mode to see what script the button calls. Your AppleScript scripts can use the do script command to carry out the action of a user clicking that button.

If you create a picture field in a FileMaker database, you can use AppleScript to copy data from other programs, provided they allow the grabbing of such graphic data (see Chapter 23 for ways to do this with Excel charts). Failing a graphics' program ability to copy pictures to a variable, you can fall back on the clipboard (especially via the Clipboard scripting addition as part of Jon's Commands, described in Chapter 33).

One other quirk reported by avid networked database scripters touches on the concept of transactions. The advice is to avoid the begin transaction command. Instead, use AppleScript's with transaction control statement (Chapter 10). Moreover, end the block by entering only the word "end," rather than "end transaction." The compiler will add "transaction" on its own, but if you script it yourself, the statement gets picked up by FileMaker (and its end transaction command), which won't properly balance the transaction block, and prevents compilation.

FileMaker Pro is the cornerstone of many professional scripters' lives, primarily because it was the first scriptable database. While its scripting quality gets better with each interim release, there are still a number of bugs that can crop up. Therefore, text you scripting applications thoroughly prior to releasing them to the hands of other users.

CHAPTER 23

Microsoft Excel

Version

5.0

Recordable

Yes.

Object Model Support

Extensive support for entering, retrieving, and manipulating data within existing spreadsheets, as well as automating the physical appearance of spreadsheets and graphics.

Supports Whose Clauses

Yes.

Important Application Concepts

A major new concept has come along with version 5 of Excel: the Workbook. A workbook can contain multiple worksheets, charts, and macro sheets (now called modules). The primary effect on scripting is that objects have a new containment hierarchy, meaning that you may address multiple worksheets (preferably by name) within a single workbook.

If you script macros, especially if you did so with Excel 4, the new version marks a transition away from the old macro language to Microsoft's Visual Basic language. While you can still use Excel 4-style macros with Excel 5, Microsoft makes it clear that this will be the last round. Therefore, it appears to be a good idea to wean yourself away from the Excel 4 language.

Scripting Overview

The scripting dictionary for Excel 5 is gargantuan. It's even too large to display its entire contents in Script Editor's dictionary window. Many of the new commands are AppleScript versions of Visual Basic commands (called methods and functions), giving scripters ready access to those commands.

This version also defines dozens of new objects, some of which are pieces of other containing objects (e.g., the Interior of a cell or drawing object). But even the Page Setup dialog is an object, whose settings (as properties) can be adjusted quite easily by script.

When scripting Excel, it is wise to remember that the primary means of exchanging information between a script and Excel is via the cells of a worksheet. In other words, to use an Excel function to achieve some calculation of a value obtained from outside of Excel, it is best to place that value in one cell, and insert the function formula in another cell (pointing to the data in the first cell); then retrieve the value from the cell containing the formula.

If you are new to scripting Excel, the primary annoyance will be the required convention for naming cells and ranges. While you've probably used the A1-style of cell references in your worksheet formulas, any such references in an AppleScript script must be in the R1C1 format. In fact, while it is possible to refer to individual cell objects, I find it more convenient to treat every such object as a range, whether for one or dozens of cells.

Between the enlarged scripting dictionary and the extensive Visual Basic language included with Excel 5, scripting this application could become someone's career. This book can't possibly cover every aspect of scripting this version, so I'll focus instead on what should be the basic data manipulation tasks for scripting a spreadsheet of Excel's caliber.

Retrieving Information

For the following script series, open the Bookstore Inventory sample workbook that comes with Excel 5. We'll extract a number of pieces of information from a typical spreadsheet table of data to demonstrate data retrieval syntax. Keep the Event Log window open at all times so you can see the commands and resulting data from the worksheet.

```
-- Excel Retrieve
tell application "Microsoft Excel"
    Activate Worksheet "Inventory"

    -- data from single cell
    Value of Range "R2C3"

    -- data from cells in a row
    Value of Range "R1C1:R1C7"
```

```
    -- data from cells in a column
    Value of Range "R1C1:R5C1"

    -- data from cells in a three-column by three-row block
    Value of Range "R2C1:R4C3"

    -- raw value of a cell
    Value of Range "R2C5"

    -- formated value of a cell
    text of Range "R2C5"

end tell
```

Notice that there is a big difference between the value of the cell and what you may see in a cell (its text). Raw values for many kinds of values (especially dates and times) are stored in Excel in the form of serial numbers that are meaningless outside of Excel. But if the spreadsheet designer has assigned a human-readable format to the data, you can extract that form by getting the text property of a cell or range.

Scripts can create charts, which can then be copied to AppleScript variables (as raw data) for transfer to other programs that accept such PICT-formatted data (e.g., a picture field of FileMaker Pro). Here is a script that generates a temporary chart from data in Bookstore Inventory, and copies the chart to a variable called myChart:

```
    -- Excel Charting
    tell application "Microsoft Excel"
        Activate -- so we can watch
        Activate Worksheet "Income Statement"
        -- select discontiguous selection for charting
        Select Range "R4C2:R15C2,R4C15:R15C15"
        Create New Chart
        -- set properties of new chart
        tell first Chart
            set Type to xl3DColumn
            set SubType to 4
            set Title to "Bookstore Income 1993"
            set HasTitle to true
            set HasLegend to false
        end tell
        -- grab color chart as data for placement in another document
        set myChart to first Chart
        Delete ActiveSheet -- remove new chart from workbook
    end tell
```

Notice the syntax for selecting a discontiguous range of cells—all one string, and a comma-delimited list of ranges. This script avoids the ChartWizard, which is also scriptable. We had difficulty capturing a chart that was created as a chart object, as script recording demonstrated for us. But the method shown here (consistent with Excel 4) works fine.

Excel 5 uses the printed version of the chart to pass back to an AppleScript variable. As long as the document is set to print in color (the default setting for LaserWriter drivers), then the chart data will be of the color version.

Finally, if the destination for the chart is a program that supports the Clipboard, but not PICT data, then you can use the CopyPicture command in your script to copy a selected chart to the Clipboard (provided Excel is active at the time).

Inserting New Information

To demonstrate entering data into cells, the following script uses several data range techniques to build a new workbook and spreadsheet from scratch. In practical application, you would probably not use every command style here, since you can enter information more efficiently with fewer calls. Study the sequence of the script prior to running it—the script may run quickly, without you seeing the specific results of each call. Feel free to create a new scratch script window and extract individual statements to see precisely how they work.

```
-- Excel Insert
tell application "Microsoft Excel"
    Activate

    -- creating new workbook, capturing reference for later use
    set newBook to Create New Workbook

    -- reduce number of sheets
    repeat until (count of Sheets) = 5
        Delete last Sheet
    end repeat

    -- assign name to a sheet
    set Name of Sheet 1 to "Test Lab"

    -- insert data in single cell
    set Range "R1C2" to "Q1"

    -- insert data in cells of same row
    set Range "R1C3:R1C6" to {{"Q2", "Q3", "Q4", "Total"}}

    -- insert data in cells of same column
    set Range "R2C1:R5C1" to {1991, 1992, 1993, 1994}

    -- insert data in cells of rectangular range
    set Range "R2C2:R5C5" to {{10, 20, 30, 40}, ¬
        {11, 21, 31, 41}, {12, 22, 32, 42}, {13, 23, 33, 43}}

    -- insert formula in single cell, then fill right
    set FormulaR1C1 of Range "R6C2" to "=SUM(R[-4]C:R[-1]C)"
```

```
    Select Range "R6C2:R6C5"
    AutoFill Range "R6C2" Destination Selection

    -- alternate, quicker method:
    -- insert same relative formula in range of cells
    set FormulaR1C1 of Range "R2C6:R6C6" to "=SUM(RC[-4]:RC[-1])"

    -- SAVING the workbook --
    -- have user enter filename from outside Excel (AS 1.1 'new file' OSAX)
    set newFileName to new file with prompt "Save Workbook as..."
    -- or with Excel file save dialog
    set newFileName to file ¬
        GetSaveAsFilename Title "Save Workbook as..."
    -- which sets result to false if Canceled,
    -- so you must manually check and bail out if canceled by user
    if newFileName is false then error number -128
    -- now do the actual file saving
    Save newBook In newFileName -- workbook reference from earlier

end tell
```

Some of the formatting, especially the list of lists formats for entering complete row(s) of data, is far from intuitive. This may also present some problems when the data you wish to insert into a spreadsheet comes from an application (e.g., FileMaker Pro) that does not supply data in the necessary list of lists format. For example, if you extract a series of cells from a FileMaker Pro record, they will be in a straight list format. You can then force Excel to make the data into a list of lists. Here's a skeleton of how this would work:

```
tell application "FileMaker Pro"
    activate
    Show Layout "Quarter Budget Summary"
    copy (Cells 3 thru 6 of Record 1 as list) to thePlan
    copy (Cells 8 thru 11 of Record 1 as list) to theActual
    makeTheChart(thePlan, theActual)
    activate
end tell

on makeTheChart(thePlan, theActual)
    tell application "Microsoft Excel"
        activate
        open file "Macintosh HD:Projects Charting"
        set Value of Range "R2C2:R2C5" to {thePlan}
        set Value of Range "R3C2:R3C5" to {theActual}
        (* stuff here to create and copy chart *)
    end tell
end makeTheChart
```

By placing the variables (which are themselves lists) inside list braces, the script passes a list of a list to Excel.

Back in the script that demonstrates insertion syntax, we also see methods of inserting formulas into both a single cell and to a range of cells. Just as with referencing cells and ranges, formulas inserted via AppleScript must be in the R1C1 format, rather than the more comfortable A1 format.

Finally, we see a method of saving a document. The script demonstrates two different save file dialog boxes: one from AppleScript's new file scripting addition; the other from within Excel itself. Neither dialog is particularly special, but you can judge which one you prefer. The Excel version does, however, allow you to change the text of the Open button in the dialog, even though it does not handle dialog canceling as you might expect. One potential advantage of using Excel's dialog is that your script is not dependent on the new file scripting addition. In your scripts, you should use just one of these styles.

Massaging Information in a Document

For the final excursions into Excel, you will need to open a workbook supplied on the companion disk (Handbook Scripts:Chapter 23). It includes the worksheet created in the previous script, as well as some additional goodies.

The first script begins by demonstrating two ways to ask the user to open a workbook file. The same pros and cons accompany these AppleScript and Excel dialog examples as in the save file examples, above. We follow with some fancy worksheet formatting, including using Excel's powerful automatic formatting. Once the data in the sheet is pretty, we make a slew of changes to the Page Setup dialog for that sheet and print a screen preview. The last bit of script displays an Excel custom dialog, which is controlled via a macro.

```
-- Excel Format & Print
tell application "Microsoft Excel"
    Activate

    -- OPEN a workbook
    -- have user select filename from outside Excel (AS 1.1 choose file OSAX)
    set fileName to choose file with prompt ¬
        "Locate "Excel Formatting Workbook":" of type "XLS5"
    -- or with Excel file save dialog
    set fileName to file ¬
        GetOpenFilename Title "Locate "Excel Formatting Workbook"" FileFilter "XLS5"
    if fileName is false then error number -128
    -- make sure you've opened the desired workbook
    if not (fileName contains "Excel Formatting Workbook") then
        display dialog ¬
            "Make sure you open only the workbook requested." buttons {"Cancel"}
    end if
```

```
-- now do the actual file opening
Open fileName

-- insert a row above Row 1
Activate Sheet "Test Lab"
Select Row 1
Insert Selection Shift xlDown

-- add title and set autoFormat
set Range "R1C3" to "Results by Quarter"
Select Range "R1C1:R7C6"
AutoFormat Selection Format xl3DEffects1 ¬
    with number, Font, Alignment, Border, Pattern and Width
set Size of Range "R1C3" to 18

-- select columns for adjustment of column width and formatting
Select Range "C2:C5"
set ColumnWidth of Selection to 5
set HorIzontalAlignment of Selection to xlCenter
Select Range "R8C1" -- to deselect columns

-- adjust several settings in Page Setup for current sheet
tell PageSetup of ActiveSheet
    set Orientation to xlLandscape
    set FitToPagesWide to 1
    set FitToPagesTall to 1
    set CenterHorizontally to 1
    set CenterVertically to 1
    set Zoom to 200
end tell

-- print (with Preview turned on)
Print ActiveSheet with Preview

-- call macro in workbook that displays Excel dialog box also in workbook
-- if user clicks "OK" then we close workbook without saving changes
if Evaluate "'Excel Formatting Workbook'!YesNo()" then
    Close Workbook "Excel Formatting Workbook"
end if
end tell
```

The dialog box is located on the workbook sheet named Decision Dialog (Figure 23.1). What makes the dialog appear is the Visual Basic macro called YesNo(), located on the Decision Code module. To get the ball rolling, the AppleScript script calls upon Excel to evaluate the YesNo() macro. The format of parameters to the **evaluate** command is very strict. The name of the workbook containing the macro must be in single quotes, followed by an exclamation point delimiter between the workbook name and the name of the macro.

The macro name must include the parentheses (and any arguments that may be sent along). The entire argument to the Evaluate command is then placed inside quotes.

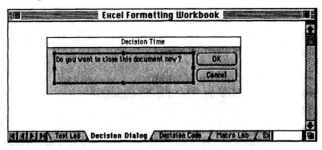

Figure 23.1 The Excel dialog box in its editing form.

The Visual Basic macro code, located in the Decision Code module of the workbook, is rather simple:

```
Function YesNo()
    YesNo = DialogSheets("Decision Dialog").Show
End Function
```

It is designed as a function, because I want to retrieve the results of the user clicking on a button in the dialog. A click of the OK button returns True, while the Cancel button returns False. Therefore, I can use those values as returned values from the Evaluate command in my AppleScript script. If the user clicks the OK button, the Excel macro returns True, so my script closes the workbook without saving changes.

While we're on the subject of macros, we come to the last script, which demonstrates how to call Excel 4-style macro functions, Excel 4-style macros, and Excel 5-style macros, from an AppleScript script. All three scripts perform similar tasks (filling down a series of numbers). The macros are located in the Excel Formatting Workbook on modules Excel 4 Code and Excel 5 Code. All work is done on the Macro Lab sheet. Close all workbooks before running this script:

```
-- Excel Macros & Functions
tell application "Microsoft Excel"
    Activate
    -- OPEN a workbook
    set fileName to file ¬
        GetOpenFilename Title "Locate "Excel Formatting Workbook"" FileFilter "XLS5"
    if fileName is false then error number -128
    -- make sure you've opened the desired workbook
    if not (fileName contains "Excel Formatting Workbook") then
        display dialog ¬
            "Make sure you open only the workbook requested." buttons {"Cancel"}
```

```
        end if
        -- now do the actual file saving
        Open fileName

        -- bring Macro Lab sheet front and center
        Activate Sheet "Macro Lab"

        -- evaluate Excel 4 function
        copy 10 to Range "R3C1"
        Select Range "R3C1:R13C1"
        Evaluate "DATA.SERIES(2,1,1,1,,FALSE)"

        -- evaluate Excel 4 macro
        Evaluate "RUN('Excel Formatting Workbook'!Series.of.ten)"

        -- evaluate Excel 5 Visual Basic macro
        Evaluate "'Excel Formatting Workbook'!VBSeriesOfTen()"
    end tell
```

By far the slowest running of these three styles is the one in which the AppleScript script calls the function. Most of the delay is in the multiple statements that must reach Excel. The other two run quickly, because all the manipulation is performed within Excel after a single call.

Some cautions about the Excel 4 **evaluate** commands are in order. When evaluating an Excel 4 function, you must observe capitalization of function name and any arguments as they appear in the Excel worksheets or macro sheets. As for running macros, the RUN command must be a part of the **evaluate** command parameters, with the name of the workbook (in single quotes) and macro as arguments to the RUN command. Excel 5 macros are a bit easier to call, as shown both in this script and the one involving the dialog box, earlier.

We're not quite finished with Excel. Excel 5 gives you the power to execute AppleScript statements or call an AppleScript script (saved as a script or application) from within Excel. The basic methodology is to create a Visual Basic macro that uses the Visual Basic **MacScript** command. In the example workbook in the Excel 5 Code module is a macro that does just this:

```
'
' A Visual Basic handler that runs an AppleScript statement
' and script saved as an application
'

Sub runASScript()
    MacScript "beep 3"
    ' Substitute your pathname to Sample Script App
    MacScript "Macintosh HD:Sample Script App"
End Sub
```

We've included a sample application, called Sample Script App, which you can open from this macro (you'll probably have to change the pathname to the app in the Visual Basic script for it to run correctly). More importantly for users of your solution, you can place a call to the macro in the Excel Tools menu. To do so, create the macro, and then:

1. Choose Macro from the Tools menu.
2. Select the new macro from the list in the dialog.
3. Click the Options button.
4. Assign a name for the macro as you'd like it to appear at the bottom of the Tools menu.
5. Click OK for the Options and Macro dialogs.

Excel shares a lot of this external application calling with the Windows version. Therefore, as you explore these realms of the Visual Basic vocabulary, you will encounter many terms that are more at home in Windows rather than in the Apple event world of the Macintosh. Still, Microsoft has managed to install enough wires for us to do the job.

CHAPTER 24

Microsoft Word

Version

6.0

Recordable

Yes.

Object Model Support

Adequate support for manipulating document text objects, but other attributes require extensive use of Word Basic language.

Supports Whose Clauses

Yes.

Important Application Concepts

From the AppleScript point of view, Microsoft Word 6 is a relatively standard implementation of a text processor. About the only out-of-the-ordinary concepts to be aware of are those of the style sheet and document section, both of which have been Microsoft Word fixtures for many generations.

Scripting Overview

If you have worked with Microsoft Excel 5's scripting dictionary, you may be startled to see such a comparatively bare offering from the Word camp of Microsoft Office 4.2. Commands don't extend much beyond the expected "standard application" commands that Apple recommends. Objects are limited predominantly to text oriented objects. So what about the rest of the depth of Word 6?

Taking full advantage of the automation of Word 6 requires diving into the Word Basic macro language built into the program. This is new for Microsoft Word. Surprisingly, it does not share a lot with Visual Basic you find in Excel, so even without AppleScript, MS Office macro writers have to contend with much inconsistency (we AppleScript scripters are not alone in that regard!). As with Excel's Visual Basic, the documentation for Word Basic is almost entirely located in on-line help. While this is good for looking up things, it's not so easy to browse through to learn your way.

Fortunately, you don't have to master Word Basic to use it from AppleScript scripts. Because Word 6 is recordable, you can try many procedures with the AppleScript recorder on to see the multitude of Word Basic commands called with the do script command. This includes such tasks as adjusting Page Setup settings, changing margins, inserting footers, and so on.

If you create long projects containing many document files, your scripts may often be standalone droplets that perform the same tasks on whatever document files need adjustment, such as changing the footer text for different draft numbers. Batch processing of files is a quite valid reason to script a word processing program.

Retrieving Information

Microsoft Word observes most of the same text extraction facilities that you learned with Scriptable Text Editor. One helpful addition to the object dictionary is the line object. A line is a physical line of a document, not related to paragraph ending characters or other virtual line characteristics of other programs (like HyperCard).

In the following script are several examples of syntax for opening a file and retrieving various pieces of text. This script and sample text file are located in the Handbook Scripts:Chapter 24 folder. Run this script with the Event Log window open so you can see each statement and the format of content returned by Word.

```
-- Word Retrieve
tell application "Microsoft Word"

    -- open a file chosen by the user
    set fileToOpen to choose file with prompt ¬
```

```
        "Open "Bill of Rights -- MS Word 6"" of type "W6BN"
    open fileToOpen

    -- retrieve single character
    character 3

    -- retrieve range of characters as list
    characters 1 thru 17 of paragraph 5

    -- retrieve range of characters as string
    text from character 1 to character 17 of paragraph 5

    -- retrieve single word, indexed from beginning of document
    word 40

    -- retrieve range of words as list
    words 40 thru 45

    -- retrieve range of words as string (indexed from start of paragraph)
    text from word 40 to end of paragraph 2

    -- retrieve line indexed within a paragraph object
    line 2 of paragraph 2

    -- retrieve text of an empty paragraph
    paragraph 3

    -- retrieve text of a paragraph
    paragraph 4

    -- character count of a paragraph
    length of paragraph 2

    -- word count of a paragraph
    count words of paragraph 8

    -- paragraph count of document
    count paragraphs of document 1
end tell
```

There is nothing out of the ordinary here.

Inserting New Information

For inserting text into a document, Word is also pretty standard, using the text insertion point model we learned with Scriptable Text Editor. The basic sequence is to select the insertion point between two characters, and then set that selection to whatever you wish to insert. As a rule in scriptable text processing programs that support the insertion point, this methodology is safer than trying to copy text to a spot before or after some known object where you're never quite sure how word spacing will be handled.

After the examples of inserting and deleting objects in the following script, it adjusts the justification property of a particular paragraph. But when it comes to doing something more complicated, such as inserting a header, the script requires that we call Word Basic commands via **do script** to accomplish the tasks. Inserting a header, for example, is a modal operation in Word, so the script opens the header viewer. The script also demonstrates how to insert special header characters (date and page number) into various locations in the header—again all via Word Basic, since the AppleScript dictionary does not support these operations.

There is no way you should be expected to know which Word Basic commands to call. And fortunately, you can open a separate script editor window to experiment with AppleScript recording a manual sequence equivalent to see how Word performs these tasks in Word Basic. For many commands that come back in a recorded script, you will see a long string of parameters to the commands. It's a good idea to use the Word on-line help material to look up the Word Basic command reference for any such commands so you can better understand what these parameters mean. Most of the time, parameters are optional, in which case you only have to include in your script the ones whose values you need to change (more about this later).

In issuing the **do script** command to Word, the name of the Word Basic command and all parameters must be within a quoted string. If, as happens in the following script, a parameter, itself, must be inside quotes, then you must use the in-string quote symbol (\") to signify each internal quote. In both **do script** commands in the following script, we have the additional burden of inserting a variable value into the parameters being passed to Word Basic. Notice how the parameter string is broken around the variable name, which is left "in the open," as it were. This is necessary so that AppleScript can evaluate the contents of the variable, and pass the evaluated value along with the Word Basic parameter.

Here is the script that demonstrates various types of object and file insertion:

```
-- Word Insert
tell application "Microsoft Word"

    -- set view to Page view for later
    do script "ViewPage"

    -- establish insertion point for next text entry
    set selection to insertion point before word 1

    -- set font info prior to entering data
    set size of selection to 36
    set style of selection to bold

    -- enter new text at insertion point
    set selection to return & "Bill of Rights" & return & return
```

```
-- delete a line (blank in this case)
delete paragraph 3

-- right justify newly entered title
set justification of paragraph 2 to right

-- insert a header with centered date and
-- right-aligned page number
do script "ViewHeader"
set selection to "Historical Documents" & tab
do script "InsertDateField"
set selection to tab & "Page "
do script "InsertPageField"
do script "CloseViewHeaderFooter"

-- create new document and insert an external file
-- choose file with AS dialog, then assemble Word Basic command
activate
set newDoc to make new document -- need reference later
set fileToInsert to (choose file with prompt ¬
    "Select any text file" of type "TEXT") as string
do script "InsertFile .Name = \"" & fileToInsert & "\""

-- prompt user for file name for saving, then save
-- with Word Basic command
-- (AppleScript Save command saves only a copy,
-- while Word command also places doc in File menu.)
set fileToSave to new file with prompt "Save file as..." as text
do script "FileSaveAs .Name = \"" & fileToSave & "\""

-- close window after saving
close first window saving no

end tell
```

One important note about using the Word Basic command for saving the file, rather than the more typical AppleScript **save** command: only the Word Basic version saves the document as if choosing Save As from the File menu. The action (unless you change one of the parameters not shown above) automatically inserts the file name into the list of most recently used files in the File menu and saves the window you're seeing to the file.

Massaging Information in a Document

Some text manipulation is possible via plain AppleScript, such as the first item in the following script, which exercises Word's whose clauses. The statement here is similar to one we saw in Chapter 18's Scriptable Text Editor, but Word requires a slight modification to the compound whose clause to work properly.

Here, we had to find a different method of testing for whether a paragraph is not empty, because the test for the contents being an empty string didn't do the trick. Instead, we test for the length being greater than zero.

Other massaging items we demonstrate here are search-and-replace, adjusting margins, and doing some fancy graphical borders around selected paragraphs. All these require calls to Word Basic commands. One command in particular, FileDocumentLayout, is an important one, because it contains parameters for everything available in the two panels of the Document Layout dialog in Word.

```
-- Word Format & Print
tell application "Microsoft Word"
    activate

    -- change style based on whose clause
    set style of every paragraph whose length > 0 ¬
        and word 1 = "Article" to bold

    -- do search-and-replace
    do script "EditReplace .Find = \"ARTICLE\", .Replace = \"ELEMENT\", " & ¬
        ".MatchCase = 1, .WholeWord = 1, .ReplaceAll"

    -- adjust left and right margins
    -- Chr$(34) is a double quote symbol for "inches"
    do script "FileDocumentLayout .LeftMargin = \"1.5\" + Chr$(34), " & ¬
        ".RightMargin = \"2\" + Chr$(34)"

    -- demo fancy borders for subheads controlled from AppleScript
    repeat with i from 1 to count of paragraphs of document 1
        if length of paragraph i > 0 and word 1 of paragraph i is "Element" then
            set selection to paragraph i
            do script "FormatBordersAndShading .Shadow = 1, " & ¬
                ".TopBorder = 8, .LeftBorder = 8, .BottomBorder = 8, " & ¬
                ".RightBorder = 8, .TopColor = 15, .LeftColor = 15, " & ¬
                ".BottomColor = 15, .RightColor = 15, " & ¬
                ".Background = 16"
        end if
    end repeat

    -- print an open document
    print window "Bill of Rights -- MS Word 6"

end tell
```

An important formatting fact about the above script has do to with the way long parameter strings to Word Basic commands are broken into shorter lines. Recall that the command and parameters must be in one long string. To break such a string into multiple lines entails breaking the string with a quote mark, appending an ampersand concatenation symbol (&), and then the soft return (Option-Return). Each subsequent line must begin and end with a quote mark.

Access to Word Basic macros is via the **do script** command. While you can trigger any Word Basic macro by name, you cannot pass arguments to an existing macro (except via the Clipboard), nor can a macro return any values to an AppleScript script. If your script must perform a macro with values that vary from run to run, you can either call the individual commands of Word Basic via a series of **do script** commands, or you can also assemble the text of the Word Basic macro in your script (assigning values as needed), and then pass the entire string as the parameter to a **do script** command. Word runs the text through the Word Basic interpreter to execute the commands.

Conversely, a Word Basic macro can use its **MacScript** command to execute AppleScript statements or run scripts (saved as compiled scripts or applications). This is the same **MacScript** command that is in Excel 5's Visual Basic vocabulary (Chapter 23). Here is the Word Basic version of the AppleScript-calling macro in Visual Basic:

```
Sub MAIN
  MacScript "beep 3"
  MacScript "Macintosh HD:Sample Script App"
End Sub
```

You may have to alter the pathname to the sample script application to make it work on your Mac.

And on the subject of printing, the object reference for the **print** command is not a document name, but rather the window name. Use Word Basic commands to adjust Page Setup settings.

CHAPTER 25

WordPerfect

Version

3.1

Recordable

No.

Object Model Support

Modest text suite objects. No WordPerfect objects.

Supports Whose Clauses

No.

Important Application Concepts

To accomplish any automation beyond simple document opening, text retrieval, text insertion, and document saving, you'll have to acquaint yourself with Word-Perfect macros. AppleScript accesses no unique features of WordPerfect.

Scripting Overview

For an industrial strength word processing program, WordPerfect's scriptability is very limited, especially in comparison to Microsoft Word 6. Without support for ranges of objects and whose clauses, WordPerfect in many instances provides even less scripting support than Scriptable Text Editor.

While you can trigger WordPerfect macros via the AppleScript do script command, the macros themselves are intended for performing action, rather than returning information about application or document settings. With version 3.1, you can pass parameters to a WordPerfect macro, but the syntax is anything but obvious (nor described in either the dictionary or Macro Help on-line document).

At the root of script parameter passing is a reserved set of WordPerfect global variables, named ScriptVar02, ..., ScriptVar50. If your script passes two parameters to the macro, WordPerfect automatically assigns them to ScriptVar01 and ScriptVar02 in left-to-right order. These variables can then be used as arguments to any applicable WordPerfect command. When calling a macro without parameters from a script, use the plain do script command, with the macro name and all parameters (separated by commas) must be encased inside AppleScript list braces. See the last script in this chapter for an example of this out-of-the-ordinary syntax.

Be careful with the macro's ScriptVar variables. Remember that they are global, so their contents extend beyond the life of the running macro. It is best to assign an empty string to these globals at the end of each macro that calls them.

Also be careful in deciding which macros to call from AppleScript. Macros that prompt the user for input with WordPerfect's Get String command will likely hang WordPerfect before the full dialog appears. It is safer to use AppleScript user interface elements (display dialog, FaceSpan, HyperCard) for prompts, and then pass the data as parameters to the macro.

Do script works only with macros: you cannot directly call WordPerfect macro language commands from AppleScript. Fortunately, WordPerfect allows you to write macros that behave globally among all open documents. As a result, you could write a number of macros that perform actions you like to do in many documents, and create a kind of library of macros you frequently and reliably call from your AppleScript script via the do script command. Still, none of these macros will be able to return any information to your script.

Be aware, too, that in the version 3.1 I examined, there were several errors in the scripting dictionary. The selection property of a document, for instance, is not accessible via script. Some commands, such as make, do not return any information about the newly created object, as the dictionary says they do.

Finally, as a script does its job on a WordPerfect document, you will likely experience unexpected behavior in the way the script leaves your document scrolled or portions of the document selected. It's a bit disconcerting at first if you have not witnessed this in other scriptable programs.

Retrieving Information

Except for ranges of some objects and whose clauses, text retrieval via script from a WordPerfect document is relatively standard stuff. While you can get the range of text, this returns only the characters, and not the formatting.

In the following script (Handbook Scripts:Chapter 25) are syntax examples for opening a document, retrieving certain text objects, and obtaining object counts. Run the script with the Event Log window showing so you can view results of each statement.

```
-- WordPerfect Retrieve
tell application "WordPerfect"

    -- open a file chosen by the user
    set fileToOpen to choose file with prompt ¬
        "Open "Bill of Rights -- WordPerfect"" of type "WPD3"
    open fileToOpen

    -- retrieve single character
    character 3

    -- retrieve range of characters as string
    text from character 1 to character 17 of paragraph 5

    -- retrieve single word, indexed from beginning of document
    word 40

    -- retrieve range of words as list
    words 40 thru 45

    -- retrieve range of words as string (indexed from start of paragraph)
    text from word 40 to end of paragraph 2

    -- retrieve line indexed within a paragraph object
    line 2 of paragraph 2

    -- retrieve text of an empty paragraph
    paragraph 3

    -- retrieve text of a paragraph
    paragraph 4

    -- retrieve text of a specific page
    text of page 2

    -- character count of a paragraph
    count characters of paragraph 2

    -- word count of a paragraph
    count words of paragraph 8

    -- paragraph count of document
    count paragraphs of document 1
end tell
```

In some other scriptable word processing programs, the statement words 50 thru 45 return the words as items in an AppleScript list. WordPerfect's scripting doesn't seem to know much about lists.

Inserting New Information

WordPerfect does not allow scripters to select text or insertion points between characters. Therefore, you can enter text in one of three ways:

- copying text to an existing object (to replace)
- copying text to a spot at the beginning of an existing object
- copying text to a spot at the end of an existing object

The syntax for specifying the relative locations is very critical, so observe the examples in the following script carefully. Making adjustments to formatting of inserted text must be done after the new text is there.

In this script, we see how to insert data before and after existing text, adjust font and paragraph formatting, create a new document, and save a document.

```
-- WordPerfect Insert
tell application "WordPerfect"

    -- enter new text before existing text
    copy return & "Bill of Rights" & return & return ¬
        to beginning of paragraph 1

    -- enter new text at bottom of document
    copy return & "The End" to end of last character

    -- set font info of existing text
    set size of paragraph 2 to 36
    set style of paragraph 2 to bold

    -- delete a line (blank in this case)
    delete paragraph 3

    -- right justify newly entered title
    set justification of paragraph 2 to right

    -- copy raw text segment from original document,
    -- then create new document and insert passage
    copy text from paragraph 1 to paragraph 8 to textData
    make new document
    copy textData to document 1

    -- prompt user for file name for saving, then save
    set fileToSave to new file with prompt "Save file as..." as text
    save document 1 in fileToSave

    -- close window after saving
    close first window saving no

end tell
```

If you need to automate the saving of documents in formats other than Word-Perfect, consult the macro language on-line help system for appropriate calls to be made in a macro (or record a macro in WordPerfect to get some idea of the commands involved).

Massaging Information in a Document

As mentioned earlier, most automated data manipulation requires WordPerfect macros. The following script calls a macro that is stored with the Bill of Rights document for WordPerfect on the companion disk. We also demonstrate a poor man's version of a whose clause—cycling through a repeat loop to do the job. Finally, we print a document by printing its containing window.

```
-- WordPerfect Format & Print
tell application "WordPerfect"
    activate

    -- in place of whose clause, go through slow,
    -- iterative repeat loop to find matching text for
    -- style adjustment
    repeat with i from 1 to count of paragraphs of document 1
        if word 1 of paragraph i = "Article" then
            set style of paragraph i to bold
        end if
    end repeat

    -- summon macro I wrote and attached to document file
    -- to display WordPerfect's Find & Change dialog.
    Do Script {"Search & Replace","Article","Element"}

    -- print an open document
    print window "Bill of Rights -- WordPerfect"

    -- print single page
    print page 2

end tell
```

Making changes to things such as Page Setup can be done via the macro language. If you do batch processing of documents (e.g., opening a daily folder-ful of downloaded text documents to be formatted, saved, and mailed via PowerTalk), you could set up a series of global macros to perform very specific tasks, and then call them in the desired sequence from your AppleScript script.

MacWrite Pro

Version

1.5v1

Recordable

No.

Object Model Support

None in the strict sense. Objects are part of messages.

Supports Whose Clauses

No.

Important Application Concepts

Because of the limitations to what formatting you can control directly via scripting, your best chances of applying formatting (changing fonts, indents, line spacing, etc.) is by way of MacWrite Pro style sheets. At best, however, you will be able to apply existing style sheets—none of the items within a style sheet is programmable via AppleScript.

Scripting Overview

MacWrite Pro's scripting mindset is entirely different from any other scriptable text processor I've seen. Rather than define an object model consisting of documents, paragraphs, characters, and the like, the MacWrite Pro dictionary consists entirely of commands. Each command works with a particular kind of object. Thus, you can obtain the number of characters for an entire document, but not the number of paragraphs.

Without the ability to specify most objects, data insertion and retrieval is heavily dependent on a text selection in the document. Beyond selecting whole paragraphs by number, all other selections (characters, words, multiple paragraphs) are made by specifying the character count of the starting and ending characters of the desired selection. Searching for text also selects the found chunk, but once it's found, you can't use the scripting language to determine where it is or whether it meets desired criteria (e.g., is the found word the first word of a paragraph, or is it embedded elsewhere?).

There are occasional errors in the dictionary (some specified results do not come back). Moreover, the counting systems for character locations and other objects are inconsistent. Selection locations and paragraph numbers start with zero; pages start with one.

By and large, you will find the advanced features of MacWrite Pro out of bounds to scripters. Inserting or editing headers and footers is not possible; nor can a script change a view. And despite the fact that Claris ships a healthy set of XTND translators with this capable word processor, no script can automatically save a document with this version in a form other than native MacWrite Pro.

Given the enormous disparity in AppleScript support, it is difficult to believe that MacWrite Pro and FileMaker Pro come from the same company.

Retrieving Information

In the following script, only the file opening process is standard AppleScript fare. After that, example statements demonstrate the syntax for selecting text and extracting it. When you run this script with the Event Log window open, you see all the calls and intermediate results prior to getting the selected text.

Notice that because selection and paragraph counting start with zero, everything seems off by one. And as for obtaining various character and word counts, we demonstrate AppleScript statistical kludges to get results, which may not always be 100% accurate.

```
-- MacWrite Pro Retrieve
tell application "MacWrite Pro"
    activate

    -- open sample file via AS file dialog
    open (choose file with prompt ¬
        "Select "Bill of Rights -- MacWrite Pro":" of type "MWPd")

    -- retrieve single character
    set selection starting 2 ending 3
    get chars

    -- retrieve range of characters as string
    set par5Start to item 1 of (get paragraph sel 4)
    set selection starting par5Start ending par5Start + 17
    get chars
```

```
-- retrieve text of an empty paragraph (carriage return only)
select paragraph 2
get chars

-- retrieve text of a paragraph (including carriage return)
select paragraph 3
get chars

-- character count of a paragraph (including carriage return)
select paragraph 3
count of (get chars)

-- word count of a paragraph (average 6 chars per word)
select paragraph 10
round (count of (get chars)) / 6

-- character count of entire frontmost document
text length
end tell
```

To test the accuracy of the word count, try it on some other paragraphs, and then use MacWrite Pro's built-in word counting facilities to compare the results.

Inserting New Information

The following script demonstrates ways of inserting new text into an existing document as well as inserting a text file into a new document. Along the way, we demonstrate how to select multiple paragraphs—hardly a straightforward task given MacWrite Pro's lack of object definitions. Deleting text means selecting it and then putting an empty string into the selection.

Adjusting font size and style involves using the quite limited do menu command. Rather than allow scripters to access any menu item, the dictionary limits the choices to a selected few. See the dictionary listing for details.

```
-- MacWrite Pro Insert
tell application "MacWrite Pro"
   activate

   -- establish insertion point for next text entry
   set selection starting 0

   -- enter new text at insertion point
   put chars return & "Bill of Rights" & return & return

   -- select multiple paragraphs for later formatting
   set endOfSelection to item 2 of (get paragraph sel 2)
   set selection starting 0 ending endOfSelection

   -- set font info of selection
   do menu item size36point
   do menu item bold
```

```
-- delete a paragraph (empty line in this case)
select paragraph 2
put chars ""

-- create new document and insert an external file
-- choose file with AS dialog
new document
insert file (choose file of type "TEXT")

-- save with MWPro's file save dialog
save document

-- close window after saving
close document saving no
```

end tell

Invoking the save document command brings up MacWrite Pro's own Save dialog, which allows the user to select a different file type, if desired—something you cannot script.

Massaging Information in a Document

Unlike the samples with Microsoft Word and WordPerfect, the following script does not show how to change the style of paragraphs that meet certain criteria. MacWrite Pro doesn't give us that level of scriptability.

A script can, however, control a search and replace function, allowing a script to pass parameters for both strings.

```
-- MacWrite Pro Print & Format
tell application "MacWrite Pro"
    activate

    -- do search-and-replace
    display dialog "Replace:" default answer ""
    set replaceText to text returned of result
    display dialog "With:" default answer ""
    set withText to text returned of result
    change all by finding replaceText ¬
        replacing with withText

    -- print an open document (user sees print dialog)
    print

    -- set to print only page 2 (no print dialog)
    set printer options starting 2 ending 2
    print
end tell
```

In the two print syntax examples, you see that you can either allow the user to see the print dialog box or, by setting some printer options, avoid the dialog. The latter may be more desirable in an automated setting.

CHAPTER 27

TouchBase Pro

Version

4.0

Recordable

No.

Object Model Support

Good support for entering, retrieving, and manipulating data within existing databases. Not intended for scripted creation of database designs or formats.

Supports Whose Clauses

Yes, among the best.

Important Application Concepts

Familiarity with the differences between the List and Detail views of a Touch-Base contact file is helpful in planning a scripting foray. Data in a TouchBase file can be thought of as a fairly standard table, with each row of the table containing the raw data for a given person. The Detail view is the window you can use to see the entries for all the "cells" in the row. In this case, there are a total of

475

47 cells (or columns to the database), some of whose names are hardwired and some of which may be customized.

Like many kinds of databases, a List view allows the database designer to designate which fields of data are readily viewable in a row-and-column view. When you point to a row that may show only four fields of information, the entire record of 47 fields is also underneath—but just the designated fields appear in the list.

In addition to the 47 fields you see in the Detail view, a list view allows you to specify special fields that show extractions of some fields and combinations of others. For instance, while the database stores an address as six component pieces, a list view can combine them into one for viewing purposes. As helpful as this is for manually working with a contact file, the column settings of views are of little significance for scripting, because you can access various fields and values (including the combined values) without having to change the view.

Extracting records that meet certain criteria is one of TouchBase's strengths, and while the scripting method is different from the manual one, the concept of the selection comes into play for many kinds of operations. Understanding the implications of limiting views to selections meeting search criteria will come in handy.

Finally, the designers of the AppleScript access to TouchBase focus on data manipulation rather than database manipulation. Scripting support in this program implies that any customization of fields, export field selection, and printing templates have all be done manually before a script ever touches the contact file.

Scripting Overview

Between the nature of the data stored in a TouchBase contact file and the excellent support for whose clauses, your scripts will probably get a workout in this arena. You can ask TouchBase to act on files that meet multiple selection criteria (even Boolean AND and OR decisions) with wild abandon (but follow the examples below for parenthesis placement).

Let's look now at the columns defined by a default TouchBase contact file. Why it's important to list them is that you may need to call a cell by number, such as cell 19 of row 30. Here, then, are the columns in the order they appear in the database:

1	"Salutation"
2	"First Name"
3	"Middle Name"
4	"Last Name"
5	"Company"
6	"Title"
7	"Work Street 1"
8	"Work Street 2"

9	"Work City"
10	"Work State"
11	"Work Zip Code"
12	"Work Country"
13	"Home Street 1"
14	"Home Street 2"
15	"Home City"
16	"Home State"
17	"Home Zip Code"
18	"Home Country"
19	"Phone 1"
20	"Phone 2"
21	"Fax"
22	"Custom 1"
23	"Custom 2"
24	"Custom 3"
25	"Custom 4"
26	"Custom 5"
27	"Custom 6"
28	"Custom 7"
29	"Custom 8"
30	"Notes"
31	"Date 1"
32	"Date 2"
33	"Number 1"
34	"Number 2"
35	"Custom Check 1"
36	"Custom Check 2"
37	"Custom Check 3"
38	"Custom Check 4"
39	"CheckBox 5"
40	"Marked"
41	"Modified"
42	"UniqueID"
43	"Preferred Listing Flag"
44	"Preferred Listing String"
45	"Created"
46	"Preferred Address Flag"
47	"Preferred Phone Flag"

Columns beyond number 39 are not modifiable—they contain data that Touch-Base manages as you work with the file.

While the table method is easy enough to understand once you've been through a product like TableServer, TouchBase defines a more powerful way of working with data. A concept that you encounter only in scripting contact managers such as TouchBase is that of the *person*. A person object is equivalent to an entry in the database. It has a name (which is the complete name of the individual) and an index number from the beginning of the database. But a person object goes beyond just a single row of data cells. A person lets you access various pieces and combinations of data that you don't even see from any of the manual views. For instance, you can treat the area code of all phone numbers as separate properties for searching and editing.

A person object is defined by a rather complex record of data. Some fields of this record are deeply nested, and point to other records that hold data. If you examine the contents of a record, you may not even see all the data you know is in the record—although you can extract that data in specific forms and modify it via script as well.

The scripting dictionary is only of partial help in figuring out the accessible pieces of a person object. Over and above the properties are properties of elements—many of which are not intuitive. Therefore, here is a list of useful string data items you can extract from a person object (run this script on a sample database with the Event Log window showing):

```
-- TouchBase Person Object
tell application "TouchBase™ Pro"
    unique ID of person 3
    name of person 3
    preferred address of person 3
    preferred phone number of person 3
    salutation of person 3
    first name of person 3
    last name of person 3
    middle name of person 3
    job title of person 3
    company name of person 3
    last modified of person 3 -- date record last changed
    label of person 3 -- mailing label data

    phone number 1 of person 3 -- work phone
    country code of phone number 1 of person 3
    area code of phone number 1 of person 3
    local number of phone number 1 of person 3
    extension of phone number 1 of person 3
    phone number 2 of person 3 -- home phone
        -- same sub items as for "phone number 1"
    FAX number 1 of person 3 -- in format for Apple Telephony Suite
        -- same sub items as for "phone number 1"

    address 1 of person 3 -- complete work address
    address 2 of person 3 -- complete home address
    address 3 of person 3 -- same as "phone number 2"
    address 4 of person 3 -- same as "FAX number 1"
```

```
        postal address 1 of person 3 -- same as address 1
        room number of postal address 1 of person 3
        building number of postal address 1 of person 3 -- street number
        street of postal address 1 of person 3
        city of postal address 1 of person 3
        state of postal address 1 of person 3
        country of postal address 1 of person 3
        postal code of postal address 1 of person 3
        postal address 2 of person 3 -- same as address 2
            -- same sub items as "postal address 1"
    end tell
```

You can see examples of the data returned by each of these items (except where the data fields are empty in the database, in which case the values return as empty strings). Some of these items are read-only (especially the ones containing multi-lined values), but most of the ones you'd want to set with data from other sources are settable.

While scripting gives you ready access to the data, be prepared to exploit TouchBase's import and export facilities, which are also partially scriptable. Moving large quantities of data into and out of TouchBase will be much more efficient via import and export than working with contact file data record-by-record. For example, to extract many records for mail merging with a scriptable word processor program, the most efficient method is to script TouchBase to export the selected records, and then script the word processor to start its mail merging procedure, using the exported data file from TouchBase.

All examples in the remainder of this chapter rely on one of the sample file that comes with TouchBase 4.0: Sample Contacts. If you no longer have this file on your disk, re-install it from the master disks.

Retrieving Information

The purpose of the retrieval examples in the following script is to demonstrate various ways to extract and select information in a contact file. At first, we examine the column and row nature of the table structure of such a file. These values are in traditional AppleScript lists.

Next, we show one of two ways to work with a subset of records. The first uses a whose clause to select records for viewing in the contact file window. Once those records are visible, we consider that group a selection, and any data extraction comes from the selection of the window—an important distinction, because oddly the window object, itself, returns all records.

A different kind of data selection follows, where we get two values from the same selection of data. Rather than make any changes to the records displayed in the view, all selections (here with a compound whose clause) are made on the data, with the script taking care of both making the selection from all records, and then extracting the desired data from those selected records. Both retrieval statements here return lists, one for names, the other for phone numbers. A script could then cycle through the lists with a repeat loop, confident that item 1 of both lists came from the same record.

Just so you can see how complex the person record is, we near the end of the script by extracting one full record. Feel free to study its structure in the Event Log window, but don't get overly concerned if you can't figure it out. Use the settings in the previous listings to reach specific items within a record.

```
-- TouchBase Retrieve
tell application "TouchBase™ Pro"
    activate

    -- open a contact file
    set fileToOpen to (choose file with prompt ¬
        "Locate the "Sample Contacts" file:" of type "SUDB")
    open fileToOpen

    -- retrieve field names (as list)
    name of every column

    -- retrieve record from entire database (as list)
    row 15

    -- make selection, then get row of that selection
    set selection of window 1 to (every person ¬
        whose (last name starts with "C"))
    row 2 of selection of window 1

    -- retrieve specific properties from person records
    -- that meet multiple criteria (parallel lists)
    set selectedNames to name of (every person ¬
        whose (first name begins with ¬
        "B" and company name contains "Aldus"))
    set selectedNumbers to preferred phone number of ¬
        (every person whose (first name begins with ¬
            "B" and company name contains "Aldus"))

    -- retrieve a person record
    person 12

    -- restore to full selection
    set selection of window 1 to every person
end tell
```

The script closes by restoring the view of the contact file window so that all records are showing. If you adjust the view in a script, it is good practice to restore the full listing at the end of the script.

Inserting New Information

You can script new entries in the database by creating either a new row or a new person. For the person, the accompanying data must be in a list with items matching their locations in the order of columns. When no data goes into a cell, there must be an empty string in the data parameter. Fortunately, you don't have to supply a 47-item list—you can stop when you've supplied all the data you intend. One potential downside to creating a new entry this way is that TouchBase does not assign the entry a unique ID number for the person. Such IDs can come in handy for other scripting tasks.

As a result you may want to consider the alternative method of creating a new entry. The demo script that comes with TouchBase presents a confusing record as the **with data** parameter. My preference is to create a new person with just the first and last name properties. After that, set individual fields of that person with the data being supplied by the script. This process is longer and slower, but far simpler to figure out than the complex person record.

Further along the script, we show a way to clone a person when the script needs to adjust only a few items. This is convenient when the script enters lots of people from the same company—just the name and perhaps phone fields change.

Next, the script demonstrates a sure-fire way to adjust data within a person's record. The reason for the tests about the existence of the person and that there is only one person by that name is that TouchBase will return an execution error if the script tries to set data to a person that doesn't exist or if there are more than two persons with the same name (although no two records will ever have the same ID). Notice the technique here to direct four **set** commands to various types of user fields within the same person object. After running the script, open the Detail view for the Cookie Monster person to see how these custom fields were adjusted by the script.

```
-- TouchBase Insert
tell application "TouchBase™ Pro"
    activate

    -- create new record with list data
    set newData to {"", "Sam", "", "Malone", "Cheers"}
    make new row in window 1 with data newData

    -- create basic new entry via person record
    make new person in window 1 with data ¬
        {first name:"Cookie", last name:"Monster"}

    -- then get its ID to set various properties
    set newID to unique ID of person (count of people of window 1)
    set company name of person id newID to "CTW"
    set street of postal address 1 of person id newID to "200 Sesame Street"
    set city of postal address 1 of person id newID to "Anytown"
```

```
        set state of postal address 1 of person id newID to "FL"
        set postal code of postal address 1 of person id newID to "30029"
        set phone number 1 of person id newID to "303-555-3943"

        -- clone one person to make a new one for another person
        -- at the same company
        set model to (first person where (company name is "CTW"))
        make new person in window 1 with data model
        set newID to unique ID of person (count of people of window 1)
        set first name of person id newID to "Oscar"
        set last name of person id newID to "Grouch"
        set phone number 1 of person id newID to "303-555-3911"

        -- modify user field values of known person
        -- but first make sure there is a valid record
        if person "Cookie Monster" exists then
            -- and that there is only one record by this name
            if (count (every person whose ¬
                (first name is "Cookie" and last name is "Monster"))) = 1 then
                -- direct a bunch of statements to a particular person object
                tell person "Cookie Monster"
                    set user field "PullDown" to "Furry Creature"
                    set user field "Keyword" to "Student"
                    set user field "Custom 3" to "Blue"
                    set user field "Custom Check 4" to "Yes"
                end tell
            end if
        end if

        -- delete single known record
        delete person "Sam Malone"

        -- delete whomever meets criteria
        delete (every person whose (company name is "CTW"))

    end tell
```

The last two statements demonstrate deleting different amounts of people. You can do it individually, or by a group that meets selection criteria. There are no warnings before deleting, and any changes are automatically written to disk, so your script may want to prompt the user prior to performing any deletions.

Massaging Information in a Document

The final TouchBase script demonstrates two ways of exporting data to files that can be used for tasks such as mail merging in word processing programs. One function in TouchBase that is not scriptable is setting the fields to be exported. These settings must be adjusted in the Export dialog prior to a scripted export (or the Import dialog for a scripted import). If you automate the same export process every time (except for different record selection), then this won't be a problem once the field mapping is done; but for frequent exporting of different fields, you will have to remember to set the mapping manually.

Unlike some other commands, the export command relies on the selected items in a window's view for the records being exported. Thus, in one example, we select all records, while in the other, we get those whose last names start with the letter "C". It is up to your script to prompt the user for the name and location of the export file (or you can hard-wire the parameter if you want to completely automate the process).

```
-- TouchBase Export & Print
tell application "TouchBase™ Pro"
    activate

    -- export entire database with mail merge header line
    set selection of window 1 to every person
    set exportFile to (new file with prompt "Export as...")
    export into exportFile

    -- export only selected records
    -- with alternate way of nesting new file command
    set selection of window 1 to (every person whose ¬
        (last name begins with "C"))
    export into (new file with prompt "Export as...")

    -- print selected records
    print (every person where company name contains "Aldus") ¬
        format listing template "Company & Phones"

end tell
```

As the last sample statement, we print records which we select with a whose clause. Although the dictionary shows the print command to have two optional parameters (format and template), both are required. Unfortunately, not all formats supplied with TouchBase have selectable templates (such as the Detailed Form), so the print command generates errors, preventing scripted printing of those formats. Unlike the export command, above, the print command works on the entire database, rather than records selected in the current view. Also notice that the format parameter requires constants (the names of the formats as illustrated by icons in the Print dialog), so do not place the format names in quotes.

CHAPTER 28

HyperCard

Version

2.2

Recordable

No.

Object Model Support

Excellent support for working with all HyperCard objects.

Supports Whose Clauses

No.

Important Application Concepts

The more comfortable you are with HyperCard's objects and their message-passing hierarchy, the easier it will be to script stacks from outside HyperCard. By virtue of HyperCard's scriptability, all stacks that run under HyperCard 2.2 or later are also scriptable. This goes for stacks saved as standalone applications, which also have the full AppleScript dictionary and implementation available.

Scripting Overview

The AppleScript implementation of HyperCard is one of the best of the scriptable applications I've seen. Much of this has to do with the emphasis that Apple put on HyperCard's ability to execute AppleScript scripts from within HyperCard, as well as from without. This chapter focuses primarily on controlling HyperCard and stacks from outside HyperCard, but much of what is said about the language syntax applies equally to AppleScript scripts that you may write from inside HyperCard.

As we've seen in some other programs that have their own internal programming languages, HyperCard supplies a number of AppleScript equivalents to commands, but not everything is there. Yet HyperCard lets us get to anything in the HyperTalk language by way of the **do script** and **evaluate** AppleScript commands, as well as invoking any menu command. Passing values back and forth between scripts is just about as easy as passing parameters among AppleScript handlers.

For those HyperTalk commands that have AppleScript equivalents, the precise syntax is not always the same. The most common difference is that any prepositions that are part of the HyperTalk version must be omitted in the AppleScript version. For example, the typical dial command in HyperTalk looks like this:

    dial "555-1212" with modem "ATDT"

The AppleScript equivalent is:

    dial "555-1212" modem "ATDT"

The AppleScript dictionary is usually very clear about the parameters for commands. Table 28.1 lists all HyperTalk commands and functions under headings that indicate whether there is direct AppleScript support for them. For the few items that are implemented a bit differently in AppleScript, their AppleScript equivalent is shown in parentheses next to the item.

Table 28.1 HyperTalk Commands Available via AppleScript and via do Script

AppleScriptable

answer	ask
ask file	ask password
beep	choose tool
click	close
close file	close printing
create menu	create stack
debug	dial
doMenu	drag
find	go
help	hide menubar
hide window	hide part
lock error dialogs	lock messages
lock recent	lock screen
open document	open file
open printing	open report printing

Table 28.1 (*continued*)

Apple Scriptable

play	play stop
pop card	print <expr>
print field	print card
print card from	push card
read from file for	read from file until
reset menubar	reset paint
reset printing	show menubar
show window	show part
unlock error dialogs	unlock messages
unlock recent	unlock screen
unmark all	visual
wait for	wait until
write to file	

abbreviated date	charToNum
clickH	clickLoc
clickText	clickV
commandKey	date (short date)
diskSpace	foundText
heapSpace	long date
mouse	mouseClick
mouseH	mouseLoc
mouseV	numToChar
optionKey	random
result (return value)	screenRect
seconds (elapsed time)	selectedLoc
shiftKey	stackSpace
sum	systemVersion
ticks	time (short time)
value	

Require Do Script

add	answer file
answer program	convert
delete	disable
divide	do

Table 28.1 (*continued*)

Require Do Script

edit script	enable
exit	export paint
find chars	find string
find whole	find word
flash	global
go <relative> card	hide picture
hide groups	import
mark	multiply
palette	pass
picture	print file
print marked cards	push background
push stack	put
reply	request
return	save
select	send
show cards	show marked cards
show picture	show groups
sort	start using
stop using	subtract
type	unmakr
wait while	
abbr date	abbrev date
clickChunk	clickLine
destination	foundChunk
foundField	foundLine
length	long time
me	menus
number	offset
param	paramCount
params	secs
selectedButton	selectedChunk
selectedField	selectedLine[s]
selectedText	sound
stacks	target
version	windows

AppleScript access to object properties is very complete. Only a handful of the hundreds of properties across all objects are not directly available—predominantly location properties which may be obtained from the bounds property for each object. The other syntactic difference to know about is that the **number** property is known in AppleScript as the **index** property. Therefore, card number 200 has an index property of 200, meaning it is the 200th card from the front of the stack.

One dictionary entry about the **ask** command may be a bit unclear, so we'll look at it briefly here. The single **ask** command lets AppleScript perform three different kinds of HyperTalk ask procedures. Despite what the dictionary says, the first parameter is the string that appears in any of the dialogs. What determines the type of dialog (standard ask dialog, ask password, or ask file) is the **as** parameter. Here, then, are the three possibilities:

ask dialog:

```
ask <prompt string> [ with <default answer> ] as dialog
```

ask password:

```
ask <prompt string> as password
```

ask file:

```
ask <prompt string> [ with <default answer> ] as putfile
```

Other choices listed for the **as** parameter do not affect the dialog.

The sample scripts for the rest of the chapter rely on a sample stack, named Chapter 28 Lab, provided on the companion disk in Handbook Script:Chapter 28. It contains not only objects the scripts expect, but samples of handlers that one of the scripts interacts with. As always, run the scripts with the Event Log showing so you can see the commands and results for a series of actions.

Retrieving Information

The first script, below, shows how closely the AppleScript implementation for obtaining information from a stack maps to the HyperTalk equivalents. Often, the syntax is identical, while other times, the difference is little more than a dropped preposition.

```
-- HyperCard Retrieve
tell application "HyperCard"
    activate

    -- open sample stack
    go stack "Chapter 28 Lab" in new window

    -- retrieve name property of stack
    name of stack 1
```

```
-- retrieve card count
count every card

-- retrieve field contents
background field 1

-- retrieve hilite property of checkboxes
hilite of background button "Sample 2"
hilite of card button "Sample 4"

-- using "do script" to retrieve
-- an unsupported function
set windowList to (do script "the windows")

-- again, to see what's selected in a popup button
set chosenColor to ¬
    (do script "the selectedText of card button \"Sample 3:\"")

end tell
```

At the end of the script are two statements that show you how to access functions and properties that are not directly supported in AppleScript. The parameter of the **do script** command must evaluate to the HyperTalk statement you'd be executing if the script were in HyperTalk. That sometimes means, as in the last statement, constructing a parameter with in-line quotes (\") because the HyperTalk command would require the quotes around the object name. When the statement(s) you're executing with the **do script** command return values, they may be captured by your AppleScript variables, as shown in the last two statements.

Inserting New Information

Setting HyperCard object properties from AppleScript is virtually the same as from HyperTalk as evidenced by the two commands that change button hilites. But missing from the AppleScript vocabulary is a way to select text within a field. **Do script** substitutes nicely, allowing you to "write HyperTalk" in the AppleScript editor.

When text is selected in a field, you can obtain the text of the selection by asking for the contents of that selection. Contents is the only property of a selection object.

```
-- HyperCard Insert
tell application "HyperCard"
    activate
    go card 1

    -- write data to a field
    copy "Hello, from AppleScript and HyperCard!" to card field 1
```

```
-- change hilite of a checkbox
set hilite of background button "Sample 2" to false

-- change hilite of radio button cluster
set hilite of card button "Choice 3" to true

-- use "do script" to hilite some text
do script "select word 3 to 5 of card field 1"

-- find out what text is hilited
contents of selection

-- create new card at end of stack,
-- then put card number into field
go card (count every card)
do menu "New Card"
copy index of current card to background field 1


end tell
```

The final task of this script is to demonstrate how to create a new card via the do menu command. Also notice that the HyperTalk expression this card is translated in AppleScript as current card. We also reinforce the concept of the index property standing in for the HyperTalk version's number property.

Massaging Information in a Document

In the final script, we look at a variety of ways an AppleScript script communicates with a stack, particularly how it triggers user-defined handlers and functions. Each of the script fragments calls a handler someplace in the Chapter 28 Lab stack. Some handlers are in Hypertalk, some in AppleScript. Some also involve working with HyperTalk global variables so you can see how to extract and set global information from outside HyperCard (or from an AppleScript script inside HyperCard).

The first pair of statements show that calling a handler in a stack is the same, whether the handler is in AppleScript or HyperTalk. Because we're calling both of them from AppleScript, any parameters are in parentheses. Just as the handlers in the stack extend the vocabulary of the stack, so too do the handlers extend the vocabulary of things you can call from outside.

Next comes a longer fragment that ultimately calls a function in the stack script. While you can use either the do script or evaluate commands and receive data back (via the HyperTalk script's return command), the evaluate command returns numerical data in the same form it left the stack. Do script tends to coerce any number to a real value, which may be undesirable if you expect only integers. In this example, we also round the returned values to the nearest whole degree.

One further example of evaluating a user-defined function demonstrates how it is sometimes necessary to assemble parameters with in-line quotes around values. In the calculation of the number of the day in a year, the date value must be passed as a quoted string, or the numbers will be evaluated as a series of divisions.

```
-- HyperCard Scripts & Globals
tell application "HyperCard"
    activate
    go card 1

    -- execute background HyperTalk script handler
    showBgText("This came from AppleScript via HyperTalk bg handler.")

    -- execute card AppleScript script handler
    showCdText("This is here thanks to an AppleScript cd handler.")

    -- evaluate a HyperTalk function (in stack script)
    display dialog ¬
        "Enter a Farenheit temperature to convert to Celsius:" default answer "32"
    set tempF to text returned of result
    if tempF is not "" then
        set tempC to round (evaluate "FtoC(" & tempF & ")")
        display dialog (tempC as string) & " degrees Celsius."
    end if

    -- evaluate a HyperTalk function requiring a string parameter
    evaluate "dayofyear(\"9/11/95\")"

    -- set a HyperTalk global from AppleScript
    set variable "sampleGlobal" to "This is a test."

    -- get a HyperTalk global from a HyperTalk handler
    set myVal to variable "sampleGlobal"

end tell
```

The last two demonstrations show ways of working with HyperTalk global variables. Not listed in the HyperCard dictionary is an object called **variable**. This is the HyperTalk global variable, and you can get or set the value of any global via this **variable** object. The variable name requires quotes (something you're not used to in HyperTalk), and values can be any number or string.

To prove this works, display the Variable Watcher window in HyperCard (type "vw" into the Message Box, and press Return). Scroll to the bottom, where you'll see sampleGlobal listed with the value set from the script, above. You can use this same syntax in AppleScript handlers attached to HyperCard objects, too.

QuarkXPress

Version

3.3

Recordable

No.

Object Model Support

Complex Object Model, resulting in good scripting control over most elements of a document, if you can master the object hierarchy. Some advanced objects (e.g., groups, libraries, page sections) are not supported.

Supports Whose Clauses

Yes.

Important Application Concepts

Scripting QuarkXPress shows you more about the internal workings of the product than you normally see as a non-scripting user. Understanding basic QuarkXPress concepts such as the different kinds of boxes and style sheets is essential to learning the further depths of object organization. Because many of the properties of objects revolve around size and location on a page, you should also have a good grasp of measurement methods and choices available in the product.

Scripting Overview

Of all the scriptable applications I've examined over one and a half years, QuarkX-Press comes with more documentation (as XPress documents) about its scripting support than any other program. Not only is there a lot of documentation, but it is extraordinarily useful in figuring out the product's scripting depth. Although the company would supply me with only a stunted demonstration version of the program (despite months of requests and assurances that I'd see the real thing), the software was fully scriptable, even if I was unable to save a document for the companion disk that you'd be able to open with the full product.

A key principle for successful QuarkXPress scripting is having a solid mental model of the object hierarchy. Quark supplies a map of the hierarchy in the "Advanced Scripting Document" file nested in the "For Advanced Scripting" folder. Of the many object paths on the map, the most important trail is the one that goes application → document → spread → page → boxes → text. Equally important are hierarchical relationships of the more specific box and text objects (e.g., text box, line box, and picture box elements of the generic box object).

The hierarchy comes into play when creating references to objects. Recall that the job of an object reference is to pinpoint—among the potentially tens of thousands of objects that can be accessed from your Mac at any given moment—exactly which object you want to work with. In a deep hierarchy such as QuarkXPress, that means that references could get rather long:

```
paragraph 1 of text box 1 of page 1 of document 1 of application "QuarkXPress"
```

Therefore, in the sample script that Quark supplies, you often see nested tell statements directed to documents or boxes that simplify the statements you make to objects contained by those outer objects:

```
tell application "QuarkXPress™ "
  tell document 1
    -- statements adjusting document settings
  end tell

  tell page 1 of document 1
    -- statements adjusting page properties
  end tell

  tell story 1 of text box 1 of page 1 of document 1
    -- statements directed to story object
  end tell
end tell
```

This is good practice, especially for the deep object hierarchy in this product.

When perusing the dictionary for objects, pay close attention to whether there is an inherits property. In some ways this is a bogus property, because you cannot retrieve this information from the object. But it does reveal vital information about the parent or containing object (and its properties) of the particular object in question. In other words, when the text box object says it inherits both the containing box and box property objects, it means that any property of either of those objects can also apply to a specific text box object. Therefore, to determine all the properties for a text box, you have to look in the containing box and box properties listings. In turn, such an object may point even higher up the hierarchy, as the box property object does when it points to the base object. You can also check the "Chapter 4-Advanced Scripting" file in Quark's "For Advanced Scripting" folder. It painstakingly lists all the properties for each object.

While we're on the QuarkXPress dictionary, let's look for a moment at the two QuarkXPress suites: the primary one and the ancillary one. The primary suite contains the objects your scripts will be working with—the kinds of objects you see in a document, such as text boxes, pages, images, guides, and so on. While the majority of the properties for these objects are common AppleScript objects (strings, integers, booleans, lists, etc.), some are more complex, requiring either records or what Quark calls *ancillary objects*.

An ancillary object is not something physical in a document, but rather a collection of properties that help define a phyical object. For example, the text inset property of a text box is shown to be of a fixed rectangle class. What may be confusing is that if you look at the value returned for the text inset property, it appears to be an AppleScript list. Consider the following script and result notations:

```
tell application "QuarkXPress™ "
    text inset of text box 1 of page 2 of document 1
        -- result: {"0.014\"", "0.014\"", "0.014\"", "0.014\""}
    class of result
        -- result: measurements rectangle
end tell
```

In the dictionary entry of ancillary objects, the fixed rectangle lists nine properties that control its specifications, four of which are the top, left, bottom, and right measurements that appear in the pseudo-list result. But even as we dig deeper, we find that none of the properties returns what appears to be the string of a single measurement:

```
tell application "QuarkXPress™ "
    -- reference gets even longer...
    bottom of text inset of text box 1 of page 2 of document 1
        -- result: "0.014\""
    class of result
        -- vertical measurement
    result = "0.014\""
        -- result: false
end tell
```

The class of a single measurement is, itself a special object class belonging to QuarkXPress, but not further defined. Any manipulation with these values will require coercion to a string (to strip away the in-line quote) and then to a real number. We do this later in this chapter.

Fortunately, QuarkXPress is more forgiving when setting values of these types. Therefore, we can set an individual or group value by passing strings, and letting QuarkXPress perform the necessary coercion to the desired measurement values:

```
tell application "QuarkXPress™ "
    tell text box 1 of page 2 of document 1
        set bottom of text inset to "0.05\""
        text inset -- to see if change was made
            -- result: {"0.014\"", "0.014\"", "0.05\"", "0.014\""}
        set text inset to ¬
            {"0.025\"", "0.025\"", "0.050\"", "0.025\""}
    end tell
    text inset of text box 1 of page 2 of document 1
        -- result: {"0.025\"", "0.025\"", "0.05\"", "0.025\""}
    class of result
        -- result: measurements rectangle
end tell
```

The point of this exercise is to make you aware to check the ancillary objects list for further properties when a physical object's property listing shows a class you don't recognize (e.g., it's not a string or boolean).

Retrieving Information

Beyond the retrieval of property information, which we covered in the previous section, data retrieval from a QuarkXPress document is straightforward, provided you know the distinction among text, story, and image objects.

From any text box, you can retrieve the entire contents or any typical text processing object (paragraph, line, word, character). But it is important to know that a text box contains both a story and text. When a text box is something that displays self-contained hunk of text, the story and text are the same. But if the story runs across multiple linked text boxes, then the returned values for these two objects are different. The text of a text box for a given page returns the contents only that appears in the text box you've named; but the story for a text box returns the entire story, no matter how many further linked text boxes it runs across. When referring to a story of a text box, you must refer to the story by number. In the vast majority of cases, there will be only one story in a text box, but you still must label it as such:

```
story 1 of text box "Body" of page 3
```

Moreover, when you retrieve the story of any text box in the linked sequence, QuarkXPress returns the entire story, even if it started on a previous page. Therefore, to limit the returned contents to just what is visible in a particular linked text box, request the text of the box, not the story.

Retrieving an image from an image box is similar to retrieving text from a text box. You may wish to pick up a PICT from a QuarkXPress document and carry it to another document or application. You can do so by getting image 1 of the box, as in:

```
set thePICT to image 1 of picture box 4
```

At that point, the variable contains the actual PICT data (it looks ugly in the Result window or, if small enough, in the Event Log window). But, this is precisely the data some other programs expect for their picture fields (e.g., File-Maker Pro) or inserts.

Inserting New Information

The sample script supplied by Quark shows many good examples of creating new objects. A solid piece of advice in their advanced scripting documentation is to create objects and set properties of the new object in the same make <object> statement, using the with properties parameter. All objects you can create from a script can accept the property record parameters:

```
make vertical guide at end with properties {position: "0.25\""}
```

Assigning data to text and picture boxes takes on an additional twist, as demonstrated in Quark's sample script. You can set these objects to their straight data or to the contents of a file. Therefore, the following syntax structures are all valid:

```
set story 1 of text box 1 of page 1 to <string>

set story 1 of text box 1 of page 1 to <formatted text data>

set story 1 of text box 1 of page 1 to <file reference>

set image 1 of picture box 1 of page 1 to <PICT data>

set image 1 of picture box 1 of page 1 to <file reference>
```

You can, for instance, pick up formatted text or picture data from a document in another program (if the source program supports such data grabbing), and drop it into the appropriate kind of box in the QuarkXPress document. Or if the script needs to get its data from a file, the program figures out the appropriate translation to capture the formatted data from the word processing or graphics file. Thus, your script doesn't have to worry about file types or other nonsense.

One other non-intuitive tip has to do with line breaks within paragraph objects. These are the soft returns you create in a paragraph by holding down the Shift key while pressing Return. In QuarkXPress, the soft return character is ASCII 7. To replicate this action in a script, you must use the ASCII character command (Apple scripting addition) to "type" that character, as in:

```
tell application "QuarkXPress™ "
  tell text box 1 of page 1 of document 1
```

```
      copy (ASCII character 7) to after word 7 of paragraph 4
   end tell
end tell
```

If the paragraph in which such a character is entered is set for justified align-ment, you may have unexpectedly wide word spacing result in the line contain-ing the soft return. But the behavior is no different for the scripted version than from manual entry of the same character.

Massaging Information in a Document

One characteristic of a QuarkXPress document that doesn't surface in Quark's own documentation is the importance of object names, particularly boxes. When you consider that a long document could have literally thousands of boxes scattered about, your scripting adventures could get rough when it comes time to get, put, or massage stuff in a particular box. Relying on box numbering (numbering is based on layering, with the frontmost layer being number 1) is hazardous, particularly if a document changes after a script has been written to control it.

Compounding the problem for the scripter is that QuarkXPress does not provide a way for the document creator to assign names to objects. If it weren't for scripting, there would be no need to name such items, so this lack of naming facilities shouldn't be much of a surprise. To see if a document has any named boxes, run the following script:

```
tell application "QuarkXPress™ "
   name of every generic box of document 1
end tell
```

Unless the document had been previously adjusted by a scripter, the results will undoubtedly be a list of empty strings, like

```
{"", "", "", "", "", ""}
```

which obviously came from a simple document. Try this same command on a document such as the scripting documentation files to see how many boxes there might be in a common document.

Naming boxes is at best a tedious process, since the job must be done via scripting. Use the following script to ease the pain. It shows each page of a document, and selects each text box, giving you a chance to enter a name for the box.

```
-- Quark Text Box Naming
tell application "QuarkXPress™ "
   activate
   tell document 1
      repeat with i from 1 to count of pages
         set current page to page i
```

```
            repeat with j from 1 to count of text boxes of page i
                if name of text box j of page i = "" then
                    set current box to text box j of page i
                    display dialog ¬
                        "Assign a name to the selected box:" ¬
                            default answer "" ¬
                            buttons {"Cancel", "Skip", "OK"} ¬
                            default button "OK"
                    if button returned of result is "OK" then
                        set name of text box j of page i to ¬
                            text returned of result
                    end if
                end if
            end repeat
        end repeat
    end tell
end tell
```

This script is written for text boxes, but you can easily modify it for picture boxes, if naming them would help your scripting task.

Using object names should always be a priority, particularly for boxes and documents. The examples in this chapter show document references by number for the sake of making it easier on your trying various scripts on any document. But if you are scripting a process on a particular document—e.g., for automating a repetitive procedure—your script should address the document(s) by name. Just as with boxes, anytime there are potentially multiple layers of objects involved, name references are much safer.

The final data massaging subject we'll address has to do with making adjustments to measurements derived from a QuarkXPress document. Recall the discussion earlier in the chapter in which we examined the details of a typical measurement value. If we obtain a rectangle of an object, the value may come back looking like a list, but the class of the object is something entirely different—and unfriendly to typical AppleScript data manipulation.

In the following script, the goal is to subtract one inch from the top measurement value of a particular text box. As written, it works nicely with the "Catalog Layout" sample QuarkXPress file (located in Sample Documents folder of the Apple Events Preview folder inside the QuarkXPress folder).

```
-- Quark Formatting
tell application "QuarkXPress™ "
    activate
    -- select box to hilite it for demo purposes
    set current box to text box 5 of document 1
    -- get measurements value, and coerce it to AppleScript list
    set theBounds to (bounds of text box 5 of document 1) as list
    -- extract first item, coercing to string along the way
```

```
        set theTop to (item 1 of theBounds) as string
        -- strip away in-line quote (inches) mark, but keep as text string
        set theTop to (characters 1 thru ((count of theTop) - 1) of theTop as text)
        -- prepare for math
        set theTop to theTop as real
        -- subtract 1
        set theTop to theTop - 1
        -- rebuild first item of list with new value and in-line inch mark
        set item 1 of theBounds to (theTop as text) & "\""
        -- pass list to QuarkXPress, which takes care of coercion to measurement
        set bounds of text box 5 of document 1 to theBounds
    end tell
```

A good deal of this script is concerned with coercing various values to the classes needed for the ultimate math. We can shorten it a bit by using the extract number OSAX from the GTQ OSAXen collection:

```
-- Quark Alternate
tell application "QuarkXPress™ "
    activate
    -- select box to hilite it for demo purposes
    set current box to text box 5 of document 1
    -- get measurements value, and coerce it to AppleScript list
    set theBounds to (bounds of text box 5 of document 1) as list
    -- use GTQ 'extract number from' OSAX to get just
    -- the number from the first item value
    set theTop to (extract number from (item 1 of theBounds) ¬
        in format "###.###'\""")
    -- subtract 1
    set theTop to theTop - 1
    -- rebuild first item of list with new value and in-line inch mark
    set item 1 of theBounds to (theTop as text) & "\""
    -- pass list to QuarkXPress, which takes care of coercion to measurement
    set bounds of text box 5 of document 1 to theBounds
end tell
```

The GTQ scripting addition is smart enough to extract just the digits we need, and return the value as a real, all set for us to perform the math.

A number of high-powered publishing companies script QuarkXPress with AppleScript, Frontier, or both to assemble complex layouts from a variety of source files. That includes the *USAToday* daily newspaper by Gannett. The more you can set up manually in a template, the easier it is to let the automation merely grab text and picture files, composing page after page of a large document on a regular basis as the source files are updated.

Getting Help with Application Scripting

When you're stuck with an application scripting problem, it's not always easy to get help. Your best long-term investment you can make to assure support for AppleScript is a modem and an account on a commercial on-line service.

Help with Applications

Virtually none of the free phone support you get for applications covers AppleScript scripting. In my experience, most support technicians don't know a thing about AppleScript, even if they'd like to help you.

The first place to go for help is to the vendor's on-line support forum. Many software companies maintain a presence on America Online, CompuServe, eWorld, and sometimes all of these places (and more). It's not uncommon for the engineer who did the AppleScript implementation to help out here. For example, Leonard Rosenthal, a principal of Aladdin Systems, has helped many users with questions about scripting StuffIt and SITcomm (a scriptable communications program). Even if someone from the company can't help, other active users of the product, who regularly hang out on these forums, usually can. For application-specific help, seek out a vendor forum.

General Help

Not all companies maintain a formal presence on line, but they do check into some of the gathering places for scripters. While I haven't been on every on-line service to check their scripting sections, the two most active public on-line areas I've seen are the AppleScript forum on America Online (keyword: APPLESCRIPT) and the AppleScript Internet list server.

The latter is a free bulletin-board like forum that uses the Internet electronic mail system as its conduit. That means that as long as your on-line service offers e-mail access to the Internet (they all do), then you can receive and submit messages to the list server. Any message you send to the server is rebroadcast as an Internet e-mail message to the approximately 300 users who "subscribe" to the list. Most questions receive answers within a matter of hours.

To subscribe to the AppleScript list server, send an e-mail message to the following Internet address:

LISTSERV@dartmouth.edu

The subject of the message must be the word:

subscribe

and the body of the message should be:

subscribe macscript *yourName*

An automated system that receives this message will set you up as a subscriber, and alert you with your first message when you are officially part of the group.

Be aware, however, that some commercial online services charge extra for messages that pass to and from the Internet. With dozens of messages coming through each day, this could get costly, even though the list subscription, itself, is free. Of course, you only have to download the messages you want to, based on the subject lines, but you can't always tell how some discussion threads may have incorporated important information that is slightly off the topic.

As an alternative, you might wish to sign up to the digest, which sends summaries of various threads discussed on a near daily basis. To subscribe to the digest, send a message to the same e-mail address, above. Label the subject of the message as:

digest

and enter the message to read:

set macscript digest

There is talk periodically about transforming the list server into a UseNet newsgroup, a more formal on-line forum which requires Internet access such as that provided by CompuServe, America Online, and Delphi. As of this writing, however, participants voted to keep the list server in publication.

It is unfortunate that we scripters are pretty much on our own. Apple, for instance, provides only fee-based support for AppleScript. But as happened with HyperCard, the scripting community largely supports itself. Somewhere out there is at least one other user who has either conquered the problem you're having, or will assume the challenge to uncover a solution for you. A connection to one or more of these scripting virtual communities will pay for itself over and over.

PART V

Essential Applescript Add-Ons

CHAPTER 31

Building User Interfaces for Scripts

Scripts you create with a script editor don't have much in the way of user interface elements in them. About the only items supplied with AppleScript are the display dialog windows and the standard file dialog boxes. Except for processes that are meant to run invisibly, we Mac users expect something special in the way of user interfaces for programs. Two primary options along these lines are the FaceSpan interface builder and HyperCard 2.2.

FaceSpan

As of this writing, FaceSpan is available only as part of the bundle you get from Apple when you buy the AppleScript Scripter Kit. FaceSpan (first released under the name FrontMost) is a third-party product, created by Software Designs Unlimited, Inc. (Chapel Hill, NC), the same folks who produce WindowScript for HyperCard (published by Heizer Software). FaceSpan consists of two key ingredients:

- FaceSpan development application
- FaceSpan extension

You use the development application (whose programming language is AppleScript) to create applications. FaceSpan's primary contribution is providing an easy way to lay out windows and their contents (various types of fields and buttons, text lists, PICT art, icons, popup menus, scroll bars, boxes, lines, and QuickTime movies). You also have complete control over menus for the application. An application (called a *project* in the FaceSpan vernacular) can have as many windows as are needed for your user interface.

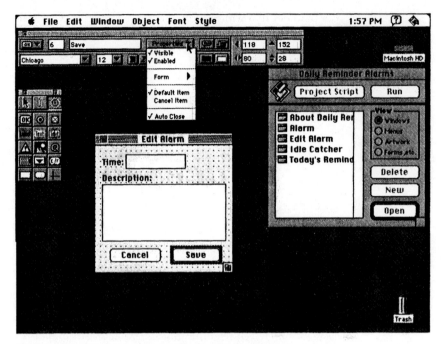

Figure 31.1 The FaceSpan authoring environment.

FaceSpan Construction Environment

The ease with which you create the windows is the remarkable story of FaceSpan. Figure 31.1 shows a typical FaceSpan project in the construction mode. For each object in the window (field, label, button, etc.), the object brower window (across the top) shows key properties of the object for simple editing. You can even assign Balloon Help text to each object, just by clicking the Balloon Help button in the browser, and filling in the text that is to go into the object's balloon (Figure 31.2).

(a)   (b)

Figure 31.2 The FaceSpan entry window for Balloon Help (a) and the results in the running application (b).

Each object in a window can have its own script (very much like HyperCard, but with more types of objects). User interaction with menus and items in windows triggers messages, which AppleScript handlers in various objects intercept and execute. Scripts, of course, can communicate with other scriptable applications.

Once you've finished a FaceSpan application, you can save it two ways. One is as a miniature application, which requires that the FaceSpan extension be present in the user's Extensions folder. An advantage to this method is that all your FaceSpan miniature applications can take advantage of a single extension. But you can also save a FaceSpan app as a complete application, which builds the powers of the FaceSpan extension into the file. The application is larger by about 256K, but it means that anyone with the AppleScript Run-time software extensions can run the application. By purchasing the AppleScript Scripter's Kit, you automatically have a royalty-free license to distribute both the FaceSpan extension with a miniature application and complete applications. FaceSpan-based applications are, themselves, scriptable applications from any OSA-compliant scripting language.

A Sample Application

To demonstrate how FaceSpan can dress up a script, we built a user interface for the Reminder Alarm Agent script from Chapter 15. The application is included on the accompanying disk (Handbook Scripts:Chapter 31).

The total project consists of four windows that the user sees: (1) display all alarms stored in the alarm data file (Figure 31.3); (2) enter data for a new alarm (Figure 31.4); (3) display the reminder when the alarm goes off (Figure 31.5); and (4) an About window (Figure 31.6). A fifth, unseen window captures the system Idle messages, which trigger the alarms.

All data is stored as a project-level property, taking advantage of the persistence of properties in FaceSpan applications (commensurate with that of AppleScript apps). This property, and the one that holds the list of alarms yet to ring for the day, behave like global variables within the objects of the project. The only non-intuitive part of scripting for these project properties

Figure 31.3 Alarm list window.

Figure 31.4 Alarm data entry window.

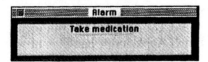

Figure 31.5   Alarm message window.

is that scripts in other objects (windows, buttons, fields) must refer to the properties preceded by the word "my," to tell AppleScript that the variable is found
within the project.

To use Daily Reminder Alarms:

1. Start Daily Reminder Alarms from the Finder. If you receive an alert
    indicating that all alarms have passed, click the Stay Open button.

2. Choose Show List from the Reminders menu. The first time you use it,
    the list will be empty.

3. Click the New button to enter a reminder for later. Consult Balloon
    Help for more information on acceptable data entry values.

4. You can then close all windows, and let the program display the alarm
    when its time comes.

Place an alias to the application in your Startup Items folder so it launches
automatically each time you start your Mac.

Designing a FaceSpan Application

Creating a user interface for a script is a different proposition from writing
the AppleScript code that does the scripting work. The Daily Reminder
Alarms program is a good example. While the core functionality of the agent
aspect of the product (in the Idle handler) is largely the same as in the
script-only version of Chapter 15, considerably more thought went into the
way to present information and allow users to interact with it. A lot more
AppleScript code went into the FaceSpan application to accommodate this
interaction—things like presenting the list of data in a nicely formatted co-
lumnar format and inserting user-entered data into the alarm data file in
proper chronological sort order. That's not to mention even more work to
validate time entries that users could enter. Fortunately, FaceSpan takes

Figure 31.6   About box.

care of much of the worries about the way interface elements look by providing script-less ways of setting element properties.

Still, designing a script that has a user interface around it requires different thinking about the script. Without a user interface beyond a few Display Dialogs, the script writer tends to focus on the What of the script—what the script does; for a true Macintosh-like interface, the scripter writer must pay even closer attention to the How of the script—how the application looks and behaves for the user.

In working with FaceSpan, you may also want to keep Script Editor open. Since the AppleScript extension doesn't have debugging support built in, FaceSpan's script editor doesn't either. While you get comparable syntax checking and a shade better feedback for run-time errors in FaceSpan, you may find yourself wanting to take advantage of the Script Editor's event log in the early stages of script development. Therefore, it is possible you may fine-tune tricky handlers that work with other applications, and then copy the handlers to the FaceSpan object of your choice.

HyperCard

The arrival of HyperCard 2.2 at the very end of 1993 coincided with the release of AppleScript 1.1 and FaceSpan. As evidenced by the level of Object Model and OSA support built into HyperCard (described in Chapter 28), HyperCard is also a candidate for creating user interfaces for AppleScript applications, especially those that can take advantage of Hyper-Card's own data storage facilities.

Figure 31.7 shows a script window for HyperCard, and its popup menu that allows you to decide which scripting language—HyperTalk, AppleScript, User-Talk, QuicKeys, or other installed OSA-compliant language—is being used for that object. In other words, it is possible to script a button to carry out its tasks in AppleScript, while it calls functions or other commands in the stack script written in HyperTalk.

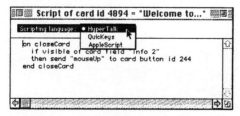

Figure 31.7 HyperCard script window
and OSA component pop-up.

A significant advantage of HyperCard as a user interface builder for an AppleScript script is that the script can use whatever XCMDs are available commercially and in the public domain. That includes externals for multi-user stacks, client-server applications, and other connectivity solutions. HyperTalk is also far easier than AppleScript for string manipulation inside a script.

If you are familiar with HyperTalk and are trying to use AppleScript (or vice versa), you will experience a moderate learning curve as you discover that the ways you perform key operations (such as assigning a value to a variable) are different in each language, while in other cases a few keywords are used in opposite ways. Making the transition from HyperTalk to AppleScript may be harder in some respects, because HyperTalk is far more forgiving to the casual programmer (accepting singular and plural versions of some keywords, for instance), while AppleScript often allows only one way to accomplish a certain task.

HyperCard allows you to save stacks (including those that use OSA scripts) as standalone applications (which are fully OSA-scriptable). The overhead for this privilege is about 650K, but some scripters may prefer HyperCard's extreme ease of use, especially with the improved user interface elements of version 2.2 and after.

FaceSpan or HyperCard?

Choosing between FaceSpan and HyperCard for your user interface builder in AppleScript may not be easy. FaceSpan has a clear advantage because of the comparatively smaller size of finished applications, while HyperCard's ready availability of external commands and data storage are attractions for its abilities. If you are serious about AppleScript scripting, you will want both tools on hand.

CHAPTER 32

Third-Party Scripting Tools

In this chapter, we'll take a look at three third-party tools. The first two are substitutes for the very plain Script Editor that ships with all of Apple's Apple-Script software; the third is an extraordinary add-on that lets you script virtually any operation in any application in the OSA-scripting language of your choice.

ScriptWizard

Authors of large scripts are easily frustrated by Apple's Script Editor, which provides little in the way of help for navigating through scripts. Without so much as even a way to search for a handler or string, it can take quite a bit of scrolling to locate what you're looking for. The first third-party editor replacement to reach the market was ScriptWizard (Full Moon Software, P.O. Box 700237, San Jose, CA 95170). ScriptWizard brings not only traditional script searching abilities, but also a modicum of enhanced debugging.

Figure 32.1 shows the ScriptWizard main script window that has a very large script in it. A popup menu lists all the handlers and properties in the script. To zip to the top of any handler, simply select the handler name in the list. You can also search the contents of a script. The search Command-key equivalents are the same as for HyperCard, so if you have experience with that editor, searching will be natural for you in ScriptWizard. Moreover, ScriptWizard includes a search-and-replace function.

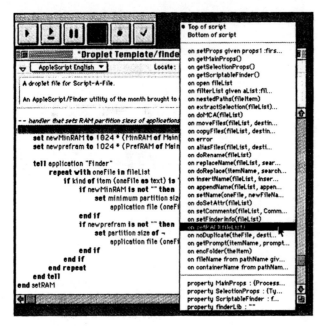

Figure 32.1   ScriptWizard editing window.

As you test a script, you can elect to "single-step" through it, and view variable values along the way . In the version I've been using so far (1.0.1), not all variables appear in the list (e.g., counting variables of repeat loops). Also, you do not see a program pointer in the script, so you cannot tell exactly which line is executing. Moreover, execution does not necessarily step one statement at a time—but rather from external Apple event to the next. One other feature of the variable watcher window that is missing is the ability to view the contents of large variables. Unlike the HyperCard variable watcher menu, clicking on a line of a variable in the list does not display the contents of the variable below the list.

ScriptWizard is also somewhat slower than Script Editor for opening and scrolling through large scripts. But you may like the navigation and search facilities to abandon the original Script Editor.

Scripter

Nearing completion as this edition goes to press is another editor replacement called Scripter (Main Event Software, 1814 Belmont Rd., NW, Washington, D.C. 20009). Scripter goes significantly further than ScriptWizard 1.0.1 in providing line-by-line debugging of AppleScript.

Figure 32.2 shows a typical screen for single-stepping through a script, watching each line execute (note the pointer in the editor window showing which line is about to execute). The log window (bottom) is set to show each statement and any result that may come back (the same kind of results you see in Apple's Script Editor Event Log window).

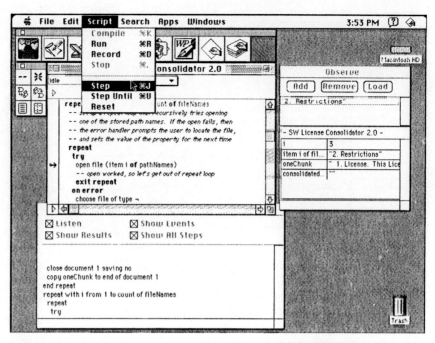

Figure 32.2   A typical Scripter window setup for true single-step debugging.

To the right is a window that acts as a variable watcher as you single-step a script. While you must manually enter the names of items you want to track (or drag-and-drop them if you're using System 7.5), you can also enter expressions that depend on variables. For instance, in the figure, I have entered not only the repeat loop counter variable (i), but also an expression that depends on the value of i and a property defined at the head of the script. As you step through a script, you can switch windows from the script to the variable watcher, and add or remove variables and expressions at will or change values of variables. Double-clicking on an item in the value column displays the complete contents in a field just below the buttons. You can save Observe windows, so you needn't re-list your variable for each debugging session.

Other handy Scripter features include a window that lets you test simple statements, instead of having to open an entire script window. The icon palette provides space for preloading of your most frequently scripted applications, simplifying the location of the programs' dictionaries when you need them.

The creators of Scripter also expended a great deal of effort in providing a series of windows to lead authors to build script statements by clicking on sublistings from an application'sdictionary (e.g., double click on a command, then view another window to double-click on an object, another for its properties, and so on). The profusion of windows to accomplish this may intimidate some, and Scripter is at the mercy of the quality of the dictionary—which, as we've seen, is not guaranteed. Experienced scripters will probably stick to the plain old dictionary as a vocabulary reference and write their own script statements. But the debugging abilities of Scripter certainly make it a worthy replacement for Script Editor.

PreFab Player

Throughout many chapters of this book, particularly in Part III's tours through scriptable applications, you've read my complaints about lack of AppleScript support for various features in programs. Or, you've probably detected a sigh of resignation about having to learn an application's scripting or macro language to take full advantage of automation.

One way around the lack of scripting support is using macro programs, such as QuicKeys (CE Software) and Tempo (Affinity). Both utilities work well with AppleScript, and QuicKeys even has a number of nicely crafted extensions that facilitate scripting such processes as mounting servers without the user having to be there to enter a password. QuicKeys even shows up in script editors' OSA language popup menus. The difficulty, however, is that you must still learn another language to accomplish scripting of otherwise non-scriptable items. And integrating script objects written in multiple languages takes a bit of thought to implement well.

Filling the gap is a comparatively new product from PreFab Software (34 Bartlett St., Somerville, MA 02145), called PreFab Player. Written specifically to work with scripting environments such as AppleScript and UserLand Frontier, Prefab Player lets your scripts do the things that an application's own scripting lacks—even if what the programs lacks is scripting of any kind. All of the script writing stays within the same script editor window your main script uses, and the vocabulary for Player's powers is an extension to the existing Apple-Script (or Frontier) syntax.

The Product

Installation of Player inserts one extension and two scripting additions into the Extensions folder. The extension is the "application" that your scripts call whenever they need the help of Player to type or click on something. Also in that application are 30 AppleScript verbs that let you script a wide variety of actions from your AppleScript scripts.

To show the range of manual actions that are scriptable via Player, here is a list of operations you can script, regardless of a program's scriptability:

Choose from a menubar menu.
Including hierarchical menus and with the equivalent of holding down any modifier key.

Choose from a popup menu.
Also including hierarchical menus and modifier keys.

Click on a button.
Buttons of virtually any style: standard, radio, and checkbox. Also, whether a modifier key should be pressed while clicking the button.

Click on any dialog or window item.
As specified by the Dialog Manager, each little gizmo in a dialog is an item, including gauges. Here you can perform the equivalent of such a click with or without a modifier key, and any number of repetitions.

Click anywhere.
Either according to the coordinate system of the frontmost window or the entire screen. Also in one command, you can specify a series of click locations or objects.

Drag the pointer.
Either between two points, or in a sequence of points—with or without a modifier key being pressed.

Type any string.
With your choice of modifier keys.

Test for existence of objects.
Necessary at times in a script, you can check for whether a particular menu item, popup menu, button, dialog window item, or window is present prior to performing any action.

Obtain attributes of menubar menu items, popup menus, buttons, dialog items, or windows.
Results consists of records with fields appropriate for the type of object. Most items are about the physical nature of the object, such as location, visibility, dimensions, and so on.

Set a checkbox state.
So you know for sure whether you're checking or unchecking a checkbox button.

Set the target window.
So your statements go to the items in the desired dialog window.

Set delays for typing or mouse actions.
Some programs can't handle quick actions, so you can slow things down a bit to make sure the program doesn't miss a thing.

Set tolerance for partial string matching and case sensitivity.
When calling menu items, for instance, you can forget the trailing ellipsis and still get away with it. These settings apply to calls to any objects.

A Sample Script

Back in Chapter 25, I lamented the fact that you could only go so far scripting search-and-replace in WordPerfect 3.0a. At best, you could trigger via Apple-Script the WordPerfect Find/Change dialog (Figure 32.3), leaving it to the user

Figure 32.3 The WordPerfect Find/Change
dialog can be scripted with Player.

to enter the search-and-replace strings. That is hardly the way to automate a
batch process that needs to perform a search-and-replace across several documents every day.

By employing PreFab Player, however, we can have AppleScript (either in a
standalone script or in a front end by FaceSpan or HyperCard) enter the search
and replace values into the WordPerfect dialog and click the right button. In
the following Player-adapted script, we prompt the user for the values with display dialog commands, but in a truly automated environment, the values might
be stored as properties or hard-wired into the script.

```
-- Player/WordPerfect
-- REQUIRES PreFab Player software
-- establish variables for search and replace strings
set searchString to text returned of (display dialog ¬
    "Replace the following string..." default answer "")
set replaceString to text returned of (display dialog ¬
    "With..." default answer "")

-- bring WordPerfect to the front
tell application "WordPerfect" to activate

-- turn Player loose on WordPerfect
tell application "PreFab Player™ "
    -- select a menu item
    do menu menu item "Find/Change" of menu "Edit"
    -- enter first value into first field
    type searchString
    -- advance the text insertion pointer to next field
    type tab
    -- enter second value
    type replaceString
    -- click the desired button
    click button "Change All"
    -- close the window via Command-W
    type "w" holding command
end tell
```

The sequence of steps in the PreFab Player portion is identical to the manual steps you'd take, except the script can insert values that come from elsewhere in the script. To accomplish the same with QuicKeys would have required writing a separate script in the QuicKeys language, and then modifying it to accept parameters (the search and replace strings) passed from the main script. One advantage the QuicKeys method has is that you can record the procedure to get most of the script (prior to the modifications). But I believe the benefit of keeping the entire process within a single language and script outweigh the recording ability.

Side Effects

As the PreFab Player clearly indicates in its documentation, some windows and programs are easier to script than others. Some programs (including control panels) don't use standard Dialog Manager calls to create their windows. Usually you can still access items by clicking at coordinate points in the dialog boxes (and a utility for quickly uncovering those coordinates is included with Player).

One other element of using PreFab Player is that unlike the usually silent and invisible work of well-supported AppleScript commands in programs, anything you script via Player appears on screen as if being run by the Invisible Man. Therefore, users of the scripts see dialogs appear, fields fill in, and buttons hilite while the script runs. To some users, this is comforting, while to others it represents visual clutter. It definitely provides visual feedback that a script is running, unlike plain AppleScript scripts.

Because PreFab Player does such an excellent job of filling scripting gaps in applications, my greatest fear is that application developers won't make the effort to improve the OSA-scriptability of their products. If they feel that anyone can script their product, no matter how poorly the scripting implementation, they may not have the incentive to do better. As good as PreFab Player is—it is a permanent component of my personal scripting toolbelt—it is not a substitute for good Object Model implementations in our applications.

Third-Party Scripting Additions

In this chapter, we'll look at the details of four scripting addition collections included on the companion disk (Handbook Scripts:Chapter 33). I have se-lected these sets because they supplement the standard OSAXes with some much-needed functionality. They were all written by programmers who are dedicated to making AppleScript a pivotal part of customization and automat-ion tasks. You can find contact information in associated documentation or the script dictionaries. Consult the authors about any problems or suggestions you may have for improvement. At the end of the chapter, I will also discuss issues surrounding the proliferation and potential conflict of scripting additions that wind up in a programmer's Scripting Additions folder.

Jon's Commands

As a member of the original AppleScript team at Apple, Jon Pugh was among the first to jump into the open distribution of scripting additions. His original Clipboard OSAX saved many an early scripter's behind.

That OSAX and several others are now grouped together into a single script-ing addition called Jon's Commands. Some items in the set are no longer nec-essary with the advent of the scriptable Finder, but many individual commands are very useful. Here is a list of those commands (items now available in scrip-table Finder or System 7.5 are in parentheses):

```
(deleteFile)
(renameFile)
(moveFile)
(sound volume)

clipboard info
     -- result: list of lists of data type & size.

set the clipboard to <any data>

the clipboard
     -- result: data from the clipboard.

execute FKEY <name or number of FKEY resource>

screen list:
     -- result: list of screen info objects.
Properties:
   screen size
   bounds
   color depth
   in color

(finder selection)

keys pressed
     -- result: list of key names.

machine environment:
     -- result: environment record object
Properties:
   machine
   CPU type
   System version
   FPU
   Color Quickdraw
   AppleTalk version
   keyboard
   Data Access Manager
   software power off
   logical RAM
   physical RAM
   active scripts
   virtual memory

play sound <sound resource name or ID number, ¬
   sound file reference, or sound descriptor>
```

Consult the dictionary for Jon's Commands to see the specifics about parameters and values of items in the screen info and environment record objects.

The most valuable of the collection is the clipboard facility. All too many scriptable products either require a scriptable Clipboard (and don't allow data to be passed any other way) or go to the opposite extreme, and ignore the Clipboard altogether. In an ideal scripting world, where every application implements the Object Model correctly, there would be no need for the Clipboard. But the OSA-scripting world is far from ideal, and the Clipboard commands in Jon's Commands make many cross-application solutions scriptable that would otherwise not be. The nature of the commands make you treat the Clipboard like a global object:

```
set the clipboard to "foo"
get the clipboard
```

But as you can see in the dictionary, the Clipboard is not defined as an object. It's just there, and the commands offer avenues to the data and attributes. If you should have acquired Jon's earlier Clipboard OSAX, you should remove it from your Scripting Additions folder after installing Jon's Commands.

GTQ OSAXen

Greg T. Quinn has created perhaps the most extensive collection of scripting additions. His preferred plural for the OSAX term is OSAXen.

On the companion disk is an extensive documentation file that details the 65 OSAXes, several of which are now covered by the scriptable Finder. Still, there are dozens of useful extensions that will surely help many scripters. Each OSAX is a separate scripting addition file. Here are some highlights:

```
current date in seconds
    -- result: seconds since midnight 1/1/1904
date string for <date> [ in short | long | abbreviated format ]
    -- result: string of date in desired format (e.g., "3/4/95")
time string for <date> [ with/without seconds ]
    -- result: string of time in desired format (e.g., "12:33:02")

does font exist <font name string> [ of size <integer> ]
    -- result: Boolean
font information for <font file> [ returning <format> ]
    -- result: variety of records depending on whether format is
    -- font families, styles, PostScript, or all.
list fonts
    -- result: list of font name strings (fonts installed on local machine)

format number <number> in format <string>
    -- result: <string> in format specified by Excel-like number format in parameter
```

choose from list <list>[prompt <string>][multiple selections <boolean>] ¬
   [ok button <string>][cancel button <string>] ¬
   [empty lists <boolean>][initially select <list>]
   -- *result: list of selected items (or false if none selected)*

offsets of <string> in <string>[case sensitive | insensitive]
   -- *result: list of integers for all locations of substring in larger string*

request attention [message <string>][sound file <file specification>] ¬
   [sound number <small integer>][timeout <integer>]
   -- *result: true if user switches to script application before timeout*
set printer to <string>[named <string>][using <port>][zone <string>]
   -- *result: none*

sort <list>[in <direction>][order <list>][case sensitivity <boolean>]
   -- *result: list in sorted order*

play movie in <file>[using name <string>][at position <point>] ¬
   [at volume <small integer>]
   -- *result: none*
play <sound specification>[in <file>][at volume <small integer>]
   -- *result: none*
record sound to <file>[named <string>][quality <quality>] ¬
   [at position <point>]
   -- *result: none*

access privileges for <file>
   -- *result: record containing items such as*
   -- *owner name, group name, and various access rights*
list links [on <string>][in zone <string>][starting at <small integer>] ¬
   [for <small integer>]
   -- *result: list of all linkable applications*
list nodes [object <string>][type <string>][zone <string>]
   -- *result: list of all addresses meeting criteria*
volume mounting info for <volume name string>
   -- *result: record of use name and login method*

available dialects
   -- *result: list of records for all OSA dialects installed on local machine*

add picture <picture> to <file>[id <small integer>][name <string>] ¬
   [replacing allowed <boolean>]
   -- *result: resource ID of added picture*
add resource <resource> to <file>[id <small integer>] ¬
   [replacing allowed <boolean>]
   -- *result: resource ID of added resource*
add string list <list> to <file>[id <small integer>][name <string>] ¬
   [replacing allowed <boolean>]
   -- *result: resource ID of added STR# resource*

extract picture [from <file>][index <small integer>] ¬
  [id <small integer>][name <string>]
  -- *result: picture resource*
extract resource [from <file>] of type <string> ¬
  [index <small integer>][id <small integer>][name <string>]
  -- *result: resource*
extract string list [from <file>][index <small integer>] ¬
  [id <small integer>][name <string>]
  -- *result: list of strings*

Additional sets of commands control using a CD-ROM drive as an audio player and PowerTalk. There are so many goodies in this collection, that you'll be hard-pressed to figure out which ones to install. Several commands here make up for glaring omissions in the AppleScript that Apple delivers—particularly date and number formatting. As with any third-party OSAX, you must exercise care when using them in your scripts: use comments to identify the commands that are not common to all AppleScript runtime software installations. See the discussion, below, about managing OSAX libraries.

Donald's Commands

Another member of the original AppleScript team is Donald Olson, who may know more about the innards of OSAXes than anyone else in the universe. His collection is divided into individual OSAX files, so you can bring only those you need into the Scripting Additions folder.

The six scripting additions in the basic collection work primarily at deeper levels of scripting than many other OSAXes you see. Here are the basic six grouped by functionality:

OSAX Name	*Command Syntax*
GetHandlers OSAX	handlers of <script object>
	[names only <Boolean>]
	-- *Result: list of handler names and handler text*
GetProperties OSAX	properties of <script object>
	[names only <Boolean>]
	-- *Result: list of property names*
SetHandler OSAX	set handler <handler name>
	[of <script object>]
	[to <handler string>]
	-- *Result: the modified script*
SetProperties OSAX	set property <property name>
	[of <script object>]
	[to <any value>]
	-- *Result: the modified script.*

OSAX Name	*Command Syntax*
Mouse OSAX	MouseXY
	-- Result: mouse's point
	ButtonDown
	-- Result: Boolean
SetCurrentDir OSAX	SetCurrentDir <container specification>

The first two commands allow a script to retrieve information about any script object: the handlers in a script and a script's properties. The same items can be set with the following two commands. In other words, a script can modify itself or another script. These operations are best suited to experienced scripters and programmers, particularly since the changes made to any script (even when saved to disk via the store script command) do not appear in the script if you re-open it in a script editor. Moreover, if you open the modified script and re-compile it, the changes go away (much like property values).

While the application of the mouseXY command should be obvious, the SetCurrentDir may not. So many times you want to make it easier for a user of a script to locate or save files in specific folders that your script knows about. Without any outside intervention, the file dialog will point to the last folder accessed by the application. But to help direct the dialog to a different folder, use the SetCurrentDir command prior to calling other file dialog commands, such as choose file or new file.

MountVolume OSAX

One last entry in this chapter for third-party scripting additions is something that Apple would probably never release, because it has potential network security breach implications. If you try to mount a server via the scriptable Finder (or via a tell statement to an application running on a different Macintosh), the user invariably gets the log-on dialog, which requires manual intervention for selecting Guest or Password access, and entering a password when necessary.

While you could script the server logon process with PreFab Player (via the Chooser), the results may vary, especially as the number of servers available in the list changes from minute to minute (you can only click at a location in the list, which could be wrong tomorrow). A better way is to use the MountVolume addition, written by Jay Lloyd (e-mail address:JLLOYD@applelink.apple.com). Here is the dictionary entry for the single command:

```
MountVolume
      Volume string -- The volume to mount.
      Server string -- The server on which the volume resides.
      [Zone string] -- The zone in which the server resides.
      [Username string] -- The username with which to mount the volume.
      [Password string] -- The password of the user.
   Result: string -- An error message, or an empty string if successful.
```

With this command, you can log on as a guest in the same zone by supplying only the required parameters. Or, as indicated, you can script an intervention-less logon to a password-protected server and volume, provided you are granted access and know the password. Despite the security implications of such a command, there are times when unattended server mounting is critical, such as remounting a backup server that is unavailable for awhile.

I have experienced some difficulties with this OSAX particularly when trying to mount two volumes from the same server, so be sure to use the services of the scriptable Finder to verify that server mounting took place as desired. To unmount any server, use the scriptable Finder's put away command.

Managing Scripting Additions

Active scripters are justifiably concerned about the proliferation of OSAXes and potential conflicts when two OSAXes have the same command name. This is especially a problem when an OSAX may contain multiple commands, none of which are indicated in the file name.

At the moment, there are no automatic solutions to avoiding scripting addition clutter. Nor can your script know whether a call to an OSAX is being caught by the desired OSAX or another one that contains a command with the same name. Moreover, even if you are vigilant in maintaining your own Scripting Additions folder as streamlined as possible, there is no way of knowing if other people running your script have conflicts in their Scripting Additions folder.

Until the OSA architecture is fortified with an OSAX management mechanism, the best advice is to avoid using third-party OSAXes for scripts you intend to distribute to a wide audience over whose machines you have no control. In many corporate environments a systems integrator may have more control over what gets put into the Scripting Additions folder of each machine on a network, so all that is necessary is an installer that makes sure the OSAXes are copied to the Scripting Additions folder (you can use AppleScript and scriptable Finder as an installer, of course).

Distributing Scripts and OSAXes

A number of issues arise when it comes to giving or selling a script to another person when that script requires an OSAX that is not part of the AppleScript runtime package.

The primary consideration is the licensing issue surrounding third-party OSAXes (i.e., ones you did not create). Most OSAXes you find on bulletin boards—and all the ones located on the companion disk to this book—are the property of their authors. None of these authors minds if you use their OSAXes for your own personal use on your single machine. But if you start duplicating the OSAX for other users, even when your scripts rely on those OSAXes, you must make sure you have permission to do so. Typically, OSAX authors don't make a big deal within corporate environments or for consultants who develop scripting solutions for clients. Still, it is a good idea to send an e-mail message to the author(s) to see if there are any licensing fees involved (typical license fees, if any, are token amounts). And don't even think about distributing the third-party OSAX in a commercial product without a license from the OSAX author. Therefore, while Random House has licensed or received permission to include the OSAX files on the companion disk, the license extends to your own personal, private use of them. Any distribution beyond the companion disk would require permission or license from the OSAX authors. So much for the legal stuff.

Onto a more serious concern. Unfortunately, we cannot embed an OSAX into a script, so that both the OSAX and script go as a team from disk to disk. The problem with this disconnection is that if you copy a script to another machine (your own or someone else's), you may easily forget to bring along any non-standard OSAXes. Attempting to run the script on the other machine will cause all kinds of head-scratching execution errors.

One way to alert you or your script user to the problem is to have your script check for the presence of the necessary OSAX files in the Scripting Additions folder. The following handler does just that:

```
-- CheckOSAX Handler
-- sample call to handler, with each OSAX file name in the list
checkOSAX({"MountVolume", "Jon's Commands", "Steve's OSAXen"})

-- generic function
on checkOSAX(OSAXTest)
  tell application "Finder"
    set OSAXList to ¬
      name of every item of folder ¬
      "Scripting Additions" of extensions folder
    set failedTest to ""
    repeat with oneItem in OSAXTest
      if oneItem is not in OSAXList then
        set failedTest to failedTest & tab & oneItem & return
      end if
    end repeat
    if failedTest is {} then
      return true
    else
      display dialog "The following item(s) are missing from your Scripting Additions folder:" & ¬
        return & failedTest buttons {"OK"} default button "OK"
      return false
    end if
  end tell
end checkOSAX
```

If you plan to use this function in a script for distribution to other users, you should beef up the message that alerts the user of what's wrong, perhaps suggesting whom to call to report the problem.

Remember that all this handler checks is whether the OSAX files are present. It doesn't dig any deeper to see if a particular OSAX file contains a desired command. Therefore, even this kind of checking won't investigate some of the potential conflicts cited earlier in this chapter. It does, however, let you know whether a proper installation was made for your script and accompanying OSAX file(s).

AppleScript Quick Reference

AppleScript Commands

activate *referenceToApplication*

>>> activate application "SteveHD:Applications:Microsoft Excel" ¬
>>> of machine "Steve's Big Mac"

copy *expression* to *variableOrReference*

>>> copy paragraph 1 of document "Sample 6.1" to oneGraph

count [of] *directParameter* [each *className*]

>>> count {1, 1.5, 2} each real
>>> *-- result: 1*

[**get**] *expressionOrReference*

>>> get words 1 thru 3 of document "Preamble"
>>> *-- result: {"We", "the", "people"}*

run *variableOrReference*

>>> run application "Scriptable Text Editor"

launch *variableOrReference*

>>> launch application "Scriptable Text Editor"

set *variableOrReference* to *expression*

>>> set oneGraph to paragraph 1 of document "Sample 6.1"

Scripting Addition Commands

AGStart

>>> AGStart

ASCII character *integer0to255*

> ASCII character 65
> *-- result: "A"*

ASCII number *characterAsString*

> ASCII number "G"
> *-- result: 71*

beep [*numberOfBeeps*]

> beep 4

choose application [with prompt *promptString*] ¬
> > [application label *appListLabel*]

> > choose application with prompt "Select a scriptable application:" ¬
> > application label "Apps"
> > *-- result:application "Microsoft Excel" ¬*
> > *of machine "Giga Server" of zone "MIS Dept"*

choose file [with prompt *promptString*] [of type *fileTypeList*]

> > choose file with prompt "Select a document:" ¬
> > of type {"TEXT", "XLS4"}
> > *-- result: alias "HD:Documents:Overhead Template"*

choose folder [with prompt *promptString*]

> > choose folder with prompt "Select a destination folder:"
> > *-- result: alias "Macintosh HD:Letters:"*

close access *fileReference*

> close access myFileRef

current date

> > get current date
> > *-- result: date "Friday, June 11, 1993 4:23:26 PM"*

display dialog *string* [default answer *string*] ¬
> > [buttons *buttonList*] [default button *integer* | *string*] ¬
> > [with icon *integer* | *string*]

> > display dialog "What is your name?" default answer ""
> > *-- result: {text returned:"David", button returned:"OK"}*
> > display dialog "What color would you like?" ¬
> > buttons {"Red","Green","Blue"} ¬
> > default button 1 with icon 1
> > *-- result: {button returned:"Blue"}*

get eof *fileReference*

> > get eof myFile
> > *--result: 233 (length of file)*

info for *fileOrFolderReference*

> info for alias "HD:Applications:Crystal Caliburn™ "
> *-- result: {name:"Crystal Caliburn™ 1.02", ¬*
> *creation date:date "Friday, October 8, 1993 5:01:00 AM", ¬*
> *modification date:date "Sunday, September 18, 1994 2:34:50 PM", ¬*
> *icon position:{0, 0}, visible:true, size:1712761, folder:false, alias:false, ¬*
> *locked:false, file creator:"fXcR", file type:"APPL", short version:"1.02", ¬*
> *long version:"1.02 (US), Copyright©1993 LittleWing CO.LTD. ¬*
> *All Rights Reserved."}*

list folder *folderReference*   [invisibles *Boolean*]

> list folder "Hard Disk:System Folder:"
> *-- result: {"Apple Menu Items", "Clipboard",..., "System"}*

list disks

> list disks
> *-- result: {"Hard Disk", "Backup Floppy", "Alice to Ocean"}*

load script *fileReference*

> load script file "HD:System Folder:Script Libraries:StringLib"
> *-- result: **<<script>>***

log *expression*

> log

max monitor depth

> max monitor depth
> *-- result: 16*

min monitor depth

> min monitor depth
> *-- result: 1*

monitor depth

> monitor depth
> *-- result: 8*

new file [with prompt *string*] [default name *string*]

> set myFile to new file with prompt "Store information in:" ¬
> default name "Backup"
> *-- result: alias "HD 160:System Folder:Backup"*

open for access *fileOrAliasReference*   [write permission *Boolean*]

> open for access file "Test File" with write permission
> *-- result: 9496 (file reference number)*

offset of *containedString* in *containerString*

    offset of "people" in "We the people"
      -- *result: 8*

path to   apple menu | apple menu items | control panels | desktop | extensions | frontmost application | preferences | printmonitor | printmonitor documents | startup disk | startup items | system folder | temporary items | trash ¬ [as *class*]

    path to control panels
      -- *result: alias "HD 160:System Folder:Control Panels:"*

random number [*number*] [from *number* to *number*] [with seed *string*]

    random number from 3 to 30
      -- *result: 12*

read *fileReference*   [from *startInteger*] ¬
      [for *numberOfBytes* | to *endInteger* ¬
      | until *includedDelimiter* | before *excludedDelimiter*] ¬
      [as *dataType* | *class* [using delimiter[s] *delimiterList*]]

    read myFile from 201 for 100
      -- *result: 100 characters of text from file*

round *realNumber* [rounding up | down | toward zero | to nearest]

    round 35.74 rounding down
      -- *result: 35*

run script *variableOrReference*

    run script alias"HD:Scripts:DateRecord"

scripting components

    scripting components
      -- *result: {"QuicKeys", "AppleScript"}*

set eof *fileReference* to *integer*

    set eof myFile to 512

set monitor depth *<numberOfColorBits>*

    set monitor depth 32

set volume *<integer0thru7>*

    set volume 3

start log

    start log

stop log

    stop log

store script *scriptObject* in *aliasReference* [replacing ask | yes | no]
>>>   store script transactionLog ¬
>>>   in alias "Server:Shared Objects:Transaction Log"¬
>>>   replacing yes

time to GMT
>>>   (time to GMT)/hours
>>>   *-- result: -8.0*

write *expression* to *fileReference* ¬
>>>   [for *numberOfBytes*] [starting at *integer*]
>>>   write "Fred" to myFile starting at eof

Scriptable Finder Commands

clean up [all | *itemReference* [by *propertyLabel*]]
>>>   clean up window of startup disk by name

close *objectReference*
>>>   close folder "AppleScript™ Utilities" of folder "Development" ¬
>>>   of startup disk

computer *gestaltSelector* [has *valueToTest*]
>>>   computer "kbd"
>>>   *-- result:: 12 (PowerBook ADB keyboard)*

copy *expression* to | into *objectReference*
>>>   copy item "Letter to Natalie" of startup disk to desktop

count (of) [each | every] *className* [(in | of) *objectReference*]
>>>   count of containers of desktop
>>>   *-- result: 4*

data size of *objectReference* [as *className*]
>>>   data size of comment of file "Letter to Joe" of startup disk
>>>   *-- result: 54*

delete *itemReference*
>>>   delete file "Joe's Letter" of folder "Documents" of startup disk

duplicate *objectReference* [to *locationReference*] ¬
>>>   [replacing (conflicts | existing items)]
>>>   duplicate file "Howdy" of startup disk to desktop replacing conflicts

eject [*diskReference*]
>>>   eject disk "Backup"

empty [*trashReference*]

> empty trash

erase *diskReference*

> erase disk "Scratch Disk"

exists *objectReference*

> if file "Apple Photo Access" of extensions folder exists then ...

[get] *objectReference* [as *className*]

> modification date of folder "Documents" of startup disk as string
> -- *result: "Fri, Aug 12, 1994, 11:27 AM"*

make [new] *className* [at *containerReference*] ¬
> [with properties {*propertyLabel:propertyValue* ¬
> [, *propertyLabel:propertyValue*] ... }] ¬
> [to | with data *objectReference*]

> make folder in startup disk with properties {name:"Today's Files", shared:true}
> -- *result: folder "Today's Files" of startup disk of application "Finder"*

move *objectReference* to *containerReference* ¬
> [replacing conflicts | existing items]

> move (every document file in folder "Letters" of startup disk ¬
> whose modification date < todayZeroHour) to folder ¬
> "Backup" of disk "Archive"

number of *className* [(in | of) *objectReference*]

> number of alias files in apple menu items folder

open *objectReference* [using *applicationReference*]

> open folder "Documents" of startup disk

print *objectReference*

> print every item of folder "Print Me"

put *expression* to | into *objectReference*

> put "Joe's Letter" into name of item "Letters" of startup disk

put away *objectReference*

> put away item "Anderson Invoice" of trash

quit

> quit

restart

> restart

reveal *objectReferenece*

> reveal folder "March 1995" of folder "Correspondence" ¬
> of folder "Documents" of startup disk

select *objectReference*

> select every folder of startup disk whose modification date < (current date)

set *objectReference* to *expression*

> set name of folder "untitled folder" of startup disk to "Databases"

shut down

> shut down

sleep

> sleep

sort *referenceList* by *propertyLabel*

> sort items of startup disk by modification date
>> -- *result: (references to all items with the most recent first)*

update *objectReference*

> update startup disk

Reference Forms

Property References

[the] *propertyLabel* <*of objectOrRecord*>

> bounds of window 1

Indexed References

[the] *className* [index] *index* <*of objectOrItem*>

> paragraph 12 of first document

[the] (first | second | third | fourth | fifth | sixth |
seventh | eighth | ninth | tenth) *className* <*of objectOrItem*>

> third paragraph of document 1

[the] *index*(st | nd | rd | th) *className* <*of objectOrItem*>

> the 234th word

[the] (last | front | back) *className* <*of objectOrItem*>

> first word

Relative References

[*className*] (before | [in] front of) *baseReference*

    word before paragraph 3

[*className*] (after | [in] back of | behind) *baseReference*

    window behind window 1
    after word 1 of document 1

Name References

className [named] *nameString* <*of objectOrItem*>

    row "William McKinley"

ID References

className id *IDvalue* <*of Object*>

    background field id 23

Middle Element Reference

middle *className* <*of objectOrItem*>

    middle word of paragraph 1

Arbitrary Element References

some *className* <*of objectOrItem*>

    some item of {20, 40, "sixty", 80, 100}

Every Element References

every *className* <*of objectOrItem*>

    every cell of row 12 of table 1

pluralClassName <*of objectOrItem*>

    words of paragraph 1

Range References

className *startIndex* (thru | through) *stopIndex*

    word 1 thru 3 of paragraph 1

pluralClassName *startIndex* (thru | through) *stopIndex*

    words 1 thru 3 of paragraph 1

every *className* from *boundaryReferrence1* to *boundaryReference2*

    every character from word 1 to word 2

pluralClassName from *boundaryReferrence1* to *boundaryReference2*

    characters from word 1 to word 2

Filtered References

reference whose | where *BooleanExpression*

```
every word whose first character is "s"
every word where it is "sea"
```

Value Classes

Class Name	Example
Boolean	true
Integer	25
List	{2, "Michael", 34.5}
Real	25.0
String	"Steve"
Date	date "Friday, June 11, 1993 4:23:26 PM"
Record	{name:"Joe", age: 32, weight: 166}
Reference	table "States" of application "TableServer"
Class	string
Constant	pi
Data	{«data ...» ... }

Control Statements

Tell

tell *reference* to *statement*

tell *reference*
    [*statement*] ...
end [tell]

If-Then-Else

if *BooleanExpression* then *statement*

if *BooleanExpression* [then]
    [*statement*] ...
end [if]

if *BooleanExpression* [then]
    [*statement*] ...
else
    [*statement*] ...
end [if]

if *BooleanExpression* [then]
    [*statement*] ...
else if *BooleanExpression* [then]
    [*statement*] ... ...
end [if]

if *BooleanExpression* [then]
    [*statement*] ...
else if *BooleanExpression* [then]
    [*statement*] ... ...
else
    [*statement*] ...
end [if]

Repeat

repeat
    [*statement*] ...
end [repeat]

repeat *numberOfTimes* [times]
    [*statement*] ...
end [repeat]

repeat until *BooleanExpression*
    [*statement*] ...
end [repeat]

repeat while *BooleanExpression*
    [*statement*] ...
end [repeat]

repeat with *counterVariable* **from** *startValue* **to** *stopValue* ¬
[by *stepValue*]
    [*statement*] ...
end [repeat]

repeat with *loopVariable* **in** *list*
    [*statement*] ...
end [repeat]

Exit

exit [repeat]

Try-Error

try
    [*statementToTest*] ...
on error [*errorMessage*] [number *errorNumber*] ¬

[from *offendingObject*] [to *expectedType*] ¬
[partial result *resultList*]
[global *variableID* [, *variableID*] ...]
[local *variableID* [, *variableID*] ...]
[*statementHandlingError*] ...
end [try | error]

Timeout

with timeout [of] *numberOfSeconds* seconds [s]
[*statement*] ...
end [timeout]

Transaction

with transaction [*sessionID*]
[*statement*] ...
end transaction

Considering

considering *attribute* [, *attribute* ... and *attribute*] ¬
[but ignoring [, *attribute* ... and *attribute*]]
[*statement*] ...
end considering
(*attributes*: case, white space, diacriticals, hyphens, punctuation,
application responses)

Ignoring

ignoring *attribute* [, *attribute* ... and *attribute*] ¬
[but considering [, *attribute* ... and *attribute*]]
[*statement*] ...
end ignoring

Operators

Connubial Operators

Syntax	*Name*	*Operands*	*Results*
+	Plus	Integer, Real	Integer, Real
−	Minus	Integer, Real	Integer, Real
*	Multiply	Integer, Real	Integer, Real
/	Divide	Integer, Real	Integer, Real

Syntax	Name	Operands	Results
+ (Option-/)			
div	Integral Division	Integer, Real	Integer
mod	Modulo	Integer, Real	Integer, Real
§	Exponent	Integer, Real	Real
&	Concatenation	All (See below)	List, Record, String
as	Coercion	(See below)	(See below)
[a] ref[erence] [to]	A Reference To	Reference	Reference

Comparison Operators

Syntax	Name	Operands	Results
= is equal[s] [is] equal to	Equal	All	Boolean
≠ (Option-=) is not isn't isn't equal [to] is not equal [to] does not equal doesn't equal	Not equal	All	Boolean

>
[is] greater than
comes after
is not less than
  or equal [to]
isn't less than
  or equal [to]
	Greater than	Date, Integer, Real, String	Boolean

<
[is] less than
comes before
is not greater than
  or equal [to]
isn't greater than
  or equal [to]
	Less than	Date, Integer, Real, String	Boolean

>= ≥ (Option->)	Greater than or equal to	Date, Integer, Real, String	Boolean

Syntax	Name	Operands	Results
[is] greater than or equal [to] is not less than isn't less than does not come before doesn't come before			
<= ≤ (Option-<) [is] not less than or equal [to] is not greater than isn't greater than does not come after doesn't come after	Less than or equal to	Date, Integer, Real, String	Boolean

Containment Operators

Syntax	Name	Operands	Results
contain[s]	Contains	List, Record, String	Boolean
does not contain doesn't contain	Does not contain	List, Record, String	Boolean
is contained by	Is contained by	List, Record, String	Boolean
is not contained by isn't contained by	Is not contained by	List, Record, String	Boolean
start[s] with begin[s] with	Starts with	List, String	Boolean
end[s] with	Ends with	List, String	Boolean

Boolean Operators

Syntax	Name	Operands	Results
and	And	Boolean	Boolean
or	Or	Boolean	Boolean
not	Not	One Boolean	Boolean

Subroutines and Handlers

Positional Parameters

subroutineName ([*parameterValue*] [, *parameterValue*] ...)
on | to *subroutineName* ([*parameter*] [, *parameter*] ...)
    [global *variableID* [, *variableID*] ...]
    [local *variableID* [, *variableID*] ...]
    [*statement*] ...
end [*subroutineName*]

Labeled Parameters

subroutineName [[of | in] *directParameter*] ¬
    [*subroutineParamLabel parameterValue*] ... ¬
    [given *labelName:parameter* [, *labelName:parameter*] ...] ¬
    [with *labelForTrueParam* ¬
    [, *labelForTrueParam*, ... and *labelForTrueParam*]] ¬
    [without *labelForFalseParam* ¬
    [, *labelForFalseParam* , ... and *labelForFalseParam*]]
(*labelNameParameters*: above, against, apart from, around, aside from, at,
beneath, below, beside, between, by, for, from, instead of, into, on, onto,
out of, over, through, thru, under)
on | to *subroutineName* [[of | in] *directParameter*] ¬
    [*subroutineParamLabel parameter*] ... ¬
    [given *labelName:parameter* [, *labelName:parameter*] ...]
    [global *variableID* [, *variableID*] ...]
    [local *variableID* [, *variableID*] ...]
    [*statement*] ...
end [*subroutineName*]

Return

return *expression*

Command Handler

on | to *commandName* [[of] *directParameter*] ¬
    [[given] *paramLabel: parameter* [, *paramLabel: parameter*] ...]
    [global *variableID* [, *variableID*] ...]
    [local *variableID* [, *variableID*] ...]
    [*statement*] ...
end [*commandName*]

Script Objects

Property Definition
property | prop *propertyLabel: initialValue*

Droplet Handler
on open *fileList*
    [*statement*] ...
end open

Predefined Variables
it
me
pi
result
return
space
tab

AppleScript Objects
application
machine
zone
paragraph
word
character
item
text item

AppleScript Property
text item delimiters default: {""}

Required Apple Events

    open
    print
    quit
    run

Index